# VIETNAM AND AMERICA

## READINGS AND DOCUMENTS

### EDITED BY ROBERT BUZZANCO

#### UNIVERSITY OF HOUSTON

PEARSON CUSTOM PUBLISHING

Printed in the United States of America

10 9 8 7 6 5 4 3

*Please visit our website at www.pearsoncustom.com*

ISBN 0–536–02678-5

BA 990845

PEARSON CUSTOM PUBLISHING
160 Gould Street/Needham Heights, MA 02494
A Pearson Education Company

# Copyright Acknowledgments

# *Contents*

## Documents

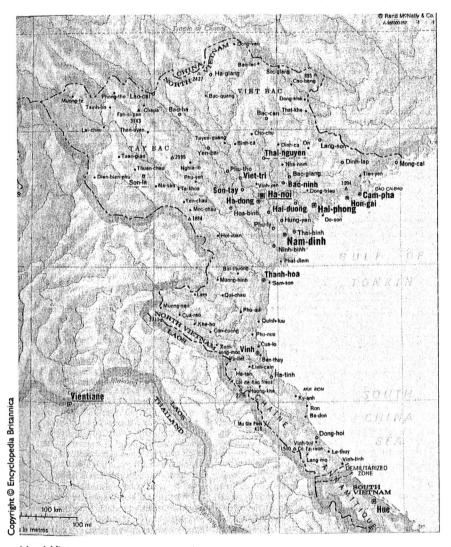

**North Vietnam**

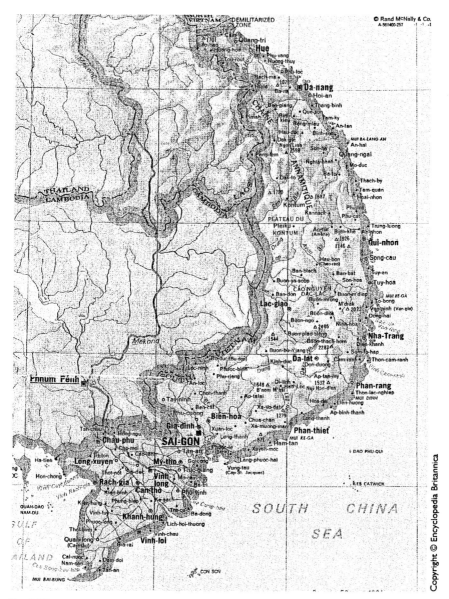

South Vietnam

# Readings

# Song of Napalm
## Bruce Weigl

*for my wife*

After the storm, after the rain stopped pounding,
we stood in the doorway watching horses
walk off lazily across the pasture's hill.
We stared through the black screen,
our vision altered by the distance
so I thought I saw a mist
kicked up around their hooves when they faded
like cut-out horses
away from us.
The grass was never more blue in that light, more
scarlet; beyond the pasture
trees scraped their voices into the wind, branches
crisscrossed the sky like barbed wire
but you said they were only branches.

Okay. The storm stopped pounding.
I am trying to say this straight: for once
I was sane enough to pause and breathe
outside my wild plans and after the hard rain
I turned my back on the old curses. I believed
they swung finally away from me . . .

But still the branches are wire
and thunder is the pounding mortar,
still I close my eyes and see the girl
running from her village, napalm
stuck to her dress like jelly,

3

her hands reaching for the no one
who waits in waves of heat before her.

So I can keep on living,
so I can stay here beside you,
I try to imagine she runs down the road and wings
beat inside her until she rises
above the stinking jungle and her pain
eases, and your pain, and mine.

But the lie swings back again.
The lie works only as long as it takes to speak
and the girl runs only as far
as the napalm allows
until her burning tendons and crackling
muscles draw her up
into that final position
burning bodies so perfectly assume. Nothing
can change that, she is burned behind my eyes
and not your good love and not the rain-swept air
and not the jungle-green
pasture unfolding before us can deny it.

# From *In the Jaws of History*
## Bui Diem
## with David Chanoff

### Epilogue

Except for the special circumstances that put me close to the center stage of the war in Vietnam, and except for the sheer luck that spared me much of the suffering endured by others, I am not different from other Vietnamese of my generation. In terms of dreams and aspirations, frustrations and disappointments, my life story is essentially theirs.

Vietnamese of my generation came of age in the early forties with the hope that after almost a century as second-class citizens in their own country, they would have a chance to recover their dignity and achieve their independence from France. They dreamed also of peace and a decent life for themselves and their children. It was their misfortune that instead of independence, peace, and a decent life, they saw only revolution, war, and destruction. For three decades they existed in the maelstrom. And even now, when Vietnam no longer has to deal with foreign invaders, their misery continues. Theirs has been a tragedy of historic proportions.

In an interview with Walter Cronkite in 1963, President John Kennedy said, "In the final analysis, it's their war and they are the ones who will either win it or lose it." Much as we might like to, there is no getting away from Kennedy's judgment. The South Vietnamese people, and especially the South Vietnamese leaders, myself among them, bear the ultimate responsibility for the fate of their nation, and to be honest, they have much to regret and much to be ashamed of. But it is also true that the war's cast of characters operated within a matrix of larger forces that stood outside the common human inadequacies and failings. And it was these forces that shaped the landscape on which we all moved.

First among these root causes was the obduracy of France, which in the late forties insisted on retaining control of its former colony rather than conceding independence in good time to a people who hungered for it. Second was the ideological obsession of Vietnam's Communists. Not content with fighting to slough off a dying colonialism, they relentlessly sought to impose on the Vietnamese people their dogma of class warfare and proletarian dictatorship. Finally came the massive intervention by the United States, inserting into our struggle for independence and freedom its own overpowering dynamic. These three forces combined to distort the basic nature of Vietnam's emergence from colonialism, ensuring that the struggle would be more complex and bloodier than that of so many other colonies which achieved nationhood during mid-century.

Caught in the midst of these powerful forces, Vietnam's nationalists found themselves in a succession of precarious situations. In most cases they were forced to choose among unpalatable alternatives; often, indeed, they saw no choice at all. With their survival at stake, they were forced to take refuge in a series of uneasy and uncomfortable compromises that little by little eroded their legitimacy. From one experience to another—first with the French and Bao Dai, then with Ngo Dinh Diem, then with the Americans and the military—they tried to carve out a role for themselves and establish their influence. But always they were pushed to the periphery, and the influence they wielded was never enough to affect the ultimate course of events. To myself and others, for a time it seemed we might be able to develop the nation's economy and build a functioning democracy, even while waging war. But eventually the room to make this kind of contribution diminished, and in the end, against a mechanized North Vietnamese invasion army equipped by the Soviets, all that remained was an alley fight for survival. By then Vietnam's nationalists had been forced to take their place alongside all the other Vietnamese who could only stand by and watch their fate unfold in front of them.

As I look back on the external forces that shaped our lives, it is the American intervention that stands out. French colonialism, after all, is dead and gone, a subject for historians who prefer the inert remains of the past to the passions of the present. As for Vietnamese communism, no one but the fervid or the blind any longer argues the merits of a system that has brought in its wake only war and deprivation and mass flight. (Not that having been right comforts us as we house our refugees and send what sustenance we can back to our families.) But American intervention is a living issue. In the train of failure in Vietnam, and in the face of hard choices elsewhere, the questions of its correctness and its morality still inform American foreign policy debates. Americans still seek to learn the lessons of intervention, and so do America's smaller allies, who cannot help but see in the fate of Vietnam intimations of their own possible futures.

For critics of the Vietnam War, the original decision to intervene was wrong, a result, as one of them put it, of a "steady string of misjudgments." It was wrong because American policymakers in the sixties failed to assess correctly the vital interests of the United States, because they exaggerated the geopolitical importance of Vietnam, and because they had an inflated concept of American capabilities.

Although it is neither my business nor within my competence to pass judgment on how the United States defined its interests at that time, it is my impression that such arguments are made on a distinctly *a posteriori* basis. I remember vividly the political atmosphere in the United States in the summer of 1964, the summer of the Tonkin resolution and Barry Goldwater's nomination, when I first visited this country. At that time the Johnson administration and practically the entire Congress were in favor of the commitment to defend Vietnam (the resolution passed in the Senate, 98 to 2, and in the House, 416 to 0). And so, *mirabile dictu*, were the national news media.

Moreover, the context of international affairs in that period provided good reasons for this nearly unanimous opinion, reasons that went beyond the specific perception of North Vietnamese aggressiveness. It was then the aftermath of the Communist attack in Korea, and China's Communist leaders were broadcasting the most belligerent and expansionistic views, even as they attempted to establish a Peking-Jakarta axis with Indonesia's pro-Communist President Sukarno. For the fragile governments of Southeast Asia the situation seemed serious indeed. Although twenty-five years later it became fashionable among some Americans to belittle Communist threats to the region's stability, among the responsible governments at the time there was deep anxiety.

Even for those South Vietnamese who thought they saw the inherent dangers in American intervention, there was still nothing illogical about it. The American interest in Vietnam, even its land intervention, seemed a natural extension of U.S. policies in Europe (the Marshall Plan, the Berlin airlift, Greece) and Asia (Korea) aimed at preventing the expansion of combined Soviet and Chinese power (at least until the early 1960s, no one could imagine that the two Communist giants would become antagonists). And for the Europeans who were able to rebuild their countries and save their democratic institutions, for the Germans in Berlin, for the Greeks, and for the South Koreans, those policies were not wrong. Nor were they based on misjudgments of geopolitical realities. In Vietnam the policy failed. But that is not to say that it was wrong there either. The disastrous mistakes that were made were mistakes in implementation rather than intention. But the thrust of the policy of containment and protection, that I do not think can be faulted. It is, on the contrary, something for Americans to be proud of.

The more vocal critics of the war in the sixties and seventies character-ized the intervention, not just as wrong, but also as immoral. Their charge was based primarily on the theory that the war in Vietnam was a civil war, and that consequently American intervention was an act of aggression against people who were fighting to free themselves from an oppressive regime and unify their country in accord with the aspirations of the great majority of decent-minded Vietnamese.

It is my own belief that this theory held the field for so long primarily because it was a powerful attraction to the many Americans who were angry at their own government and society and were looking for issues to hang their anger on. Certainly, the facts that refuted it were readily available. From early on, both Saigon and Washington knew beyond a doubt that the National Liberation Front—the Vietcong—was a creation of the Commu-nist party, and that without North Vietnamese organization, leadership, sup-plies, and, starting in 1964, without the North Vietnamese regular army, there would have been no revolution to speak of and no war. It was one of my greatest frustrations that our firm knowledge of this—both from widespread and incontrovertible evidence and also from personal experience among many of us of communist "front" techniques—made no impact on popular understanding in the West. Regardless of what was there to be seen, people saw only what they wished.

After the war, when propaganda no longer mattered, the party dropped its pretense. "Our Party," said Le Duan in his 1975 victory speech, "is the unique and single leader that organized, controlled, and governed the entire struggle of the Vietnamese people from the first day of the revolution." Dur-ing the war, the North Vietnamese never openly admitted they had troops in South Vietnam. (Le Duc Tho even kept up the pretense with Henry Kissinger, although Kissinger knew the situation as well as he knew his own name, and Tho, of course, knew that he knew it.) But afterward the party treated this subterfuge simply as an excellent piece of public relations and its own role as a matter of intense pride. As the North Vietnamese general Vo Ban told French television interviewers in 1983, "In May 1959 I had the privilege of being designated by the Vietnamese Communist Party to unleash a military attack on the South in order to liberate the South and reunify the fatherland."

During the heyday of the antiwar movement, I marveled at the innocence of its spokesmen in believing something different from this. I wonder even now if they ever feel shame for their gullibility and for their contribution to the tragedy. But they are not heard from. It was, after all, only one chapter in their lives, as it was only a chapter in the book of American history.

The issue of morality, then, comes down to whether it was moral for the United States to have supported an admittedly flawed South Vietnamese regime in its attempt to survive against a totalitarian antagonist. Here, too, the answer seems to me self-evident. However unpalatable leaders like Nguyen Van Thieu might have been, South Vietnam was full of pluralistic ferment and possibilities for change and development. It was a place where good people could hope for something better to evolve, where they could even fight for it, as so many strong-minded opposition politicians, intellectuals, and writers did. None but ideologues can compare such a place with the chilling police state that destroyed it. And none, I think, can fairly question the morality of the effort to prevent its destruction.

To my mind, the lessons of American intervention in Vietnam have to do not so much with the geopolitical or moral underpinning of the war, but rather with the way the intervention was implemented. The real question was not whether to intervene, but how to intervene effectively.

In this book I have described in some detail the process by which the Johnson administration decided to bring an American land army to Vietnam. The salient feature of that confused and unclear process (as Bill Bundy characterized it) was not that it was ill planned and based on no comprehensive strategy. It was the startling attitude of American decision makers toward their ally. At the top levels of the administration, the State Department, and the Pentagon, there is no evidence to suggest that anyone considered the South Vietnamese as partners in the venture to save South Vietnam. In a mood that seemed mixed of idealism and naïveté, impatience and overconfidence, the Americans simply came in and took over. It was an attitude that would endure throughout the remainder of the conflict. The message seemed to be that this was an American war, and the best thing the South Vietnamese could do was to keep from rocking the boat and let the Americans get on with their business.

The military consequences of this orientation were that the United States took the entire burden on itself instead of searching for ways to make a decisive impact while limiting its exposure. Had the South Vietnamese been consulted in early 1965, it is likely they would have preferred either no intervention or a limited effort sufficient to stabilize the military situation and block the infiltration routes from North Vietnam. An agreement among the United States, South Vietnam, and Laos, allowing U.S. troops to be stationed along the seventeenth parallel as a barrier, would have been quite feasible at the time. With that done, an immediate Vietnamization program could have been undertaken to strengthen and upgrade the South Vietnamese army.

Could such a simple strategy have worked? That is one of the "what if" questions with which the Vietnam War abounds. Colonel Harry Summers, in *On Strategy,* his uncompromising review of American military planning, concludes that it would have, that in fact, isolating the South Vietnamese battlefield from North Vietnamese reinforcement and resupply was the only logical objective for American arms. Whatever the imponderables of war, this approach would at least have had the virtue of establishing the United States as a peace-keeping force protecting South Vietnam from outside aggression. It would have reduced American casualties and precluded the involvement of American firepower in the disconcerting people's war that was such a nightmare for the GIs to fight and that created such powerful antagonism in the arena of international public opinion.

On the political level, too, this American failure to regard the South Vietnamese as people worthy of partnership had destructive results. It meant that the United States never pursued a consistent policy aimed at encouraging the development of a viable democracy in South Vietnam. Certainly, such a thing was possible. Between 1965 and 1967 the South Vietnamese drafted and adopted a constitution, elected a president, vice president, and legislature, and successfully held many local elections—all of this in the middle of a war. It was a substantial achievement, but it would not have happened except that during those years the impulse toward democracy in South Vietnam and the objectives of the Johnson administration coincided.

Unfortunately, thereafter "stability" became the American watchword. As long as the Saigon government demonstrated a modicum of equilibrium, that was all that was asked of it. Several years of progress toward decent government might erode, corruption and autocracy might swell, but these things were not a primary American concern. By 1969 Henry Kissinger and Richard Nixon had embarked on a complex chess game, manipulating big-power diplomacy, military force, and secret negotiations in an attempt to extricate the United States from its quagmire. Amidst this constellation of variables, they needed a government in Saigon that was stable and predictable. If Thieu provided them with that, then whatever else he might do was essentially irrelevant.

It was a fatal error on two counts. First, stigmatized as undemocratic and corrupt, South Vietnam was deemed unworthy of support by an ever-increasing percentage of the American public and Congress. Second, within South Vietnam itself, the unpopular nature of the regime produced apathy, cynicism, and finally, in the anticorruption movement, outrage. Charles Mohr, veteran correspondent of the *New York Times*, summed it up succinctly in a seminar at the American Enterprise Institute. "We lost the war in Vietnam," he said, "not because we did not bring enough pressure to bear on our enemy, but because we did not bring sufficient pressure on our ally." Admittedly, bringing pressure for reform and democracy is a delicate business. But in situations where the United States has significant leverage, the role of catalyst for change, of prodding contending factions toward consensus, beckons to American diplomacy.

To successfully play such a role, there are two prerequisites. One is the will to carry out a strong and consistent advocacy. The other is the determination to accept the consequences if in the end American pressure proves unavailing. The United States must find a way to say to a Ngo Dinh Diem or a Nguyen Van Thieu (or a Ferdinand Marcos or an Augusto Pinochet), "We have no alternative but to stand by our own values. If for your own reasons you find you cannot bring yourselves toward conforming with them, then we are very sorry, but we will have no choice but to leave you to your own devices." With all its power and prestige, the United States simply cannot allow itself to yield to the tyranny of the weak, to authoritarians who believe their importance is so vast that the United States cannot help but support them. If Vietnam has one single lesson to teach, it is that people cannot be saved in spite of themselves. Far better to get out and cut losses before ensnaring treasure, lives, prestige, and all in the service of those whose rule means violent discord and social breakdown.

In Vietnam I always believed that among decent and reasonable people there could be no disagreement about things like corruption, economic and social reforms, and democratic procedures. I believe the same is true elsewhere. Another *New York Times* man, A. M. Rosenthal, in reflecting on his decades of covering American diplomacy, had this to say: "What should our policy be? Simply to act in our belief and interest. Our belief is political freedom and our interest is political freedom. We will not be able to achieve them for others all of the time or even much of the time. But what we can do is stand up for what we believe in, all of the time. . . . That requires two things: vision and constancy. Haitians, Filipinos, Koreans, Afghans seem to have no great confusion about what they really seek from us. Neither do the Czechoslovaks or the Poles." Neither, he might have added, did the South Vietnamese.

The experience of Vietnam suggests that a policy such as Rosenthal recommends would not be simple idealism. After Vietnam it is natural to question the extent to which the United States can sustain any major commitment to a foreign nation unless that nation is capable of eliciting moral support from an idealistic and essentially antimilitaristic American public. The suggestion is that geopolitical considerations by themselves constitute an insufficient grounding for stable, long-term policy. From this perspective, a democratic commitment in foreign policy is not mere idealism; it is also pragmatic self-interest.

From 1965 through 1967, Lyndon Johnson's administration acted according to this concept of idealistic pragmatism. From time to time other administrations did too, but never consistently and never strongly. For all the rhetoric, the American commitment to democracy in South Vietnam was a timid and wavering and sometime thing. That is another way of saying that in South Vietnam American policy neglected the human dimension. It did not accord its allies their requisite dignity as human beings. (I am not speaking here of the thousands of Americans who worked devotedly alongside the Vietnamese.) At the decision-making level, Vietnam was regarded primarily as a geopolitical abstraction, a factor in the play of American global interests. That was true about the way the United States intervened in the war with its land army. It was true about the way the United States conducted the war. And it was especially true about how the United States left the war.

Of all the successive phases of U.S. involvement—the intervention of 1965, the Americanization of the war, then its Vietnamization, and finally the disengagement—it is the disengagement that will stick longest in the minds of the South Vietnamese. Major mistakes were made during the war by everyone concerned. But the manner in which the United States took its leave was more than a mistake; it was an act unworthy of a great power, one that I believe will be remembered long after such unfortunate misconceptions as the search and destroy strategy have been consigned to footnotes.

It was not that the leave-taking itself was a disgrace. The United States fought long and hard in Vietnam, and if in the end circumstances required that it withdraw, it may be considered a tragedy but hardly an act of shame. The same cannot be said, however, for the manipulative and callous manner with which the American administration and the American Congress dealt with South Vietnam during the last years of the war. It was not one of America's finest hours, and there are plenty of lessons in it for both the United States and for other nations, particularly small ones that must rely on the United States for their defense.

As for Henry Kissinger, the architect of the Paris agreement, one can sympathize with his desire for "flexibility," that is, for control. Kissinger was in the middle, attempting to maneuver disparate and obstinate parties (including the North Vietnamese, South Vietnamese, Soviets, Chinese, even, on occasion, his own president) toward the same end. But he had taken on himself an awesome responsibility, negotiating not just for the global interests of the United States but for the existence of South Vietnam. In this context, he and Richard Nixon avoided holding frank discussions on common strategies with the South Vietnamese. They knew that Nguyen Van Thieu could do nothing without American support, yet they chose the unnecessary expedient of keeping developments to themselves until the last moment, then bringing to bear the heavy tactics of promises and threats. They treated a dependent ally of twenty years with finesse and then brutality, instead of with the openness the relationship required.

The fact that Kissinger and Nixon may have believed they had a viable agreement, or at least the best they could get, does not in my view justify their conduct toward South Vietnam. But at the same time, as unique as the

Nixon administration's diplomatic style was, it was in effect just another aspect, another face of the American policy that had obtained in Vietnam from the beginning, informed by worthy motives but without an understanding of the human beings who would be affected by its geopolitical goals.

The congresses that in 1973, 1974, and 1975 washed their hands of Vietnam shared fully in this same guilt. Although senators and representatives talked a good deal then about credibility and moral obligation, in fact what they did was to make a geopolitical decision on the basis of what they saw as American self-interest. They did so in callous disregard of the consequences their actions would have on a nation of twenty million people, and they did so although it was no longer a matter of American blood, but only of some hundreds of millions of dollars.

"Is it possible for a great nation to behave this way?" That was the question an old friend of mine asked me in Saigon when news came in August of 1974 that Congress had reduced the volume of aid. He was a store owner whom I had gone to school with in North Vietnam, a totally nonpolitical person. "You are an ambassador," he said. "Perhaps you understand these things better than I do. But can you explain this attitude of the Americans? When they wanted to come, they came. And when they want to leave, they leave. It's as if a neighbor came over and made a shambles of your house, then all of a sudden he decides the whole thing is wrong, so he calls it quits. How can they just do that?" It was a naïve question from an unsophisticated man. But I had no answer for it. Neither, I think, would William Fulbright, or George McGovern, or the other antiwar congressmen.

In the end, though, the culpability is hardly theirs alone. So many thought they knew the truth. The newsmen—as arrogant as any—Kissinger, Thieu, Nixon, myself as well. But none of us knew the truth or, knowing it, took it sufficiently to heart. Not we, and certainly not the implacable and ruthless ideologues who were our enemies. The truth is in the millions of Vietnamese families that have suffered the most horrible tragedies, people who understood what was happening only in the vaguest way. The truth of this war lies buried with its victims, with those who died, and with those who are consigned to live in an oppressed silence, for now and for the coming generations—a silence the world calls peace.

# The Failed Search for Victory: Vietnam and the Politics of War

## Lawrence J. Bassett and Stephen E. Pelz

Two weeks before the United States's defeat at the Bay of Pigs, John Kenneth Galbraith, John F. Kennedy's new Ambassador to India, warned the President against "the surviving adventurism in the Administration. . . ." The always frank Galbraith recalled that the "futile campaign to the Yalu ruined the Democrats in 1950. . . . We Democrats with our reputation for belligerence and our basically hostile press have far less margin for mistakes than had the Republicans." During the following months, Galbraith also told Kennedy that South Vietnam was "a can of snakes," and speculated that Premier Ngo Dinh Diem's desperate efforts to cling to power might falter and draw the United States deeper into Indochina. Galbraith recommended that Kennedy send an emissary to explain the problem of Diem's pigheadedness to the State Department— "with pictures. . . . We are increasingly replacing the French as the colonial military force and we will increasingly arouse the resentment associated therewith." "Incidentally," he continued, "who is the man in your administration who decides what countries are strategic? I would like to have his name and address and ask him what is so important about this [Vietnamese] real estate in the space age." Galbraith concluded that "it is the political poison that is really at issue. The Korean war killed us in the early 50s; this involvement could kill us now."

John F. Kennedy himself decided that South Vietnam was strategically vital. He did so because he viewed the world and the methods for dealing with it differently from Galbraith, although he certainly agreed with the Ambassador about the domestic political dangers of ordering American infantry units to fight in South Vietnam. While Galbraith called for continuing a "conservative, thoughtful, nonbelligerent stance" toward the world, Kennedy wanted to lead his South Vietnamese allies to victory over the

Vietnamese Communists without sending large numbers of American troops into battle. To this end the President stated repeatedly and publicly that the United States would help suppress the insurgency in South Vietnam; he warned the Soviets both publicly and privately against assisting the guerrillas; he increased economic aid to South Vietnam; he enlarged the South Vietnamese Army and police forces; he increased the number of American military advisers, logistic units, and pilots from approximately 700 to approximately 16,700; he allowed a number of the advisers to participate in combat; he ordered assistance to the South Vietnamese for covert raids against North Vietnam; he helped launch the South Vietnamese strategic hamlet program; he encouraged the South Vietnamese military to assume political power; and he rejected suggestions that he try to neutralize South Vietnam—a solution which he had been willing to accept in Laos.

Early in his career Kennedy had formed an image of South Vietnam as a nation whose nationalist elite was caught between French colonialists and Communist insurgents. Since Kennedy believed Americans were not seen as colonialists, he expected that American advisers would be able to work with Vietnamese nationalists to establish and defend a pro-Western state in South Vietnam. Drawing the containment line at the South Vietnamese border was all the more important, because he had reluctantly accepted a neutralized Laos. In his determined search for victory in Vietnam, President Kennedy kept trying different tactics and personnel, but his efforts played into the hands of the National Liberation Front (NLF), a coalition of anti-Diem groups for which the Communists provided most of the leaders. By giving Diem money and men, Kennedy backed a system of landlord rule in the countryside, which was deeply unpopular with the peasants, and by aiding the South Vietnamese security forces in their attempts to impose Diem's will on the villages, he identified the Americans with a repressive *ancien regime.*

Peasants joined the NLF in increasing numbers, because the NLF cadres helped them achieve a rural revolution. Kennedy's program of industrialization, rural aid, resettlement, and helicopter assaults carried little appeal in the countryside. Kennedy nonetheless persisted in his quest for victory in Vietnam, even after repeated warnings that his methods were failing. He did so in part because he and his small senior staff did not spend much time searching for the realities behind the flow of daily cables from Saigon. Given the current state of documentation, Kennedy's motives for this persistent quest for victory must remain something of a mystery. It appears, however, that he persevered in Vietnam not only to preserve his credibility as a successful practitioner of containment but also to maintain his reputation as an anti-Communist in the face of Republican attacks at home.

Indochina had a special meaning for Kennedy, because it was the first issue on which he had gained some recognition as an expert on foreign policy. He formed his views during a brief trip to the Middle East and Southeast Asia in October 1951, and he never changed them. Both he and his brother Robert concluded that unrest in the area stemmed from nationalist revolutions against exploitative, white colonialists and that, in some areas, such as Indochina, the Communists were winning over the nationalists by default. When Congressman Kennedy arrived in Saigon, Vietnam, he doubted the French predictions of victory and took an immediate dislike to Bao Dai, the French puppet ruler, whom he described as looking as if he were "fried in Crisco." When Kennedy returned home, he reported that "the majority of the people are on the side of the guerrillas," and he urged the French to permit Vietnam to establish "a non-communist native government so that it can move safely toward independence."

Kennedy appears to have relied heavily in the 1950s on the views of Edmund A. Gullion, a young foreign service officer who shared Kennedy's doubts about French willingness to work with Vietnamese nationalists (in 1963 Kennedy considered sending Gullion to Saigon as Ambassador). Gullion argued that a grant of independence would produce a "feeling of nationhood" for Vietnam and give the fledgling French-trained officer corps of the Vietnamese army an ideal around which to rally. Even with the Communist-led Vietminh in control of much of the countryside, Gullion believed that the Communists lacked appeal as social revolutionaries, because Vietnam did not suffer the "grinding poverty" of other Southeast Asian nations. Gullion concluded that "the principal communist appeal is to nationalism." Kennedy thought the harsh methods of the Communist cadres alienated the nationalist elite, which was sitting on the fence between the two conquerors—the French and the Communists. The hope of the future, he believed, rested in this educated nationalist minority and in a trained corps of military officers, because the semiliterate peasantry's "main concern is their bowl of rice." The peasants would follow leaders who provided them with economic security and national independence.

In 1953 Senator Kennedy asked the Eisenhower Administration to use foreign aid to force a French grant of independence to the Vietnamese, and a year later he told the Senate that it would be "self-destructive . . . to pour money, material, and men into the jungles of Indochina," unless the people there supported the cause of the West wholeheartedly. If the French granted them freedom and recruited "a reliable and crusading native army with a dependable officer corps," then victory might be possible in Vietnam—the key to all of Southeast Asia. And if American troops tried to prop up the French colonial regime, Kennedy predicted they would suffer the same fate as the French, making it necessary "to move back to a secondary line."

After the French withdrawal from Vietnam in 1954–1955, events in South Vietnam seemed at first to confirm Kennedy's diagnosis. Kennedy claimed that Ngo Dinh Diem and "a determined band of patriotic Vietnamese around one man of faith, President Diem," had released and harnessed "the latent power of nationalism to create an independent, anti-Communist Vietnam." In reality, far from being a full-fledged nationalist, Diem had served the Japanese during World War II. Yet in 1956 Kennedy praised the new South Vietnam with a barrage of mixed clichés such as "the cornerstone of the Free World in Southeast Asia, the keystone to the arch, the finger in the dike," "a proving ground of democracy in Asia," "a test of American responsibility and determination." And he concluded, "We must supply capital . . ., technicians . . ., [and] guidance to assist a nation taking those first feeble steps toward the complexities of a republican form of government."

In spite of considerable American economic and military aid, Diem was in trouble by 1959. In 1957–1958 he had restored landlord-gentry rule to many of the rural areas and put his northern and central Vietnamese Catholic Can Lao party members in control of much of the government, army, and police. In 1959 the southern Vietminh began reclaiming the countryside for the peasants, while decrying the harsh rule of "American Diem's" minions. In Long An province, not far from Saigon, for example, armed squads drove Diem's officials almost completely out of the villages with a campaign of terror which killed twenty-six people during the New Year's celebration of 1960. Vietminh cadres established peasant committees in the liberated areas and encouraged the newly empowered peasants to reduce land rents and redistribute the land of those Diemist officials who had fled. By 1961 the campaign had swayed about 80 percent of South Vietnam's villages toward their side, and Diem's government had to rely almost totally on American economic and military assistance to replace the taxes and recruits lost in the villages.

The Vietminh offensive in South Vietnam appeared to confirm Kennedy's picture of world politics in 1961. Although the United States was far superior to the Soviet Union in nuclear weaponry, Kennedy believed the United States faced a challenge to the global balance of power from both the Soviets and the Chinese Communists, who he claimed were merely vying with one another over the best way to bury the West. Because the Soviets possessed hydrogen bombs, Kennedy complained, Eisenhower's reliance on nuclear weapons represented a dangerous illusion; neither side could use such weapons for fighting conventional and brushfire wars. Kennedy therefore adopted a flexible response strategy to counter Communist-led insurgencies like the one in South Vietnam. The President and Secretary of State Dean Rusk also became particularly alarmed by the aggressive rhetoric of the People's Republic of China, which seemed to be gaining influence in Hanoi in 1962.

Kennedy had other reasons for taking the NLF challenge seriously. He had learned during the 1950s that he could win political rewards by advocating an anti-Communist counter-offensive. After all, he had grown up in the Massachusetts politics of anti-Communism, and Bay State voters had provided some of Joseph R. McCarthy's most loyal supporters. As a young congressman Kennedy had actually joined Republicans in criticizing the Democrats for losing East Germany, Poland, and China to the Soviets. He had also made headlines by pursuing alleged Communists in labor unions, and during his senatorial campaign of 1952, he charged that Henry Cabot Lodge, Jr., was soft on Communism. During his political campaigns he solicited support from a wide range of anti-Communist ethnic organizations—Italians, Poles, Germans, Hungarians, Czechs, Greeks, Lithuanians, and Russians.

The political arithmetic was simple—ethnic voters had supported Truman by a two-to-one margin in 1948, but they shifted in large numbers to Eisenhower in 1952. Due in part to his public McCarthyism, Kennedy was one of the few Democrats to buck the Republican tide in 1952. Although ethnic voters did not support McCarthyism in larger proportions than the general population, McCarthyism became the bridge over which formerly loyal Democratic voters in critical electoral college states left the decaying New Deal coalition. In 1956, 35 percent of Catholic *Democrats* voted against Stevenson. Kennedy knew good politics when he saw it. During his campaign, Kennedy portrayed himself as the man who could stand up to the Communists better than the Republicans, whom he accused of losing both Cuba and the Cold War. In the electoral college, Kennedy achieved a net gain of 22 votes due to the fortuitous concentration of ethnic blocs in key Northern and Midwestern states, and these votes were critical in the very close election of 1960.

The Republicans would hold Kennedy to his campaign promises of victories in the Cold War. In 1960, Richard M. Nixon had predicted that Kennedy was "the kind of man Mr. Khrushchev will make mincemeat of," and during his final briefing of the President-elect, Eisenhower told Kennedy he had to intervene militarily in Laos, with or without allies, if the Laotians appealed to the Southeast Asian Treaty Organization (SEATO). Kennedy had sought a second meeting with Eisenhower during the transition because he himself was leaning toward escalation in Laos, where leftist guerrillas were defeating American-backed rightists. For Eisenhower, an independent Laos was vital for holding the rest of Southeast Asia. According to one participant in this meeting, however, Eisenhower did leave an opening for a peaceful solution by saying that a coalition government which included the Communists might succeed in keeping Laos neutral indefinitely, but Kennedy concluded from this meeting that Eisenhower would prefer United States military intervention to any substantial Communist success in Laos. During this second meeting neither Eisenhower nor Kennedy thought Vietnam required emergency measures, for they did not mention the country.

At the start of his Administration, Kennedy believed Indochina demanded decisions. In spite of the best efforts of Central Intelligence Agency advisers, America's allies in Laos were in disarray, and the neutralist factions there were tilting toward cooperation with the Communists; the NLF was making steady gains in South Vietnam; Diem's regime was almost completely dependent upon the United States for funds; and the 675 American advisers in South Vietnam could not stir Diem's security forces to fight effectively. With Eisenhower's support, Kennedy might have declared the region a vital security zone and stationed regular American armed forces in South Vietnam, Laos, and Thailand, exposing those units to attrition by the guerrillas. Or he might have decided to increase military, economic, and political aid and advice to the Laotians and Vietnamese and rely on them to hold the line, exposing only American advisers to danger. Or, finally, he might have tried to negotiate a neutralization agreement with the Communist powers, leaving American allies in Laos and Vietnam to fight on with American dollar aid only, while drawing the military containment line at the Thai border. Kennedy chose the middle course—escalation short of sending United States combat troops—though he had to retreat from Laos and apply his strategy to South Vietnam.

Why did Kennedy intervene in Southeast Asia? Domestic politics played its part, but international factors were also important. Kennedy perceived the Laotian civil war as yet another Sino-Soviet challenge, and he became even more alarmed when Premier Nikita Khrushchev placated the Chinese by declaring Soviet support for wars of national liberation. Khrushchev added to Kennedy's uneasiness in 1961 by increasing Soviet airlifts to Congolese and Laotian insurgents and by augmenting aid to Castro's Cuba and to North Vietnam. Even more disturbing was Khrushchev's threat to resume the Berlin blockade. In October, just before the Berlin crisis eased, Kennedy told Arthur Krock of the *New York Times* that "it was a hell of a note . . . that he had to try to handle the Berlin situation with the Communists encouraging foreign aggressors all over the place . . . in Viet-Nam, Laos, etc."

In early 1961 Kennedy believed the United States lacked the strength to intervene with conventional forces in both Southeast Asia and Europe simultaneously, and, with the Berlin crisis looming, he certainly wanted enough troops available for service in Europe. Landlocked Laos presented difficult logistical problems, and the anticommunist Laotians showed little desire for combat. General Maxwell D. Taylor and Walt W. Rostow of the National Security Council (NSC) staff urged the President to commit the United States to direct military intervention if the Communists renewed their Laotian offensive. Kennedy demurred, replying that President Charles de Gaulle of France "had spoken with feeling of the difficulty of fighting in this part of the world." He also "emphasized the reluctance of the American people and of many distinguished military leaders to see any direct involvement of U.S. troops in that part of the world." Consequently, Kennedy chose to negotiate, and in April 1961 the Soviets and Chinese agreed to meet in Geneva to discuss Laos.

By careful maneuvering, Kennedy was able to limit Republican criticism of his plan for a Laotian coalition government. He neutralized Eisenhower by having British Prime Minister Harold Macmillan appeal directly to the ex-President, and on July 20 he arranged for General Douglas MacArthur to lecture congressional leaders on the inadvisability of deploying American troops in Southeast Asia. Kennedy hoped he could persuade the South Vietnamese and Thais to send their own forces into Southern Laos, if the need arose. Rostow concluded that Kennedy wanted "indigenous forces used to the maximum," and "should we have to fight, we should use air and seapower to the maximum and engage minimum U.S. forces on the Southeast Asian mainland." The Geneva Conference on Laos began in May 1961 and lasted until June 1962, when the conferees agreed to set up a neutral government. Although they promised to respect Laotian neutrality and avoid establishing foreign military bases in Laos, by late 1962 both sides were covertly violating the agreement. Nevertheless, the shaky arrangement held together, decreasing the need for overt American intervention after June 1962.

Kennedy's concessions in Laos raised the stakes for him in South Vietnam. During the Laos negotiations, Dean Rusk told Andrei Gromyko that "there must be a cessation of the increasingly open attacks against South Viet Nam by the DRV [North Vietnam]. . . . Both the Soviets and the DRV should understand that we are deeply committed to South Vietnam and cannot and will not accept its destruction." In spite of Rusk's claim, the Eisenhower Administration had not formally committed Kennedy to defend South Vietnam. The SEATO treaty required only that member nations consult with one another and meet common dangers according to their own "constitutional processes." Eisenhower had conditioned the large United States aid program on proper performance by Diem—a performance which Elbridge Durbrow, the United States Ambassador in Saigon, 1960–1961, found lacking. Eisenhower's policy toward South Vietnam left Kennedy with options other than to support a Diemist regime, but Kennedy was determined to help the South Vietnamese defeat the Communists.

Even before deciding to negotiate a Laotian settlement, Kennedy had gradually increased American military and economic aid to South Vietnam. At the outset of his Administration Kennedy had expressed doubt that Eisenhower had been doing enough in South Vietnam, and he asked his NSC staff, "How do we change morale; how do we get [South Vietnamese] operations in the north [North Vietnam]; how do we get moving?" In order to shift "from the defense to the offense," Kennedy authorized a 50,000-man increase in ARVN, sent in more American training staff, deployed 400 Green Berets to lead 9,000 border tribesmen against North Vietnam's infiltration routes, ordered the Central Intelligence Agency to organize commando raids against North Vietnam, armed the South Vietnamese provincial Civil Guard forces with heavy weapons, and added $42 million to an aid program which was already spending $220 million per year. In May 1961 Diem assured Vice President Lyndon B. Johnson that this impressive military and economic buildup would enable the ARVN to go on the offensive. Kennedy also prompted SEATO to declare publicly that it would refuse to "acquiesce in [a] takeover of [South Vietnam by] . . . an armed minority . . . supported from outside. . . ." In spite of these emergency actions, 58 percent of South Vietnam was under some degree of Communist control in May 1961, according to the Department of Defense.

When Kennedy personally tried to warn off the Russians, however, he hit a roadblock. At the Vienna summit in June, Kennedy brought up Khrushchev's speech in support of national liberation wars, and he told the Soviet leader that the "problem was how to avoid direct contact between [the] two countries as we support respective groups; [he] referred to Vietnam guerrilla activity and said we do not believe they represent [the] popular will. . . ." Khrushchev said the Soviets found it necessary to support such wars, because they were the only way oppressed peoples could throw off their oppressors. He also warned that American meddling in such wars might bring the "terrible prospect of mutual destruction." While Kennedy found Khrushchev to be threatening in this encounter, the young President may well have misperceived the degree of Soviet aggressiveness. During the Vienna summit, Kennedy gave as good as he got, and Khrushchev's moves in Germany, Laos, and the Congo might well have been defensive. In Berlin, the East Germans were losing growing numbers of refugees to the West; in Laos, the Communists were counterattacking against an American-backed rightist offensive; and in the Congo, Eisenhower had winked at the Belgian-sponsored Katanga secession and had driven Patrice Lumumba, a nationalist leader, to seek Soviet military aid. Even Khrushchev's much quoted speech called for disarmament negotiations and increased East-West trade, not just national liberation wars. The Soviet Union was not a principal opponent in South Vietnam.

Who was the enemy in South Vietnam? The People's Republic of China was hardly a consistent or enthusiastic ally of the Vietnamese Communists, for Beijing had joined Moscow in forcing Ho Chi Minh to accept the division of Vietnam during the 1954 Geneva Conference, and the Chinese Communists continued to compete with the North Vietnamese for influence over the Pathet Lao in Laos. Until 1960 the Chinese had not been enthusiastic about reviving the insurgency in South Vietnam. Given this record, the majority of the North Vietnamese preferred to lean to the side of the more distant Russians rather than to the side of the nearby Chinese. And just before Kennedy decided to escalate American efforts drastically in South Vietnam, Zhou Enlai walked dramatically out of the Twenty-second Congress of the Communist Party of the Soviet Union on October 23, 1961. As the Sino-Soviet dispute widened in 1961–1963, the North Vietnamese were able to play off both Communist powers to secure somewhat increased aid, but even the Chinese stressed that the independent strength of internal revolutionaries, not outside aid, was the prerequisite for victory in national liberation wars. Although the 1950s' line of peaceful coexistence did disappear from Communist rhetoric, neither the Chinese nor the Russians wanted to press national liberation wars to a direct superpower confrontation, and both recognized the centrality of indigenous sources to revolutionary success.

The North Vietnamese were not even the primary enemy in South Vietnam, for they hoped to avoid a full-scale conventional war with the American-advised Army of the Republic of Vietnam (ARVN). They planned to mobilize the peasantry by a socio-political campaign and convert urban dwellers and disgruntled ARVN officers to their cause by nationalistic appeals, and then set up a coalition government after a general uprising and coup. In order to appeal to nationalists, the North Vietnamese urged the Southern Vietminh to organize the NLF. After the coup, the North Vietnamese probably planned to ease the Americans out of the country and then move the noncommunist elements out of the coalition. This program would let Hanoi finish its new five-year economic plan for the north by 1966. The North Vietnamese, then, did not constitute the *primary* enemy in South Vietnam during the Kennedy Administration, though they certainly provided leadership, some supplies, and encouragement to southern NLF fighters.

The two main enemies of the United States in South Vietnam were the peasants, who supported the NLF for reasons which Kennedy did not understand, and the southern Vietminh (later NLF) leaders who had suffered or gone into exile under Diem. Under Ho Chi Minh's direction from 1945 to 1954 the southern Vietminh had established the legitimacy of their movement by helping to defeat the Japanese, by driving the French colonialists from the country, and by extending the Vietminh revolution to at least 60 percent of the South, only to see Diem re-impose landlord control in the rural areas and arrest those suspected of Communist connections or opposition sympathies. By 1961 the NLF-inspired peasants were steadily liberating themselves from Diemist rule, while supplying their village militias with arms purchased or captured from the ARVN or brought home by numerous

ARVN deserters. Although they received trained leaders from among the southerners who had fled North and returned, and although they received some arms from China, the NLF-led peasants could sustain a guerrilla campaign and control the countryside without major infiltration or arms shipments from North Vietnam or China.

The NLF had so many advantages that the insurgency spread rapidly. Its land program carried great appeal in the Delta region, where tenant farmers comprised the great majority, as well as in central Vietnam where landholdings were very small. Tenants customarily paid around 50 to 60 percent of their crop to the landlord, in addition to taxes and bribes, leaving them far poorer than Kennedy and Gullion supposed. The Diemists also represented an old, Westernizing, landlord regime, symbolized by Catholicism, which distinguished it from the majority of its Confucian, Buddhist, and Animist countrymen. By the fall of 1961, the peasant revolutionaries had won control of the villages in many regions of South Vietnam, although some experts have maintained that the Delta region was still hotly contested as late as 1963. Walt Rostow and Roger Hilsman, Kennedy's principal counter-insurgency war theorists, did not understand the attraction of the people's war strategy for the peasantry. They believed the Communists were primarily terrorists and guerrilla fighters, whose challenge was as much military as socioeconomic, though Rostow stressed the military side of the struggle more than Hilsman. If Kennedy had felt politically free to do so, and if he had understood the strength of the people's war strategy, he might well have accepted coalition governments in both Laos and South Vietnam and drawn the counter-insurgency line instead in Thailand, a country which had not suffered the social divisions of colonialism and which did not suffer from a major insurgency.

By fall 1961 Diem's regime was in far deeper trouble than Kennedy had realized. In September, NLF armed forces tripled their attacks and consolidated their hold on much more of the countryside. Diem requested a bilateral security treaty with the United States and, with less enthusiasm, the dispatch of regular American combat forces. Kennedy then sent General Taylor, his personal military counselor, and Rostow of the NSC staff, two hawkish advisers, to South Vietnam to explore the seriousness of the setback and the need to meet Diem's requests. After their return the President began to consider his options. Through early November, the debate among Kennedy's principal advisers centered on a variety of escalatory alternatives. There were five main policies suggested, each of which reflected the organizational origins of its sponsor. Defense Secretary Robert S. McNamara and the Joint Chiefs of Staff recommended sending 40,000 regular United States troops to deal with the NLF, and 205,000 if the North Vietnamese and Chinese intervened with regular troops. The Joint Chiefs believed that regular American troops were quite capable of dealing with lightly armed guerrillas and that North Vietnamese and Chinese logistical difficulties and American air attacks could prevent the Communists from mounting a conventional campaign in South Vietnam on the scale of Korea. McNamara also wanted to warn North Vietnam that it would suffer "punitive retaliation" if it continued to support the southern guerrillas.

McGeorge Bundy, Kennedy's National Security Adviser, joined Taylor and Rostow in arguing for a second alternative. They believed a smaller commitment of American troops—on the order of 5,000 to 25,000—would deter the North Vietnamese from aiding the NLF, and they expected this deployment to galvanize the South Vietnamese effort, provided that Kennedy also agreed to send a large number of American advisers, helicopters, tactical bombers, transport planes, logistical detachments, and intelligence units. Taylor believed helicopters and improved intelligence efforts would allow ARVN to move from static defensive positions to active pursuit of the guerrillas. McGeorge Bundy claimed that the United States was already committed to the survival of South Vietnam and that a victory there would "produce great effects all over the world." He contrasted South Vietnam with Laos: "Laos was never really ours after 1954. South Vietnam is and wants to be. Laotians have fought very little. South Vietnam troops are not U.S Marines, but they are usable."

Taylor, Rostow, and Edward Lansdale predicted that spreading American advisers throughout the South Vietnamese government would spur ARVN to action and shorten military reaction times, which had been slow because of Diem's personal control of all military movements. General Lansdale was a CIA agent who had helped direct the successful counter-insurgency effort of Ramon Magsaysay in the Philippines, and he had also helped advise Diem during the latter's consolidation of power in South Vietnam. "A U.S. operating presence at many working levels," Lansdale predicted, would force the South Vietnamese "to get their house in order." This proposal reflected Kennedy's continuing desire to use local troops in Southeast Asia, though it bowed slightly toward the Pentagon by including small formations of American combat troops. This recommendation also reflected Taylor's belief that air mobility and tactical bombing provided a way for technologically superior forces to take the offensive in limited wars.

The State Department was much more ambivalent about Diem's regime and offered a third alternative: a hard line on Diem to go with more advisers and aid. As McGeorge Bundy summarized Dean Rusk's views, the Secretary of State "knows we may lose, and he knows we want no Korea but he . . . thinks we *must* meet Khrushchev in Vietnam or take a terrible defeat." Nevertheless, Rusk had grown frustrated with Diem's repeated rejection of Ambassador Frederick Nolting's requests to revise the military command arrangements which prevented ARVN generals from responding quickly to NLF attacks (and also from mounting a coup against Diem). Rusk feared Diem's continued refusal to "trust [his] military commanders" and "to consolidate non-communist elements into [a] serious national effort" would eventually make him "a losing horse."

Sterling Cottrell, the head of State's Vietnam task force, which oversaw day-to-day implementation of Vietnam policy in 1961, was less polite, when he called Diem "an oriental despot." Ambassador Galbraith added that Diem's family dictatorship was marked by "intrigue, nepotism . . . , corruption . . . , administrative paralysis and steady deterioration." George C. McGhee, the counselor at the Department of State who had run the American counter-insurgency program during the Greek civil war in the 1940s, had argued earlier that South Vietnamese insurgents derived support from inside the country and therefore American regulars would not be of much help, since "alien troops simply lack the bases for discriminating between friend and foe. . . ." State Department officials urged the use of foreign aid as a lever to force Diem to revise his chain of command and broaden his government.

Kennedy's political advisers warned him against the dangers of sending American troops into combat and offered a fourth alternative. Senator Mike Mansfield, a former supporter of Diem, feared the Chinese might overwhelm American troops with regulars of their own, while Diem and the South Vietnamese would regard the deployment of United States regulars as a "revival of colonial force." Mansfield argued that the way to secure the South Vietnamese countryside was to introduce "democratic practices at the village and provincial levels" and couple them with economic and social reforms. "If the necessary reforms have not been forthcoming over the past seven years . . . then I do not see how American combat troops can do it today . . . we must . . . avoid another Korean-type involvement on the Asian mainland." Mansfield recommended a different solution: give Diem all the money and weapons he needed, but let him do the job, while keeping the number of Americans in the field extremely limited. Theodore Sorensen, the President's political alter-ego, later explained the rationale for this position. No effective way seemed to exist to use a division of American troops against "guerrilla-terrorist tactics," and the South Vietnamese government in any case had a 10 to 1 manpower advantage. Sorensen concluded:

> This battle must be won at [the] village level; and thus only the Vietnamese can defeat the Viet Cong. . . . Troops of a different country, color and culture are not as suitable or effective . . . as long as the local troops are in the preponderance. If such troops have the will, we can supply the weapons, training and financing—no more should be needed.[48]

W. Averell Harriman, the head negotiator at the talks on Laos, suggested a fifth, very different alternative. He advised that the Soviet Union was interested in stabilizing Southeast Asia, at least for a time, and that the United States should agree to reduce its military presence in South Vietnam as peace was restored in the area. For their part, the North Vietnamese and the NLF would agree to a cease-fire, accept a strong United Nations Control Commission, and achieve eventual reunification, possibly through elections. Harriman's proposal was not likely to have appealed to the NLF leaders, for unlike the Communists in Laos, they would have gotten no role in a coalition government. Galbraith and Chester Bowles, the former Under Secretary of State whose influence was waning rapidly, also backed the idea of an independent, neutral South Vietnam; otherwise, Bowles warned, "we are headed full blast up a dead end street."

Kennedy briefly considered the neutralization proposal, but in the end he did not pursue it, or even order preliminary diplomatic contacts with the North Vietnamese or the NLF. He rejected neutralization, even though the international reasons for maintaining a hard line had moderated. By November 1961 the Berlin crisis had eased considerably, while the Sino-Soviet split had worsened. Even so, Rusk and McNamara warned that a retreat from South Vietnam would destroy SEATO and undermine the credibility of American commitments elsewhere. But they also added that "extreme elements" would seize on such a withdrawal "to divide the country and harass the Administration." After the failure of the Bay of Pigs invasion in April 1961, the Republicans began charging that Kennedy was yielding ground to the Communists around the world. They criticized him for canceling air strikes during the Bay of Pigs operation; for talking "big" and then backing "down when the chips were down" in Laos; for agreeing to negotiate on Berlin; and for failing to respond to the construction of the Berlin Wall in August. Senator Barry Goldwater made the cover of *Time* magazine in the summer of 1961 by criticizing Kennedy's softness. The President moved to head off criticism. In October, he told Sorensen to ask Walter Lippmann, Joseph Alsop, and other columnists how to counter increasing Republican charges of appeasement, and he publicly urged Americans to display "national maturity" in the face of temporary gains and setbacks in the Cold War.

Kennedy ruled out neutralization, but he also vetoed the Pentagon's plan to send regular combat troops to South Vietnam. Although the proposal for troops had gained wide support within the Administration, Taylor reported that Kennedy was "instinctively" against it. The CIA supported the President by predicting that the North Vietnamese would match American deployments with increased infiltration. On November 11, Kennedy vetoed sending regular combat troops. Instead, he decided to increase economic aid as well as send more advisers to ARVN and to South Vietnamese intelligence and government agencies. The United States also promised air reconnaissance, air transport, and helicopter units to improve ARVN reactions to NLF movements. Kennedy ordered that American advisers be assigned to ARVN field battalions, rather than division headquarters (thereby allowing them to help plan and direct operations). The President also followed Lansdale's advice by seeking the insertion of American advisers into the South Vietnamese government to provide operational guidance at all levels. The advisory effort, he said, "should be substantial otherwise we will give the wrong impression. . . . Are we prepared to send in hundreds and hundreds of men and dozens and dozens of ships? If we would just show up with 4 or 5 ships this will not do much good. . . . As I said on Saturday concerning Laos—we took actions which made no difference at all." In return for all of this United States assistance Diem would have to mobilize his nation fully, broaden his government, and give his generals the power to move troops without prior clearance from Saigon. Kennedy directed Ambassador Nolting to tell Diem that the "missions being undertaken by our own forces . . . are more suitable for white foreign troops than garrison duty or seeking out of Viet Cong personnel submerged in the Viet-Nam population." Nevertheless, Kennedy had committed Americans to fly helicopters and planes and accompany ARVN troops when they engaged the NLF.

In mid-November, Kennedy tried to dissuade Bundy, Taylor, Rostow, McNamara, and the Joint Chiefs from their campaign to send regular troops by telling them foreign troops were only "a last resort." The President added that he did not want a war with China. He did agree to allow the Pentagon to plan for the introduction of SEATO troops, but that was as far as he would go. Vietnam, he explained, was unlike Korea, because it was not a clear-cut victim of aggression, and, consequently, neither the Democrats in Congress nor the British nor the French would support SEATO intervention there. And the United States did not have enough troops to go around. Nor was it clear why American soldiers should be sent into South Vietnam, but not into Cuba: "The President said that he could even make a rather strong case against intervening in an area 10,000 miles away against 16,000 guerrillas with a native army of 200,000, where millions have been spent for years with no success." The Joint Chiefs remained unconvinced, replying that they favored invading Cuba as well. The Chiefs doubted that the Lansdale counter-insurgency approach would work, for Vietnam was not like the Philippines or Malaya. They told General Taylor in October that the Malay counter-insurgency campaign was not comparable to Vietnam, because the Thais and British were able to control Malaya's borders; because colonial police were able to isolate ethnic Chinese insurgents from the majority of the population; because food was scarce, enabling strategic hamlet programs to work; and because the British, not the Malays, were in command. In January 1962 the Joint Chiefs reiterated their request for the dispatch of regular American troops, but by then the alternative program was well under way.

Diem expressed disappointment and anger. He had requested a bilateral alliance and massive aid, not an Americanization of his government. He told Nolting, "Viet Nam did not want to be a protectorate." After tense negotiations, he agreed only to *consult* American advisers whom he helped select, and he avoided significant changes in his military command structure, because he remained fearful of a coup. Kennedy was trapped by the contradictions in his own policy toward Diem. He could not force a supposedly independent nationalist leader to accept American tutelage without appearing to undermine him, and Diem was already publicizing Kennedy's demands. Kennedy gave way. On December 15, the two governments announced their joint partnership—but on Diem's terms. A solid political foundation was essential to successful prosecution of the war, but the State Department had lost another round in its fight to make Diem more efficient, democratic, and popular. And on February 18, 1962, Robert F. Kennedy confirmed the State Department defeat by declaring unconditionally during a visit to Saigon, "We are going to win in Viet-Nam. We will remain here until we do win."

Diem regained some favor with Washington by accepting another part of the Kennedy plan for South Vietnam—strategic hamlets. Roger Hilsman, director of the State Department's Bureau of Intelligence and Research, correctly concluded that the villages of South Vietnam willingly provided supplies and the great majority of recruits to the NLF. He argued that the South Vietnamese government had to provide villagers with civic action programs and physical security by creating fortified hamlets linked by radio. The strategic hamlets would receive developmental aid and close police scrutiny. In addition, the hamlets' own militias would defend them and call in roving Civil Guard units if the NLF attacked. Because they lacked food and replacements, the NLF bands would have to attack in strength, rather than starve, and the Civil Guard and newly mobile ARVN could then crush them by ambush or conventional engagement.

While Hilsman had a somewhat more accurate perception of the insurgency than the Pentagon, his proposed solution proved unrealistic. His proposed village militias consisted of the fathers, uncles, and brothers of the NLF village guerrillas, and his expectation that one relative would starve or even shoot another in return for a medical clinic, a school, and a new well was strange at best. Diem, and his brother Ngo Dinh Nhu, who was in charge of the secret police and internal security, pushed the hamlet program rapidly as a means of reclaiming the villages. Land reform was notably absent and other benefits slow in coming, while the peasants often had to purchase the building materials and barbed wire which they used to fence themselves in.

At first, the military side of Kennedy's counter-insurgency campaign appeared to show progress. Aided by helicopters and growing numbers of American advisers, the ARVN bedeviled the NLF in the first half of 1962. With ARVN's fortunes appearing to prosper, the Kennedy Administration flirted briefly with negotiations. In July 1962, Harriman, who was just wrapping up the Laos settlement, offered the North Vietnamese a neutrality agreement similar to the one he had just concluded for Laos. Ho Chi Minh replied that the NLF had already suggested such a plan: the United States would withdraw its advisers; a cease-fire would go into effect; the great powers would guarantee the neutralization and independence of Vietnam; the Vietnamese would establish a coalition government, which would include both Diem and the NLF; and the coalition government would end the strategic hamlet program, hold free elections, and begin talks to reunify the country. In late 1962 the NLF also offered a cease-fire which did not first require the withdrawal of the Americans. Given the strength of the NLF in the countryside, free elections would almost certainly have resulted in a government dominated by the NLF. Although the NLF proposal opened the prospect of a decent interval between the time of American withdrawal and the time of a prospective defeat of Diem, Kennedy rejected the NLF offer. The President preferred to seek victory, rather than accept defeat, however much disguised or delayed.

By the end of 1962 Kennedy had sent 11,000 American military personnel to South Vietnam, along with 300 military aircraft, 120 helicopters, and additional heavy weapons. American pilots helped to fly combat missions, and the Americans supplied napalm bombs to the South Vietnamese air force. At Binh Hoa in January 1962 an air strike killed five civilians, including a two-year-old boy, a five-year-old girl, and a seven-year-old boy. If their parents had not been active supporters of the NLF before the raid, they most probably joined after this tragedy. Kennedy put General Paul D. Harkins, a former tank officer, in charge of the military assistance program in Saigon, and Harkins adopted a strategy based on the United States Army's tradition of achieving victory via attrition and destruction of the enemy's army. Harkins left the problem of village militias largely to the Vietnamese Civil Guards and Self Defense Corps, while he tried to break the enemy's will by using ARVN regulars to smash the enemy's main guerrilla forces. Taylor and Harkins wanted to put continuous pressure on the NLF regulars by exploiting American air mobility—a strategy which they believed had worked against guerrillas in both Greece and Korea. When ARVN succeeded in surrounding the NLF regulars with overwhelming numbers, they were supposed to use artillery and air strikes to flush them into combat with superior blocking forces.

For a variety of reasons ARVN could not implement this strategy. Its divisions were trained and armed to deter a conventional invasion from the north, and they were unsuited to chase lightly armed guerrillas who disappeared into the countryside. Nor did many of the units in the field want to fight. A number of senior officers were mercenaries who had served in the colonial French Army, and Diem compounded the problem by putting his favorite officers in charge of the best units and keeping them in garrison, while sending poorly trained units into combat. American advisers could not energize ARVN because they did not speak Vietnamese, control promotions, make aid allocations (which came through Diem), or command troops (as they had done in Korea). Intelligence operations also faltered. American and South Vietnamese intelligence officers sought order-of-battle information on regular NLF units, rather than try to identify members of the local village militias and political committees, who were the mainstays of the insurgency. In 1962 air mobility allowed ARVN to achieve some early surprise victories, but the NLF soon adapted to the helicopters by making quicker hit-and-run attacks and placing heavy machine guns in village tree lines. Even if ARVN had been able to destroy the main force units which they were vainly chasing, they would still have faced the much more numerous village militias. The only solution to the village militias was to occupy the villages, reduce land rents, and recognize the NLF's land redistributions. But American military advisers believed in the Clausewitzian goal of destroying their enemy's army, not clearing and holding peasant villages, and Diem believed in control by his bureaucrats and the landlords, not reform for peasant hamlets.

Given the advanced state of the NLF revolt, Kennedy's counterinsurgency strategy was proving unworkable. As 1962 gave way to 1963, the strategic hamlet program also developed trouble. Diem, Nhu, and Harkins had pushed the program far out into enemy territory, resettling some hamlets in which as many as one-third of the men were missing—they had probably joined the NLF. The sullen strategic hamlet militias often did not defend their villages against the insurgents, and the Self-Defense Corps and Provincial Civil Guard units were unable or unwilling to take on company-sized NLF attacks. By the spring of 1963 only 1500 of 8500 strategic hamlets remained viable. By contrast, in June 1963 the NLF was levying taxes in 42 of South Vietnam's 44 provinces.

Organizational problems also undermined Kennedy's strategy. General Lyman Lemnitzer, the Chairman of the Joint Chiefs of Staff, and General Earle G. Wheeler, Army Chief of Staff, proved unsympathetic to counterinsurgency ideas. Kennedy failed to appoint anyone of stature to ride herd in South Vietnam on Harkins, Diem, and Nhu, while in Washington the

successive Vietnam task force directors also lacked the rank to force independent government departments to coordinate their activities. Consequently
the military campaigns and strategic hamlet programs did not mesh well.
Kennedy kept most of the decisions in his own hands, and he lacked the time
or energy to be an effective Vietnam desk officer. Nor could he play the role
of an Under Secretary of State or Defense in seeking intelligence or reviewing
policy, except in crises such as occurred during the fall of 1961. Most NSC
staffers were primarily European-oriented generalists who lacked Asian
expertise or the time to develop a sophisticated set of questions which would
have revealed the nature of the NLF revolution. The NSC staff members
maintained the illusion of being in touch by having mountains of cables
routed through the White House, but they lacked the time and background
to put them in their proper perspective. Sorensen is correct in saying that
Vietnam "never received the attention it should have . . . at the highest levels." Kennedy remained convinced that the methods of counter-insurgency
would gradually bring victory in the countryside. In his State of the Union
message of 1963, he confidently declared, "The spearpoint of aggression has
been blunted in Viet-Nam."

In early 1963 Kennedy's optimism waned briefly after Senator Mansfield
reported on his recent trip to Southeast Asia. Mansfield warned that the
United States might ultimately be forced to accept a dominant combat role if
Kennedy did not withdraw the American advisers. Mansfield's prediction
reportedly angered the President, who was even less pleased when he heard of
the very poor ARVN showing in combat at Ap Bac in the Delta. With the
American press present, a large ARVN force, aided by American-donated
helicopters and armored personnel carriers, allowed a much smaller NLF
force to escape. In the process, the NLF inflicted heavy casualties on ARVN
and shot down five helicopters. Three American advisers died. Kennedy was
puzzled by "the Vietnam troops and their lack of courage," and he asked his
aides to reassess the rice paddy war. Hilsman and Michael V. Forrestal, the
NSC staffer assigned to expedite Vietnam policy, saw no need to "make any
sudden and dramatic change," though they questioned Harkins's penchant
for large-scale operations. The generals themselves remained optimistic.
Wheeler reported that "[we] are winning slowly on the present thrust," and
Harkins trumpeted that "improvement is a daily fact . . . and we are confident of the outcome."

Besides ARVN and strategic hamlet failures, Kennedy had to contend
with charges that the United States was using "dirty-war" tactics in Vietnam.
Kennedy had indeed ordered a limited, experimental program of trail clearing and crop destruction using defoliants and herbicides such as Agent
Orange. In doing so, he not only set an unfortunate precedent for much
larger applications of chemicals during the Johnson Administration but he

also provided the NLF and North Vietnam with an opportunity to launch a propaganda campaign and appeal to the International Control Commission. It was a high political price to pay for a program which proved militarily worthless.

Much worse problems arose when South Vietnamese troops fired into a crowd of Buddhists in Hué on May 8, 1963. The Buddhist marchers were flying religious banners during a celebration of Buddha's birthday, in spite of a ban on such symbols issued by Diem's brother, Ngo Dinh Thuc, the Archbishop of Hué. The ARVN killed nine marchers and wounded many others, triggering Buddhist demonstrations and self-immolations. In the major South Vietnamese cities students took to the streets to support Buddhist charges of religious discrimination and authoritarianism against the Ngos. Diem and Nhu countered with raids on pagodas, mass arrests, and martial law, each of which provoked more marches and self-immolations, creating a cycle which would persist through the Ngos' collapse in November. Madame Ngo Dinh Nhu, the security chief's wife and Diem's sister-in-law, callously dismissed the immolations as "barbecues" and offered to supply matches and gasoline in the future. The Kennedy Administration attempted repeatedly to induce Diem to compromise with the Buddhists. Diem said he would seek reconciliation, but he never kept his promise.

During his first two years in office Kennedy had tried to minimize the seriousness of the Vietnam problem, and he had largely succeeded. In spite of Sorensen's advice, Kennedy chose not to make a major speech at the end of 1961 explaining his decision to escalate, and thus he delayed public debate. As American advisers went into combat, congressmen yielded to Kennedy's appeals for support and Congress routinely approved increases in American aid programs to South Vietnam. In the summer of 1963, however, the Buddhist crisis brought increasingly critical newspaper reports from Homer Bigart and David Halberstam of the *New York Times* and Neil Sheehan of United Press International. At first Kennedy believed that having the American mission in Saigon bring reporters "into our confidence" would generate an "accurate story [of] our Viet-Nam program," but the journalists' well-founded distrust of the Diem regime and the American mission doomed the effort. In late October Kennedy even tried to persuade *New York Times* publisher Arthur H. Sulzberger to remove Halberstam from South Vietnam, but to no avail. Vietnam became a big story in August and September 1963, and increasingly the criticism included both Kennedy and Diem. Kennedy finally had to conclude, "The way to confound the press is to win the war."

As the election campaigns for 1964 began, bipartisan support for Kennedy's foreign policy broke down. During the summer and fall of 1963, conservatives attacked the foreign aid bill, the American wheat sale to the

Soviet Union, and the nuclear test ban treaty. Nelson Rockefeller, Nixon, and Goldwater were waiting for Kennedy to make serious mistakes in South Vietnam and then exploit such errors in the presidential campaign. Senator Richard Russell of Georgia, a member of the President's own party, presaged the debate by chiding the Administration for "trying to fight this [Vietnam] problem as if it were a tournament of roses." He called for the "dirty-tricks department" to offer rewards for NLF guerrillas—dead or alive. To Kennedy, experienced as he was in the politics of anti-Communism, these criticisms foreshadowed another debate about "who lost China?"

While Kennedy watched the Buddhist crisis in South Vietnam with growing dismay, he faced a similar crisis closer to home: the civil rights conflict in the American South. The civil rights issue worried Kennedy's pollsters and political advisers, who warned that he might lose critical Southern and Midwestern votes in the next election. By August 1963, half of those polled said he was pushing integration too fast. Louis Harris's analysis of the 1960 results indicated the Republicans might make real inroads in the region in 1964, and a Lubell survey of former Kennedy voters in Birmingham, Alabama, turned up only one white who would again vote for Kennedy.

The probable political loss of the South made the retention and expansion of the Democratic vote in the North vital, but Kennedy's advisers warned him he was in trouble there as well. States such as Ohio, Indiana, and Wisconsin, with their large ethnic blocs, were critical to victory, but Harris warned that urban Poles and Italians required "immediate and hard work" by the Democrats, because they were frustrated by their stagnant wages and by increased competition from blacks for jobs and housing. Harris concluded that the Republicans might win in 1964 by adding Southern segregationist and Northern working-class voters to their traditional strength in the Western states. Ithiel de Sola Pool, a pollster and political analyst, reported that Kennedy had successfully appealed to these "urban Catholic Democratic" swing voters in 1960 with a hard line on Cold War containment. At the same time, however, mass public opinion placed limits on the possibility of military escalation, since surveys showed that the average American feared the Democrats as the party of war. This mass opinion actually remained inattentive to the Vietnam issue through 1963, but the potential for a strong reaction remained everpresent, especially if escalation occurred or defeat loomed. In any case, it was the swing votes, and not mass opinion, which counted in the Electoral College. The Republican party turned demonstrably further to the right as Barry Goldwater moved ahead of Nelson Rockefeller in the polls, and Republican pundits predicted that Goldwater's states' rights stand would win the formerly solid South and Northern white ethnics over to the Republican banner in 1964.

Thus, in addition to Kennedy's personal and ideological commitment to containment in South Vietnam, there also existed a political imperative to quiet the Buddhist crisis, stabilize the South Vietnamese regime, and convince the South Vietnamese to fight effectively. But Kennedy had little luck with Diem. In fact, Kennedy's efforts to persuade Diem to mollify the Buddhists aggravated the underlying conflict between Saigon and Washington. Diem resented the rapid American advisery buildup and the American advisers' penchant for meddling in Vietnamese decisions. The South Vietnamese dictator also feared—quite correctly—the Americans might encourage his enemies among the South Vietnamese generals to depose him. The CIA reported that Diem might request a reduction in the number of American advisers. When asked about Diem's complaints at a news conference, Kennedy responded that withdrawal of the advisers would be premature, with "still a long, hard struggle to go" and no "brightening in the skies that would permit us to withdraw troops or begin to by the end of this year." Actually, back in 1962 when the war seemed to be going well, the Pentagon had prepared plans for an orderly withdrawal. If Kennedy had wanted to, he might have used these plans to implement a withdrawal of aid and advisers in stages as a means of forcing the generals and Diem to reform.

During June and July intelligence officials warned Kennedy that Diem had alienated the nationalist elites which Kennedy had identified in the 1950s as vital to building a stable Third World. Thomas Hughes of the State Department reported that discontent was widespread in the civil bureaucracy, in the military establishment, among students, and even within the Catholic hierarchy. Hughes, Hilsman, and the CIA warned that a coup against Diem was a distinct possibility, and Hughes and the CIA assured Kennedy that "a reasonably large pool of . . . experienced and trained manpower" existed which "could provide reasonably effective leadership for the government [of South Vietnam] and [for] the war effort."

On June 27 the Administration announced the nomination of Henry Cabot Lodge, former senator from Massachusetts and Republican candidate for Vice President in 1960, as Ambassador to Saigon. According to the CIA, a "considerably disturbed" Diem correctly interpreted the appointment to mean "that the United States [now] planned to wield a 'big stick.' . . ." Lodge's appointment also gave the Administration political sea room to act against Diem; one magazine predicted Lodge's appointment would "make the Republicans think twice before attacking Administration policy in troublesome South Viet Nam." Lodge arrived in Saigon on August 22, the day after Nhu's American-trained Special Forces raided Buddhist pagodas in Saigon, Hué, and elsewhere and made mass arrests. Diem had presented Lodge with a fait accompli: he had curbed the Buddhists before Lodge could press him to accommodate them. Rumors even circulated that Diem and

Nhu were considering serious negotiations with North Vietnam. Kennedy had instructed Lodge to persuade Diem to treat his non-Communist opponents better, and if Diem resisted, work for Diem's removal. In fact, since July a group of ARVN generals led by Duong Van Minh, Tran Van Don, and Tran Thien Khiem had been exploring with American CIA agents the possibility of an American-supported coup.

In Washington, many senior officials were on vacation at the time of the August raids on the pagodas, and the anti-Diem faction in the White House and State Department urged swift action. Forrestal urged the President to "move before the situation in Saigon freezes." With the aid of George Ball, the Under Secretary of State, who was filling in for Rusk, Harriman, Hilsman, and Forrestal persuaded Kennedy over the telephone to instruct Lodge on August 24 to compel Diem to drop Nhu from his administration and accept American advice on how to run his government and army. If Diem did not comply, then the United States was to give "direct support" to the ARVN generals in the event of Diem's ouster. Kennedy assured Lodge, "We will back you to the hilt on actions you take to achieve our objectives." Perhaps with the Bay of Pigs fiasco in mind, Kennedy did want time to review plans for the coup to assure that the American-backed generals would succeed. He warned Lodge on August 29, "I know from experience that failure is more destructive than the appearance of indecision. . . . When we go, we must go to win. . . ." Consequently, Kennedy reserved the right to "change course and reverse previous instructions." But he continued to allow the Ambassador wide discretion in the execution of his Vietnam policy, authorizing Lodge to suspend aid to Diem "at a time and under conditions of your choice." Although Lodge was eager to act immediately, the ARVN generals were unable to line up enough military support in the Saigon area to risk a coup.

Kennedy continued to apply pressure to Diem. On television on September 2 he remarked that the war could not be won without popular support from the South Vietnamese, and, he added, "in my opinion, in the last 2 months, the government has gotten out of touch with the people." Kennedy predicted that Diem could only regain such support "with changes in policy and perhaps with [changes in] personnel." Otherwise, the chances for victory "would not be very good." But Kennedy disagreed "with those who say we should withdraw. That would be a great mistake. . . . Forty-seven Americans have been killed in combat with the enemy, but this is a very important struggle even though it is far away." Between October 2 and October 5, Kennedy signaled his displeasure with Diem by applying a variety of "selective pressures": Kennedy canceled some future economic aid shipments; threatened to cut off American support for Nhu's Special Forces, unless they were placed under the command of the ARVN General Staff and moved from Saigon into the field; recalled the CIA station chief in Saigon, who was too closely identified with Nhu; and announced publicly that 1,000 American advisers would be withdrawn from South Vietnam by the end of 1963 and all American advisers would be out by the end of 1965, provided that the war in the countryside continued to go well.

By cutting aid to Diem, Kennedy helped revive—apparently unwittingly—the ARVN generals' interest in a coup. On October 3, Duong Van Minh, Chief of the General Staff, asked for reassurance that the Americans would not oppose a coup, and he suggested the possibility that the plan might include the assassination of two Ngo brothers, Nhu and Can. Lucien Conein, Minh's CIA contact, assured him that Washington would provide economic and military assistance to a new regime which promised to cooperate with the United States, regain popular support, and try to win the war. CIA Director John McCone neither encouraged nor deplored the recommendation for the assassination of Diem's brothers, although he did warn Saigon that Diem himself should not be killed. On October 25, Lodge alerted Kennedy that a coup would occur sometime before November. In the days just before the coup, Kennedy and McGeorge Bundy worriedly questioned Lodge about prospects for success and the possibility of achieving plausible deniability of the American role in the coup. Once the attempted overthrow began, however, they told Lodge it was "in the interests of the U.S. Government that it should succeed."

On the morning of November 1, Lodge met for the last time with Diem. A few hours later the coup finally began, with CIA agent Conein at coup headquarters to report to the embassy, advise the coup leaders, and distribute cash, if needed. At 4:30 p.m. that same day a frantic Diem telephoned the United States Ambassador. Lodge relayed an offer of safe conduct out of the country from the coup leaders, but he claimed disingenuously that the United States government had no policy toward the coup. While Diem and Nhu escaped to the Cholon section of Saigon, both to die the following day at the hands of General Minh's lieutenants, Lodge went to bed. On November 8, Washington officially recognized the new military regime in Saigon. A week later, in response to a *New York Times* editorial which suggested a negotiated settlement of the war, Rusk instructed Lodge to tell the generals that the United States government "cannot envisage any points that would be negotiable." The Secretary of State reassured the South Vietnamese government that North Vietnam would have to end its "subversive aggression" and allow the new South Vietnamese regime to "extend its authority throughout South Vietnam before the United States would withdraw."

The events of 1963 shattered one expectation—that Diem would listen to American advice, reform his government, and win the war—and created another—that the generals would do the same. Before the coup Kennedy and his Washington advisers simply assumed that the ARVN generals would be an improvement over Diem, but they were wrong. Many of the members of the South Vietnamese Military Revolutionary Council had been collaborators with the French colonialists, and Robert Thompson, the British counter-insurgency expert, thought they "lacked the experience or ability to command much more than a regiment, let alone a country." Within three months, another military faction overthrew Minh and the Revolutionary Council, starting a topsy-turvy pattern of coup and counter-coup which continued for some time. Even the Buddhist protest marches and self-immolations continued to occur.

Before Minh fell, however, Kennedy himself died. His remarks prepared for delivery on November 22 in Dallas, Texas, a destination he never reached, included the words: "We in this country in this generation are—by destiny rather than choice—the watchmen on the walls of world freedom. . . . Our assistance to . . . nations can be painful, risky and costly, as is true in Southeast Asia today. But we dare not weary of the task." And in another speech he intended to deliver that night can be seen the outline of his anticipated 1964 campaign. The New Frontier had gotten the country moving again—America's economy was growing, its space effort thriving, its military power expanding, and its containment policy working from Berlin to Latin America to Southeast Asia. On the day he died he still hoped for victory in South Vietnam and vindication of the doctrine of counter-insurgency.

Why did Kennedy persist in Vietnam under such unpromising conditions? After all, many leaders, ranging from Charles de Gaulle and Douglas MacArthur to Mike Mansfield and John Kenneth Galbraith, had warned Kennedy against a deepening Vietnam adventure. He chose to ignore their warnings. His defenders claimed that the Eisenhower Administration left him no choice but to pursue the war in Vietnam. But he might well have drawn the containment line in Thailand, while letting Diem fight his own battles with generous grants of money and arms. Instead, he sent in 16,000 advisers, 100 of whom had died by the end of 1963; he sponsored the strategic hamlet program; he unleashed a war of attrition against the NLF; and he allowed the military to use napalm, defoliation, and helicopter envelopment tactics, rather than a clear and hold strategy. Why did he do it? Both Khrushchev and Mao Zedong may have helped to draw him in, for they had exaggerated their support for national liberation wars, thereby lending substance to Kennedy's fears. In fact, however, the fragmentation of the Communist world was accelerating in these years, as Kennedy could read in his own intelligence reports. If Kennedy had negotiated a deal on South Vietnam, he might have encouraged détente with the Soviet Union and hastened a Sino-Vietnamese split.

Kennedy's self-confident definition of the South Vietnamese problem was an important reason for his persistence. The President believed that Diem and the generals constituted a third force of nationalists who could lead peasants and workers in a fight against Communism. Because Americans were nation-builders, not colonialists, they could persuade the South Vietnamese to apply American technology, tactics, and organizational techniques to the problems of the Vietnamese countryside, wracked by continued underdevelopment, terrorism, and guerrilla warfare. The struggle would be long and hard, but success would come eventually—if only the right combination of Vietnamese nationalist leaders could be found. The misapplied analogs of Greece and Malaya reinforced his belief in nation-building and counter-insurgency. Kennedy's image of Vietnam proved false. In the minds of the peasants, Diem and the generals represented the old regime. The people of the countryside craved land, power, and the promise of economic justice and national liberation, not wells, clinics, films, strategic hamlets, or infantry sweeps through their villages. The NLF program also contained more political and economic change and less coercion and violence than Kennedy comprehended. Kennedy's expectations for the future were unrealistic as well. American advisers could not transform the ARVN into an effective force, nor persuade Diem and Nhu to appeal to the peasantry.

Kennedy's decision-making system failed to correct the President's false image of Vietnam's prospects. His small staff lacked an understanding of the socio-economic appeal of the Chinese and Vietnamese revolutions to the peasantry. The NSC did not produce an accurate picture which would shatter the President's strongly held image of a nationalist elite waiting for outside inspiration to mobilize a neutral peasantry against Communist terrorists. Although Kennedy's collegial style of decision-making has received considerable praise, it did not work very well in the case of Vietnam. Until the Buddhist crisis of 1963 Kennedy usually treated Vietnam as a fairly routine foreign policy problem, which he assumed he could handle with limited resources. His staff, with the exception of the hyperactive Walt Rostow, tended to coast along the lines of established policy, recommending more of the same. Not until November 1961 did a major review of the options emerge. Even then, however, the list of options which were staffed out and fully considered was incomplete, for none of the key debaters, with the brief exception of Harriman, was a serious advocate of neutralization and a retreat to Thailand. Kennedy never gave negotiations a chance. Nor were there many advocates for withholding advisers while giving Diem enough money and arms to sink or swim on his own. Instead of a sophisticated image of the problem of rural revolution in Southeast Asia, ingrained Cold War thinking about the credibility of containment shaped Administration deliberations. Consequently, the debate always centered on escalation, with Kennedy curbing the hawks in the Pentagon and choosing counter-insurgency.

The politics of anti-Communism also played a large role in shaping Kennedy's decisions. He had survived and prospered in the McCarthyite atmosphere of the fifties, and he feared the loss of swing anti-Communist votes to the Republicans and the Dixiecrats in the increasingly turbulent politics of the sixties. The lesson of the so-called loss of China remained with him, and the Republicans repeatedly peppered him with charges of appeasement on a host of issues. During the 1960 campaign he had promised to turn the tide of the Cold War, and he was preparing to claim considerable progress in 1964. With Laos neutralized, Cuba hostile, and East Berlin sealed off, Vietnam became a testing ground by his own definition. Though some of his defenders have claimed he would have withdrawn the United States from Vietnam after his re-election in 1964, they underestimate the degree to which Kennedy had committed himself and the country to supporting a non-Communist Vietnam. Kennedy would have had to admit the failure of his major counter-insurgency effort, which was designed to discourage national liberation wars everywhere. More likely than withdrawal was a continued search for the right combination of means and men to win the war in South Vietnam. Kennedy would probably have ruled out sending in United States Army infantry divisions, but short of that limit, he would probably have continued to make a major effort to succeed.

In any case, by late 1963 Kennedy had radically expanded the American commitment to Vietnam. By putting American advisers in harm's way and allowing the press to chronicle their tribulations and casualties, he helped to engage American patriotism in a war against the Vietnamese people. By arguing that Vietnam was a test of the West's ability to defeat the people's war strategy and a test of American credibility in the Cold War, he raised the costs of withdrawal for his successor. By launching a strategic hamlet program, he further disrupted peasant society. By allowing Harkins and the ARVN to bomb, shell, search, and destroy, he made so many recruits for the NLF that he encouraged North Vietnam and the NLF to move the war into its final military phase. By participating in Diem's removal, he brought warlord politics to Saigon. By downplaying publicly the American role in Vietnam, he discouraged a constitutional debate about the commitment of American advisers to battle. By publicly and privately committing the United States to the survival of an anti-Communist state in South Vietnam, he made it much more difficult to blame the South Vietnamese government for its own failures and to withdraw. And by insisting that military victory was the only acceptable outcome, he ignored the possibility that negotiations might lead to an acceptable process of retreat. Kennedy bequeathed to Lyndon B. Johnson a failing counter-insurgency program and a deepened commitment to the war in South Vietnam.

# From *Tactics, Grand Tactics, and Strategy*

## Harry Summers

The first, the supreme, the most far-reaching act of judgment
that the statesman and commander have to make is to
establish . . . the kind of war on which they are embarking;
neither mistaking it for, nor trying to turn it into, something
that is alien to its nature. This is the first of all strategic questions
and the most comprehensive.

Clausewitz, On War[1]

As military professionals, it was our job to judge the true nature of the Vietnam war, communicate those facts to our civilian decision-makers, and to recommend appropriate strategies. As Clausewitz said, that was the first strategic question and the most comprehensive. It is indicative of our strategic failure in Vietnam that almost a decade after our involvement the true nature of the Vietnam war is still in question. There are still those who would attempt to fit it into the revolutionary war mold and who blame our defeat on our failure to implement counterinsurgency doctrine.[2] This point of view requires an acceptance of the North Vietnamese contention that the war was a civil war, and that the North Vietnamese regular forces were an extension of the guerrilla effort, a point of view not borne out by the facts.

As Professor Raymond Aron recently pointed out, it is essential to distinguish the First Indo-China war between France and the Viet Minh from the Second Indo-China war between North Vietnam and South Vietnam.[3] The first was a revolutionary war. The second was not. The forces that besieged Dien Bien Phu grew out of the guerrilla movement; the forces that captured Saigon did not grow out of the Viet Cong but were the regular armed forces of

North Vietnam. This critical difference validates the official U.S. government position that the Vietnam war was caused by aggression from the North.[4]

To have understood the true nature of the Vietnam war required not only a strict definition of the enemy, it also required a knowledge of the nature of war itself. As we saw in Part I, our understanding was clouded by confusion over preparation for war and the conduct of war, by fears of nuclear war, by fears of Chinese intervention, and by the misconception that we were being challenged by a whole new kind of "revolutionary" war that could only be countered by the "strategy" of counterinsurgency. Reviewing the literature on Vietnam in search of "lessons," Professor of History Joe Dunn concluded that while "George Santayana reminded us that 'those who cannot remember the past are condemned to repeat it,' some would argue that Gaddis Smith's rejoinder is more applicable: 'One of the most somber aspects of the study of history is that it suggests no obvious ways by which mankind could have avoided folly.'"[5]

There are many ways to look at the war in Vietnam. One way (Santayana's) suggests that by a proper understanding and application of military art we could have influenced the outcome. Another (Gaddis Smith's) would have it that we were caught up in a kind of Greek tragedy where the end was perordained and where there were "no obvious ways by which [we] could have avoided folly." There is an attraction—some would say a fatal attraction—in the Gaddis Smith approach. In the face of failure it is easy to salve your conscience with the notion that nothing you could have done would have made any difference, that fate rather than your action or inaction had predetermined the end. For example, there are those who would blame our failure in Vietnam on the forces of history or on the tide of human events. But, as we will see, it was four North Vietnamese Army corps, not "dialectical materialism," that ultimately conquered South Vietnam.

As Alexander Solzhenitsyn said, "We must not hide behind fate's petticoats." We must reject Gaddis Smith in favor of Santayana and believe that a thorough knowledge of the art of war through what Clausewitz called "critical analysis"—can influence the course of events. Critical analysis, according to Clausewitz, consists of three different intellectual activities—the discovery and interpretation of facts, the tracing of effects back to their cause, and the investigation and evaluation of the means employed. "Critical analysis is not just an evaluation of the means actually employed, but of *all possible means*," said Clausewitz. "One can, after all, not condemn a method without being able to suggest a better alternative."

Clausewitz further observed that "[we see] things in the light of their result, and to some extent come to know and appreciate them fully only because of it."[6] In retrospect, our entire approach to the war would have been different if at the beginning we could have foreseen the North Vietnamese tanks rumbling through the streets of Saigon on 1 May 1975. The North Korean conventional attack in June 1950—and the North Korean tanks rumbling through Seoul—left no doubt as to the nature of that war and the nature of the proper U.S. response. But the North Vietnamese, evidently learning from the Korean war that an overt attack could precipitate a massive U.S. military response, began the war on the different key. Unlike the North Koreans who had pulled their communist cadres out of South Korea in April 1948 and opted for a conventional attack, the North Vietnamese opened their campaign with a guerrilla attack. One reason undoubtedly was fear of the U.S. response to an open attack, but there were other reasons as well. Unlike Korea, where the South Korean leader Syngman Rhee personified Korean nationalism and the North Korean leader Kim Il-sung was seen as a Soviet puppet, in Vietnam the situation was reversed. Ho Chi Minh had captured the cloak of Vietnamese nationalism during the struggles with the French, while the South Vietnamese leader Ngo Dinh Diem (and his successors) were tainted with a civil service and army structure inherited from French colonialism. Another factor was that in Korea the Americans were seen as the liberators from Japanese colonialism, in Vietnam they were identified with the former French regime.[7]

All of these things combined tended to cloud our perception of how to counter North Vietnamese aggression. Judged by the results of the war, the basic mistake (as we will see) was that we saw their guerrilla operations as a strategy in itself. Because we saw it as a strategy, we attempted to understand it in terms of "people's war" theories of Mao Tse-tung, and devised elaborate theories of counterinsurgency. We attempted to counter it by using such models as the British model in Malaysia. These theories and models had some relevance for the government of South Vietnam which ultimately had to neutralize the internal threat to its existence, but they had only secondary relevance to the United States. Ironically, we had seen this clearly in Korea. While we could protect them from external attack, internal security was a problem only they could solve. We could aid them with political advice and economic and military assistance, but the task was primarily theirs. As we will see in a later chapter, it was not until the end that we rediscovered this fact in Vietnam.

Where did we go wrong? It can be argued that from the French withdrawal in 1954 until President Diem's assassination in 1963, the American response was essentially correct. The task at hand was one of assisting South Vietnam to become a viable nation state, and the U.S. military advisors contributed to that end. In December 1963, the nature of the war began to change. The North Vietnamese made a decision to intervene directly both with military assistance and guerrilla cadres. In the late summer of 1964, the North Vietnamese again escalated the war by sending regular North Vietnamese Army forces south. In his analysis of the Vietnam war, Brigadier General Dave Palmer identifies this crucial turning point:

> By committing its regular forces to a cause which had previously been cloaked in the guise of an internal war, Hanoi dramatically altered the entire thrust and scope of the conflict. It was a key command decision. Indeed, it may well have been *the* key command decision of the war.[8]

Although it was not so dramatic, nor so obvious, as the North Korean invasion of South Korea in June 1950, the North Vietnamese had launched a strategic offensive to conquer South Vietnam. As in Korea, our initial response was defensive, relying primarily on South Vietnamese ground forces and limited U.S. air support. By mid-1965 it had become clear that this was not enough. U.S. combat troops were needed to stabilize the situation. In November 1965, the 32nd, 33rd and 66th regiments of the North Vietnamese Army clashed head-on with the U.S. 1st Cavalry Division in the Ia Drang Valley in central Vietnam. After ten days of heavy fighting the North Vietnamese were in full retreat. As General Palmer reports:

> On a strategic scale, a brilliant spoiling attack had completely derailed Hanoi's hopes of earning a decisive victory before full American might could be deployed to South Vietnam. Moreover, in a head-on clash between an American and a North Vietnamese division, on the enemy's chosen ground, the NVA unit had been sent reeling in retreat. For the moment, at least, an adverse tide had been reversed.[9]

Now was the time for the United States to take the offensive. Although in theory the best route to victory would have been a strategic offensive against North Vietnam, such action was not in line with U.S. strategic policy which called for the *containment* rather than the destruction of communist power. As we saw earlier this policy was based at least in part on our fears of sparking a nuclear war and our fears of Chinese intervention. As General Palmer reports:

> The Johnson administration had already barricaded the one sure route to victory—to take the strategic offensive against the source of the war. Memories of Mao Tse-tung's reaction when North Korea was overrun by United Nations troops in 1950 haunted the White House. America's fear of war with Red China protected North Vietnam from invasion more surely than any instrument of war Hanoi could have fielded.[10]

While a strategic offensive against North Vietnam may not have been politically feasible, we could have taken the tactical offensive to isolate the battlefield. But instead of orientating on North Vietnam—the source of war—we turned our attention to the symptom—the guerrilla war in the south. Our new "strategy" of counterinsurgency blinded us to the fact that the guerrilla war was tactical and not strategic. It was a kind of economy of force operation on the part of North Vietnam to buy time and to wear down superior U.S. military forces. As Norman Hannah, a career State Department Foreign Service Officer (FSO) with long experience in Southeast Asia wrote in 1975, "In South Vietnam we responded mainly to Hanoi's simulated insurgency rather than to its real but controlled aggression, as a bull charges the toreador's cape, not the toreador."[11]

We thought we were pursuing a new strategy called counterinsurgency, but actually we were pursuing a defensive strategy in pursuit of a negative aim—a strategy familiar with Clausewitz in the early nineteenth century. In his chapter on purpose and means in war Clausewitz discusses various methods of obtaining the object of war. One way is what Clausewitz calls "the negative aim." It is, he said, "the natural formula for outlasting the enemy, for wearing him down."[12] In a later chapter, Clausewitz discusses the relationship between the negative aim and the strategic defensive. "The aim of the defense must embody the idea of waiting," he said. "The idea implies . . . that the situation . . . may improve . . . Gaining time is the only way [the defender] can achieve his aim."[13] Basic to the success of a strategic defense in pursuit of the negative aim, therefore, is the assumption that time is on your side. But the longer the war progressed the more obvious it became that time was *not* on our side. It was American rather than North Vietnamese will that was being eroded. In his review of General Westmoreland's biography, Hannah writes:

> . . . [General] Westmoreland mentions several factors that prolonged the war, but . . . we are entitled to conclude that he did not regard these factors likely to be decisive. Indeed, he tells us he suffered these impediments because he believed that "success would eventually be ours." But it was not. Why not?
>
> General Westmoreland does not directly answer the question but the answer emerges without being stated. We ran out of time. This is the tragedy of Vietnam—we were fighting for time rather than space. And time ran out.[14]

In the introductory chapter to this book we posed the question—how could we have done so well in tactics but failed so miserably in strategy? The answer we postulated then—a failure in strategic military doctrine—manifested itself on the battlefield. Because it did not focus on the political aim to be achieved—containment of North Vietnamese expansion—our so-called strategy was never a strategy at all. At best it could be called a kind of grand tactics.

As a tactic it was extremely effective. As Professor Chalmers Johnson wrote in 1973, two years before the fall of Saigon:

Both Lin Piao and Vo Nguyen Giap identified the Vietnam war as a test case for the efficacy of people's war. The United States too saw the war as a test of methods for resisting people's war. Therefore, any study of people's war is obliged to consider Vietnam and try to find out how the test came out. . . .

None of the people's wars of the sixties did very well, including the one in Vietnam. Vo Nguyen Giap himself has admitted a loss of 600,000 men in fighting between 1965 and 1968. . . . Moreover, by about 1970 at least 80 percent of the day-to-day combat in South Vietnam was being carried on by regular People's Army of Vietnam (PAVN) troops. . . . Genuine black-pyjama southern guerrillas . . . had been decimated and amounted to no more than 20 percent of the communist fighting force.[15]

But tactical success is not necessarily strategic success, and tactical failure is not necessarily strategic failure. As we saw earlier, Clausewitz had said 150 years ago that military victory is only an end when it leads directly to peace—i.e., the political object of the war. Ironically, our tactical successes did not prevent our strategic failure and North Vietnam's tactical failures did not prevent their strategic success, and in strategic term, people's war *was* a success. It caused the United States to deploy against a secondary force and exhaust itself in the effort. It also caused the Army of South Vietnam to deploy in such a manner that it could not be massed to meet a conventional North Vietnamese cross-border conventional attack.

As was noted earlier, there are those who still question the true nature of the war, including many who actually fought there. Clausewitz warned of the "*vividness* of transient impressions,"[16] and most American military experience was during 1965–1970 when we were supposedly pursuing "counterinsurgency." Few experienced the North Vietnamese conventional attacks in 1972 and 1975. Most of the writings on the war also miss its true nature. Analysis after analysis condemns the United States for its overreliance on conventional methods. Yet these conventional tactics were militarily successful in destroying guerrilla forces. They were so successful that, according to press reports, the North Vietnamese imitated these same tactics to suppress the insurgent movement in Cambodia. From bitter experience they knew that such tactics worked. The reason for the confusion is that our announced strategy was counterinsurgency. The analysts, seeking the cause of our strategic failure, naturally focused on counterinsurgency. But since the insurgency itself was a tactical screen masking North Vietnam's real objectives (the conquest of South Vietnam), our counterinsurgency operations could only be tactical, no matter what we called them.

Our failure as military professionals to judge the true nature of the Vietnam war had a profound effect. It resulted in confusion throughout the national security establishment over tactics, grand tactics and strategy, a confusion that continues to this day. As author and strategist Herbert Y. Schandler commented, "The President had one view, the JCS another, and the field commander had another."[17]

In order to sort out this confusion the remaining chapters of this book will analyze our strategic defeat in terms of the classic principles of war. These principles can provide what Colonel Charles A. Hines describes as "military planning interrogatories"—i.e., an analytical framework to reduce general principles and theoretical postulations to pragmatic and operational situations.[18] Such an approach will present the Vietnam war in its true light—not as something new and unique with no lessons for the future, but as a war best understood in terms of war itself. In so doing it should illuminate the tasks that America may have to face on future battlefields. As Army Chief of Staff General Edward C. Meyer emphasized on 4 June 1980:

> The keystone of our contribution toward peace is total competence in waging war. That expertise can only come from an ardent study of tactics and strategy. It demands that we develop a full appreciation for applying the principles of war in our decision process . . .[19]

## Notes

1. Clausewitz, *On War*, I:1. pages 88–89.
2. Not only was it not the cause of our defeat, it had little to do with the North Vietnamese victory. As Lieutenant Colonel Stuart A. Herrington put it in a recent book (*Silence Was a Weapon*. Novato, California: Presidio Press, 1982): "Like us, Hanoi had failed to win the 'hearts and minds' of the South Vietnamese peasantry. Unlike us, Hanoi's leaders were able to compensate for this failure by playing their trump card—they overwhelmed South Vietnam with a twenty-two division force."
3. Raymond Aron, "On Dubious Battles," *Parameters: Journal of the US Army War College*, Vol. X, No. 4, December 1980, pp. 2–9.
4. President Lyndon B. Johnson, Press Conference, 28 July 1965, in *Why Vietnam* (Washington, D.C.: USGPO, 1965), p. 5.
5. Joe P. Dunn, "In Search of Lessons: The Development of a Vietnam Historiography." *Parameters: Journal of the US Army War College*, Vol. IX, No. 4, 1979, p. 37.
6. Clausewitz, *On War*, II:5, pp. 156, 161, 164–65.
7. See Selig S. Harrison, *The Widening Gulf: Asian Nationalism and American Policy* (New York: The Free Press, 1978), particularly pp. 100–1, 135, 138.
8. Palmer, *Summons of the Trumpet*, p. 62.
9. *Ibid*, p. 103.
10. *Ibid*, p. 110.

11. Norman B. Hannah, "Vietnam: Now We Know," Anthony T. Bouscaren (ed), *All Quiet on the Eastern Front* (New York: Devin-Adair, 1977), p. 149.

12. Clausewitz, *On War*, I:2, p. 94.

13. *Ibid*, VIII:8, pp. 613, 614.

14. Norman B. Hannah, *All Quiet on the Eastern Front*, p. 146.

15. Johnson, *Autopsy on People's War*, pp. 46–48.

16. Clausewitz, *On War*, I:3, p. 108.

17. Interview with Colonel (USA, Retired) Herbert Y. Schandler, 13 November 1980.

18. Interview with Colonel Charles A. Hines, U.S. Army: Strategic Analyst, USAWC, on 24 December 1980.

19. Letter, Office of the Chief of Staff U.S. Army, 4 June 1980.

# The Vietnam War and Soviet-American Relations, 1964–1973: New Russian Evidence

## Ilya V. Gaiduk

The Vietnam War stands out among Cold War crises for its scale, length, intensity, and global repercussions. The literature on the war and the American role in it encompasses thousands of volumes, from political memoirs to soldiers' eyewitness accounts to historical and journalistic studies, to novels and political science treatises.[1] With the passage of time, ever more documents have been declassified, enabling more thorough and comprehensive analyses. Now that there is substantial access to archives in the former USSR, researchers have at their disposal a whole set of previously unavailable materials which shed new light on unresolved issues as well as on problems which have either escaped the attention of Western scholars or have not yet been analyzed in detail. One of those problems relates to the Soviet Union's participation in the Vietnam conflict, particularly the nature of Soviet-American relations during the war and Moscow's role as a potential mediator. Although many U.S. researchers have studied these problems and, on the basis of the documents analyzed, drawn certain conclusions, their analyses of the subject were far from exhaustive and quite often insufficiently corroborated by the necessary archival sources.

The present article assesses Soviet policy toward Vietnam and the war's impact on U.S.-Soviet relations from 1964 to the early 1970s on the basis of materials bearing on this subject in the archive of the former Communist Party of the Soviet Union Central Committee (CPSU CC)—a repository now known as the Storage Center for Contemporary Documents (SCCD, or TsKhSD, in its Russian acronym)—located in the CC's former headquarters in Staraya Ploschad' (Old Square) in Moscow. This report was originally prepared for presentation at the January 1993 Moscow Conference on New

51

Evidence on Cold War History, organized by the Cold War International History Project (CWIHP) in cooperation with the Institute of General History of the Russian Academy of Sciences and SCCD. Subsequently, the author expanded his research into a far broader study of Soviet involvement in the Vietnam conflict, utilizing sources in both Russian and American archives (the latter during a CWIHP fellowship for research in the United States); that study, *The Soviet Union and the Vietnam War*, is scheduled for publication by Ivan R. Dee (Chicago) in Spring 1996.

The SCCD archives contain materials related to a broad range of the former CPSU CC's work, primarily correspondence with a wide range of Soviet organizations and establishments dealing with various socio-economic, domestic, and foreign policy issues. The archive collections (*fondy*) include a considerable number of documents on the subject of the Vietnam War and Soviet-American relations which were sent to the CPSU CC—mostly to the CC International Department and the CC Socialist Countries' Communist and Workers' Parties Department—by the Soviet Ministry of Foreign Affairs, Defense Ministry, and Committee of State Security (KGB). Considerably less frequently encountered, alas, is documentation illuminating recommendations, draft decisions, and top-level decision-making. Thus, the top leadership's decisions and the mechanism of decision-making on this level are only indirectly reflected in the SCCD materials. This unfortunate gap, naturally, creates problems for historians trying to determine how policy was actually made by the top Soviet leadership on important foreign policy questions, and necessitates continued efforts to increase access to materials in Russian archives that remain off-limits, particularly the so-called Kremlin or Presidential Archives, known officially as the Archive of the President of the Russian Federation (APRF).

At the same time, the SCCD materials enable historians not only to reconstruct many events related to the Vietnam War during the period in question, and to present matters which were previously interpreted only inferentially, but also to assess the development of U.S.-Soviet relations in close interconnection with the conflict in Southeast Asia. This last factor is of obvious import, for one can hardly study U.S.-Soviet relations during the Vietnam War in isolation from an understanding of relations between the Soviet Union and North Vietnam (the Democratic Republic of Vietnam, or DRV), between the Soviet Union and the People's Republic of China (PRC), and between the DRV and PRC. All those interconnected relations crucially influenced the relevant Soviet policies.

The escalation of the conflict in Vietnam after the Tonkin Gulf incident in August 1964 and the February 1965 attack by armed units of the National Front for the Liberation of South Vietnam (NFLSV, also known as the NLF) on the base of American military advisers in Pleiku (triggering

U.S. aerial bombardment of North Vietnam in retaliation), coincided with a certain cooling in Soviet-North Vietnamese relations. This chill between Moscow and Hanoi, in turn, was partly attributable to the growing differences between the USSR and the PRC, the two chief patrons and supporters of the Vietnamese struggle against the Saigon regime.[2] Besides the impact of the Sino-Soviet split, the tension in Soviet-North Vietnamese relations during this stretch was also tied to the relatively moderate stand adopted by the then Soviet government, under the leadership of Nikita S. Khrushchev prior to his downfall in October 1964. Owing to the palpable improvement in Soviet-American relations following the shared fright of the 1962 Caribbean (Cuban missile) crisis, the Kremlin sought to minimize Soviet involvement in the Vietnam conflict, which was not only problematic from the viewpoint of possible foreign-policy advantages but was also fraught with possible new clashes between the USSR and the USA. Moreover, the Soviet leaders were apprehensive of radical views held by North Vietnam's leaders, who had a clearly pro-Chinese orientation.

The extent of the difference in the positions held by the two countries became clear after a visit to Moscow in Jan.-Feb. 1964 by a delegation of the Workers Party of Vietnam (WPV), led by Le Duan, the party's First Secretary. The DRV Communists came out in support of their Chinese colleagues with such zeal and expressed such radical ideas about the role of the national liberation movement in Third World countries that their Moscow interlocutors were obliged to switch from "the patient explanation of the CPSU stand and the general line of the world communist movement" to direct warnings about the possible consequences such views could have for "the Vietnamese friends'" relations with the Soviet Union.[3]

Further evidence that the two sides were slowly but surely drifting apart surfaced during a July 1964 visit to Moscow by an NLF delegation at the invitation of the Soviet Afro-Asian Solidarity Committee. The representatives of the patriotic forces of South Vietnam presented to the Soviet leaders a number of requests and proposals, including requests for increased supplies of arms and ammunition. They also expressed a desire that a permanent mission of the NFLSV be opened in the USSR. The CPSU CC viewed skeptically all those requests. In his report to the CC about that delegation's visit, D. Shevlyagin, deputy head of the CC International Department, advised that no definite answer about the opening of such a mission be given and that all talks be held exclusively via the North Vietnamese state agencies. In view of this, it was decided not to receive the delegation at the CPSU CC, for that would have raised the awkward necessity for the Kremlin leaders to state in clear terms their stand on the above-mentioned issues. CC Secretary Boris Ponomarev, who was the curator of relations between the CPSU and other parties, accepted that advice.[4]

Meanwhile, faced with the Soviet leadership's unwillingness to plunge into the Southeast Asian conflict, Hanoi redoubled its efforts to improve relations with China. According to the information of the Soviet Defense Ministry, PRC and DRV officials opened talks in 1964 on a bilateral treaty of military cooperation. North Vietnam hosted a delegation of PRC military leaders, led by the Defense Minister, and in December 1964 a bilateral treaty was signed which provided for the introduction of PRC troops to the DRV.[5] Prior to that, the DRV General Staff had informed the Soviet military attaché in Hanoi that there was no longer any need for Soviet military experts to stay in the country and they should leave the DRV without replacement by other Soviet advisors as soon as they completed their current business.[6] The rapprochement between Hanoi and Beijing was facilitated by common views on the need to fight against "U.S. imperialism." Although the North Vietnamese leaders never fully trusted China (as later conflicts demonstrated), coolness in relations with the Soviet Union predetermined their official position.[7]

Khrushchev's ouster in October 1964 marked a turning point in Soviet-North Vietnamese relations.[8] For reasons that remain unclear, the Soviet Union made an about-face and again oriented itself toward closer cooperation with North Vietnam. Probably Leonid I. Brezhnev and his entourage feared a loss of Soviet influence in the region, particularly in the context of the mounting differences between Beijing and Moscow which threatened to develop into an open conflict. In that context, the consolidation of China's position in Southeast Asia at the USSR's expense posed a potential threat to the Soviet authority in the world communist movement.[9] Furthermore, the assassination of U.S. President John F. Kennedy in November 1963 and advent to power of Lyndon B. Johnson (whose election as president in 1964 was regarded in the USSR as an indicator of greater right-wing influence in American politics) dimmed the hopes of improvement in Soviet-American relations that had arisen in the last year of Kennedy's life. This development offered a certain freedom of action to Moscow's new leadership, which had reverted to the policy of confrontation—a policy which was, in turn, facilitated by Johnson's escalation of U.S. involvement in Vietnam.

From late 1964 on, Soviet policy with respect to Vietnam pursued several goals. First and foremost, the USSR emphasized moral and political support to what it described as the Vietnamese people's war against American aggression. The Soviet mass media now promptly and frequently carried official statements by Soviet leaders denouncing U.S. aggressive actions in Southeast Asia, no longer delaying as it had with TASS's statement on the Tonkin Gulf incident. Steps were taken to expand contacts both with Hanoi and representatives of the South Vietnamese patriotic forces, and, accordingly, the CPSU CC now approved the opening in Moscow (at the Soviet

Afro-Asian Solidarity Committee), on 24 December 1964, of a permanent mission of the NFLSV.

Second, Soviet material assistance (economic and, primarily, military) to the DRV and NLF expanded. Soviet military supplies in the period from 1963 to 1967 (particularly after 1965) exceeded one billion rubles, according to the data of the Soviet Embassy in Hanoi.[10] Prior to 1965, German models of arms were sent to North Vietnam from the Soviet Union, but from then on the Kremlin provided only Soviet-made arms to the "Vietnamese friends," including the latest designs of surface-to-air missiles, jet planes, rockets, and field artillery, as well as a large array of especially sophisticated arms and combat hardware for the DRV air defense system.[11] And Soviet economic and military assistance to Vietnam kept on increasing. According to estimates of the Soviet Embassy in Hanoi, by 1968 Soviet material assistance accounted for 50 percent of all aid to the DRV, and as of 1 January 1968 the total value of Soviet assistance over that period was in excess of 1.8 billion rubles, with military supplies accounting for 60 percent.[12]

Such a turnabout in Soviet policy with respect to cooperation with Vietnam was received with satisfaction by the Hanoi leaders, who increasingly stressed the importance of Soviet moral, political, and material assistance in their conversations with the officials of the Soviet Embassy and those of other socialist countries. However, the North Vietnamese leaders' appreciation for this largesse by no means signified that they would now take the USSR's side in the Sino-Soviet dispute, or otherwise rely exclusively on only one communist patron. Rather, after Moscow changed its attitude to the DRV, Hanoi took steps to secure maximum profit by exploiting its friendship with *both* of its mighty allies—the PRC and the USSR—as they competed for influence in Southeast Asia. Precisely this policy was pursued by the WPV Central Committee grouping which was formed in late 1964-early 1965 and included Le Duan, Pham Van Dong, and Vo Nguyen Giap.[13] This group sought to rid North Vietnam of China's excessive wardship, on the one hand, and, on the other, to avoid any kind of dependence on the Soviet Union. As a result, in that period reports by Soviet representatives in Vietnam, the USSR Defense Ministry, and the KGB regarding reduced Chinese influence in the DRV were accompanied by complaints of insincerity, egoism and unmanageability on the part of "the Vietnamese friends."

For instance, back in 1966, in his analysis of the prospects of Soviet-Vietnamese relations, Soviet Ambassador in Hanoi Ilya Shcherbakov pointed out: "Just as before, the Embassy believes that the process of promotion of our relations with the WPV and the DRV will hardly be steady or rapid in view of the policy pursued by the Vietnamese comrades. This was, regrettably, confirmed in the past few years. Even the manifestation of a more serious discord between the WPV and the Communist Party of China will not probably mean automatic or proportionate Soviet-Vietnamese rapprochement. The year 1966 showed once more that we are obliged constantly to display initiative and unilaterally, as it were, drag the Vietnamese comrades to greater friendship and independence." The ambassador then stressed the "general positive nature" of the WPV's tendency for independence but pointed to its negative aspects, primarily to indications that the Vietnamese conducted its foreign policy, including its relations with Moscow, from a narrow, nationalistic viewpoint. Soviet aid was regarded by Hanoi exclusively from the standpoint of their benefit to Vietnam, rather than for the good of the international socialist cause.[14]

This undercurrent of tension in Soviet-North Vietnamese relations, produced by what Moscow viewed as Hanoi's parochial perspective, cropped up repeatedly. In 1966, for example, the North Vietnamese expressed indignation at the partial reduction of Soviet and U.S. military contingents in Germany. Why? Because, they explained, the Soviet troops had allegedly been transferred to the Soviet-Chinese border, which provoked tensions there and diverted Beijing from North Vietnamese military requirements, and the U.S. troops were immediately transferred to South Vietnam.[15]

The Vietnamese side's egoism and its desire (in the words of a Soviet Embassy political letter) "to have a monopoly on the correct assessment and methods of solution to the Vietnam conflict," often verged on cynicism. Indicative in this respect was a complaint by the Soviet Ministry of Commercial Shipping, dated 18 July 1966, sent to the CPSU CC, in connection with the actions by the Vietnamese in Haiphong, the DRV's chief port. The port authorities, the ministry complained, had artificially delayed the unloading of Soviet vessels, evidently believing that the longer they held the large-tonnage vessels flying the Soviet flag in the port and its vicinity, the less risk of damage they would run of U.S. bombing raids. Moreover, they usually placed those Soviet vessels in close proximity to the most dangerous areas (e.g., near anti-aircraft guns), in hopes of ensuring their safety during air raids. Moreover, during air raids Vietnamese military boats lurking behind Soviet vessels fired at the enemy, thus making the Soviet "shields" the targets of U.S. bombers (and those vessels contained loads of cargoes meant as assistance to "the embattled Vietnamese people"). The clearly outraged ministry officials demanded that Soviet commercial vessels be kept out of danger while discharging their noble mission.[16]

No less complicated was the situation concerning Soviet-North Vietnamese military cooperation. The USSR Defense Ministry and embassy in Hanoi repeatedly informed Moscow about "the Vietnamese friends' insincere attitude" toward the Soviet Union, the Soviet people, and the Soviet Defense Ministry. They pointed out that they received slanted reports from the

People's Army of (North) Vietnam regarding the situation in South Vietnam, belittling the role and importance of Soviet military assistance to the DRV and discrediting the performance of Soviet arms and military hardware. They also reported that the North Vietnamese had raised obstacles in the way of Soviet military experts who wished to inspect U.S. military hardware, and displayed other signs of distrust and suspiciousness toward Soviet Defense Ministry representatives. The Soviet leadership was informed about violations of storage rules for Soviet military hardware, wasteful use of missiles and ammunition, and neglect of Soviet experts' advice on the rules of exploitation of military hardware, which led to its spoilage. All this coincided with Hanoi's requests for more assistance, but the DRV leaders evidently saw no contradiction in this: It was pointed out in the 1970 political report of the Soviet Embassy in Hanoi that, while "attaching great importance to the Soviet military assistance, the command of the People's Army of Vietnam at the same time regarded it exclusively as the obligatory discharge of its internationalist duty by the Soviet Union."[17]

All the above-mentioned facts suggest how complicated and contradictory Soviet-Vietnamese relations were, and demonstrate the great discrepancy between the scale of Soviet assistance to Vietnam and the degree of Soviet influence on Hanoi's policy. As a Vietnamese journalist in his conversation with M. Ilyinsky, an *Izvestia* correspondent, put it: "Do you know," the Vietnamese journalist asked, "what is the Soviet Union's share in total assistance, received by Vietnam, and what is the share of Soviet political influence there (if the latter can be measured in percent)? The respective figures are: 75–80 percent and 4–8 percent." The Soviet journalist noted: "If the Vietnamese journalist has exaggerated the former figures (by 15–20 percent), the share of Soviet influence is probably correct."[18]

Sino-Vietnamese relations were no less complicated and contradictory. That Moscow monitored their development closely is testified to by the vast number of reports in the CPSU CC archives on this subject, sent by the Soviet Embassy in Hanoi, the KGB, and the Military Intelligence Agency (GRU) of the General Staff of the Soviet Armed Forces. An early sign of the incipient discord between the two countries seems to have appeared in a still-classified 21 February 1966 KGB report to the CPSU CC stating that Chinese leaders were concerned about the WPV's increasingly independent foreign policy, especially in relations with the PRC and the conduct of the war.[19] And the Soviet Embassy in Hanoi pointed out in its 1966 report that, although the WPV tendency to settle the Vietnam issue independently from China was not yet pronounced, the DRV's trust in Beijing had already been undermined. However, the report admitted that one could hardly hope for the WPV leadership to display initiative to opt for one patron over the other, for "the comrades probably have not yet risen to the level of clear-cut choice." In view of this, the Soviet Embassy set itself the task "to render all-round assistance to the Vietnam leadership in its adoption of an independent stand on the issues of home and foreign policy." That "independent" policy naturally was meant to be independent from China, for the report then underlined the need "to react more firmly to any action by Vietnamese comrades which may be directly or indirectly damaging to Soviet-Vietnamese friendship."[20]

Sino-Vietnamese contradictions tended to sharpen as the DRV leadership came to realize the need for a diplomatic settlement with the USA. The DRV's consent to hold talks with Washington in 1968 profoundly irritated Beijing, which was dead-set against any compromise settlement leading to a cessation of hostilities. To advance its more militant policy, the Chinese leaders began to expand separate contacts (bypassing Hanoi) with the NLF, urging it to carry on protracted warfare. Moreover, the PRC started to obstruct carriages of Soviet arms and ammunition delivered by rail through Chinese territory, with the express aim of undermining Soviet-Vietnamese relations. Although the PRC leadership's approach to the talks issue later softened, Sino-Vietnamese relations remained strained.

Although discord between the Beijing and Hanoi leaderships affected Sino-Vietnamese relations, no major conflict between the two countries threatened a complete rupture during the course of the war. Vietnam still needed Chinese assistance and support, so it took steps to reduce or contain the level of tensions. The DRV's party and government leaders, as before, regularly visited Beijing to discuss with "the Chinese friends" important foreign policy issues. No matter how riled, Hanoi carefully avoided giving categorical assessments of Chinese policy—either regarding the world communist movement or Soviet-Chinese relations. "The WPV leaders realize full well," the Soviet Embassy in Hanoi explained to Moscow, "that China is situated quite close to Vietnam, whereas the Soviet Union is far away. Vietnam would be hard put to do without Chinese assistance in its struggle and in future peaceful construction. So it would be premature to ask the Vietnamese now to state their clear-cut position with respect to the USSR and China."[21] And the following fact is quite indicative: Hanoi named Xuan Thuy, well-known for his pro-Chinese views and a past president of the Vietnamese-Chinese Friendship Association, as the head of the DRV delegation to the Paris talks. The details of relations among the USSR, DRV, and PRC also throw light on the Soviet Union's relations with the USA. Soviet leaders could hardly react indifferently or simplistically to the Vietnam conflict and the dramatic escalation of American military activity in Southeast Asia. From a purely propaganda viewpoint, the conflict played into Soviet hands. While U.S. support for an unpopular neo-colonial regime in Saigon offered a ripe target for condemnation and undermined Washington's international stature, the USSR could simultaneously pose as a consistent fighter for the triumph of a just cause, acting in the spirit of proletarian internationalism—as evidenced by its moral-political, economic, and military assistance to North Vietnam—and also as a potential mediator in the forging of a peaceful settlement. Furthermore, the likely protracted nature of the conflict promised to sap the strength of the Soviet Union's principal rivals, distracting the United States and China and thereby enhancing Soviet security interests in other regions (especially Europe and the Soviet Far East).

Yet the Vietnam War also presented long-term difficulties and dangers for Moscow, especially to the extent that there was a real threat of its escalating from a local into a world war, if (as was sometimes speculated) the USA were driven to desperation and resorted to the use of nuclear weapons. In that case, the USSR could hardly have kept neutral—and yet retaliating against the United States might have led to disastrous consequences. All the same, even if no nuclear conflict broke out, the risk of a direct clash between the two superpowers arising from the Southeast Asian crisis was too great and this was precisely what the Soviet leadership wished to avoid at all costs. Plus, to the extent Kremlin leaders genuinely desired an improvement in relations with Washington, the war would inevitably serve as a distraction and potential sticking point. There were naturally other "pros" and "cons" which Moscow must have taken into account in determining its policy toward the struggle: Military factors constituted one major positive incentive favoring a more active Soviet involvement, according to archival documents. There were two principal, interconnected perceived opportunities: Vietnam offered a live battlefield testing ground for Soviet military hardware, including the latest models, and also a chance to obtain a windfall of hard information about up-to-date U.S. weaponry, by inspecting the war booty captured or obtained by the DRV forces. The North Vietnamese air defense was fully equipped with modern Soviet hardware, whose effectiveness was shown by the fact that even the Vietnamese personnel managed to operate it successfully, despite a frequent lack of training or competence. Those systems were being constantly improved, taking into account the capabilities of U.S. warplanes.[22] Apart from the anti-aircraft defense system, the archival documents note, the North Vietnamese used the Soviet-made Grad artillery shelling systems, which were highly effective in attacks on U.S. bases, airfields, ammunition depots, etc.,[23] as well as MiG-21 jets.

The Soviet military also relished the opportunity to pore over the latest U.S. military hardware. In accordance with a Soviet-North Vietnamese agreement signed in the spring of 1965, the Vietnamese undertook to transfer to the USSR models of captured U.S. military hardware for inspection. All difficulties notwithstanding, according to the data of the Soviet Embassy in Hanoi, a total of 700 models were delivered to the USSR between May 1965 and January 1967. The embassy pointed out that the work done was very valuable: the CPSU CC adopted a decision to apply in Soviet industry of a number of selected and studied models.[24]

However, apart from obvious assets the USSR gained in the course of the Vietnam War, its expenditures were likewise enormous, primarily in the sphere of ever increasing material assistance to Vietnam. (See the figures cited above.) In 1966–1968 the Soviet Union undertook to render to the DRV economic assistance to the tune of 121.6 million rubles, but in fact the assistance was far greater in view of Hanoi's incessant requests for additional supplies. In 1968 Soviet assistance to the DRV totaled 524 million rubles, with 361 million rubles transferred as a gift. Soviet assistance in 1969 was planned to remain on the same level (525 million rubles), but with the opening of peace talks and reduction of the scale of hostilities in Vietnam, part of the funds originally assigned for military deliveries was reallocated for other purposes, so Soviet assistance to Vietnam in 1969 totaled 370 million rubles and in 1970, 316 million rubles.[25]

One negative factor, from the Soviet leaders' viewpoint, in decision-making on aid to the DRV was what they saw as the Vietnamese allies' unmanageability and unpredictability. Hanoi's independent course in relations with the USSR hardly inspired Moscow to greater enthusiasm in its support for the war, and as time went on, those Vietnamese properties might have led to undesirable consequences—perhaps an open break. So from that standpoint, at least, Moscow had every reason to favor an early cease-fire and political solution.

In fact, the hope for a peaceful settlement was shared by both Soviet and American leaders, and their tactics on this issue, paradoxically enough, were surprisingly similar. However, the Soviet government backed a settlement on Hanoi's terms, whereas the U.S. sought to ensure the maximum consideration of the Saigon government's interests. Moreover, of course, as a direct participant in the conflict, the United States could not possibly play the part of an arbiter, which remained a privilege of the Soviet Union. For this reason, with U.S. armed forces directly involved in hostilities, the Johnson Administration was obliged to rely on intermediaries in its attempts to convince Hanoi to sit down at the negotiating table rather than pursue a purely military outcome. And in this respect Washington pinned much of its hopes on the Soviet Union.[26]

U.S. leaders had every reason for such hopes, for they believed that since the USSR rendered massive and ever-growing military and economic assistance to Vietnam (of which Washington was well aware),[27] so the Soviet Union could exert leverage on the DRV leadership. Both Johnson and, after January 1969, his successor Richard M. Nixon were convinced that Moscow would press Hanoi to agree to open negotiations, once Washington: 1) demonstrated to the Soviet Union that the Vietnam War was hardly in its interests; 2) seduced it by the promise of cooperation with the United States; or, better still, 3) warned it that if Soviet cooperation were not forthcoming the United States might resort to rapprochement with China—or some optimal combination of all those approaches. When in retirement, Johnson disclosed his calculations as president in a conversation at his Texas ranch with Soviet citizens that was reported to the Kremlin leadership by the KGB in December 1969. The USSR could be instrumental in helping the United States to bring the Vietnam War to a conclusion, Johnson argued, for "if we take Soviet strategic, not tactical, interests, the end of the Vietnam War fully accords with the Soviet Union's interests," considering that, "after all, it is the United States, not Vietnam, which is the main partner of the USSR." And Johnson rejected the argument that the Soviet Union was not in a position to exert pressure on the DRV as groundless from the viewpoint of realpolitik. "It's highly doubtful for a country supplying Vietnam with 75 percent of [its] arms not to have real levers of influence on it," the ex-president was quoted as saying.[28]

Thus, the problem, from the U.S. perspective, consisted only in discovering how best to approach Moscow. The United States might have acted through official channels, since although Soviet-American relations were rather cool at that time, they were maintained. And the United States certainly probed what could be done in that direction. For instance, at an August 1966 meeting between Colonel C. C. Fitzgerald, a military attaché of the U.S. Embassy in Moscow, with officers of the Department of External Relations of the Soviet Defense Ministry, the American stressed the important role the USSR could play in the settlement of the Vietnam conflict as the initiator of and active mediator in peace negotiations. Col. Fitzgerald drew the attention of his interlocutors to the Johnson Administration's constant efforts to open talks, stating that the visit to Moscow of Senator Mike Mansfield and Averell Harriman's appointment as a special presidential advisor aimed at precisely this purpose.[29] However, worried that a formal, top-level overture to Moscow might result in a rebuff or even denunciation by the Kremlin leaders, the White House opted not to run the risk, but to first sound out Soviet officials in order to ascertain their attitudes and try to reach agreement unofficially. Regrettably, we do not yet have access to all the documents, including the still-classified "special dossiers" (*osobaya papki*) at SCCD, as well as KGB, Foreign and Defense Ministry, and Presidential Archive materials, that are necessary to reconstruct fully from Soviet sources all of the many conversations and probes connected to various diplomatic efforts aimed at ending the Vietnam conflict in 1965–67, including, perhaps most importantly, the so-called MARIGOLD and SUNFLOWER initiatives (to use the secret U.S. government code names), in both of which the Soviet Union played an important role.[30] An initial survey of the SCCD archives disclosed only cryptic traces of Soviet contacts with potential intermediaries. For instance, documents failed to clarify what was discussed in conversations with L. Mulkern (vice-president for international relations of the Bank of America), who asked for assistance in establishing unofficial contacts between U.S. President Johnson and the Soviet government, or with Marshall D. Shulman (then an associate of Harvard University's Russian Research Center), both of which were recorded by the KGB (the latter with the recommendation that Shulman be advised that his information had to be confirmed by the U.S. President). While the documents encountered during this early stage of research left these and many other questions unresolved, they certainly pointed at the high intensity of unofficial Soviet-U.S. contacts apparently related to the war (either directly or through mediators, as, for instance, through the services of Austrian Ambassador in the USSR Vodak) in the summer-autumn of 1965.[31]

Moscow's seeming reluctance to meet Washington half-way in its diplomatic efforts was probably at least partly attributable to the fact that the Kremlin was acutely aware of its limited ability to exert influence on Hanoi's policy—an awareness due in large measure to the complete and objective information sent to Moscow by the Soviet Embassy in the DRV, led by Ambassador Shcherbakov. Perusing the great number of minutes of conversations between Soviet Embassy officials and Vietnamese leaders, WPV members, and Vietnamese citizens, as well as informational letters and reports sent to the Soviet Foreign Ministry and the CPSU CC, one gets the impression that decision-making on the Vietnamese issue was largely produced in accordance with recommendations and draft decisions sent by the Soviet Embassy in Hanoi—not by the Politburo, the CC Secretariat, nor the Foreign Ministry—and only later were those recommendations and draft decisions rubber-stamped by the top Soviet leaders. This conclusion, albeit preliminary, is based on ample documentary evidence, when, for instance, the Soviet Ambassador sets out a number of ideas in his political letter to Moscow about what should be done, and later the same considerations were put forward as the official views of the CPSU and Soviet government in conversations with Pham Van Dong or Nguyen Duy Trinh.[32] So Moscow obviously deemed it advisable to consult the Soviet Ambassador in Hanoi before adopting decisions.

Take the following two examples. The political letter[33] of the Soviet Embassy in the DRV, entitled "Soviet-Vietnamese Relations After the Talks Held in April 1968," prepared for Moscow Center on 1 September 1968, assessed the results and significance of the opening of the Paris peace talks. Regarding the situation as favorable for achieving a settlement in the best interests of the Vietnamese people, the Ambassador, who signed the letter, believed that the prime task at the moment was "to help the Vietnamese comrades to put an end to the hostilities this year and switch over to a political settlement of the Vietnamese issue." With this aim in view, Shcherbakov believed, it would be advisable to invite a higher-level DRV government delegation to Moscow in October and "try once more to analyze jointly the situation and convince the DRV government to express its opinion on the whole package of the Vietnamese settlement."

Soon afterward, V. Chivilev, the Soviet charge d'affaires in the DRV, presented Pham Van Dong with a letter of invitation from Brezhnev and Alexei Kosygin for a DRV party and government delegation to visit the Soviet Union. The date of the visit was later settled and a decision was adopted on a visit to the USSR by a Vietnamese government delegation led by Le Duan in November 1968. Though the materials on the visit remain inaccessible, it seems highly likely that Soviet leaders followed the recommendations of their man in Hanoi.[34]

Another example of the importance of the Soviet ambassador's advice in decision-making dates to early 1974. CC Secretary Boris Ponomarev, who was in charge of the Party's international relations, submitted to the CPSU CC Secretariat a memorandum, entitled "On a Proposal to the Vietnamese Friends," in which he raised the issue of establishing and promoting relations between the CPSU and the communist parties of several Southeast Asian countries by making use of the authority wielded by the WPV in the communist movement in the region. In other words, he suggested possible Soviet penetration of Thailand, Indonesia, Malaysia, and the Philippines. After inconclusive discussion of the proposal, Ponomarev, along with CC secretaries Suslov, Kirilenko, Demichev, Katushev, and Rakhmanin, decided to consult the Soviet Ambassador in Hanoi on the matter.[35]

The new importance attached to the role of ambassadors and embassies in the process of decision-making on foreign-policy issues reflected a general trend, typical of the Brezhnev era: the growing influence of the bureaucratic apparatus, especially medium-level officials, on policy-making. Since top Soviet leaders had little idea of the reality in Vietnam, they willingly entrusted decision-making in the sphere of current policy to experts, signing ready-made decisions or intervening only in extraordinary situations.[36]

Thus, indirect evidence suggests that in defining its stand on the Vietnam War, Moscow largely drew on the opinion of its diplomatic representatives in the DRV. And in 1965–1966 the Soviet Embassy was far from optimistic about the prospects for a peaceful settlement. Meetings and conversations between the Soviet Embassy officials and members of the diplomatic corps and journalists accredited in Hanoi revealed that North Vietnam's leaders were fully committed to continuing the hostilities against the USA. Indicative in this respect was a conversation at the WPV CC on 23

August 1966 between Soviet charge d'affaires P. Privalov and Nguyen Van Vinh, Chairman of the Committee for the Unification of the Country. Gen. Vinh firmly believed that the situation was hardly favorable for opening North Vietnamese-U.S. talks. "Had we been defeated by the Americans," Vinh said, "we would have had no other choice than to agree to hold talks, but we are confidently dealing blows at the enemy and winning decisive victories. What would it mean for us to hold talks now? That would mean losing everything. . . ."[37] This viewpoint was shared by the entire WPV top leadership. That is why the Soviet Embassy's report for 1966 included very cautious forecasts about possible changes in the DRV stand. The embassy, in the belief that it was necessary to "exert and broaden, with the support of all peace-loving forces and the socialist countries, strong political and diplomatic efforts in order to bring the matter to the settlement of the conflict in the current year," suggested that the USSR might eventually have to elaborate and present its own peace plan to the Vietnamese comrades. That supposition was made on the basis of what the embassy viewed as a certain coincidence of the CPSU and WPV "assessment of the situation and active promotion of politico-diplomatic struggle for Vietnam."[38]

In that contest, the USSR sought to evade the issue of acting as a formal mediator at the U.S.-DRV talks (which was what the USA sought). The only role the Soviet Union was then prepared to play was that of a "postman," who would carry both sides' messages, and that of "a night watchman" by offering an opportunity for unofficial meetings between U.S. and North Vietnamese embassy officials in Moscow.[39] At the same time, Moscow spared no effort to convince its "Vietnamese friends" of the need to switch from military to political-diplomatic methods to attain a settlement.

The USSR undertook the mission of "a postman" and "a night watchman" very reluctantly, probably for fear of being turned into an official mediator. At least it did not wish to perform those functions on a permanent basis. So the United States had to use the services of other countries, in particular, Poland, Canada, India, etc. However, early in 1967 a new flurry of activity was observed in Moscow. In Jan.-Feb., DRV Foreign Minister Nguyen Duy Trinh received Shcherbakov and familiarized him with the gist of President Johnson's letter to Ho Chi Minh, handed over at a regular meeting in Moscow of representatives of the DRV and the US embassies. And Ho Chi Minh's reply, according to Trinh, was to be sent along the same channels.[40] Those facts make it possible for us to suppose that by 1967, meetings of diplomats of the two warring parties were held in Moscow on a regular basis.

As to its function of "a postman," in 1967 Moscow regularly supplied Hanoi with information regarding the requests and offers of U.S. representatives, conveyed during meetings with Soviet diplomats, and delivered messages between the two sides. For instance, on 24 April 1967, "Vietnamese comrades" were informed about a request of the U.S. Embassy in Moscow that the Soviet government take the necessary steps for the DRV government to give access to representatives of the international commission of the Red Cross to American POWs then held in North Vietnam. And on April 28, the DRV leaders learned that Johnson envoy Averell Harriman had handed over a U.S. statement on the withdrawal of U.S. troops from the demilitarized zone to the Soviet charge d'affaires in the United States.[41] There is no doubt that Hanoi also received exhaustive information about the June 1967 Glassboro summit between Kosygin and Johnson.

In 1967, too, the Soviet Union failed to convince the Vietnamese leaders to hold talks with the USA on a peaceful settlement. The Soviet Embassy in Hanoi believed that the DRV leadership would accept the idea of such a settlement only under the following conditions: a worsening of the military situation; U.S. acceptance of North Vietnam's main demands; a change in China's attitude to the Vietnam War; and finally, the socialist countries' clear declaration to the North Vietnamese that they could not afford to bear the ever growing burden of that war for reasons of an international nature or for fear of its protracted nature. So in assessing the results of the Soviet-Vietnamese talks in April 1967 and the subsequent DRV policy, the Soviet Embassy drew the conclusion that at that juncture, "not a single [one] of the above-mentioned situations makes the Vietnamese comrades take the road of active searching for ways to a peaceful settlement."[42]

Nevertheless, summing up the results of 1967, Soviet diplomats in Hanoi reached the optimistic conclusion that the year 1968 would be the most favorable for starting the process of settlement. They strongly denounced Hanoi's rejection of Johnson's San Antonio formula—so-named after a speech in the Texas city on 29 September 1967 in which LBJ declared that Washington would stop bombing North Vietnam when assured that this would "lead promptly to productive discussions"—pointing out that that formula could not be regarded as "insurmountable" and advising that the DRV leadership take steps to snatch the diplomatic initiative. In order to convince Hanoi to change its intractable stand on talks with Washington, the Soviet Embassy advised Moscow to inform the North Vietnamese at their next summit with Soviet leaders that the USSR could not afford to pursue a policy of brinkmanship with respect to the United States by getting more deeply involved in the Vietnam conflict, and that therefore the best plan for both the Soviet Union and Vietnam would be if the hostilities drew to a close in 1968.[43] The fact that talks on the settlement of the Vietnam issue in fact finally started in 1968 may be regarded as a matter of pure coincidence. At the same time, the Soviet Embassy in Hanoi was farsighted in its assessments—what mattered was not that its forecasts had proved correct but rather the factors on which those forecasts were based. And in this respect, the Soviet Embassy had every reason to hope that the pressure exerted by Moscow on the Vietnamese leaders to accept a political rather than military solution, would finally bear fruit.

Preliminary U.S.-North Vietnamese talks opened on 13 May 1968, followed on 18 January 1969 by the official quadripartite (U.S.-South Vietnam-North Vietnam-NLF) Paris negotiations. Soviet diplomats justifiably regarded the event as their own success, at least in part. "Without acting as an official mediator," the Soviet Embassy in the DRV pointed out, "the Soviet Union rendered an important service for the two sides to sit down at the negotiating table and open official talks. The USSR spared no effort to convince world opinion and national governments to support an end to bombing raids on the DRV, and exerted pressure on the USA. At the same time it emphasized to the Vietnamese comrades that the year 1968 was most favorable for a number of reasons for launching the process of the political settlement of the Vietnam issue."[44]

The USSR did much to organize the Paris meeting, including influencing the choice of venue. The record of a conversation between V. Chivilev, Soviet acting charge d'affaires, and Le Duan, First Secretary of the WPV CC, held on 2 May 1968, suggests that on the eve of the opening of U.S.-DRV peace talks, the Vietnamese side offered Paris as the venue with due regard for the Soviet opinion. By that time Soviet diplomacy had already performed "a certain amount of work with the French." The main factor behind Hanoi's choice of the French capital, Le Duan told Chivilev, was "the opportunity to maintain contacts with Moscow from it."[45]

The same factor was taken into account by Moscow, which faced the task of keeping the sides at the negotiating table. With this aim in mind, the Kremlin exerted constant pressure on North Vietnam not to disrupt the process. On 13 June 1968, the CPSU CC and Soviet government sent a letter to the WPV CC and DRV government stressing that the Paris talks were vitally important for achieving a settlement of the Vietnam issue. The Soviet leaders also emphasized that they were living through an important period from the viewpoint of opportunities for diplomatic struggle, offering to put the entire weight of Soviet authority in the world in order to triumph in the political and diplomatic contest.[46] In an effort to influence the North Vietnamese side and as a hedge against the DRV's sometimes unpredictable behavior, the Soviet Embassy in Hanoi offered to send experts on Vietnamese affairs to the Soviet Embassy in Paris.[47] Moreover, Moscow reached an agreement with the DRV leadership for the Vietnamese regularly to inform Moscow on the situation at the talks and their future strategy, tactics, and plans. In turn, the USSR gave the Vietnamese exhaustive information about U.S. intentions. Nevertheless, despite its promises, Hanoi on several occasions confronted Moscow with a *fait accompli*. Yet, having "forgotten" to inform its ally about a planned action, the Vietnamese leadership nevertheless insisted on Moscow's immediate support. This happened, for instance, when the NLF published its program of ten points and established the Provisional Revolutionary Government of South Vietnam (RSV PRG). Although Le Duc Tho met with Kosygin on the eve of the program's publication (during a stopover in Moscow on his way to Paris), the leading DRV negotiator never mentioned the planned steps.[48]

However, in attempting to convince Soviet leaders to exert greater pressure on Vietnam to achieve progress in the talks, U.S. officials often forced an open door. Assessing the steps taken by Moscow for the settlement of the Vietnam conflict alongside the difficulties it encountered in dealing with Hanoi's foreign policy, one may reasonably conclude that the USSR did its utmost to ensure a favorable outcome of the talks, naturally with due account of its own interests.

Moscow continued to play an important role at the Paris talks after Nixon came to power in 1969. The Soviet leaders kept abreast of the latest developments and did their best to influence the Vietnamese position through the services of the USSR embassies in Hanoi and Paris. At his regular meetings with the leaders of the DRV and NLF delegations, the Soviet Ambassador in France, V. Zorin, asked the Vietnamese what questions they considered it necessary for him to raise in his conversations with the U.S. delegation. At the same time, Zorin expressed his "desire" for the Vietnamese side to put forward some specific proposals on military issues and for the NLF to elaborate a specific diplomatic program. Simultaneously, the Soviet ambassador in the DRV, Shcherbakov, warned "the Vietnamese friends" against following an extremist path, such as the temptation to pursue a purely propagandist policy or to resort exclusively to military methods in relations with the USA.[49]

Richard Nixon's victory in the 1968 elections marked a turning point in U.S. policy toward the USSR, as the incoming administration made every effort to obtain greater Soviet involvement and cooperation in the process of achieving a peaceful settlement in Vietnam. The newly elected U.S. president and his national security adviser, Henry A. Kissinger, decided that all problems in Soviet-American relations were linked to the Soviet stand on the Vietnam issue. And if efforts in Moscow did not quickly or sufficiently pay dividends, Nixon and Kissinger were prepared not to miss an opportunity to play "the Chinese card" to make the Soviet leaders more tractable. Like his predecessors, Nixon was convinced that the USSR had unlimited control over Hanoi's policy and that as soon as it issued the appropriate orders, the Vietnamese leaders would be ready, willing, and obliged to conclude the talks. As a result, each time the Paris talks reached a blind alley, the White

House turned to Moscow to help find an acceptable escape route. After a meeting with Kissinger on 12 June 1969, when the American openly asked the USSR for assistance to overcome the latest crisis in the talks, Soviet Ambassador in the United States Anatoly F. Dobrynin reported to Moscow: "All indications are that his [Nixon's] attempts to convince the USSR to help the USA in the settlement of the [Vietnam] conflict, will be repeated in the future, and this will probably be felt in the course of our talks with this administration on other international issues, if not directly, then at least in the form of procrastination in the course of such talks or in decision-making on other issues."[50]

In this respect, however, former CIA chief William Colby was probably right when he wrote in his memoirs about his deep skepticism with respect to the Soviet Union's ability to exert pressure on its friends, who were "stubborn and full of determination."[51] Nevertheless, in spite of its limited opportunities, the USSR managed to make a considerable contribution to the peaceful settlement of the Vietnam conflict. So the signing of the bilateral agreement by the DRV and USA, on 27 January 1973, on the end of hostilities and restoration of peace in Vietnam, irrespective of all its weak points, was an important result of the efforts of Soviet diplomacy as well.

In conclusion, in assessing Soviet policy toward the Vietnam War in the 1964–1973 period, including in the sphere of Soviet-American ties, it may be asserted that in spite of all the difficulties, complications, and human costs associated with the conflict in Southeast Asia, the superpowers avoided grave crises, upheavals, or direct confrontations in their bilateral relations—thus preserving a degree of general international stability and paving the way toward the U.S.-Soviet détente of the early-mid-1970s.

## Notes

1. Space precludes a full listing of relevant titles here: for detailed references see Ilya V. Gaiduk, *The Soviet Union and the Vietnam War* (Chicago: Ivan R. Dee, forthcoming [1996]).

2. According to data of the Soviet Ministry of Foreign Affairs, in the period from 1961 to 1966 the Soviet Union supplied the NLF via the DRV as disinterested assistance 130 recoilless weapons and mortars, 1400 machine guns, and 54,500 fire-arms with ammunition. Prior to 1965 the USSR supplied to North Vietnam German models of arms. (Top Secret Memorandum of the Southeast Asia Department, USSR Foreign Ministry, "Soviet Moral and Political Support of and Material Aid to the South Vietnam Patriots," 24 March 1966, SCCD, fond (f.) 5, opis (op.) 50, delo (d.) 777, listy (ll.) 58–59.) This aid supplemented the economic assistance Moscow rendered to the DRV. China, in turn, in the period from 1955 to 1965, supplied the DRV with economic assistance to the total value of 511.8 million rubles, including 302.5 million rubles as gift. (Memorandum of the

Ministry of Foreign Trade, "CPR's [Chinese People's Republic's] Economic Assistance to the Socialist Countries," 30 March 1966, SCCD, f. 5, op. 58, d. 254, l. 172.)

3. Telegram to the Soviet Ambassador to France, SCCD, f. 4, op. 18, d. 582, St.-95/462 g., 14 February 1964.

4. International Department of the CPSU CC to the CC, 25 July 1964, SCCD, f. 4, op. 50, d. 631, l. 163–164.

5. Memorandum from USSR Ministry of Defense to the CPSU CC, 14 July 1967, SCCD, f. 4, op. 59, d. 416, l. 119–120.

6. Top Secret Memorandum from the Soviet Embassy in the DRV, "On the Political Situation in South Vietnam and the Position of the DRV," 19 November 1964, SCCD, f. 4, op. 50, d. 631, l. 253.

7. See, e.g, Gabriel Kolko, *Anatomy of a War: Vietnam, the United States and the Modern Historical Experience* (New York: Pantheon, 1986), 157.

8. For further analysis of the impact of Khrushchev's overthrow on Soviet policy toward Vietnam, see the paper presented by Ilya V. Gaiduk to the conference on the Vietnam War held in October 1993 at the Lyndon B. Johnson Library, Austin, Texas.

9. A memo, sent to the CPSU CC by I. Shchedrov, a *Pravda* correspondent in Southeast Asia, may serve as an indirect basis for such suppositions. In it Shchedrov analyzes the situation in the region in the first half of the 1960s from the viewpoint of Soviet and Chinese influence on the events in Vietnam, Laos and Cambodia. He not only criticizes the Soviet Union's restraint, shown before the end of 1964, and expresses concern in view of stepped-up activities by the PRC in those countries, but also offers a series of measures to improve the situation. In their time the top CPSU leadership familiarized themselves with that memo, and the following note by Boris Ponomarev testifies to this: "Please read this memo and submit proposals and measures on issues which call for them." (SCCD, f. 5, op. 58, d. 264.)

10. Political Report of the Soviet Embassy in Hanoi for 1966, SCCD, f. 5, op. 58, d. 263, l. 148.

11. Memorandum, "Soviet Moral and Political Support," SCCD, f. 5, op. 50, d. 773, l. 59; Soviet Embassy in Hanoi Political Report for 1966, SCCD, f. 5, op. 58, d. 263, l. 148.

12. Soviet Embassy in Hanoi, Political Report for 1967, SCCD, f. 5, op. 59, d. 331, l. 26.

13. Shchedrov Memorandum, SCCD, f. 5, op. 58, d. 264, l. 96.

14. Soviet Embassy in Hanoi, Political Report for 1966, SCCD, f. 5, op. 58, d. 263, l. 130.

15. Memorandum of Conversation between Soviet Embassy in Hanoi interpreter M. Isaev and Ho Hai Thuy, 25 October 1966, SCCD, f. 5, op. 58, d. 261, l. 167.

16. Memorandum from USSR Ministry of Commercial Shipping for the CPSU CC, 18 July 1966, SCCD, f. 5, op. 58, d. 263, l. 38–41. The report by the Ministry of Commercial Shipping was a source of concern by the Soviet leadership. It was decided to make use of the information contained in it, in

the course of talks with the DRV party and government delegation to be held in Moscow (SCCD, f. 5, op. 58, d. 263, l. 43).

17. Soviet Embassy in Hanoi, Political Report for 1970, SCCD, f. 5, op. 62, d. 495, l. 109.

18. Memorandum from *Izvestia* correspondent M. Ilyinskii for CPSU CC, 29 January 1968, SCCD, f. 5., op. 60, d. 368, l. 19.

19. Memorandum from Committee of State Security (KGB), 21 February 1966, SCCD, f. 5, op. 6, d. 511. Regrettably, this document is kept in a "special dossier," so we have had no opportunity as yet to study it.

20. Soviet Embassy in Hanoi, Political Report for 1966, SCCD, f. 5, op. 58, d. 263, l. 141, 259.

21. Soviet Embassy in Hanoi, Political Report for 1970, SCCD, f. 5, op. 62, d. 495, 1. 104.

22. A memo by Defense Minister Grechko to Brezhnev serves as testimony to this fact. Grechko wrote that on 30 March 1968 a U.S. F-111A plane was brought down by an anti-aircraft Dvina complex in the area of Hanoi. He also mentioned measures, adopted by Soviet experts to improve the anti-aircraft complexes after they had obtained information about the use of high-speed aircraft (up to 3700 km per hour) by the US air forces (SCCD, f. 5, op. 60, d. 232, 11. 9–10).

23. Memorandum of Conversation between Deputy Chief of the USSR Foreign Ministry Southeast Asia Department S. Nemchina and Head of the NFLSV Permanent Mission in Moscow Dang Cuong Minh, 2 September 1967, SCCD, f. 5, op. 59, d. 416, l. 139.

24. Memorandum from the Soviet Embassy in the DRV, 14 March 1967, SCCD, f. 5, op. 59, d. 329, l. 43.

25. Memorandum from the State Committee on the Economic Relations (GKES), "On the Economic and Technical Assistance to the Democratic Republic of Vietnam," 29 July 1966, SCCD, f. 5, op. 58, d. 263, ll. 54–55; Soviet Embassy in the DRV, Political Report for 1968, SCCD, f. 5, op. 60, d. 375, l. 48; Soviet Embassy in the DRV, Political Report for 1969, SCCD, f. 5, op. 61, d. 459, l. 123; Soviet Embassy in the DRV, Political Report for 1970, SCCD, f. 5, op. 62, d. 495, 1. 104.

26. Washington's first attempts to reach agreement with the DRV leaders were made back in 1962, under President Kennedy's administration, so we can only suppose what could be the results of those contacts, had President Kennedy been alive. A. Goodman, for instance, believes that as a result of President Kennedy's assassination, the USA lost an opportunity to reach agreement with Hanoi. (A.E. Goodman, *The Lost Peace: America's Search for a Negotiated Settlement of the Vietnam War* (Stanford, CA: Stanford University Press, 1978), 14.)

27. To this testifies the KGB information of President Johnson's talks with Italian Foreign Minister A. Fanfani (SCCD, f. 5, op. 50, d. 690, l. 93).

28. KGB Memorandum, 11 December 1969, SCCD, f. 5, op. 61, d. 558, 1. 178–179.

29. Main Intelligence Administration (GRU), USSR Ministry of Defense, to CPSU CC, 23 August 1966, SCCD, f. 5, op. 58, d. 262, ll. 237–238. (For an English translation of this document, see CWIHP *Bulletin* 3 (Fall 1993) 61–62.)

30. The most complete records of these and other secret Vietnam peace efforts during the period 1964–68, based on classified U.S. government records, can be found in George C. Herring, ed., *The Secret Diplomacy of the Vietnam War: The Negotiating Volumes of the Pentagon Papers* (Austin, TX: University of Texas Press, 1983). MARIGOLD and SUNFLOWER are covered in greater detail, using additional Soviet and U.S. sources, in Gaiduk, *The Soviet Union and the Vietnam War* (forthcoming).

31. KGB Memoranda, 5 and 21 July 1965 and 7 October 1966, SCCD, f. 5, op. 6, d. 379, 389, 533.

32. Prime Minister and Foreign Minister of the Democratic Republic of Vietnam.

33. Political letters from Soviet embassies were in fact detailed reports of the situation in the respective countries, their domestic and foreign policy, and usually written in connection with particular events.

34. Political Letter, "Soviet-North Vietnamese Relations after the April 1968 Talks," 1 September 1968, SCCD, f. 5, op. 60, d. 369, l. 114; see also SCCD, f. 5, op. 60, d. 369, ll. 129, 131–132, 133.

35. Memorandum from B. Ponomarev for the CPSU CC, "On a Proposal to the Vietnamese Friends," attached to resolution of the CPSU CC Secretariat, SCCD, f. 4, op. 22, d. 1240, Art. No. 113/10, 12 February 1974.

36. Sometimes the situation looked simply ridiculous. Mentioned in the list of materials, included in "special dossiers," is the draft decision on the reply to Le Duan's personal message to Brezhnev, presented by the CC Department and the USSR Ministry of Foreign Affairs on 24 December 1974. There is the following note on the card of that document, written by Brezhnev's aide, Alexandrov: "to C-de K.U. Chernenko. Leonid Ilyich asked to hold a vote on this proposal (he has not read the text)." It turns out that top Soviet leaders signed documents either having learned the gist of the document at best, or having read only its title.

37. Memorandum of Conversation between Soviet Charge d'Affaires in Hanoi P. Privalov and Chairman of the Lao Dong Party's Committee on the Unification of the Country Nguyen Van Minh, 23 August 1966, SCCD, f. 5, op. 58, d. 264, ll. 173–174.

38. Soviet Embassy to the DRV, Political Report for 1966, SCCD, f. 5, op. 58, d. 263, l. 259.

39. For details, see Herring, ed., *The Secret Diplomacy of the Vietnam War*, and Gaiduk, *The Soviet Union and the Vietnam War* (forthcoming).

40. KGB Memorandum, 28 January 1967, SCCD, f. 5, op. 60, d. 680; Memorandum of Conversation between Soviet Ambassador Shcherbakov and DRV Foreign Minister Nguyen Duy Trinh, 15 February 1967, SCCD, f. 5, op. 59, d. 327, l. 145.

41. USSR Foreign Ministry, list of questions on which the Vietnamese comrades were informed, SCCD, f. 5, op. 60, d. 369, l. 15.

42. Soviet Embassy to the DRV, Political Letter, "Soviet-North Vietnamese Talks of April 1967 and the Policy of the PTV [Workers' Party of Vietnam] on the Settlement of the Vietnamese Problem," August 1967, SCCD, f. 5, op. 59, d. 327, l. 263.

43. Soviet Embassy to the DRV, Political Report for 1967, SCCD, f. 5, op. 59, d. 332, l. 133–138.

44. Soviet Embassy to the DRV, Political Report for 1968, SCCD, f. 5, op. 60, d. 375, l. 30–31.

45. Memorandum of Conversation between Soviet Charge d'Affaires in the DRV V. Chivilev and Le Duan, 2 May 1968, SCCD, f. 5, op. 60, d. 376, l. 47.

46. Soviet Embassy to the DRV, Political Letter, "Soviet-North Vietnamese Relations After the April 1968 Talks," SCCD, f. 5, op. 60, d. 369, l. 109.

47. Soviet Embassy to the DRV, Political Report for 1968, SCCD, f. 5, op. 60, d. 375, l. 31.

48. Soviet Embassy to the DRV, Political Report for 1969, SCCD, f. 5, op. 61, d. 459, l. 117.

49. Memorandum of Conversation between Soviet Ambassador V. Zorin and Xuan Thuy and Tranh Byu Khiem, 21 February 1969, SCCD, f. 5, op. 61, d. 460, ll. 56–60, 131–134. (For an English translation, see CWIHP *Bulletin* 3 (Fall 1993), 62–63.

50. Memorandum of Conversation between A. Dobrynin and H. Kissinger, 12 June 1969, SCCD, f. 5, op. 61, d. 558, l. 103. (For an English translation of this document, see CWIHP *Bulletin* 3 (Fall 1993), 63–67.) The contents of this conversation, as the note on the document testifies, were reported to Brezhnev, so the top Soviet leadership had been informed about Washington's intentions.

51. William Colby and James McCargar, *Lost Victory: A Firsthand Account of America's Sixteen-Year Involvement in Vietnam* (Chicago, N.Y., 1989), 335.

*Ilya V. Gaiduk, a research scholar at the Institute of Universal History (IUH), Russian Academy of Sciences, Moscow, is the author of* The Soviet Union and the Vietnam War *(Chicago: Ivan R. Dee, forthcoming). A recipient of fellowships from CWIHP and the Norwegian Nobel Institute, he originally presented the findings in this article to the January 1993 Conference on New Soviet Evidence on Cold War History in Moscow, organized by CWIHP and IUH. The author gratefully acknowledges the assistance of Oganez V. Marinin, then a staff archivist at SCCD (now at the State Archive of the Russian Federation [GARF]), in locating archival documents for this article.*

# Beijing and the Vietnam Conflict, 1964–1965: New Chinese Evidence

## Qiang Zhai

The years 1964–1965 marked a crucial period in the Vietnam War. The Gulf of Tonkin Incident and subsequent U.S. escalation of war against North Vietnam represented a major turning point in the American approach to Indochina, as the Johnson Administration shifted its focus from Saigon to Hanoi as the best way to reverse the deteriorating trend in South Vietnam and to persuade the North Vietnamese leadership to desist from their increasing involvement in the South. How did Beijing react to Washington's escalation of the conflict in Vietnam? How did Mao Zedong perceive U.S. intentions? Was there a "strategic debate" within the Chinese leadership over the American threat and over strategies that China should adopt in dealing with the United States? What was in Mao's mind when he decided to commit China's resources to Hanoi? How and why did a close relationship between Beijing and Hanoi turn sour during the fight against a common foe? Drawing upon recently available Chinese materials, this paper will address these questions.[1] The first half of the article is primarily narrative, while the second half provides an analysis of the factors that contributed to China's decision to commit itself to Hanoi, placing Chinese actions in their domestic and international context.

### China's Role in Vietnam, 1954–1963

China played an important role in helping Ho Chi Minh win the Anti-French War and in concluding the Geneva Accords in 1954.[2] In the decade after the Geneva Conference, Beijing continued to exert influence over developments in Vietnam. At the time of the Geneva Conference, the Vietnamese

Communists asked the Chinese Communist Party (CCP) to help them consolidate peace in the North, build the army, conduct land reform, rectify the Party, strengthen diplomatic work, administer cities, and restore the economy.[3] Accordingly, Beijing sent Fang Yi to head a team of Chinese economic experts to North Vietnam.[4]

According to the official history of the Chinese Military Advisory Group (CMAG), on 27 June 1955, Vo Nguyen Giap headed a Vietnamese military delegation on a secret visit to Beijing accompanied by Wei Guoqing, head of the CMAG in Vietnam. The Vietnamese visitors held discussions with Chinese Defense Minister Peng Dehuai, and General Petroshevskii, a senior Soviet military advisor in China, regarding the Democratic Republic of Vietnam's reconstruction of the army and the war plan for the future. The DRV delegation visited the Chinese North Sea Fleet before returning to Hanoi in mid-July. That fall, on 15 October 1955, Vo Nguyen Giap led another secret military delegation to China, where he talked with Peng Dehuai and Soviet General Gushev again about the DRV's military development and war planning. The Vietnamese inspected Chinese military facilities and academies and watched a Chinese military exercise before traveling back to North Vietnam on December 11.[5]

The official CMAG history states that during both of Giap's journeys to Beijing, he "reached agreement" with the Chinese and the Russians "on principal issues." But it does not explain why Giap had to make a second visit to China shortly after his first tour and why the Soviet participants at the talks changed. Perhaps disagreement emerged during the discussions of Giap's first trip, leaving some issues unresolved. In fact, according to the study by the researchers at the Guangxi Academy of Social Sciences, the Chinese and the Russians differed over strategies to reunify Vietnam. The Soviet advisors favored peaceful coexistence between North and South Vietnam, urging Hanoi to "reunify the country through peaceful means on the basis of independence and democracy." The Chinese Communists, conversely, contended that because of imperialist sabotage it was impossible to reunify Vietnam through a general election in accordance with the Geneva Accords, and that consequently North Vietnam should prepare for a protracted struggle.[6]

On 24 December 1955, the Chinese government decided to withdraw the CMAG from Vietnam; Peng Dehuai notified Vo Nguyen Giap of this decision. By mid-March 1956, the last members of the CMAG had left the DRV. To replace the formal CMAG, Beijing appointed a smaller team of military experts headed by Wang Yanquan to assist the Vietnamese.[7]

These developments coincided with a major debate within the Vietnamese Communist leadership in 1956 over who should bear responsibility for mistakes committed during a land reform campaign which had been instituted since 1953 in an imitation of the Chinese model. Truong Chinh,

General Secretary of the Vietnamese Workers' Party (VWP), who was in charge of the land reform program, was removed from his position at a Central Committee Plenum held in September. Le Duan, who became General Secretary later in the year, accused Truong Chinh of applying China's land reform experience in Vietnam without considering the Vietnamese reality.[8]

The failure of the land-reform program in the DRV dovetailed with a growing realization that the reunification of the whole of Vietnam, as promised by the Geneva Accords, would not materialize, primarily as a result of U.S. support for the anti-Communist South Vietnamese regime of Ngo Dinh Diem, who refused to hold elections in 1956. As hopes for an early reunification dimmed, the DRV had to face its own economic difficulties. The rice supply became a major problem as Hanoi, no longer able to count on incorporating the rice-producing South into its economy, was forced to seek alternative food sources for the North and to prepare the groundwork for a self-supporting economy. In this regard, leaders in Hanoi continued to seek Chinese advice despite the memory of the poorly-implemented land-reform program. There are indications that the Chinese themselves had drawn lessons from the debacle of the Vietnamese land reform and had become more sensitive to Vietnamese realities when offering suggestions. In April 1956, Deputy Premier Chen Yun, an economic specialist within the CCP, paid an unpublicized visit to Hanoi. At the request of Ho Chi Minh, Chen proposed the principle of "agriculture preceding industry and light industry ahead of heavy industry" in developing the Vietnamese economy. The Vietnamese leadership adopted Chen's advice.[9] Given the fact that the CCP was putting a high premium on the development of heavy industry at home during its First Five-Year Plan at this time, Chen's emphasis on agriculture and light industry was very unusual, and demonstrated that the Chinese were paying more attention to Vietnamese conditions in their assistance to the DRV. Zhou Enlai echoed Chen's counsel of caution in economic planning during his tour of Hanoi on 18–22 November 1956, when he told Ho Chi Minh to refrain from haste in collectivizing agriculture: "Such changes must come step by step."[10]

Donald S. Zagoria argues in his book *Vietnam Triangle* that between 1957 and 1960, the DRV shifted its loyalties from Beijing to Moscow in order to obtain Soviet assistance for its economic development.[11] In reality, the Hanoi leadership continued to consult the CCP closely on such major issues as economic consolidation in the North and the revolutionary struggle in the South. With the completion of its economic recovery in 1958, the VWP began to pay more attention to strengthening the revolutionary movement in the South. It sought Chinese advice. In the summer of 1958, the VWP presented to the CCP for comment two documents entitled "Our View on the Basic Tasks for Vietnam during the New Stage" and "Certain

Opinions Concerning the Unification Line and the Revolutionary Line in the South." After a careful study, the Chinese leadership responded with a written reply, which pointed out that "the most fundamental, the most crucial, and the most urgent task" for the Vietnamese revolution was to carry out socialist revolution and socialist construction in the North. As to the South, the Chinese reply continued, Hanoi's task should be to promote "a national and democratic revolution." But since it was impossible to realize such a revolution at the moment, the Chinese concluded, the VWP should "conduct a long-term underground work, accumulate strength, establish contact with the masses, and wait for opportunities."[12] Clearly, Beijing did not wish to see the situation in Vietnam escalate into a major confrontation with the United States. Judging by subsequent developments, the VWP did not ignore the Chinese advice, for between 1958 and 1960 Hanoi concentrated on economic construction in the North, implementing the "Three-Year Plan" of a socialist transformation of the economy and society.

The policy of returning to revolutionary war adopted by the VWP Central Committee in May 1959 did not outline any specific strategy to follow. The resolution had merely mentioned that a blend of political and military struggle would be required. During the next two years, debates over strategy and tactics continued within the Hanoi leadership.[13] Ho Chi Minh continued to consult the Chinese. In May 1960, North Vietnamese and Chinese leaders held discussions in both Hanoi and Beijing over strategies to pursue in South Vietnam. Zhou Enlai and Deng Xiaoping argued that in general political struggle should be combined with armed conflict and that since specific conditions varied between the city and the countryside in South Vietnam, a flexible strategy of struggle should be adopted. In the city, the Chinese advised, political struggle would generally be recommended, but to deliver a final blow on the Diem regime, armed force would be necessary. Since there was an extensive mass base in the countryside, military struggle should be conducted there, but military struggle should include political struggle.[14] The Chinese policymakers, preoccupied with recovery from the economic disasters caused by the Great Leap Forward, clearly did not encourage a major commitment of resources from the North in support of a general offensive in the South at this juncture.

In September 1960, the VWP convened its Third National Congress, which made no major recommendations affecting existing strategy but simply stated that disintegration was replacing stability in the South. To take advantage of this new situation, the Congress urged the party to carry out both political and military struggle in the South and called for an increase of support from the North.[15] This emphasis on a combination of political and military struggle in the South reflected to some degree the Chinese suggestion of caution.

In the spring of 1961, U.S President John F. Kennedy approved an increase in the Military Assistance and Advisory Group (MAAG) of 100 advisers and sent to Vietnam 400 Special Forces troops to train the South Vietnamese in counterinsurgency techniques. This escalation of U.S. involvement in Indochina aroused Chinese leaders' concern. During DRV Premier Pham Van Dong's visit to Beijing in June 1961, Mao expressed a general support for the waging of an armed struggle by the South Vietnamese people while Zhou Enlai continued to stress flexibility in tactics and the importance of "blending legal and illegal struggle and combining political and military approaches."[16]

1962 saw a major turning point in both U.S. involvement in Vietnam and in Chinese attitudes toward the conflict. In February, Washington established in Saigon the Military Assistance Command, Vietnam (MAC,V), to replace the MAAG. The Kennedy Administration coupled this move with a drastic increase in the number of American "advisers" and the amount of military hardware it was sending to the Diem regime, marking a new level of U.S. intervention in Vietnam.

That spring, an important debate broke out within the Chinese leadership over the estimation of a world war, the possibility of peaceful coexistence with capitalist countries, and the degree of China's support for national liberation movements. On February 27, Wang Jiaxiang, Director of the CCP Foreign Liaison Department, sent a letter to Zhou Enlai, Deng Xiaoping, and Chen Yi (the three PRC officials directly in charge of foreign policy), in which he criticized the tendency to overrate the danger of world war and to underestimate the possibility of peaceful coexistence with imperialism. In terms of support for national liberation movements, Wang emphasized restraint, calling attention to China's own economic problems and limitations in resources. On the issue of Vietnam, he asked the party to "guard against a Korea-style war created by American imperialists," and warned of the danger of "Khrushchev and his associates dragging us into the trap of war." Wang proposed that in order to adjust and restore the economy and win time to tide over difficulties, China should adopt a policy of peace and conciliation in foreign affairs, and that in the area of foreign aid China should not do what it cannot afford.[17] But Mao rejected Wang's proposal, condemning Wang as promoting a "revisionist" foreign policy of "three appeasements and one reduction" (appeasement of imperialism, revisionism, and international reactionaries, and reduction of assistance to national liberation movements).[18]

The outcome of the debate had major implications for China's policy toward Vietnam. If Wang's moderate suggestions had been adopted, it would have meant a limited Chinese role in Indochina. But Mao had switched to a militant line, choosing confrontation with the United States. This turn to the left in foreign policy accorded with Mao's reemphasis on class struggle and radical politics in Chinese domestic affairs in 1962. It also anticipated an active Chinese role in the unfolding crisis in Vietnam. With the rejection of Wang's proposal, an opportunity to avert the later Sino-American hostility over Indochina was missed.

In the summer of 1962, Ho Chi Minh and Nguyen Chi Thanh came to Beijing to discuss with Chinese leaders the serious situation created by the U.S. intervention in Vietnam and the possibility of an American attack against North Vietnam. Ho asked the Chinese to provide support for the guerrilla movement in South Vietnam. Beijing satisfied Ho's demand by agreeing to give the DRV free of charge 90,000 rifles and guns that could equip 230 infantry battalions. These weapons would be used to support guerrilla warfare in the South.[19] In March 1963, Luo Ruiqing, Chief of Staff of the Chinese People's Liberation Army (PLA), visited the DRV and discussed with his hosts how China might support Hanoi if the United States attacked North Vietnam.[20] Two months later, Liu Shaoqi, Chairman of the PRC, traveled to Hanoi, where he told Ho Chi Minh: "We are standing by your side, and if war broke out, you can regard China as your rear."[21] Clearly Beijing was making a major commitment to Hanoi in early 1963. Toward the end of the year, Chinese and North Vietnamese officials discussed Beijing's assistance in constructing defense works and naval bases in the northeastern part of the DRV.[22]

According to a Chinese source, in 1963 China and the DRV made an agreement under which Beijing would send combat troops into North Vietnam if American soldiers crossed the Seventeenth Parallel to attack the North. The Chinese soldiers would stay and fight in the North to free the North Vietnamese troops to march to the South.[23] But the precise date and details of this agreement remain unclear.

In sum, between 1954 and 1963 China was closely involved in the development of Hanoi's policy. The CCP urged Ho Chi Minh to concentrate on consolidating the DRV and to combine political and military struggles in the South. Although before 1962 Beijing policy makers were not eager to see a rapid intensification of the revolutionary war in South Vietnam, neither did they discourage their comrades in Hanoi from increasing military operations there. Between 1956 and 1963, China provided the DRV with 270,000 guns, over 10,000 pieces of artillery, nearly 200 million bullets, 2.02 million artillery shells, 15,000 wire transmitters, 5,000 radio transmitters, over 1,000 trucks, 15 aircraft, 28 war ships, and 1.18 million sets of uniforms. The total value of China's assistance to Hanoi during this period amounted to 320 million yuan.[24] 1962 was a crucial year in the evolution of China's attitudes toward Vietnam. Abandoning the cautious approach, Mao opted for confrontation with the United States and decided to commit China's resources to Hanoi. Beijing's massive supply of weapons to the DRV in 1962 helped Ho Chi Minh to intensify guerrilla warfare in the South, triggering greater U.S. intervention. By the end of 1963, Chinese leaders had become very nervous about American intentions in Vietnam but were ready to provide full support for the DRV in confronting the United States.

## China's Reaction to U.S. Escalation

In the first half of 1964, the attention of U.S. officials was shifting increasingly from South Vietnam toward Hanoi. This trend reflected mounting concern over the infiltration of men and supplies from the North and a growing dissatisfaction with a policy that allowed Hanoi to encourage the insurgency without punishment. In addition to expanding covert operations in North Vietnam, including intelligence overflights, the dropping of propaganda leaflets, and OPLAN 34A commando raids along the North Vietnamese coast, the Johnson Administration also conveyed to Pham Van Dong through a Canadian diplomat on June 17 the message that the United States was ready to exert increasingly heavy military pressure on the DRV to force it to reduce or terminate its encouragement of guerrilla activities in South Vietnam. But the North Vietnamese leader refused to yield to the American pressure, declaring that Hanoi would not stop its support for the struggle of liberation in the South.[25]

Mao watched these developments closely. Anticipating new trouble, the chairman told General Van Tien Dung, Chief of Staff of the (North) Vietnamese People's Army, in June: "Our two parties and two countries must cooperate and fight the enemy together. Your business is my business and my business is your business. In other words, our two sides must deal with the enemy together without conditions."[26] Between July 5 and 8, Zhou Enlai led a CCP delegation to Hanoi, where he discussed with leaders from the DRV and Pathet Lao the situations in South Vietnam and Laos.[27] Although the details of these talks are unknown, clearly the three Communist parties were stepping up their coordination to confront the increasing threat from the United States.

Immediately after the Gulf of Tonkin Incident, Zhou Enlai and Luo Ruiqing sent a cable on August 5 to Ho Chi Minh, Pham Van Dong, and Van Tien Dung, asking them to "investigate the situation, work out countermeasures, and be prepared to fight."[28] In the meantime, Beijing instructed the Kunming and Guangzhou Military Regions and the air force and naval units stationed in south and south-west China to assume a state of combat-readiness. Four air divisions and one anti-aircraft division were dispatched into areas adjoining Vietnam and put on a heightened alert status.[29] In

August, China also sent approximately 15 MiG-15 and MiG-17 jets to Hanoi, agreed to train North Vietnamese pilots, and started to construct new airfields in areas adjacent to the Vietnamese border which would serve as sanctuary and repair and maintenance facilities for Hanoi's jet fighters.[30] By moving new air force units to the border area and building new airfields there, Beijing intended to deter further U.S. expansion of war in South Vietnam and bombardment against the DRV. Between August and September 1964, the PLA also sent an inspection team to the DRV to investigate the situation in case China later needed to dispatch support troops to Vietnam.[31]

The first months of 1965 witnessed a significant escalation of the American war in Vietnam. On February 7, 9 and 11, U.S. aircraft struck North Vietnamese military installations just across the 17th Parallel, ostensibly in retaliation for Vietcong attacks on American barracks near Pleiku and in Qui Nhon. On March 1, the Johnson Administration stopped claiming that its air attacks on North Vietnam were reprisals for specific Communist assaults in South Vietnam and began a continuous air bombing campaign against the DRV. On March 8, two battalions of Marines armed with tanks and 8-inch howitzers landed at Danang.[32]

Worried about the increasing U.S. involvement in Vietnam, Zhou Enlai on April 2 asked Pakistani President Ayub Khan to convey to President Johnson a four-point message: (1) China will not take the initiative to provoke a war with the United States. (2) The Chinese mean what they say. In other words, if any country in Asia, Africa, or elsewhere meets with aggression by the imperialists headed by the United States, the Chinese government and people will definitely give it support and assistance. Should such just action bring on American aggression against China, we will unhesitatingly rise in resistance and fight to the end. (3) China is prepared. Should the United States impose a war on China, it can be said with certainty that, once in China, the United States will not be able to pull out, however many men it may send over and whatever weapons it may use, nuclear weapons included. (4) Once the war breaks out, it will have no boundaries. If the American madmen bombard China without constraints, China will not sit there waiting to die. If they come from the sky, we will fight back on the ground. Bombing means war. The war can not have boundaries. It is impossible for the United States to finish the war simply by relying on a policy of bombing.[33]

This was the most serious warning issued by the Chinese government to the United States, and given the caution exercised by President Johnson in carrying out the "Rolling Thunder" operations against the DRV, it was one that Washington did not overlook. Clearly, U.S. leaders had drawn a lesson from the Korean War, when the Truman Administration's failure to heed Beijing warning against crossing the 38th parallel led to a bloody confrontation between the United States and China.

The U.S. escalation in early 1965 made the DRV desperate for help. Le Duan and Vo Nguyen Giap rushed to Beijing in early April to ask China to increase its aid and send troops to Vietnam. Le Duan told Chinese leaders that Hanoi needed "volunteer pilots, volunteer soldiers as well as other necessary personnel, including road and bridge engineers." The Vietnamese envoys expected Chinese volunteer pilots to perform four functions: to limit U.S. bombing to the south of the 20th or 19th parallel, to defend Hanoi, to protect several major transportation lines, and to boost morale.[34] On behalf of the Chinese leadership, Liu Shaoqi replied to the Vietnamese visitors on April 8 that "it is the obligation of the Chinese people and party" to support the Vietnamese struggle against the United States. "Our principle is," Liu continued, "that we will do our best to provide you with whatever you need and whatever we have. If you do not invite us, we will not go to your place. We will send whatever part [of our troops] that you request. You have the complete initiative."[35]

In April, China signed several agreements with the DRV concerning the dispatch of Chinese support troops to North Vietnam.[36] Between April 21 and 22, Giap discussed with Luo Ruiqing and First Deputy Chief of Staff Yang Chengwu the arrangements for sending Chinese troops.[37] In May, Ho Chi Minh paid a secret visit to Mao in Changsha, the chairman's home province, where he asked Mao to help the DRV repair and build twelve roads in the area north of Hanoi. The Chinese leader accepted Ho's request and instructed Zhou Enlai to see to the matter.[38]

In discussions with Luo Ruiqing and Yang Chengwu, Zhou said: "According to Pham Van Dong, U.S. blockade and bombing has reduced supplies to South Vietnam through sea shipment and road transportation. While trying to resume sea transportation, the DRV is also expanding the corridor in Lower Laos and roads in the South. Their troops would go to the South to build roads. Therefore they need our support to construct roads in the North." Zhou decided that the Chinese military should be responsible for road repair and construction in North Vietnam. Yang suggested that since assistance to the DRV involved many military and government departments, a special leadership group should be created to coordinate the work of various agencies. Approving the proposal, Zhou immediately announced the establishment of the "Central Committee and State Council Aid Vietnam Group" with Yang and Li Tianyou (Deputy Chief of Staff) as Director and Vice Director.[39] This episode demonstrates Zhou's characteristic effectiveness in organization and efficiency in administration.

In early June, Van Tien Dung held discussions with Luo Ruiqing in Beijing to flesh out the general Chinese plan to assist Vietnam. According to their agreement, if the war remained in the current conditions, the DRV would fight the war by itself and China would provide various kinds of support as the

Vietnamese needed. If the United States used its navy and air force to support a South Vietnamese attack on the North, China would also provide naval and air force support to the DRV. If U.S. ground forces were directly used to attack the North, China would use its land forces as strategic reserves for the DRV and conduct military operations whenever necessary. As to the forms of Sino-Vietnamese air force cooperation, Dung and Luo agreed that China could send volunteer pilots to Vietnam to operate Vietnamese aircraft, station both pilots and aircraft in Vietnam airfields, or fly aircraft from bases in China to join combat in Vietnam and only land on Vietnamese bases temporarily for refueling. The third option was known as the "Andong model" (a reference to the pattern of Chinese air force operations during the Korean War). In terms of the methods of employing PRC ground troops, the two military leaders agreed that the Chinese forces would either help to strengthen the defensive position of the DRV troops to prepare for a North Vietnamese counter offensive or launch an offensive themselves to disrupt the enemy's deployment and win the strategic initiative.[40]

But despite Liu Shaoqi's April promise to Le Duan and Luo Ruiqing's agreement with Van Tien Dung, China in the end failed to provide pilots to Hanoi. According to the Vietnamese "White Paper" of 1979, the Chinese General Staff on 16 July 1965 notified its Vietnamese counterpart that "the time was not appropriate" to send Chinese pilots to Vietnam.[41] The PRC's limited air force capacity may have caused Beijing to have second thoughts, perhaps reinforcing Beijing's desire to avoid a direct confrontation with the United States. Whatever the reasons for China's decision, the failure to satisfy Hanoi's demand must have greatly disappointed the Vietnamese since the control of the air was so crucial for the DRV's effort to protect itself from the ferocious U.S. bombing, and undoubtedly contributed to North Vietnam's decision in 1965 to rely more on the Soviet Union for air defense.

Beginning in June 1965, China sent ground-to-air missile, anti-aircraft artillery, railroad, engineering, mine-sweeping, and logistical units into North Vietnam to help Hanoi. The total number of Chinese troops in North Vietnam between June 1965 and March 1973 amounted to over 320,000.[42] To facilitate supplies into South Vietnam, China created a secret coastal transportation line to ship goods to several islands off Central Vietnam for transit to the South. A secret harbor on China's Hainan Island was constructed to serve this transportation route. Beijing also operated a costly transportation line through Cambodia to send weapons, munitions, food, and medical supplies into South Vietnam.[43] When the last Chinese troops withdrew from Vietnam in August 1973, 1,100 soldiers had lost their lives and 4,200 had been wounded.[44]

The new materials from China indicate that Beijing provided extensive support (short of volunteer pilots) for Hanoi during the Vietnam War and risked war with the United States in helping the Vietnamese. As Allen S. Whiting has perceptively observed, the deployment of Chinese troops in Vietnam was not carried out under maximum security against detection by Washington. The Chinese troops wore regular uniforms and did not disguise themselves as civilians. The Chinese presence was intentionally communicated to U.S. intelligence through aerial photography and electronic intercepts. This evidence, along with the large base complex that China built at Yen Bai in northwest Vietnam, provided credible and successful deterrence against an American invasion of North Vietnam.[45]

The specter of a Chinese intervention in a manner similar to the Korean War was a major factor in shaping President Johnson's gradual approach to the Vietnam War. Johnson wanted to forestall Chinese intervention by keeping the level of military actions against North Vietnam controlled, exact, and below the threshold that would provoke direct Chinese entry. This China-induced U.S. strategy of gradual escalation was a great help for Hanoi, for it gave the Vietnamese communists time to adjust to U.S. bombing and to develop strategies to frustrate American moves. As John Garver has aptly put it, "By helping to induce Washington to adopt this particular strategy, Beijing contributed substantially to Hanoi's eventual victory over the United States."[46]

## Explaining PRC Support for the DRV

Mao's decision to aid Hanoi was closely linked to his perception of U.S. threats to China's security, his commitment to national liberation movements, his criticism of Soviet revisionist foreign policy, and his domestic need to transform the Chinese state and society. These four factors were mutually related and reinforcing.

### Sense of Insecurity:

Between 1964 and 1965, Mao worried about the increasing American involvement in Vietnam and perceived the United States as posing a serious threat to China's security. For him, support for North Vietnam was a way of countering the U.S. strategy of containment of China. The Communist success in South Vietnam would prevent the United States from moving closer to the Chinese southern border.

On several occasions in 1964, Mao talked about U.S. threats to China and the need for China to prepare for war. During a Central Committee conference held between May 15 and June 17, the chairman contended that "so long as imperialism exists, the danger of war is there. We are not the chief of staff for imperialism and have no idea when it will launch a war. It is the conventional weapon, not the atomic bomb, that will determine the final victory of the war."[47] At first Mao did not expect that the United States would attack North Vietnam directly.[48] The Gulf of Tonkin Incident came as a surprise to him. In the wake of the incident, Mao pointed out on October 22 that China must base its plans on war and make active preparations for an early, large-scale, and nuclear war.[49]

To deal with what he perceived as U.S. military threats, Mao took several domestic measures in 1964, the most important of which was the launching of the massive Third Front project. This program called for heavy investment in the remote provinces of southwestern and western China and envisioned the creation of a huge self-sustaining industrial base area to serve as a strategic reserve in the event China became involved in war. The project had a strong military orientation and was directly triggered by the U.S. escalation of war in Vietnam.[50]

On 25 April 1964, the War Department of the PLA General Staff drafted a report for Yang Chengwu on how to prevent an enemy surprise attack on China's economic construction. The report listed four areas vulnerable to such an attack: (1) China's industry was over-concentrated. About 60 percent of the civil machinery industry, 50 percent of the chemical industry, and 52 percent of the national defense industry were concentrated in 14 major cities with over one million people. (2) Too many people lived in cities. According to the 1962 census, in addition to 14 cities of above one million, 20 cities had a population between 500,000 and one million. Most of these cities were located in the coastal areas and very vulnerable to air strikes. No effective mechanisms existed at the moment to organize anti-air works, evacuate urban populations, continue production, and eliminate the damages of an air strike, especially a nuclear strike. (3) Principal railroad junctions, bridges, and harbors were situated near big and medium-size cities and could easily be destroyed when the enemy attacked the cities. No measures had been taken to protect these transportation points against an enemy attack. In the early stage of war, they could become paralyzed. (4) All of China's reservoirs had a limited capacity to release water in an emergency. Among the country's 232 large reservoirs, 52 were located near major transportation lines and 17 close to important cities. In conclusion, the report made it clear that "the problems mentioned above are directly related to the whole armed forces, to the whole people, and to the process of a national defense war." It asked the State Council "to organize a special committee to study and adopt, in accordance with the possible conditions of the national economy, practical and effective measures to guard against an enemy surprise attack."[51]

Yang Chengwu presented the report to Mao, who returned it to Luo Ruiqing and Yang on August 12 with the following comment: "It is an excellent report. It should be carefully studied and gradually implemented." Mao urged the newly established State Council Special Committee in charge of the Third Front to begin its work immediately.[52] Mao's approval of the report marked the beginning of the Third Front project to relocate China's industrial resources to the interior. It is important to note the timing of Mao's reaction to the report—right after the Gulf of Tonkin Incident. The U.S. expansion of the war to North Vietnam had confirmed Mao's worst suspicions about American intentions.

Deputy Prime Minister Li Fuchun became Director, Deputy Prime Minister Bo Yibo and Luo Ruiqing became Vice Directors of the Special Committee. On August 19, they submitted to Mao a detailed proposal on how to implement the Third Front ideas.[53] In the meantime, the CCP Secretariat met to discuss the issue. Mao made two speeches at the meetings on August 17 and 20. He asserted that China should be on guard against an aggressive war launched by imperialism. At present, factories were concentrated around big cities and coastal regions, a situation deleterious to war preparation. Factories should be broken into two parts. One part should be relocated to interior areas as early as possible. Every province should establish its own strategic rear base. Departments of industry and transportation should move, so should schools, science academies, and Beijing University. The three railroad lines between Chengdu and Kunming, Sichuan and Yunnan, and Yunnan and Guizhou should be completed as quickly as possible. If there were a shortage of rails, the chairman insisted, rails on other lines could be dismantled. To implement Mao's instructions, the meetings decided to concentrate China's financial, material, and human resources on the construction of the Third Front.[54]

While emphasizing the "big Third Front" plan on the national level, Mao also ordered provinces to proceed with their "small Third Front" projects. The chairman wanted each province to develop its own light armament industry capable of producing rifles, machine guns, canons, and munitions.[55] The Third Five-Year Plan was revised to meet the strategic contingency of war preparation. In the modified plan, a total of three billion yuan was appropriated for small Third Front projects. This was a substantial figure, but less than 5 percent of the amount set aside for the big Third Front in this period.[56] In sum, the Third Front was a major strategic action designed to provide an alternative industrial base that would enable China to continue production in the event of an attack on its large urban centers.

In addition to his apprehension about a strike on China's urban and coastal areas, Mao also feared that the enemy might deploy paratroop assault forces deep inside China. In a meeting with He Long, Deputy Chairman of the Central Military Commission, Luo Ruiqing, and Yang Chengwu on 28 April 1965, Mao called their attention to such a danger. He ordered them to prepare for the landing of enemy paratroopers in every interior region. The enemy might use paratroops, Mao contended, "to disrupt our rear areas, and to coordinate with a frontal assault. The number of paratroops may not be many. It may involve one or two divisions in each region, or it may involve a smaller unit. In all interior regions, we should build caves in mountains. If no mountain is around, hills should be created to construct defense works. We should be on guard against enemy paratroops deep inside our country and prevent the enemy from marching unstopped into China."[57]

It appears that Mao's attitudes toward the United States hardened between January and April 1965. In an interview with Edgar Snow on January 9, Mao had expressed confidence that Washington would not expand the war to North Vietnam because Secretary of State Dean Rusk had said so. He told Snow that there would be no war between China and the United States if Washington did not send troops to attack China.[58] Two days later, the CCP Central Military Commission issued a "Six-Point Directive on the Struggle against U.S. Ships and Aircraft in the South China Sea," in which it instructed the military not to attack American airplanes that intruded into Chinese airspace in order to avoid a direct military clash with the United States.[59] In April, however, Mao rescinded the "Six Point Directive." Between April 8 and 9, U.S. aircraft flew into China's airspace over Hainan Island. On April 9, Yang Chengwu reported the incidents to Mao, suggesting that the order not to attack invading U.S. airplanes be lifted and that the air force command take control of the naval air units stationed on Hainan Island. Approving both of Yang's requests, Mao said that China "should resolutely strike American aircraft that overfly Hainan Island."[60] It is quite possible that the further U.S. escalation of war in Vietnam in the intervening months caused Mao to abandon his earlier restrictions against engaging U.S. aircraft.

It is important to point out that the entire Chinese leadership, not just Mao, took the strategic threat from the United States very seriously during this period. Zhou Enlai told Spiro Koleka, First Deputy Chairman of the Council of Ministers of Albania, on 9 May 1965 in Beijing that China was mobilizing its population for war. Although it seemed that the United States had not made up its mind to expand the war to China, the Chinese premier continued, war had its own law of development, usually in a way contrary to the wishes of people. Therefore China had to be prepared.[61] Zhou's remarks indicated that he was familiar with a common pattern in warfare: accidents and miscalculations rather than deliberate planning often lead to war between reluctant opponents.

In an address to a Central Military Commission war planning meeting on 19 May 1965, Liu Shaoqi stated:

If our preparations are faster and better, war can be delayed. . . . If we make excellent preparations, the enemy may even dare not to invade. . . . We must build the big Third Front and the small Third Front and do a good job on every front, including the atomic bomb, the hydrogen bomb, and long-distance missiles. Under such circumstances, even if the United States has bases in Japan, Taiwan, and the Philippines, its ships are big targets out on the sea and it is easy for us to strike them. We should develop as early as possible new technology to attack aircraft and warships so that we can knock out one enemy ship with a single missile. The enemy's strength is in its navy, air force, atomic bombs, and missiles, but the strength in navy and air force has its limits. If the enemy sends ground troops to invade China, we are not afraid. Therefore, on the one hand we should be prepared for the enemy to come from all directions, including a joint invasion against China by many countries. On the other, we should realize that the enemy lacks justification in sending troops. . . . This will decide the difference between a just and an unjust war.[62]

Zhu De remarked at the same meeting that "so long as we have made good preparations on every front, the enemy may not dare to come. We must defend our offshore islands. With these islands in our hands, the enemy will find it difficult to land. If the enemy should launch an attack, we will lure them inside China and then wipe them out completely."[63]

Scholars have argued over Beijing's reaction to the threat posed by U.S. intervention in Vietnam. Much of this argument focuses on the hypothesis of a "strategic debate" in 1965 between Luo Ruiqing and Lin Biao. Various interpretations of this "debate" exist, but most contend that Luo was more sensitive to American actions in Indochina than either Lin or Mao, and that Luo demanded greater military preparations to deal with the threat, including accepting the Soviet proposal of a "united front."[64]

However, there is nothing in the recently available Chinese materials to confirm the existence of the "strategic debate" in 1965.[65] The often cited evidence to support the hypothesis of a strategic debate is the two articles supposedly written by Luo Ruiqing and Lin Biao on the occasion of the commemoration of V-J day in September 1965.[66] In fact, the same writing group organized by Luo Ruiqing in the General Staff was responsible for the preparation of both articles. The final version of the "People's War" article also incorporated opinions from the writing team led by Kang Sheng. (Operating in the Diaoyutai National Guest House, Kang's team was famous for writing the nine polemics against Soviet revisionism). Although the article included some of Lin Biao's previous statements, Lin himself was not involved in its writing. When Luo Ruiqing asked Lin for his instructions about the composition of the article, the Defense Minister said nothing. Zhou Enlai and other standing Politburo members read the piece before its publication.[67] The article was approved by the Chinese leadership as a whole and was merely published in Lin Biao's name. Luo Ruiqing was purged in December 1965 primarily because of his dispute with Lin Biao over domestic military organization rather than over foreign policy issues.[68] Luo did not oppose Mao on Vietnam policy. In fact he carried out loyally every Vietnam-related order issued by the chairman. Mao completely dominated the decision making. The origins of the "People's War" article point to the danger of relying on public pronouncements to gauge inner-party calculations and cast doubts on the utility of the faction model in explaining Chinese foreign policy making.[69]

## Commitment to National Liberation Movements:

The second factor that shaped Mao's decision to support the DRV was his desire to form a broad international united front against both the United States and the Soviet Union. To Mao, national liberation movements in the Third World were the most important potential allies in the coalition that he wanted to establish. In the early 1960s, the chairman developed the concept of "Two Intermediate Zones." The first zone referred to developed countries, including capitalist states in Europe, Canada, Japan, Australia, and New Zealand. The second zone referred to underdeveloped nations in Asia, Africa, and Latin America. These two zones existed between the two superpowers. Mao believed that countries in these two zones had contradictions with the United States and the Soviet Union and that China should make friends with them to create an international united front against Washington and Moscow.[70]

Mao initially developed the idea of the "intermediate zone" during the early years of the Cold War. In a discussion with Anna Louise Strong in 1946, the CCP leader first broached the idea. He claimed that the United States and the Soviet Union were "separated by a vast zone including many capitalist, colonial and semi-colonial countries in Europe, Asia, and Africa," and that it was difficult for "the U.S. reactionaries to attack the Soviet Union before they could subjugate these countries."[71] In the late 1940s and throughout the greater part of the 1950s, Mao leaned to the side of the Soviet Union to balance against the perceived American threat. But beginning in the late 1950s, with the emergence of Sino-Soviet differences, Mao came to revise his characterization of the international situation. He saw China confronting two opponents: the United States and the Soviet Union. To oppose these two foes and break China's international isolation, Mao proposed the formation of an international united front.

Operating from the principle of making friends with countries in the "Two Intermediate Zones," Mao promoted such anti-American tendencies as French President De Gaulle's break with the United States in the first zone and championed national liberation movements in the second zone. For Mao, the Vietnam conflict constituted a part of a broader movement across Asia, Africa, and Latin America, which together represented a challenge to imperialism as a whole. China reached out to anti-colonial guerrillas in

Angola and Mozambique, to the "progressive" Sihanouk in Cambodia, to the leftist regime under Sukarno in Indonesia, and to the anti-U.S. Castro in Cuba.[72] Toward the former socialist camp dominated by the Soviet Union, Mao encouraged Albania to persuade other East European countries to separate from Moscow.[73]

During this increasingly radical period of Chinese foreign policy, Mao singled out three anti-imperialist heroes for emulation by Third World liberation movements: Ho Chi Minh, Castro, and Ben Bella, the Algerian nationalist leader. In a speech to a delegation of Chilean journalists on 23 June 1964, Mao remarked: "We oppose war, but we support the anti-imperialist war waged by oppressed peoples. We support the revolutionary war in Cuba and Algeria. We also support the anti-U.S.-imperialist war conducted by the South Vietnamese people."[74] In another address to a group of visitors from Asia, Africa, and Oceania on July 9, Mao again mentioned the names of Ho Chi Minh, Castro, and Ben Bella as models of anti-colonial and anti-imperialist struggle.[75]

Envisioning China as a spokesman for the Third World independence cause, Mao believed that the Chinese revolutionary experience was relevant to the struggle of liberation movements in Asia, Africa, and Latin America. By firmly backing the Vietnamese struggle against the United States, he wanted to demonstrate to Third World countries and movements that China was their true friend. Victory for North Vietnam's war of national unification with China's support would show the political correctness of Mao's more militant strategy for coping with U.S. imperialism and the incorrectness of Khrushchev's policy of peaceful coexistence.

A number of Chinese anti-imperialist initiatives, however, ended in a debacle in 1965. First Ben Bella was overthrown in Algeria in June, leading the Afro-Asian movement to lean in a more pro-Soviet direction due to the influence of Nehru in India and Tito in Yugoslavia. The fall of Ben Bella frustrated Mao's bid for leadership in the Third World through the holding of a "second Bandung" conference of Afro-Asian leaders. Then in September, Sukarno was toppled in a right-wing counter-coup, derailing Beijing's plan to promote a militant "united front" between Sukarno and the Indonesian Communist Party (PKI). The Chinese behavior, nevertheless, did convince leaders in Washington that Beijing was a dangerous gambler in international politics and that American intervention in Vietnam was necessary to undermine a Chinese plot of global subversion by proxy.[76]

## Criticism of Soviet Revisionism:

Mao's firm commitment to North Vietnam also needs to be considered in the context of the unfolding Sino-Soviet split. By 1963, Beijing and Moscow had completely broken apart after three years of increasingly abusive polemics. The conclusion of the Soviet-American partial Nuclear Test Ban Treaty in July 1963 was a major turning point in Sino-Soviet relations. Thereafter the Beijing leadership publicly denounced any suggestion that China was subject to any degree of Soviet protection and directly criticized Moscow for collaborating with Washington against China. The effect of the Sino-Soviet split on Vietnam soon manifested itself as Beijing and Moscow wooed Hanoi to take sides in their ideological dispute.

After the ouster of Khrushchev in October 1964, the new leadership in the Kremlin invited the CCP to send a delegation to the October Revolution celebrations. Beijing dispatched Zhou Enlai and He Long to Moscow for the primary purpose of sounding out Leonid Brezhnev and Alexei Kosygin on the many issues in dispute: Khrushchev's long-postponed plan to convene an international Communist meeting, support for revolutionary movements, peaceful coexistence with the United States, attitudes toward Tito, and "revisionist" domestic policies within the Soviet Union. The Chinese discovered during their tour on November 5–13 that nothing basic had changed in the Soviet position: the new leaders in Moscow desired an improvement in Sino-Soviet relations on the condition that Beijing stopped its criticisms and limited competition in foreign policy, probably in return for the resumption of Soviet economic aid.[77]

Instead of finding an opportunity to improve mutual understanding, the Chinese visitors found their stay in Moscow unpleasant and the relationship with the Soviet Union even worse. During a Soviet reception, Marshal Rodion Malinovsky suggested to Zhou Enlai and He Long that just like the Russians had ousted Khrushchev, the Chinese should overthrow Mao. The Chinese indignantly rejected this proposal: Zhou even registered a strong protest with the Soviet leadership, calling Malinovsky's remarks "a serious political incident."[78] Zhou Enlai told the Cuban Communist delegation during a breakfast meeting in the Chinese Embassy on November 9 that Malinovsky "insulted Comrade Mao Zedong, the Chinese people, the Chinese party, and myself," and that the current leadership in the Kremlin inherited "Khrushchev's working and thought style."[79]

Before Zhou's journey to Moscow, the Chinese leadership had suggested to the Vietnamese Communists that they also send people to travel with Zhou to Moscow to see whether there were changes in the new Soviet leaders' policy. Zhou told Ho Chi Minh and Le Duan later in Hanoi, on 1 March 1965, that he was "disappointed" with what he had seen in Moscow, and that "the new Soviet leaders are following nothing but Khrushchevism."[80] Clearly Zhou wanted the Hanoi leadership to side with the PRC in the continuing Sino-Soviet dispute, and Beijing's extensive aid to the DRV was designed to draw Hanoi to China's orbit.

The collective leadership which succeeded Khrushchev was more forthcoming in support of the DRV. During his visit to Hanoi on 7–10 February 1965, Kosygin called for a total U.S. withdrawal from South Vietnam and promised Soviet material aid for Ho Chi Minh's struggle. The fact that a group of missile experts accompanied Kosygin indicated that the Kremlin was providing support in that crucial area. The two sides concluded formal military and economic agreements on February 10.[81] Clearly the Soviets were competing with the Chinese to win the allegiance of the Vietnamese Communists. Through its new gestures to Hanoi, Moscow wanted to offset Chinese influence and demonstrate its ideological rectitude on issues of national liberation. The new solidarity with Hanoi, however, complicated Soviet relations with the United States, and after 1965, the Soviet Union found itself at loggerheads with Washington. While Moscow gained greater influence in Hanoi because of the North Vietnamese need for Soviet material assistance against U.S. bombing, it at the same time lost flexibility because of the impossibility of retreat from the commitment to a brother Communist state under attack by imperialism.

Before 1964, Hanoi was virtually on China's side in the bifurcated international communist movement. After the fall of Khrushchev and the appearance of a more interventionist position under Kosygin and Brezhnev, however, Hanoi adopted a more balanced stand. Leaders in Beijing were nervous about the increase of Soviet influence in Vietnam. According to a Vietnamese source, Deng Xiaoping, Secretary General of the CCP, paid a secret visit to Hanoi shortly after the Gulf of Tonkin Incident in an attempt to wean the Vietnamese away from Moscow with the promise of US$1 billion aid per year.[82] China's strategy to discredit the Soviet Union was to emphasize the "plot" of Soviet-American collaboration at the expense of Vietnam. During his visit to Beijing on 11 February 1965, Kosygin asked the Chinese to help the United States to "find a way out of Vietnam." Chinese leaders warned the Russians not to use the Vietnam issue to bargain with the Americans.[83] Immediately after his return to Moscow, Kosygin proposed an international conference on Indochina. The Chinese condemned the Soviet move, asserting that the Russians wanted negotiation rather than continued struggle in Vietnam and were conspiring with the Americans to sell out Vietnam. But as R.B. Smith has observed, the Chinese "may have oversimplified a Soviet strategy which was . . . more subtle. . . . Moscow's diplomatic initiative of mid-February may in fact have been timed to coincide with—rather than to constrain—the Communist offensive in South Vietnam."[84] The Chinese criticism of the Soviet peace initiative must have confirmed the American image of China as a warmonger.

The Sino-Soviet rivalry over Vietnam certainly provided leaders in Hanoi an opportunity to obtain maximum support from their two Communist allies, but we should not overstate the case. Sometimes the benefits of the Sino-Soviet split for the DRV could be limited. For example, the Hanoi leadership sought a communist international united front to assist their war effort. They wanted Moscow and Beijing to agree on common support actions, particularly on a single integrated logistical system. They failed to achieve this objective primarily because of China's objection.[85]

## Domestic Need to Transform the Chinese State and Society:

Beginning in the late 1950s, Mao became increasingly apprehensive about the potential development of the Chinese revolution. He feared that his life work had created a political structure that would eventually betray his principles and values and become as exploitative as the one it had replaced. His worry about the future of China's development was closely related to his diagnosis of the degeneration of the Soviet political system and to his fear about the effects of U.S. Secretary of State John Foster Dulles' strategy of "peaceful evolution."[86] Mao believed that Dulles' approach to induce a peaceful evolution within the socialist world was taking effect in the Soviet Union, given Khrushchev's fascination with peaceful coexistence with the capitalist West. Mao wanted to prevent that from happening in China.

The problem of succession preoccupied Mao throughout the first half of the 1960s. His acute awareness of impending death contributed to his sense of urgency. The U.S. escalation of war in Vietnam made him all the more eager to put his own house in order. He was afraid that if he did not nip in the bud what he perceived to be revisionist tendencies and if he did not choose a proper successor, after his death China would fall into the hands of Soviet-like revisionists, who would "change the color" of China, abandon support for national liberation struggles, and appease U.S. imperialism. Mao was a man who believed in dialectics. Negative things could be turned into positive matters. The American presence in Indochina was a threat to the Chinese revolution. But on the other hand, Mao found that he could turn the U.S. threat into an advantage, namely, he could use it to intensify domestic anti-imperialist feelings and mobilize the population against revisionists. Mao had successfully employed that strategy during the Civil War against Jiang Jieshi [Chiang Kai-shek]. Now he could apply it again to prepare the masses for the Great Cultural Revolution that he was going to launch. Accordingly, in the wake of the Gulf of Tonkin Incident, Mao unleashed a massive "Aid Vietnam and Resist America" campaign across China.[87]

## *Sino-Vietnamese Discord*

In its heyday the Sino-Vietnamese friendship was described as "comrades plus brothers," but shortly after the conclusion of the Vietnam War the two communist states went to war with each other in 1979. How did it happen? In fact signs of differences had already emerged in the early days of China's intervention in the Vietnam conflict. Two major factors complicated Sino-Vietnamese relations. One was the historical pride and cultural sensitivity that the Vietnamese carried with them in dealing with the Chinese. The other was the effect of the Sino-Soviet split.

Throughout their history, the Vietnamese have had a love-hate attitude toward their big northern neighbor. On the one hand, they were eager to borrow advanced institutions and technologies from China; on the other hand, they wanted to preserve their independence and cultural heritage. When they were internally weak and facing external aggression, they sought China's help and intervention. When they were unified and free from foreign threats, they tended to resent China's influence. A pattern seems to character-ize Sino-Vietnamese relations: the Vietnamese would downplay their inher-ent differences with the Chinese when they needed China's assistance to balance against a foreign menace; they would pay more attention to problems in the bilateral relations with China when they were strong and no longer facing an external threat.

This pattern certainly applies to the Sino-Vietnamese relationship dur-ing the 1950s and the first half of the 1960s. The Vietnamese Communists during this period confronted formidable enemies, the French and the Amer-icans, in their quest for national unification. When the Soviet Union was reluctant to help, China was the only source of support that Hanoi could count upon against the West. Thus Ho Chi Minh avidly sought advice and weapons from China. But sentiments of distrust were never far below the sur-face. Friction emerged between Chinese military advisers and Vietnamese commanders during the war against the French in the early 1950s.[88] Viet-namese distrust of the Chinese also manifested itself when Chinese support troops entered Vietnam in the mid 1960s.

When Chinese troops went to Vietnam in 1965, they found them-selves in an awkward position. On the one hand, the Vietnamese leadership wanted their service in fighting U.S. aircraft and in building and repairing roads, bridges, and rail lines. On the other hand, the Vietnamese authori-ties tried to minimize their influence by restricting their contact with the local population. When a Chinese medical team offered medical service to save the life of a Vietnamese woman, Vietnamese officials blocked the effort.[89] Informed of incidents like this, Mao urged the Chinese troops in Vietnam to "refrain from being too eager" to help the Vietnamese.[90] While the Chinese soldiers were in Vietnam, the Vietnamese media reminded the public that in the past China had invaded Vietnam: the journal *Historical Studies* published articles in 1965 describing Vietnamese resistance against Chinese imperial dynasties.[91]

The increasing animosity between Beijing and Moscow and their efforts to win Hanoi's allegiance put the Vietnamese in a dilemma. On the one hand, the change of Soviet attitudes toward Vietnam from reluctant to active assistance in late 1964 and early 1965 made the Vietnamese more unwilling to echo China's criticisms of revisionism. On the other hand, they still needed China's assistance and deterrence. Mao's rejection of the Soviet proposal of a "united action" to support Vietnam alienated leaders in Hanoi. During Kosygin's visit to Beijing in February 1965, he proposed to Mao and Zhou that Beijing and Moscow end their mutual criticisms and cooperate on the Vietnam issue. But Mao dismissed Kosygin's suggestion, asserting that China's argument with the Soviet Union would continue for another 9,000 years.[92]

During February and March, 1966, a Japanese Communist Party delegation led by Secretary General Miyamoto Kenji, visited China and the DRV, with the purpose of encouraging "joint action" by China and the Soviet Union to support Vietnam. Miyamoto first discussed the idea with a CCP delegation led by Zhou Enlai, Deng Xiaoping, and Peng Zhen in Beijing. The two sides worked out a communiqué that went part of the way toward the "united action" proposal. But when Miyamoto, accompanied by Deng, came to see Mao in Conghua, Guangdong, the chairman burst into a rage, insisting that the communiqué must stress a united front against both the United States and the Soviet Union. Miyamoto disagreed, so the Beijing communiqué was torn up.[93] Clearly, Mao by this time had connected the criticism of Soviet revisionism with the domestic struggle against top party leaders headed by Liu, Deng, and Peng. It was no wonder that these officials soon became leading targets for attack when the Cultural Revolution swept across China a few months later.

In the meantime the Vietnamese made their different attitude toward Moscow clear by deciding to send a delegation to attend the 23rd Congress of the Communist Party of the Soviet Union (CPSU), which was to be held between March 29 and April 8 and which the Chinese had already decided to boycott. The Vietnamese were walking a tightrope at this time. On the one hand they relied on the vital support of Soviet weapons; on the other hand, they did not want to damage their ties with China. Thus Le Duan and Nguyen Duy Trinh traveled from Hanoi to Beijing on March 22, on their way to Moscow. Although no sign of differences appeared in public during Duan's talks with Zhou Enlai, China's unhappiness about the Vietnamese participation in the 23rd Congress can be imagined.[94]

In sum, the Beijing-Hanoi relationship included both converging and diverging interests. The two countries shared a common ideological outlook and a common concern over American intervention in Indochina, but leaders in Hanoi wanted to avoid the danger of submitting to a dependent relationship with China. So long as policymakers in Hanoi and Beijing shared the common goal of ending the U.S. presence in the region, such divergent interests could be subordinated to their points of agreement. But the turning point came in 1968, when Sino-Soviet relations took a decisive turn for the worse just as Washington made its first tentative moves toward disengagement from South Vietnam. In the new situation, Beijing's strategic interests began to differ fundamentally from those of Hanoi. Whereas the Chinese now regarded the United States as a potential counterbalance against the Soviet Union, their Vietnamese comrades continued to see Washington as the most dangerous enemy. After the withdrawal of U.S. troops from Vietnam and the unification of the country, Hanoi's bilateral disputes with Beijing over Cambodia, a territorial disagreement in the South China Sea, and the treatment of Chinese nationals in Vietnam came to the fore, culminating in a direct clash in 1979.

## Was China Bluffing During the War?

The fact that Beijing did not openly acknowledge its sizable presence in North Vietnam raised questions about the justification for Washington's restraint in U.S. conduct of war, both at the time and in later years. Harry G. Summers, the most prominent of revisionist critics of President Johnson's Vietnam policy, asserts that the United States drew a wrong lesson from the Korean War: "Instead of seeing that it was possible to fight and win a limited war in Asia regardless of Chinese intervention, we . . . took counsel of our fears and accepted as an article of faith the proposition that we should never again become involved in a land war in Asia. In so doing we allowed our fears to become a kind of self-imposed deterrent and surrendered the initiative to our enemies." Summers contends that "whether the Soviets or the Chinese ever intended intervention is a matter of conjecture," and that the United States allowed itself "to be bluffed by China throughout most of the war." He cites Mao's rejection of the Soviet 1965 proposal for a joint action to support Vietnam and Mao's suspicions of Moscow's plot to draw China into a war with the United States as evidence for the conclusion that Mao was more fearful of Moscow than Washington and, by implication, he was not serious about China's threats to intervene to help Hanoi.[95]

Was China not serious in its threats to go to war with the United States in Indochina? As the preceding discussion has shown, Beijing perceived substantial security and ideological interests in Vietnam. From the security perspective, Mao and his associates were genuinely concerned about the American threat from Vietnam (although they did not realize that their own actions, such as the supply of weapons to Hanoi in 1962, had helped precipitate the U.S. escalation of the war) and adopted significant measures at home to prepare for war. China's assistance to the DRV, to use John Garver's words, "was Mao's way of rolling back U.S. containment in Asia."[96] From the viewpoint of ideology, China's support for North Vietnam served Mao's purposes of demonstrating to the Third World that Beijing was a spokesman for national liberation struggles and of competing with Moscow for leadership in the international communist movement. If the actions recommended by Summers had been taken by Washington in Vietnam, there would have been a real danger of a Sino-American war with dire consequences for the world. In retrospect, it appears that Johnson had drawn the correct lesson from the Korean War and had been prudent in his approach to the Vietnam conflict.

## New Chinese Documents on the Vietnam War Translated by Qiang Zhai

### Document 1: Report by the War Department of the General Staff, 25 April 1964.

Deputy Chief of Staff Yang[97]:

According to your instruction, we have made a special investigation on the question of how our country's economic construction should prepare itself for a surprise attack by the enemy. From the several areas that we have looked at, many problems emerge, and some of them are very serious.

(1) The industry is over concentrated. About 60 percent of the civil machinery industry, 50 percent of the chemical industry, and 52 percent of the national defense industry (including 72.7 percent of the aircraft industry, 77.8 percent of the warship industry, 59 percent of the radio industry, and 44 percent of the weapons industry) are concentrated in 14 major cities with over one million population.

(2) Too many people live in cities. According to the census conducted at the end of 1962, 14 cities in the country have a population over one million, and 20 cities a population between 500,000 and one million. Most of these cities are located in the coastal areas and are very vulnerable to air strikes. No effective mechanisms exist at the moment to organize anti-air works, evacuate urban population, guarantee the continuation of production, and eliminate the damages of an air strike, especially the fallout of a nuclear strike.

(3) Principal railroad junctions, bridges, and harbors are situated near big and medium-size cities and can easily be destroyed when the enemy attacks cities. No measures have been taken to protect these transportation points against an enemy attack. In the early stage of war, they can become paralyzed.

(4) All reservoirs have a limited capacity to release water in an emergency. Among the country's 232 large reservoirs with a water holding capacity between 100 million and 350 billion cubic meter, 52 are located near major

transportation lines and 17 close to important cities. There are also many small and medium-size reservoirs located near important political, economic, and military areas and key transportation lines.

We believe that the problems mentioned above are important ones directly related to the whole armed forces, to the whole people, and to the process of a national defense war. We propose that the State Council organize a special committee to study and adopt, in accordance with the possible conditions of the national economy, practical and feasible measures to guard against an enemy surprise attack.

Please tell us whether our report is appropriate.

The War Department of the General Staff,

April 25, 1964.

[Source: *Dangde wenxian*[98] (Party Documents) 3 (1995), 34–35.]

## Document 2: Mao Zedong's Comments on the War Department's April 25 Report, 12 August 1964.

To Comrades Luo Ruiqing[99] and Yang Chengwu:

This report is excellent. We must carefully study and gradually implement it. The State Council has established a special committee on this question. Has it started its work?

Mao Zedong

August 12.

[Source: Ibid., 33.]

## Document 3: "Report on How Our Country's Economic Construction Should Prepare Itself Against an Enemy Surprise Attack" by Li Fuchun,[100] Bo Yibo,[101] and Luo Ruiqing,[102] 19 August 1964.

Chairman[103] and the Central Committee:

In accordance with Chairman's comments on the General Staff War Department's report of how our country's economic construction should prepare itself for a surprise attack by the enemy, we have gathered comrades with responsibility in these areas for a meeting. All of us agree that Chairman's comments and the War Department's report are extremely important. We must pay serious attention to and do our best on such an important issue concerning our country's strategic defense. The meeting has decided:

  (1) To establish a special committee on this case within the State Council. We suggest that the committee consist of thirteen people including Li Fuchun, Li Xiannian, Tan Zhenlin, Bo Yibo, Luo Ruiqing, Xie Fuzhi, Yang Chengwu, Zhang Jichun, Zhao Erlu,

Cheng Zihua, Gu Mu, Han Guang, and Zhou Rongxin. Li Fuchun serves as Director, and Bo Yibo and Luo Ruiqing Deputy Directors.

(2)  In addition to the four areas mentioned by the War Department, our preparation measures also need to include universities and colleges, scientific research and planning institutions, warehouses, government departments and institutions as well as civil shelters in cities and mines. We must follow Chairman's principle of "careful study and gradual implementation" in conducting our investigation into various areas as early as possible and pay attention to the following issues.

(a)  All new construction projects will not be placed in the First Front, especially not in the fifteen big cities with over a million population.

(b)  For those currently on-going construction projects in the First Front and particularly in the fifteen big cities, except those that can be completed and put into effective operation next year or the year after, all the rest must be reduced in size, undergo no expansion, and be concluded as soon as possible.

(c)  For existing old enterprises, especially those in cities with high industrial concentration, we must remove them or some of their workshops. Particularly for military and machinery enterprises, we must break them in two parts if possible, and shift one part to the Third and Second Fronts. If we can remove them as a whole, we must do that with careful planning and in steps.

(d)  Beginning in next year, no new large and medium-size reservoirs will be built.

(e)  For key national universities and colleges, scientific research and planning institutes in the First Front, if they can be removed, we must relocate them to the Third and Second Fronts with careful planning. If they can not be removed, we must break them into two parts.

(f)  From now on, all new projects, in whatever Front they will be located, must comply with the principle of dispersion, closeness to mountains, and concealment. They must not be concentrated in certain cities or areas.

We have divided labor to deal with the above work:

(a)  The State Economic Commission and the State Planning Commission will be responsible for the arrangement of the industrial and transportation systems.

(b) The Ministry of Railway will be responsible for preparation measures concerning railroad junctions.

(c) The Office of National Defense Industry will be responsible for the arrangement of national defense industry.

(d) The General Staff will be responsible for the division of the First, Second, and Third Fronts on the national level and for the arrangement of national defense fortifications and war preparation mobilizations.

(e) Comrade Tan Zhenlin will be responsible for preparation measures concerning reservoirs.

(f) Comrades Zhang Jichun and Han Guang will be responsible for the arrangement of universities and colleges, scientific research and planning institutes.

(g) Comrade Zhou Rongxin will be responsible for the protection of city buildings and government departments and institutions.

We will spend the months of September and October investigating the various aspects and produce detailed plans that can be implemented gradually. The special committee will synthesize the plans before submitting them to the Central Committee for inclusion in the general plan for the next year and in the Third Five-Year Plan.

(3) We propose to revive the People's Anti-Air Committee. Premier[104] should still serve as Director and Comrade Xie Fuzhi as Secretary General (Comrade Luo Ruiqing was Secretary General originally). The Ministry of Public Safety will be responsible for the daily work of the committee.

We should restore the Planning Office for the Construction of Underground Railway in Beijing and carry out an active preparation for the building of underground railway in Beijing. In the meantime, we should consider the construction of underground railway in Shanghai and Shenyang. The Ministry of Railway will be responsible for this task.

(4) If the central leadership approves the above suggestions, we propose to distribute our report along with the General Staff War Department report as well as Chairman's comments as guidelines to all Party Bureaus, to all provincial, municipal, and district Party committees, and to all Party committees within government ministries.

Please inform us whether our report is correct.

Li Fuchun, Bo Yibo, Luo Ruiqing

August 19, 1964.

[Source: Ibid., 33–34.]

## Document 4: Zhou Enlai's Conversation with Ayub Khan, President of Pakistan, 2 April 1965.

(1) China will not take the initiative to provoke a war (with the United States). (2) China means what it says and will honor the international obligations it has undertaken. (3) China is prepared. China's policies are both prudent and prepared. . . . (4) If the American madmen carry out an extensive bombing, China will not sit still and wait to be killed. If they come from the sky, we will take action on the ground. Bombing means war, and war will have no boundaries. It is impossible for the United States to resolve the issue of war simply by relying on a policy of bombing.

[Source: The Diplomatic History Research Office of the People's Republic of China Foreign Ministry, comp., *Zhou Enlai waijiao huodong dashiji, 1949–1975* (Chronology of Zhou Enlai's Major Diplomatic Activities, 1949–1975). (Beijing: World Knowledge Press, 1993), 445.]

## Document 5: Liu Shaoqi's Speech to the Central Military Commission war planning meeting on 19 May 1965.

The enemy has many contradictions, weaknesses, and difficulties. Its problems are no less than ours. If our preparations are faster and better, war can be delayed. The enemy will find it difficult to invade. If we make excellent preparations, the enemy may even dare not to invade. If it does not invade, we will not fight out. Such a prospect is not impossible. But we must work hard to achieve this goal. We must build the big Third Front and the small Third Front and do a good job on every front, including the atomic bomb, the hydrogen bomb, and long-distance missiles. Under such circumstances, even if the United States has bases in Japan, Taiwan, and the Philippines, its ships are big targets out on the sea and are easy for us to strike. We should develop as early as possible new technology to attack aircraft and warships so that we can knock out one enemy ship with a single missile. Our Red Flag 1 and Red Flag 2[105] can shoot down the enemy's high-altitude airplanes. If we have assurance to shoot down high-altitude airplanes, we can have more assurance to knock down low-altitude ones. The enemy's strength lies in its navy, air force, atomic bombs, and missiles, but the strength in navy and air force has its limits. If the enemy sends ground troops to invade China, we are not afraid. Therefore, on the one hand we should be prepared for the enemy to come from all directions, including a joint invasion against China by many countries. On the other hand we should realize that the enemy lacks reasons and justifications in sending troops. If the enemy invades us without our attacking it first, the enemy's morale cannot be high. This will decide the difference between a just and an unjust war.

In addition, there is the issue of increasing the size of troops. In order to build fortifications, we can organize some engineer units. After working for a period and completing fortifications, they can be dismissed. Troops engaged in agricultural production and divisions on semi war alert should also construct fortifications. Production troops are busy with agricultural work, but during slack seasons they should spend most of their time building fortifications. This means that they can work on fortifications for half a year in North China and for four to five months in the Yangtze valley. If war begins and we have to expand troops, we just need a mobilization. This matter will be easy. At the moment, we need to do a good job in organizing militia forces.

What we cannot have time to prepare when war begins includes fortification construction, third fronts, bases as well as communications, a reconnaissance network, and new technology. We must pay attention to these issues. We should start work on the big Third Front, the small Third Front, material storage, state-of-the-art technology, scientific investigation, and research on new weapons. If we delay work on these matters, we will find ourselves unprepared later. To do these things needs time.

As to the issues of the size of troops, the number of military regions, and a unified leadership between the local civilian government and the military, we can have time to deal with them when war begins. Some of the issues will be dealt with only after the enemy has invaded our country. In case that the enemy occupies the Longhai Railroad,[106] or the Yangtze valley, or the Jinghan Railroad,[107] or the Jinpu Railroad,[108] our country will then be divided into sections. If that happens, we have to practice a unified leadership of the party, the government and the army. But this will be decided at that time, not now. With trains and airplanes at its disposal, the enemy will not do things according to our methods. Only when that time comes will our leadership go to mountains. At present, the leadership must live in the city because it will be inconvenient if it does not live in the city. Only when a large number of enemy troops invades China and cuts us into parts will the leadership go to the mountains. It will not do that when China is not cut into parts. For instance, if the enemy does not occupy cities like Xian and Tongguan, Shaanxi[109] will not create a Shaanan Military region and a Shaanbei military region. The leadership will decide on this matter after the enemy has invaded, and there is time to do that. There is also time to mobilize troops. At present, we can begin the organization of the militia. . . . (the rest of the speech is about how to organize the militia).

[Source: *Dangde wenxian* 3 (1995), 40.]

## Document 6: Mao's Conversation with the Party and Government Delegation of the Democratic Republic of Vietnam,[110] 20 October 1965.

You are fighting an excellent war. Both the South and the North are fighting well. The people of the whole world, including those who have already awakened and those who have not awakened, are supporting you. The current world is not a peaceful one. It is not you Vietnamese who are invading the United States, neither are the Chinese who are waging an aggressive war against the United States.

Not long ago the Japanese *Asahi Shimbun* and *Yomiuri Shimbun* published several reports filed by Japanese correspondents from South Vietnam. U.S. newspapers described these reports as unfair, thus provoking a debate. I am not referring to the Japanese Communist newspaper, *Akahata*. I am talking about Japanese bourgeois newspapers. This shows that the direction of the media is not favorable to the United States. Recently the demonstration by the American people against the American government's Vietnam policy has developed. At the moment it is primarily American intellectuals who are making trouble.

But all this are external conditions. In fact what will solve the problem is the war you are fighting. Of course you can conduct negotiations. In the past you held negotiations in Geneva. But the American did not honor their promise after the negotiations. We have had negotiations with both Chiang Kai-shek and the United States. Rusk said that the United States has had most negotiations with China. But we stick to one point: the United States must withdraw from Taiwan, and after that all other problems can be easily resolved. The United States does not accept this point. China and the United States have been negotiating for ten years and we are still repeating the same old words. We will not give up that point. The United States once wanted to exchange press delegations with us. They argued that when we began with minor issues, we could better settle major problems later. We contended that only by starting from major issues could minor problems be easily resolved.

You withdrew your armed forces from the South in accordance with the Geneva Accords. As a result, the enemy began to kill people in the South, and you revived armed struggle. At first you adopted political struggle as a priority supplemented by armed struggle. We supported you. In the second stage when you were carrying out political and armed struggles simultaneously, we again supported you. In the third stage when you are pursuing armed struggle as a priority supplemented by political struggle, we still support you. In my view, the enemy is gradually escalating the war; so are you. In the next two and three years you may encounter difficulties. But it is hard to say, and it may not be so. We need to take this possibility into consideration. So long as you have made all kinds of preparations, even if the most difficult situation emerges, you will not find it too far from your initial considerations. Isn't this a good argument? Therefore there are two essential points: the first is to strive for the most favorable situation, and the second to prepare for the worst.

The Algerian experience can serve as a reference for you. Possibly in the fourth or fifth year of their war, some Algerian leaders became worried. At that time, their Prime Minister Arbas came to talk with us. They said that Algeria had a very small population of ten million. A million had already died. While the enemy had an army of 800,000, their own regular forces possessed only about 30,000 to 40,000 troops. To add the guerrillas, their total forces were less than 100,000. I told them at the time that the enemy was bound to defeat and that their population would increase. Later, after negotiations France began to withdraw its troops. Now it has completed the withdrawal, only leaving behind a few small naval bases. The Algerian revolution is a national democratic revolution led by the bourgeoisie. Our two parties are Communist. In terms of mobilizing the masses and carrying out people's war, our two parties are different from Algeria.

I talked about people's war in my article. Some of the statements refer to specific problems of ten to twenty years ago. Now you have encountered some new conditions. Many of your methods are different from our methods in the past. We should have differences. We also learn about war gradually. At the beginning we lost battles. We have not done as smoothly as you have.

I have not noticed what issues you have negotiated with the United States. I only pay attention to how you fight the Americans and how you drive the Americans out. You can have negotiations at certain time[s], but you should not lower your tones. You should raise your tones a little higher. Be prepared that the enemy may deceive you. We will support you until your final victory. The confidence in victory comes from the fighting you have done and from the struggle you have made. For instance, one experience we have is that the Americans can be fought. We obtained this experience only after fighting the Americans. The Americans can be fought and can be defeated. We should demolish the myth that the Americans cannot be fought and cannot be defeated. Both of our two parties have many experiences. Both of us have fought the Japanese. You have also fought the French. At the moment you are fighting the Americans.

The Americans have trained and educated the Vietnamese people. They have educated us and the people of the whole world. In my opinion it is not good without the Americans. Such an educator is indispensable. In order to defeat the Americans, we must learn from the Americans. Marx's works do not teach us how to fight the Americans. Nor do Lenin's books write about how to fight the Americans. We primarily learn from the Americans.

The Chinese people and the people of the whole world support you. The more friends you have, the better you are.

[Source: The People's Republic of China Foreign Ministry and the Chinese Communist Party Central Documentary Research Office, comp., *Mao Zedong Waijiao wenxuan* (Selected Diplomatic Works of Mao Zedong) (Beijing: Central Documentary Press and World Knowledge Press, 1994), 570–573.]

## Document 7: Mao's Conversation with Pham Van Dong, 17 November 1968.

Because there has been no battle to fight recently, you want to negotiate with the United States. It is all right to negotiate, but it is difficult to get the United States to withdraw through negotiations. The United States also wants to negotiate with you because it is in a dilemma. It has to deal with problems of three regions: the first is the Americas—the United States, the second is Europe, and the third is Asia. In the last few years the United States has stationed its major forces in Asia and has created an imbalance. In this regard American capitalists who have investments in Europe are dissatisfied. Also throughout its history the United States has always let other countries fight first before it jumps in at halfway. It is only after World War Two that the United States has begun to take the lead in fighting, first in the Korean War and then in the Vietnam War. In Vietnam the United States is taking the lead, but it is followed by only a small number of other countries. Whether the war is a special war or a limited war, the United States is totally devoted to it. Now it cannot afford to pay attention to other countries. Its troops in Europe, for example, are complaining, saying that there is a shortage of manpower and that experienced soldiers and commanders have been removed and better equipment has been relocated. The United States has also redeployed its troops from Japan, Korea and other areas of Asia. Did not the United States claim that it has a population of two hundred million? But it cannot endure the war. It has dispatched only several hundred thousand troops. There is a limit to its troops.

After fighting for over a dozen years you should not think about only your own difficulties. You should look at the enemy's difficulties. It has been twenty-three years since Japan's surrender in 1945, but your country still exists. Three imperialist countries have committed aggression against you: Japan, France, and the United States. But your country has not only survived but also developed.

Of course imperialism wants to fight. One purpose for its war is to put out fire. A fire has started in your country, and imperialism wants to put out that fire. The second purpose is to make money through producing munitions. To put out fire they must produce fire-extinguishing machines, which will bring about profits. Every year the United States expends over 30 billion dollars in your country.

It has been an American custom not to fight a long war. The wars they have fought average about four to five years. The fire in your country cannot be put out. On the contrary, it has spreaded. Capitalists in the United States are divided into factions. When this faction makes more profit and that faction make less profit, an imbalance in booty-sharing will occur and trouble will begin domestically. These contradictions should be exploited. Those monopolized capitalists who have made less money are unwilling to continue the war. This contradiction can be detected in election speeches made by the two factions. Especially the American journalist Walter Lippmann has published an article recently, warning not to fall into another trap. He says that the United States has already fallen into a trap in Vietnam and that the current problem is how to find ways to climb out of that trap. He is afraid that the United States may fall into other traps. Therefore your cause is promising.

In 1966, I had a conversation with Chairman Ho Chi Minh in Hangzhou. At that time, the United States had already resumed attack on North Vietnam, but had not renewed bombing. I said that the United States might end the war that year because it was an American election year. No matter which president came to power, he would encounter the problem of whether the United States should continue the war or withdraw now. I believed that the difficulties that the United States faced would increase if it continued the war. Countries in all of Europe did not participate in the war. This situation was different from that of the Korean War. Japan probably would not enter the war. It might lend some help economically because it could make money by producing ammunition. I think the Americans overestimated their strength in the past. Now the United States is repeating its past practice by overstretching its forces. It is not just us who make this argument. Nixon has also said so. The United States has stretched its forces not only in the Americas and Europe but also in Asia. At first I did not believe that the United States would attack North Vietnam. Later the United States bombed North Vietnam, proving my words wrong. Now the United States has stopped bombing. My words are correct again. Maybe the United States will resume bombing, proving my words wrong a second time. But eventually my words will prove correct: the United States has to stop bombing. Therefore I believe that it is all right for you to make several contingency plans.

In sum, in the past years the American army has not invaded North Vietnam. The United States has neither blockaded Haiphong nor bombed the Hanoi city itself. The United States has reserved a method. At one point it claimed that it would practice a "hot pursuit." But when your aircraft flew over our country, the United States did not carry out a "hot pursuit." Therefore, the United States has bluffed. It has never mentioned the fact that your aircraft have used our airfields. Take another example, China had so many people working in your country. The United States knew that, but had never mentioned it, as if such a thing did not exist. As to the remaining people sent by China to your country who are no longer needed, we can withdraw them. Have you discussed this issue? If the United States comes again, we will send people to you as well. Please discuss this issue to see which Chinese units you want to keep and which units you do not want to keep. Keep the units that are useful to you. We will withdraw the units that are of no use to you. We will send them to you if they are needed in the future. This is like the way your airplanes have used Chinese airfields: use them if you need and not use them if you do not need. This is the way to do things.

I am in favor of your policy of fighting while negotiating. We have some comrades who are afraid that you may by taken in by the Americans. I think you will not. Isn't this negotiation the same as fighting? We can learn experience and know patterns through fighting. Sometimes one cannot avoid being taken in. Just as you have said, the Americans do not keep their words. Johnson once said publicly that even agreements sometimes could not be honored. But things must have their laws. Take your negotiations as an example, are you going to negotiate for a hundred years? Our Premier has said that if Nixon continues the negotiations for another two years and fails to solve the problem, he will have difficulties in winning another term of presidency.

One more point. It is the puppet regime in South Vietnam who is afraid of the National Liberation Front of South Vietnam. Some people in the United States have pointed out that the really effective government popular among the South Vietnamese people is not the Saigon government but the Liberation Front. This is not a statement attributed to someone in the U.S. Congress. It is reported by journalists, but the name of the speaker was not identified. The statement was attributed to a so-called U.S. government individual. The statement raises a question: Who represents the government with real prestige in South Vietnam? Nguyen Van Thieu or Nguyen Huu Tho? Therefore although the United States publicly praises Nguyen Van Thieu, saying that he will not go to Paris to attend the negotiations, it in fact realizes that problems can not be solved if the National Liberation Front of South Vietnam does not participate in the negotiations.

[Source: Ibid., 580–583.]

## Notes

1. Using recent Chinese sources, Chen Jian's "China's Involvement in the Vietnam War, 1964–69," *The China Quarterly* 142 (June 1995), 357–387, provides an informative and insightful analysis of China's decision to assist Hanoi during the Vietnam War, but he does not address the historiographical

controversy of whether there was a "strategic debate" in Beijing in 1965. Fresh materials released in China in 1994 and 1995 shed new light on this issue.

2. See Qiang Zhai, "Transplanting the Chinese Model: Chinese Military Advisers and the First Vietnam War, 1950–1954," *The Journal of Military History 57* (October 1993), 698–715; idem., "China and the Geneva Conference of 1954," *The China Quarterly* 129 (March 1992), 103–122; Chen Jian, "China and the First Indochina War, 1950–1954," *The China Quarterly* 133 (March 1993), 85–110.

3. Guo Ming, ed., *Zhongyue guanxi yanbian sishinian* [The Evolution of Sino-Vietnamese Relations over the Last Forty Years] (Nanning: Guangxi People's Press, 1991), 65. The contributors in this volume are from the Guangxi Academy of Social Sciences, a major research center on Sino-Vietnamese relations in China.

4. Pei Jianzhang, chief comp., *Zhonghua renmin gongheguo waijiaoshi, 1949–1956* [A Diplomatic History of the People's Republic of China, 1949–1956] (Beijing: World Knowledge Press, 1994), 94; Hoang Van Hoan, *Canghai yisu: Hoang Van Hoan geming huiyilu* [A Drop in the Ocean: Hoang Van Hoan's Revolutionary Reminiscences] (Beijing: Liberation Army Press, 1987), 267.

5. The Writing Team on the History of the Chinese Military Advisory Group, ed. *Zhongguo junshi guwentuan yuanyue kangfa douzheng shishi* [Historical Facts about the Role of the Chinese Military Advisory Group in the Struggle to Aid Vietnam and Resist France] (Beijing: Liberation Army Press, 1990), 126–127. On 16 October 1955, Mao personally selected Peng Dehuai, Chen Geng, and Wei Guoqing as members of the Chinese delegation for the forthcoming discussions during Giap's second visit. See Mao to Liu Shaoqi, Zhou Enlai, Zhu De, and Deng Xiaoping, 16 October 1955, in the CCP Central Documentary Research Office, comp., *Jianguo yilai Mao Zedong wengao* [Mao Zedong Manuscripts since the Founding of the PRC] (Beijing: Central Document Press, 1991), 5:419. Deputy Defense Minister Chen Geng, who had served as China's chief military advisor to the Vietminh in 1950, was not mentioned during Giap's first visit; evidently, Mao wanted to present a stronger Chinese team to talk with Giap during his second trip.

6. Guo, *Zhongyue guanxi yanbian sishinian*, 65.

7. The Writing Team on the History of the Chinese Military Advisory Group, ed. *Zhongguo junshi guwentuan yuanyue kangfa douzheng shishi*, 142–143.

8. During the Vietnamese land reform, an excessive persecution of so-called landlords and rich peasants occurred, creating serious resentments among the peasant population against the party. Hoang, *Canghai yisu*, 279–285. Truong Chinh was often regarded by Western observers as a member of the "pro-Chinese" wing of the VWP.

9. Pei, *Zhonghua renmin gongheguo waijiaoshi, 1949–1956*, 94.

10. For Zhou's visit to Hanoi, see the PRC Foreign Ministry's Diplomatic History Research Office, comp., *Zhou Enlai waijiao huodong dashiji, 1949–1975* [A Chronology of Zhou Enlai's Diplomatic Activities, 1949–1975] (Beijing: World Knowledge Press, 1993), 169–170; Huang Zheng, *Hu Zhiming he Zhongguo* [Ho Chi Minh and China] (Beijing: Liberation Army Press, 1987), 182–183. Zhou's quote is taken from Han Suyin, *Eldest Son: Zhou Enlai and*

*the Making of Modern China, 1898–1976* (New York: Hill and Wang, 1994), 260.

11. Donald S. Zagoria, *Vietnam Triangle: Moscow, Peking, Hanoi* (New York: Pegasus, 1967), 102–104.

12. Guo, *Zhongyue guanxi yanbian sishinian*, 65. According to a recent study by William J. Duiker, Le Duan as General Secretary was "a powerful advocate of an aggressive strategy to achieve national reunification with the South." At the Fifteenth Plenum of the VWP held at the end of 1958, the Central Committee adopted a new policy which advocated a return to revolutionary war to unify the South. But the new line also included the ambivalence that had shaped attitudes in Hanoi from the time of the Geneva Conference. Though urging a return to revolutionary war, the Central Committee report, which was not issued until May 1959, asserted that the "political strength of the masses" would remain the principal from of struggle, although it would now be supplemented by low-level military operations conducted by local guerrilla forces and village self-defense units of the type that had been employed during the August 1945 Revolution. William J. Duiker, *U.S. Containment Policy and the Conflict in Indochina* (Stanford: Stanford University Press, 1994), 235. It is possible that China's advice for caution in waging revolutionary struggle in the South contributed to the ambivalence in Hanoi's policy.

13. Duiker, *U.S. Containment Policy and the Conflict in Indochina*, 265.

14. Guo, *Zhongyue guanxi yanbian sishinian*, 67.

15. Duiker, *U.S. Containment Policy and the Conflict in Indochina*, 266.

16. For Pham Van Dong's visit to China, see the PRC Foreign Ministry Diplomatic History Research Office, comp., *Zhou Enlai waijiao huodong dashiji, 1949–1975*, 313–314. Remarks by Mao and Zhou are taken from Guo, *Zhongyue guanxi yanbian sishinian*, 67.

17. Cong Jin, *Quzhe fazhan de suiyue* [Years of Twisting Development] (Zhengzhou: Henan People's Press, 1989), 500–502. The author is a party history researcher at the Chinese National Defense University. See also Zhu Zhongli, *Liming yu wanxia: Wang Jiaxiang wenxue zhuanji* [Dawn and Dusk: A Literary Biography of Wang Jiaxiang] (Beijing: Liberation Army Press, 1986), 394–396. The author is the wife of Wang Jiaxiang.

18. Ma Qibin, Chen Wenbin, et al. *Zhongguo gongchandang zhizheng sishinian, 1949–1989* [The Forty Years of the Chinese Communist Party in Power, 1949–1989] (Beijing: CCP Party History Material Press, 1989), 213; Cong, *Quzhe fazhan de suiyue*, 502; Zhu, *Liming yu wanxia*, 396–399.

19. Xue Mouhong and Pei Jianzhang, chief comp., *Dangdai Zhongguo waijiao* [Contemporary Chinese Diplomacy] (Beijing: Chinese Social Science Press, 1990), 159; Guo, *Zhongyue guanxi yanbian sishinian*, 69; Wang Xiangen, *Yuanyue kangmei shilu* [A Factual Record of Assistance to Vietnam against the United States] (Beijing: International Culture Press, 1990), 25. Wang Xiangen was a secretary at the headquarters of the PLA Engineering Corps in the late 1970s and is currently working with the PLA General Staff. His book contains much useful data on the role of Chinese army engineer troops in Vietnam.

20. Xue and Pei, *Dangdai Zhongguo waijiao*, 159.

21. Ibid.

22. Li Ke, "The Indelible Mark on History of Chinese Assistance to Vietnam against the United States," *Junshi lishi* [Military History] 4 (1989), 30. This bi-monthly journal is published by the Chinese People's Revolutionary Military Museum in Beijing.

23. Interview with a Chinese military history researcher, Beijing, 13 July 1995.

24. Li Ke and Hao Shengzhang, *Wenhua dageming zhong de renmin jiefangjun* [The People's Liberation Army during the Cultural Revolution] (Beijing: CCP Historical Materials Press, 1989), 409.

25. George C. Herring, *America's Longest War: The United States and Vietnam, 1950–1975* (New York: 2nd ed., Alfred A. Knopf, 1986), 117–119.

26. Xue and Pei, *Dangdai Zhongguo waijiao*, 159.

27. Present at the meetings were Zhou Enlai, Chen Yi, Wu Xiuquan, Yang Chengwu, and Tong Xiaopeng of the CCP; Ho Chi Minh, Le Duan, Truong Chinh, Pham Van Dong, Vo Nguyen Giap, Nguyen Chi Thanh, Hoang Van Hoan, and Van Tien Dung of the VWP; and Kaysone Phomvihane, Prince Souphanouvong, and Phoumi Vongvochit of the Lao People's Revolutionary Party. The PRC Foreign Ministry's Diplomatic History Research Office, comp., *Zhou Enlai waijiao huodong dashiji, 1949–1975*, 413.

28. Li and Hao, *Wenhua dageming zhong de renmin jiefangjun*, 408.

29. Chen, "China's Involvement in the Vietnam War," 364.

30. Allen S. Whiting, "How We Almost Went to War with China," *Look*, 29 April 1969, p. 76; Melvin Gurtov and Hwang Byong-moo, *China Under Threat: The Politics of Strategy and Diplomacy* (Baltimore: Johns Hopkins University Press, 1980), 160–161.

31. Li, "The Indelible Mark on History of Chinese Assistance to Vietnam against the United States," 30.

32. Gurtov and Hwang, *China Under Threat: The Politics of Strategy and Diplomacy*, 162; Herring, *America's Longest War*, 128–131.

33. The PRC Foreign Ministry Diplomatic History Research Office, comp., *Zhou Enlai waijiao huodong dashiji, 1949–1975*, 445; Xue and Pei, *Dangdai Zhongguo waijiao*, 160–161.

34. Han Huaizhi and Tan Jingjiao, chief comp., *Dangdai zhongguo jundui de junshi gongzuo* [The Military Work of the Contemporary Chinese Armed Forces] (Beijing: Chinese Social Sciences Press, 1989), 1:539–40; Li and Hao, *Wenhua dageming zhong de renmin jiefangjun*, 415; Guo, *Zhongyue guanxi yanbian sishinian*, 69–70; Li, "The Indelible Mark on History of Chinese Assistance to Vietnam against the United States," 31.

35. Han and Tan, *Dangdai zhongguo jundui de junshi gongzuo*, 539–540; Wang, *Yuanyue kangmei shilu*, 44; Li, "The Indelible Mark on History of Chinese Assistance to Vietnam against the United States," 31.

36. Xue and Pei, *Dangdai Zhongguo waijiao*, 161.

37. Wang, *Yuanyue kangmei shilu*, 45.

38. Ibid. 35, 44; Li and Hao, *Wenhua dageming zhong de renmin jiefangjun,* 422. R. B. Smith also mentions Ho's meeting with Mao in Changsha. He dates the meeting at May 16–17. His source is the diary of Ho's personal secretary. See R. B. Smith, *An International History of the Vietnam War, Volume III: The Making of a Limited War, 1965–66* (New York: St. Martin's Press, 1991), 139.

39. Wang, *Yuanyue kangmei shilu,* 46–48. According to Li Ke and Hao Shengzhang, to facilitate the transportation of materials to Vietnam, Beijing in 1965 also established a special leadership group in charge of transportation to Vietnam. Luo Ruiqing was director. Li Xiannian, Bo Yibo, Yang Chengwu, Li Tianyou, Fang Yi, Li Qiang, and Liu Xiao were vice-directors. Li and Hao, *Wenhua dageming zhong de renmin jiefangjun,* 413.

40. Li and Hao, *Wenhua dageming zhong de renmin jiefangjun,* 417.

41. Quoted in Smith, *An International History of the Vietnam War, Volume III: The Making of a Limited War, 1965–66,* 171. According to Luu Doan Huynh, from the International Relations Institute of the Ministry of Foreign Affairs of Vietnam, Beijing informed Hanoi in June 1965 that it would not be able to defend North Vietnam from U.S. air attacks. Quoted in Allen Whiting, "China's Role in the Vietnam War," in Jayne Werner and David Hunt, eds., *The American War in Vietnam* (Ithaca: Cornell University Southeast Asia Program, 1993), 71–76.

42. Xue and Pei, *Dangdai Zhongguo waijiao,* 161; Guo, *Zhongyue guanxi yanbian sishinian,* 70.

43. Li, "The Indelible Mark on History of Chinese Assistance to Vietnam against the United States," 31; Guo, *Zhongyue guanxi yanbian sishinian,* 69. For a description of the Chinese use of the Cambodian port of Sihanoukville to send military supplies to the National Liberation Front in South Vietnam between 1966–1967, see Kang Daisha, "My Days in Cambodia," in Cheng Xiangjun, ed., *Nu waijiaoguan* [Women Diplomats] (Beijing: People's Sports Press, 1995), 482–483. Kang Daisha is the wife of Chen Shuliang, who was the Chinese ambassador to Cambodia between 1962–1967. For a detailed treatment of Chinese aid to the DRV between 1965–1969, see Chen, "China's Involvement in the Vietnam War," 371–380.

44. Guo, *Zhongyue guanxi yanbian sishinian,* 71.

45. Allen S. Whiting, *The Chinese Calculus of Deterrence: India and Indochina* (Ann Arbor: University of Michigan Press, 1975), 186; idem., "Forecasting Chinese Foreign Policy: IR Theory vs. the Fortune Cookie," in Thomas W. Robinson and David Shambaugh, eds., *Chinese Foreign Policy: Theory and Practice* (Oxford: Clarendon Press, 1994), 506–523.

46. John W. Garver, "The Chinese Threat in the Vietnam War," *Parameters* 22 (Spring 1992), 73–85, quotation on 75.

47. Sun Dongsheng, "The Great Transformation in the Strategic Planning of Our Country's Economic Construction," *Dangde wenxian* [Party Documents] 3 (1995), 42–48. Sun's indirect quotation of Mao's remarks is on p. 44. *Dangde wenxian* is a bi-monthly journal published by the CCP Central Documentary Research Office and the Central Archives. It often contains important party documents. Sun Dongsheng is a researcher at the Central Documentary Research Office.

48. Mao's conversation with Pham Van Dong, 17 November 1968, in the PRC Foreign Ministry and the Central Documentary Research Office, comp., *Mao Zedong waijiao wenxuan* [Selected Diplomatic Works of Mao Zedong] (Beijing: Central Document Press and World Knowledge Press, 1994), 582.

49. Yuan Dejin, "The Evolution of Mao Zedong's Theory of War and Peace since the Founding of New China," *Junshi lishi* [Military History] 4 (1994), 36.

50. For an excellent discussion of the origins, development and consequences of the Third Front, see Barry Naughton, "The Third Front: Defence Industrialization in the Chinese Interior," *The China Quarterly* 115 (September 1988), 351–386.

51. For the complete text of the report, see *Dangde wenxian* 3 (1995), 34–35.

52. Mao to Luo and Yang, 12 August 1964, in ibid, 33.

53. For the text of the Special Committee report of 19 August 1964, see ibid., 33–34.

54. Mao's remarks are quoted in Sun, "The Great Transformation in the Strategic Planning of Our Country's Economic Construction," 45.

55. Sun, "The Great Transformation in the Strategic Planning of Our Country's Economic Construction," 44.

56. Naughton, "The Third Front," 368.

57. Mao's conversation with He Long, Luo Ruiqing, and Yang Chengwu, 28 April 1965, in *Mao Zedong junshi wenji* [Collection of Mao Zedong's Military Writings] 6 vols. (Beijing: Military Science Press and Central Document Press, 1993), 6:404.

58. For Snow's version of his conversation with Mao, see Edgar Snow, *The Long Revolution* (New York: Random House, 1971), 215–216. For the Chinese version, see the PRC Foreign Ministry and the Central Documentary Research Office, comp., *Mao Zedong waijiao wenxuan*, 544–562.

59. Li and Hao, *Wenhua dageming zhong de renmin jiefangjun*, 341.

60. Ibid., 341–342; *Mao Zedong junshi wenji*, 6:403.

61. The PRC Foreign Ministry Diplomatic History Research Office, comp., *Zhou Enlai waijiao huodong dashiji, 1949–1975*, 455.

62. Liu Shaoqi's speech at the war planning meeting of the Central Military Commission, 19 May 1965, in *Dangde wenxian* 3 (1995), 40.

63. The CCP Central Documentary Research Office, comp., *Zhu De nianpu* [Chronicle of Zhu De] (Beijing: People's Press, 1986), 537–538.

64. Harry Harding, "The Making of Chinese Military Power," in William Whitson, ed., *The Military and Political Power in China in the 1970s* (New York: Praeger, 1973), 361–385; Uri Ra'anan, "Peking's Foreign Policy 'Debate', 1965–1966," in Tang Tsou, ed., *China in Crisis*, vol. 2 (Chicago: University of Chicago Press, 1968), 23–71; Donald Zagoria, "The Strategic Debate in Peking," in ibid., 237–268; Michael Yahuda, "Kremlinology and the Chinese Strategic Debate, 1965–66," *The China Quarterly* 49 (January–March 1972), 32–75.

65. Barry Naughton has made a similar criticism. Naughton, "The Third Front," 370–371.

66. Luo Ruiqing, "The People Defeated Japanese Fascism and They Can Certainly Defeat U.S. Imperialism Too," *Peking Review*, 3 September 1965, 31–39; Lin Biao, "Long Live the Victory of People's War," ibid., 9–30.

67. Xu Yan, *Junshijia Mao Zedong* [Military Strategist Mao Zedong] (Beijing: Central Document Press, 1995), 149; Huang Yao, *Sanci danan busi de Luo Ruiqing Dajiang* [Senior General Luo Ruiqing who Survived Three Deaths] (Beijing: CCP Party History Press, 1994), 263, 265, 270–271. This book is based on sources from the Central Archives, the PLA General Staff Archives, and the Ministry of Public Security Archives.

    It is possible that the two articles published in Luo and Lin's names were written in response to Soviet arguments on war and peace. On 30 January 1965, Mao asked Yang Chengwu and Lei Yingfu, Deputy Director of the Combat Department of the General Staff, to find a person well versed in political and military issues to prepare a commentary on the book *Military Strategy* edited by Soviet Chief of Staff V. D. Sokolovsky and published by the Soviet Defense Ministry's Military Press in 1962. See Mao to Yang Chengwu and Lei Yingfu, 30 January 1965, in *Mao Zedong junshi wenji*, 6:402.

68. For a detailed discussion of the Luo-Lin dispute, see Huang, *Sanci danan busi de Luo Riqing Dajiang*, chapters 24–34. Allen Whiting attempts to establish a causal relationship between Luo's purge and China's foreign policy change in mid-1965. Citing the Vietnamese claim that China decided in June 1965 to provide no air cover for North Vietnam, Whiting argues that this timing dovetails with a major personnel change in the Chinese leadership: "At some point between May and September Luo Ruiqing fell from office, after which Lin Biao published a major treatise on guerrilla war implicitly rejecting Luo's forward strategy and with it any advanced air combat. Chinese ground support apparently came as a substitute form of help for Hanoi." Whiting, "Forecasting Chinese Foreign Policy," 516. In fact, Luo did not fall from office until December 1965.

69. Michael H. Hunt has also criticized the emphasis on factions to account for Chinese foreign policy formation. He poses the question sharply: "Does the factional model transpose on China the competitive ethos of American politics and underestimate the restraining authoritarian and hierarchical qualities of China's political culture?" See Michael H. Hunt, "CCP Foreign Policy: 'Normalizing the Field,'" in Michael H. Hunt and Niu Jun, eds., *Toward a History of Chinese Communist Foreign Relations, 1920s–1960s: Personalities and Interpretive Approaches* (Washington, DC: Woodrow Wilson International Center for Scholars Asia Program, 1995), 163–191. The quotation is on p. 170.

70. For Mao's statements on the "Two Intermediate Zones," see the PRC Foreign Ministry and the CCP Central Documentary Research Office, comp., *Mao Zedong waijiao wenxuan*, 506–509. See also Chi Aiping, "The Evolution of Mao Zedong's International Strategic Thought," in *Dangde wenxian 3* (1994), 46–52; Li Jie, "Study of Mao Zedong's International Strategic Thought," in the International Strategic Studies Foundation, ed., *Huanqiu tongci liangre* [All Is the Same in the World] (Beijing: Central Document Press, 1993), 1–16.

71. Mao Zedong, "Talks with the American Correspondent Anna Louise Strong," in *Selected Works of Mao Tse-tung* (Beijing: Foreign Languages Press, 1965), 4:99.

72. For a recent study of China's policy toward Angola and Mozambique, see Steven F. Jackson, "China's Third World Foreign Policy: The Case of Angola and Mozambique, 1961–93," *The China Quarterly* 143 (June 1995), 387–422.

73. On Beijing's attempt to divide the Soviet-led bloc, see the putative memoirs of Enver Hoxha, *Reflections on China*, 2 vols., (Tirana: 8 Nentori, 1979). For an overview of Chinese-Albanian relations, see Fan Chengzuo, "The 'Spring, Summer, Autumn, and Winter' in Chinese-Albanian Relations," *Waijiao xueyuan xuebao* [Journal of Foreign Affairs College] 3 (1993), 50–52.

74. Mao's conversation with the Chilean Journalist Delegation, 23 June 1964, in the PRC Foreign Ministry and the Central Documentary Research Office, comp., *Mao Zedong waijiao wenxuan*, 529–533.

75. Mao's talk with delegates from Asia, Africa, and Oceania on 9 July 1964, in ibid, 534–539. These delegates came to China after participating in Pyongyang in the Second Asian Economic Forum.

76. For a good discussion of anti-imperialism in Chinese foreign policy, see Edward Friedman, "Anti-Imperialism in Chinese Foreign Policy," in Samuel S. Kim, ed., *China and the World: Chinese Foreign Relations in the Post Cold War Era*, 3rd ed. (Boulder: Westview Press, 1994), 60–74.

77. Gurtov and Hwang, *China under Threat*, 161.

78. For a detailed, first-hand account of Zhou Enlai's visit to Moscow, see Yu Zhan, "An Unusual Visit: Remembering Zhou Enlai's Last Visit to the Soviet Union," *Dangde wenxian* [Party Documents] 2 (1992), 85–91. It is also included in the Foreign Ministry Diplomatic History Research Office, comp., *XinZhongguo waijiao fengyun* [Episodes of New China's Diplomacy] (Beijing: World Knowledge Press, 1994), 3:14–30. Yu Zhan was Director of the Department of the Soviet Union and Eastern Europe of the Chinese Foreign Ministry in 1964 and accompanied Zhou to Moscow.

79. The PRC Foreign Ministry's Diplomatic History Research Office, comp., *Zhou Enlai waijiao huodong dashiji, 1949–1975*, 428.

80. Zhou's conversation with Ho Chi Minh and Le Duan, 1 March 1965, in ibid., 438.

81. Smith, *An International History of the Vietnam War, Volume III: The Making of a Limited War, 1965–66*, 54.

82. The Vietnamese claim is quoted in Nayan Chanda, "Secrets of Former Friends," *Far Eastern Economic Review* (15 June 1979), 38–39. I have not seen any Chinese material that confirms the Vietnamese claim.

83. Xie Yixian, ed., *Zhongguo waijiao shi: Zhonghua renmin gongheguo shiqi, 1949–1979* [A Diplomatic History of China: The Period of the People's Republic of China, 1949–1979] (Zhengzhou: Henan People's Press, 1988), 344.

84. Smith, *An International History of the Vietnam War, Volume III: The Making of a Limited War, 1965–66*, 55.

85. Douglas Pike describes Hanoi's strategy to put the Sino-Soviet dispute to its own use in service of its war as "the alternating tilt gambit." See Douglas Pike, *Vietnam and the Soviet Union: Anatomy of an Alliance* (Boulder, CO: Westview, 1987), 54–55.

86. For Mao's reaction to Dulles' policy, see Bo Yibo, *Ruogan zhongda juece yu shijian de huigu* [Recollections of Certain Important Decisions and Events], vol. 2 (Beijing: CCP Party School Press, 1993), 1137–1157.

87. For more discussions of Mao's attempt to use the escalation of the Indochina conflict to radicalize China's political and social life, see Chen, "China's Involvement in the Vietnam War," 361–365.

88. For a description of this problem, see Zhai, "Transplanting the Chinese Model," 712–713.

89. Wang, *Yuanyue kangmei shilu*, 60–68.

90. Ibid., 74–75.

91. Guo, *Zhongyue guanxi yanbian sishinian*, 102.

92. Cong, *Quzhe fazhan de suiyue*, 607.

93. Kikuzo Ito and Minoru Shibata, "The Dilemma of Mao Tse-tung," *The China Quarterly* 35 (July–September 1968), 58–77; Smith, *An International History of the Vietnam War, Volume III: The Making of a Limited War, 1965–66*, 285–304.

94. Smith, *An International History of the Vietnam War, Volume III: The Making of a Limited War, 1965–66*, 298–299. For Zhou's reception of the Vietnamese delegation led by Le Duan, see The PRC Foreign Ministry Diplomatic History Research Office, comp., *Zhou Enlai waijiao huodong dashiji, 1949–1975*, 491.

95. Harry G. Summers, Jr., *On Strategy: A Critical Analysis of the Vietnam War* (New York: Dell Publishing Co., Inc., 1982), 93–94, 96.

96. Garver, "The Chinese Threat in the Vietnam War," 75.

97. Yang Chengwu.

98. *Dangde wenxian* is a bi-monthly journal published by the CCP Central Documentary Research Office and the Central Archives. It often contains important party documents

99. Chief of Staff.

100. Deputy Prime Minister, Director of the State Council Special Committee on war preparation.

101. Deputy Prime Minister, Deputy Director of the State Council Special Committee on war preparation.

102. Luo was also named Deputy Director of the State Council Special Committee on war preparation.

103. Mao Zedong.

104. Zhou Enlai.

105. These are the names of Chinese missiles.

106. A major railway trunk running east and west between Lianyungang and Lanzhou.

107. A major railway trunk running north and south between Beijing and Wuhan.
108. A major railway trunk running north and south between Tianjin and Nanjing.
109. A province in North China.
110. The Vietnamese delegation was led by Pham Van Dong.

*Qiang Zhai teaches history at Auburn University at Montgomery (Alabama) and is the author of* The Dragon, the Lion, and the Eagle: Chinese-British-American Relations, 1949–1958 *(Kent, OH: Kent State University Press, 1994). This article is adapted from a paper prepared for presentation at the CWI HP Conference on New Evidence on the Cold War in Asia at the University of Hong Kong on 9–12 January 1995.*

# The 1968 "Hue Massacre"
## D. Gareth Porter

### Part One

Six years after the stunning communist Tet Offensive of 1968, one of the enduring myths of the Second Indochina War remains essentially unchallenged: the communist "massacre" at Hue. The official version of what happened in Hue has been that the National Liberation Front (NLF) and the North Vietnamese deliberately and systematically murdered not only responsible officials but religious figures, the educated elite and ordinary people, and that burial sites later found yielded some 3,000 bodies, the largest portion of the total of more than 4,700 victims of communist execution.

Although there is still much that is not known about what happened in Hue, there is sufficient evidence to conclude that the story conveyed to the American public by the South Vietnamese and American propaganda agencies bore little resemblance to the truth, but was, on the contrary, the result of a political warfare campaign by the Saigon government, embellished by the U.S. government and accepted uncritically by the U.S. press. A careful study of the official story of the Hue "massacre" on the one hand, and of the evidence from independent or anti-communist sources on the other, provides a revealing glimpse into efforts by the U.S. press to keep alive fears of a massive "bloodbath."[1] It is a myth which has served the U.S. administration interests well in the past, and continues to influence public attitudes deeply today.

### The Tenth Political Warfare Battalion's Role

To unravel the official story of Hue, one must go back to the source of the original information which was conveyed to the American public about the episode.

The agency of the Saigon government given overall responsibility for compiling data on the alleged "massacre" and publicizing the information was neither the Ministry of Social Welfare and Refugees nor the Ministry of Health, as one might have expected, but the Tenth Political Warfare Battalion of the Army of the Republic of Vietnam (ARVN). It is on the word of this body, whose specific mission is to discredit the National Liberation Front without regard to the truth, that the story of the "massacre" reported by the U.S. press in 1968 and 1969 was based. Neither the number of bodies found nor the causes of death were ever confirmed by independent sources. On the contrary, as we shall see, evidence from independent sources challenges the Tenth Political Warfare Battalion's version of the facts.

The official Saigon account of the alleged massacre surfaced on April 23, 1968 when the Political Warfare Battalion released a report that over one thousand people were executed by the communists in and around Hue. The battalion's report was repeated in detail by the United States Information Service but the U.S. media ignored it.[2] One week later the U.S. Mission released a report of its own which was essentially a restatement of the ARVN report. The U.S. Mission report was said to have been the result of an investigation "by the United States and South Vietnamese authorities."[3] But the role of the U.S. advisors in the report appears to have been secondary; according to the Saigon government news agency, Vietnam Press, the report was based on data supplied by the National Police in Hue, U.S. advisers, interviews with South Vietnamese Information and Refugee officials and "records of the Tenth Political Warfare Battalion," which supplied the basic statistics on the alleged executions.[4] Vietnam Press further reported that "an officer of the Tenth Political Warfare Battalion involved in investigating the executions estimated that almost half of the victims were found buried alive."

During the months of March and April, when the alleged victims of communist execution were being uncovered, the Saigon government did not allow any journalists to view the grave sites or bodies, despite the fact that many foreign journalists were in Hue at the time. Province Chief Col. Pham Van Khoa announced at the end of February that 300 civilian government workers had been executed by the communists and had been found in common graves southeast of the city.[5] But no journalist was ever taken to see the alleged graves. In fact, French photographer Marc Riboud, who demanded several times to see the graves, was repeatedly refused permission. When he was finally taken in a helicopter to travel to the alleged site the pilot refused to land, claiming that the area was "insecure."[6] Riboud never saw the site, and when the official chronology of discoveries and map coordinates of the grave sites were finally released, there was no site resembling the one described by Col. Khoa.[7]

Stewart Harris of the *London Times* was in Hue to do a story on the alleged mass executions in late March, just at the time when, according to the official chronology, some 400 bodies were being uncovered in the area of the imperial tombs south of Hue. But instead of taking him to that site, the American political warfare officer took Harris to a village where there were no mass graves, while the Vietnamese political warfare officer took him to a grave site in Gia Hoi district, where the bodies had long since been reburied.[8] So he had to depend on the word of the Vietnamese and American officials concerning what was to be found at the grave sites.

Moreover, ARVN'S Political Warfare Department issued contradictory reports on how many bodies were actually uncovered. At the Gia Hoi High School sites, for example, the official American report, based on information furnished by the Tenth Political Warfare Battalion, gave a total of 22 mass graves and 200 bodies, for an average of nine bodies per grave.[9] But when Stewart Harris was taken to the site, he was told by his Vietnamese escort officer that each of the 22 graves held from three to seven bodies, which would have put the total somewhere between 66 and 150.[10] At about the same time, the Tenth Political Warfare Battalion published a pamphlet for Vietnamese consumption which said there were 14 graves at the high school instead of 22, which would have reduced the total still further.[11]

## A Doctor's Contradictory Findings

The elusiveness of Saigon's figures is significant in the view of the testimony of Alje Vennema, a doctor working for a Canadian medical team at Quang Ngai hospital, who happened to be in the Hue province hospital during the Tet Offensive and who made his own investigation of the grave sites.[12] Vennema agreed that there were 14 graves at Gia Hoi High School but said there was a total of only 20 bodies in those graves. Vennema also stated that the other two sites in Gia Hoi district of Hue held only 19 bodies rather than the 77 claimed by the government, and that those in the area of the imperial tombs southwest of Hue contained only 29 bodies rather than 201 as claimed in the official report.

According to Vennema, therefore, the total number of bodies at the four major sites discovered immediately after Tet was 68, instead of the officially claimed total of 477. Then, too, while he did not claim that none of these bodies was the victim of NLF execution, he said that the evidence indicated most of them were victims of fighting in the area, rather than of political killings. In the case of the sites in the imperial tombs area, he stated that most of the bodies were clothed in the threads of uniforms. He reported having talked with nearby villagers who said that from February 21 to 26 there had been heavy bombing, shelling and strafing in the immediate area. And, in contrast to the government claims that many victims had been buried alive there, Vennema said all the bodies showed wounds.

The circumstances of the official version—its political warfare origins, the refusal to allow confirmation by the press from first-hand observation, the questionable statistics—and the conflicting testimony of a medical doctor who was present at the time all point to misrepresentation of the truth by the Saigon government in its April 1968 report. In fact, the evidence suggests that the Political Warfare Battalion may have inflated the number of actual executions by the NLF by a factor of ten or more.

## The 1969 Exhumations

During 1969, as more bodies were uncovered in the villages surrounding Hue, another phase of the Saigon government campaign was launched by ARVN's political warfare officers. The first bodies were found southeast of Hue, where digging was carried out under the supervision of a "Committee for Search and Burial of Communist Victims" headed by the district chief, Major Trung. Again newsmen were not invited to watch the work while it was going on, but were later summoned by Major Trung and told that the Committee had found 135 bodies in Vinh Luu hamlet of Phu Da village and 230 bodies in seven graves in Phu Xuan village.[13]

What the district chief did not tell the reporters was that the entire area in which the grave sites were found southeast of Hue had been a battleground for many weeks early in 1968. The NLF continued to hold many of the hamlets even after being driven out of the city, and some hamlets remained in their hands for months, as American fighter-bombers carried out heavy strikes against them.

One of the four sites discovered in late March 1969, which allegedly contained 22 bodies, was between Phu My and Tuy Van villages.[14] Phy My village, only three miles east of Hue, was one of the villages occupied by communist troops during the offensive, when many young men of military age were drafted into the Liberation Army. According to a later interview with one of its inhabitants, American planes bombed the village repeatedly, destroying hundreds of homes and killing civilians.

The three other burial sites, uncovered in late March and early April, containing 357 bodies according to the Pentagon's chronology of discoveries, were located in Phu Xuan village and a short distance down the road in Phu Da village.[15] Again, Phu Xuan, 13 miles east of Hue, had been the scene of fierce fighting, including the heavy use of American air power, in the weeks after the offensive. In one all-day battle in which American air strikes were called in, some 250 communist soldiers were killed, according to an interview with the Phu Xuan village chief published in the Political Warfare Department's own newspaper, *Tien Tuyen*.[16]

The Saigon assertion that the bodies found were victims of communist execution were not convincing even to officials of the Saigon government. The Minister of Health, Tran Luu Y, after visiting the burial sites in April 1969, frankly informed the Thua Thien deputy province chief of his opinion that the bodies could be those of NLF soldiers killed in battle.[17] The Political Warfare Department's newspaper promptly denounced the minister for this skepticism.[18]

What little information was made available about the bodies discovered certainly supported the suspicion that very few were actually victims of communist execution. For one thing, Major Trung's own report on the bodies found in his district claimed only nine civil servants and 14 soldiers of the Saigon army out of a total of 365.[19] It was well known that a considerable number of the bodies were those of women and children. An American officer in Hue admitted to a *Washington Post* reporter at a mass funeral for the dead, "Some may have just gotten caught up [in the fighting]."[20] It would not be surprising indeed if the NLF had not buried many women and children killed by airstrikes or artillery fire in the hamlets which they controlled near Hue.

Another major discovery of bodies at Da Mai Creek, a heavily wooded area ten miles south of Hue, in September 1969 remains shrouded in vagueness and contradictions. Even the number of bodies found remains something of a mystery. The official Pentagon account of the discovery shows that the number was approximately 250.[21] But when Douglas Pike, the U.S. Information Agency's Vietnam specialist, reported the find a few months later, the figure had grown to 428.[22]

Moreover, the one "defector" produced by Saigon to testify on this alleged communist massacre told two very different and contradictory stories about the episode. In an interview arranged by the Saigon government for the *Baltimore Sun* late in 1969, the "defector" testified that a communist district chief who had been his friend had told him that nearly 600 people from Phu Cam and Tu Dam were turned over to pro-communist hill tribesmen to be murdered. The reason, he explained to the *Sun*, was that they had been "traitors to the revolution."[23] But this same man, in an interview with the correspondent of *Tien Tuyen* a few days later said he had been told by the same district chief that 500 "tyrants" were being taken to the mountains, not to be killed but to be reformed."[24]

Again, there is a major and direct conflict between Pike and the official Pentagon version on who the victims were and where they came from. Pike's version is that they were a group captured in a church in the Catholic district of Phu Cam in Hue on February 5, 1968 and marched five miles south, where 20 of them were executed by a people's court and then turned over to a local communist unit, which took them three and a half more miles away from Hue before being murdered.[25] But the Defense Department account shows that the group of civilians taken from the church in Phu Cam numbered only 80 to 100 people, not 400 as Pike suggests.[26] Moreover, an account originally published in the semi-official *Viet-Nam Magazine* and reprinted by the Saigon Embassy in Washington, asserts that all except the 20 people executed by the people's court were allowed to return to Hue with the warning that the NLF would some day return to Hue, and that the people should behave accordingly.[27]

These contradictions are important, given Pike's effort to argue that the skeletons at Da Mai had to be the victims of communist murder because they were a group which had been taken from Hue as prisoners. In fact, there is evidence that most of the people who left Phu Cam with the communists were not prisoners at all, but were pressed into service as stretcher-bearers, ammunition carriers, or even as soldiers for the NLF.[28] As Agence France Presse reported from Hue during the battle for the city, a number of young men, especially from the Phu Cam area, received guns or were used as stretcher-bearers to transport wounded soldiers toward the mountain camps.[29]

Again, circumstantial evidence strongly suggests that the 250 skeletons found at Da Mai Creek (not 400 as claimed by Pike) were also killed in battle or by American B-52 strikes. The *Viet-Nam Magazine* article notes in passing that the site was "in the vicinity where the communists fought their last big battle with the allies (April 30 to May 2, 1968)"[30]—a fact of which readers of the American press were never informed. The People's Liberation Armed Forces have always made a point of carrying as many of their war dead as possible from the battlefield to be buried, in order to deny their enemy tactical intelligence on casualties.

In short, the inconsistencies and other weaknesses of the various official documents, the lack of confirming evidence, and the evidence contradicting the official explanation all suggests that the overwhelming majority of the bodies discovered in 1969 were in fact the victims of American air power and of the ground fighting that raged in the hamlets, rather than NLF execution.

## Douglas Pike: Media Manipulator Par Excellence

It was in large part due to the work of one man that the Hue "massacre" received significant press coverage and wide comment in 1969 and 1970. That man was U.S. Information Agency's Douglas Pike. It was Pike who visited South Vietnam in November 1969, apparently at the suggestion of Ambassador Ellsworth Bunker, to prepare a report on Hue.[31]

During the last two weeks of November, Pike inspired, either directly or indirectly, several different newspaper articles on both Hue and the "bloodbath" theme in general. Pike himself briefed several reporters on his version of the communist occupation of Hue and at the same time circulated a translation of a captured communist document which he had found in the files and which he argued was an open admission of the mass murder of innocent civilians during the occupation of Hue.

The document was the subject of several stories in the American press. The *Washington Post*, for example, carried the Associated Press article on the document with the headline, "Reds Killed 2900 in Hue during Tet, according to Seized Enemy Document."[32] The *Christian Science Monitor* correspondent's article, under the headline, "Communists Admit Murder," began, "The Communist massacre in Hue in early 1968 represented the culmination of careful planning."[33] Both articles quoted as proof of the "admission" the following sentence from the translation: "We eliminated 1,892 administrative personnel, 39 policemen, 790 tyrants, 6 captains, 2 first lieutenants, 20 second lieutenants, and many non-commissioned officers."

No reporter questioned the authenticity of the document or the accuracy of the translation they were given. Yet the original Vietnamese document, a copy of which I obtained from the U.S. Command in Vietnam in September, 1972, shows that the anonymous author did not say what the press and public were led to believe he said.[34] In the original Vietnamese, the sentence quoted above does not support the official U.S. line that the communists admitted murdering more than 2,600 civilians in Hue. To begin with, the context in which this sentence was written was not a discussion of punishing those who were considered criminals or "enemies," but an overall account of the offensive in destroying the army and administration in Thua Thien. Two paragraphs earlier, the document refers to the establishment of a "political force whose mission was to propagandize and appeal for enemy soldiers to surrender with their weapons." It recalls that self-defense forces were so frightened when the Front's forces attacked that they tried to cross the river, with the result that 21 of them drowned. The section dealing with Phu Vang district notes the strength of the opposing forces and the locus of the attack, claiming the seizure of 12 trucks to transport food and 60 rolls of cloth for flags.

It is the next sentence which reads, "We eliminate 1,892 administrative personnel" in the official translation. But the word *diet*, translated as "eliminate" here, must be understood to mean "destroy" or "neutralize" in a military sense, rather than to "kill" or "liquidate," as Pike and the press reports claimed. As used in communist military communiques, the term had previously been used to include killed, wounded or captured among enemy forces. For example, the Third Special Communique of the People's Liberation Armed Forces, issued at the end of the Tet Offensive, said, "We have destroyed [*diet*] a large part of the enemy's force; according to initial statistics, we have killed, wounded and captured more than 90,000 enemy. . . ."[35] It should be noted that *diet* does not mean to "kill" in any ordinary Vietnamese usage, and that the official translation is highly irregular.

Moreover, the word *te*, translated as "administrative personnel" in the version circulated to newsmen, actually has the broader meaning, according to a standard North Vietnamese dictionary, of "puppet personnel," including both civilian *and* military.[36] When the document does refer specifically to the Saigon government's administration, in fact, it uses a different term, *nguy quyen*. Both the context and the normal usage of the words in question, therefore, belie the meaning which Pike successfully urged on the press.

## Pike's 'Enemies of the People' Document

If the misrepresentation of the document may be explained by a combination of bad translation and Pike's own zeal to find evidence to support the official argument, Pike himself must take sole responsibility for a second such case which occurred about the same time. Pike gave to selected reporters a list of 15 categories of what he called—and were called in the press—"enemies of the people," which were said to be targeted by the communists for liquidation. The list included two categories which suggests that the communists were out to kill Catholic leaders and landlords or capitalists in particular: "leading and key members of religious organizations still superstitious" and "members of the exploiting class." The document was given prominence in articles in the *Los Angeles Times* and *Washington Daily News* on alleged communist plans for a "bloodbath," and was again mentioned in stories dealing with Pike's own pamphlet.[37]

But again, although the document may have been authentic, the construction put on it was clearly deceptive. First of all, the document itself said nothing about "enemies of the people"[38]—a phrase introduced by Pike himself and repeated by the press as though it were in the original. And second, it did not say or imply that these 15 categories of people were to be punished, much less liquidated, as Pike suggested to reporters and later wrote in his own booklet on Hue.[39]

In fact, the document, which bore the title "Fifteen Criteria for Investigation," was simply one local cadre's notion of the kinds of people who should be watched.[40] The categories of people who were marked for repression by the NLF were quite different from the ones on the list circulated by Pike, and included neither the "leading and key members of religious organizations" nor "members of the exploiting class." And Pike should have been well aware of this, since a separate document containing the categories of people to be punished was published by the U.S. Mission in October 1967.[41]

Yet another element of the press offensive inspired by Pike's presence in Saigon was the testimony of a "rallier," or defector, from the NLF on the bloodbath issue. The technique of displaying such defectors before press conferences had been used on many occasions by Saigon's Political Warfare Department in order to make a political point which could not otherwise be convincingly documented. Although the most experienced reporters in Saigon were always skeptical of statements made by defectors put on display by Saigon, there were always journalists who were fascinated by the idea of interviewing genuine ex-communists. Thus, it was arranged for Le Xuan Chuyen, who claimed to have been a lieutenant colonel in the Vietnam People's Army before defecting in August 1966, to be interviewed by *Washington Daily News* and *Los Angeles Times* correspondents in order to publicize his views on communist plans for a postwar bloodbath. Chuyen estimated that a communist "blood debt" list included some five million South Vietnamese, of whom some 500,000 would be killed.[42]

A brief note on Chuyen's background helps to put this testimony in proper perspective. Even in his initial interrogation, this self-proclaimed "lieutenant colonel" (a rank his interrogators were inclined to question) exhibited a notable sense of political opportunism.[43] He lost no time in praising Thieu and Ky as leaders who were "daring, patriotic and have a strong sense of nationalism," and he volunteered his desire to work for the Americans or the Saigon government even before he was asked.[44] Within a few months, Chuyen was nominated to be director of the government's Chieu Hoi Center for Saigon—a position which was never mentioned in news accounts of his statement on alleged communist policies.[45]

A second alleged high-ranking communist defector, Col. Tran Van Dac, was actually Planning Adviser to the General Directorate of Political Warfare of ARVN at the time and thus hardly a disinterested witness.[46] His 1969 statement that there were three million Vietnamese on the "blood debt" list continues to be relied on by U.S. administrative apologists, including Sir Robert Thompson and Pike himself.[47]

## Part Two

### *Feed Them a Number . . .*

The major accomplishment of Pike's work was to launch the official "estimate" or 4,756 as the number of civilians killed by the NLF in and around Hue. This was no small feat because, in arriving at that figure, Pike had to statistically conjure away thousands of civilian victims of American air power in Hue. The undeniable fact was that American rockets and bombs, not communist assassination, caused the greatest carnage in Hue. The bloodshed and ruin shook even longtime supporters of the anti-communist effort. Robert Shaplen wrote at the time, "Nothing I saw during the Korean War, or in the Vietnam War so far has been as terrible, in terms of destruction and despair, as what I saw in Hue."[48] After the communist occupation had ended, Don Tate of Scripps-Howard Newspapers described bomb craters 40 feet wide and 20 feet deep staggered in the streets near the walls of the citadel and "bodies stacked into graves by fives—one on top of another."[49] Nine thousand seven hundred and seventy-six of Hue's 17,134 houses were completely destroyed and 3,169 more officially classified as "seriously damaged." (In the rest of Thua Thien province another 8,000 homes were more than half destroyed.[50]) The initial South Vietnamese estimate of the number of civilians killed in the fighting of the bloody reconquest was 3,776.[51]

When ARVN's political warfare specialists went to work, however, this initial estimate, given in a March report of the office of the provincial chief of Social Services and Refugees, was somehow replaced by a new estimate of 944, published in the Tenth Political Warfare Battalion's booklet.[52] And this was all Douglas Pike needed to transform those thousands of civilian dead into victims of a "communist massacre."

In a chart which he calls a "recapitulation" of the dead and missing, Pike begins not by establishing the number of casualties from various causes, but with a total of 7,600, which he says is the Saigon government's "total estimated civilian casualties resulting from the Battle of Hue."[53] The original government estimate of civilian casualties, however, again supplied by the provincial Social Services Office, was just over 6,700—not 7,600—and it was based on the estimate of 3,776 civilians killed in the battle of Hue.[54] Instead of using the Social Services Office's figure, Pike employs the Political Warfare Battalion's 944 figure. Subtracting that number and another 1,900 hospitalized with war wounds, Pike gets the figure of 4,756, which he suggests is the total number of victims of communist massacre, including the 1,945 "unaccounted for" in this strange method of accounting. In short, the whole statistical exercise had the sole purpose of arriving at a fraudulent figure of 4,756 victims of a "massacre."

## Pike Rewrites Policy for the NLF

The substance of Pike's own analysis is what he calls a "hypothesis" concerning the policy of the NLF leadership in Hue during the occupation of the city. The gist of the "hypothesis" is as follows: NLF policy went through three distinct phases, corresponding to different phases of the occupation: in the first few days, the NLF expected to be in control only temporarily and its mission was not to establish its own government but to destroy Saigon administrative structure. During this period, NLF cadres with blacklists executed not only civil servants and military officers but religious and social leaders as well. Then, after the third or fourth day, the communist leadership decided they could hold the city permanently, whereupon they launched a "period of social reconstruction," in Pike's words, and sought to kill all who were not proletarian in ideology and class background, in particular Buddhist, Catholic and intellectual leaders. Finally, as they prepared to leave the city late in February, they killed anyone who would be able to identify their cadres in the city.[55]

While Pike refers vaguely to various pieces of evidence which he claims support this hypothesis, he offers none of it in his published work. In any case, all the evidence available at present contradicts Pike's hypothesis from beginning to end. To begin with, captured NLF documents indicate that the Front had the mission not only of destroying the Saigon administration but of establishing a revolutionary government in Hue and planned to hold the city for as long as possible. In fact, the very document which Pike used to establish the communist admission of responsibility for mass murder of civilians specified that the Liberation Forces had the "mission of occupying Hue for as long as possible so that a revolutionary administration could be established."[56]

As for the "blacklists" for execution, Pike's claim that the list was extensive and included lower-ranking officials and non-governmental figures is contradicted by none other than Hue's chief of secret police, Le Ngan, whose own name was on the list. In 1968, soon after the reoccupation of the city, Le Ngan told former International Voluntary Services worker Len Ackland, who had worked in Hue before the offensive, that the only names on the blacklist for Gia Hoi district were those of the officers of the secret police apparatus for the district.[57]

Other lists were of those selected not for summary execution but for capture on the one hand and for reeducation in place on the other. Those who were to be captured—although not necessarily executed, according to a document called "Plan for an Offensive and General Uprising of Mui A" given to me by the Joint U.S. Public Affairs Office in June 1971—were limited to a relatively small number of Vietnamese and American officials.[58] The document says, "With regard to the province chief, deputy province chief, officers from the rank of major up, American intelligence officers and chiefs of services, if things go to our advantage, at 12 o'clock on the day some of them are arrested, they must quickly persuade others not to hide and compel them to surrender . . . and then we must take them out of the city." The captives were to remain in prison outside the city, according to the plan, until their dossiers could be studied and a determination made on their individual cases. It emphasizes that none of these higher U.S. or Vietnamese officials in Hue was to be killed unless the fighting in the first hours was unsuccessful and there was no way to conduct them out of the city—a circumstance which obviously did not arise.

The document further exempted lower-ranking officials from capture or retribution: "With regard to those ordinary civil servants working for the enemy because of their livelihood and who do not oppose the revolution, educate them and quickly give them responsibility to continue working to serve the revolution."

There was a third category of individual, those who were neither high-ranking officials nor ordinary civil servants but officials who had at one time or another been involved actively in the government's paramilitary apparatus. While these individuals were not to be given jobs, the evidence indicates that they were to be "reeducated" rather than executed as long as the NLF was assured control of the city. They were ordered in the first days of the occupation to report to their local committees but were then allowed to return home.[59]

This does not mean that there were no executions in Hue during the initial period of the occupation. Len Ackland and *Washington Post* correspondent Don Oberdorfer have documented cases of individuals who were executed when they tried to hide from the Front or resisted the new government in some way or another.[60] But these harsh measures, which may in many cases have reflected individual actions by soldiers or cadres rather than a policy decision by the Front (as when a person was shot for resisting arrest), were distinct from the mass retribution for official position or political attitude claimed by Douglas Pike. And the number of executions was relatively small, according to Hue residents interviewed by Ackland.

## Clergy and Intellectuals Executing Themselves

Pike's argument that there was a period of "social reconstruction" marked by a purge of religious figures and intellectuals is contradicted not only by the logic of NLF political strategy in Hue but by documentary evidence as well. As Pike himself pointed out in his book, *War, Peace and the Viet Cong*, published in 1969, the revolutionary government in Hue during the occupation comprised a number of leaders of the 1966 Struggle Movement against the Ky government—precisely the Buddhist and intellectual leaders he later claimed the NLF wished to systematically eliminate in 1968.[61] These were not proletarian revolutionaries eager to take vengeance on the Buddhist hierarchy and the educated elite, as Pike intimates, but representatives of those groups in Hue who had actively opposed the Thieu-Ky government and the American military occupation. It was on these strata that the NLF had based its political strategy of the broadest possible united front in Hue.

Thus, the chairman of the Revolutionary Committee in Hue was Le Van Hao, the well-known Hue University ethnologist who had earlier edited the Struggle Movement's publication *Vietnam, Vietnam.* A deputy chairman was the senior Buddhist monk in Central Vietnam, Thich Don Hau. Other 1966 Struggle Movement leaders who returned as members of the Revolutionary Committee included Hoang Phu Mgoc Tuong, formerly a teacher at Quoc Hoc High School, who became secretary general of the new committee; Nguyen Dac Xuan, who had been dispatched by the Struggle Movement in Hue to organize "student commandos" in Danang in 1966; and Ton That Duong Ky, a Hue University professor.

These veterans of the Buddhist protests of 1966 were joined in the revolutionary regime by other well-known figures from educational institutions in Hue, such as Mrs. Nguyen Dinh Chi, former principal of the respectable Dong Khanh Girls' School, who was a deputy chairwoman of the "Alliance" group formed later in 1968. Ton That Duong Thien, a teacher at Nguyen Du High School, directed operations in Gia Hoi district, and many others from the Hue educated elite accepted positions of responsibility in the revolutionary administration.[62]

The "Plan for an Offensive" also confirms that the political strategy of the Front was to rely on Buddhist clergy and laity for support in Hue. In a section dealing specifically with religious groups, the document says, "We must seek by every means to struggle to unite with and win over the Buddhist masses and monks and nuns."

As for the Catholics of Hue, the evidence from both communist documents and eyewitness testimony shows that the NLF's policy was not directed against the Catholic Church. The captured "Plan for an Offensive" does refer to "isolating reactionaries who exploit Catholicism in Phu Cam." In Vietnamese communist terminology, however, "isolate" means to act to cut off the influence of the individual in question in community affairs. It does not mean execution or even imprisonment necessarily, contrary to what the American political warfare specialists may argue.

The document specifies that only those priests who were found to "hide the enemy" were subject to any form of punishment, and the specific treatment was to depend on the degree to which the individual had opposed the revolution in the past.

In Gia Hoi district, which the NLF controlled for 26 days, one Catholic priest told Len Ackland that not one of his parishioners was harmed by the Front.[63] The only two Catholic figures identified by the Saigon regime as having been killed by the NLF are two French Benedictine priests, Father Guy and Father Urbain. It was reported by sources from the Thien An Monastery, however, that NLF forces occupied the monastery for several days when Father Guy and Father Urbain were still present and that neither they nor any other priests were harmed. The two were reported by Agence France Presse to have fled from heavy American bombing of the monastery on February 25—two days after the NLF forces had withdrawn.[64] The spot where their bodies were found was in the area in which Dr. Vennema says villagers reported heavy American bombing at the time the two priests were said to have been killed.[65] Moreover, the official Saigon government account is again marred by a major contradiction. The Political Warfare Battalion pamphlet claims that both Father Urbain and Father Guy were arrested and forced to remove their tunics before being taken to the area of the Dong Khanh tombs, where they were killed and buried. But the priest who recovered the body of Father Urbain is quoted in the same pamphlet as saying that he recognized it from the laundry number on his tunic!

Douglas Pike's notion of an NLF plan to purge Vietnamese society through mass executions is so bizarre and unrelated to the reality of NLF policy that it tells us more about Pike's own mind than it does about the movement he claims to be describing. Likewise, his suggestion that the Front tried to eliminate anyone who knew the identity of previously underground cadres in Hue appears to be based more on Pike's conception of how the Mafia operates than on any understanding of how the NLF operates. Obviously, cadres whose identities were well-known could not have remained in the city when the NLF evacuated it. Others, who did not reveal themselves even after the NLF takeover of Hue, no doubt remained behind.[66]

Pike apparently made no effort to inquire into what in fact did happen in the later period of the communist occupation. Saigon officials in Hue told Len Ackland in 1968 that those who were killed by the NLF when it prepared to leave the city in the face of Saigon and U.S. military pressure were officials and anti-communist political party leaders who had earlier been on the list for reeducation.[67] At that point, the NLF was faced with the choice of leaving those individuals to carry on their war against it, or eliminating them while the NLF was still in control of the city, or taking them out of the city for reeducation. There is no doubt that some of those previously marked for reeducation were executed during the latter part of the occupation, although the number appears to have been many times less than the Saigon government and Douglas Pike claim. Others who had been marked for reeducation were taken out of the city toward the mountains for that purpose. The charge that these prisoners were systematically killed is supported neither by evidence or by logic.

Pike's "hypothesis," therefore, must be judged unworthy of serious consideration. It represents ill-formed speculation undisciplined by attention to the available documentary evidence, much less to the revolutionary strategy and tactics about which Pike claims to be an expert. Yet Pike's pamphlet must be considered a political warfare success, for his interpretation of events in Hue remains the dominant one for journalists and public figures.

## Conclusion

The issue which historians must weigh in the NLF occupation of Hue is not whether executions took place but whether they were indiscriminate or the result of a prearranged "purge" of whole strata of society, as charged by political warfare specialists of the Saigon and U.S. governments. Equally important is the question of whether it was the NLF or U.S. bombing and artillery which caused the deaths of several thousand Hue civilians during the battle for the city.

The available evidence—not from NLF sources but from official U.S. and Saigon documents and from independent observers—indicates that the official story of an indiscriminate slaughter of those who were considered to be unsympathetic to the NLF is a complete fabrication. Not only is the number of bodies uncovered in and around Hue open to question, but more important, the cause of death appears to have been shifted from the fighting itself to NLF execution. And the most detailed and "authoritative" account of the alleged executions put together by either government does not stand up under examination.

Understanding the techniques of distortion and misrepresentation practiced by Saigon and U.S. propagandists in making a political warfare campaign out of the tragedy of Hue is as important today as it was when U.S. troops were still at war in Vietnam. It goes to the heart of the problem of facing the truth about the Vietnamese revolution and the American efforts to repress it by force. The screen of falsehood which has been erected around the Tet Offensive in Hue was and is but another defense mechanism for the U.S. government and much of the American public as well to avoid dealing honestly with the real character of the struggle there.


D. Gareth Porter is a fellow of the International Relations of East Asia Project, Cornell University, and is concurrently a staff member of the Indochina Resource Center in Washington, D.C.

## Notes

1. For a study of the earlier underpinnings of this strategy, see D. Gareth Porter, "Bloodbath; Myth or Reality?" *Indochina Chronicle* No. 19, September 15, 1973.
2. Joseph Dees, "Survivors Relate Communist Mass Murders of 1,000 in Hue," IPS (USIS) dispatch, April 23, 1968.
3. *New York Times*, May 1, 1968; *Washington Post*, May 1, 1968.

4. Vietnam Press, May 1, 1968. The UPI story on the report indicated that it was based solely on information supplied by the police, failing to mention the role of the Political Warfare Battalion. *Washington Post*, May 1, 1968. *The New York Times* did not mention the source of the information. It is safe to say, therefore, that no American newspaper reader learned that the ARVN Tenth Political Warfare Battalion played the key role in compiling the story.

5. *New York Times*, February 29, 1968.

6. *Le Monde*, April 13, 1968.

7. "Chronology of Graves Discovered, Vicinity of Hue (Civilian Deaths in Tet 1968)," obtained from the Office of the Assistant Secretary of Defense for Public Affairs, February 1970.

8. *New York Times*, March 28, 1968.

9. "Chronology of Graves Discovered."

10. *New York Times*, March 28, 1968.

11. Vu Cuong Sat cua Viet Cong tai Co Do Hue (Communist Murder in Hue), Tenth Political Warfare Battalion of ARVN, 1968, p. 13.

12. Alje Vennema, "The Tragedy of Hue," unpublished manuscript, 1968, pp. 19–23.

13. "Chronology of Graves Discovered," site 22.

14. "Villagers Returning to Hue," UPI, in *San Francisco Chronicle*, December 8, 1968; "South Vietnamese Farmer Stoically Works Fields," *Washington Post*, January 4, 1970.

15. "Chronology of Graves Discovered," sites 21, 13 and 14.

16. *Tien Tuyen*, January 27, 1969.

17. *Tien Tuyen*, May 3, 1969.

18. Ibid.

19. Vietnam Press, April 12, 1969.

20. *Washington Post*, May 5, 1969.

21. "Chronology of Graves Discovered," site 25.

22. Douglas Pike, *The Viet-Cong Strategy of Terror* (Saigon: U.S. Mission, Vietnam, 1970), p. 29.

23. *Baltimore Sun*, October 12, 1969.

24. *Tien Tuyen*, October 17, 1969.

25. Pike, op. cit., pp. 28–29.

26. "Chronology of Graves Discovered."

27. Embassy of Viet-Nam, Washington, D.C., *Vietnam Bulletin*, Viet-Nam Information Series, No. 28, April, 1970, p. 6.

28. Agence France-Presse dispatch, February 15, 1968, in L'Heure Decisive (Paris: Dossiers AFP-Laffont, 1968), p. 153.

29. Ibid.

30. *Vietnam Bulletin*, loc. cit.

31. This is what Pike told Benedict Stavis of Cornell University in an interview on September 10, 1973. Letter from Stavis to the author, September 10, 1973.

32. *Washington Post*, November 25, 1969.

33. *Christian Science Monitor*, December 1, 1969.

34. "Tien Chien Thang Hue tu Ngay 31.1, 23.3" (Information on the Victory in Hue from January 31 to March 23), Xerox copy obtained from the Combined Documents Exploitation Center, Saigon. The document, it should be noted, is far from being a high-level report or analysis of the Tet Offensive in Hue. It is handwritten, sketchy, and clearly done at the local level for local consumption.

35. *Nhan Dan*, February 28, 1968.

36. *Tu Dien Tieng Viet* (Vietnamese Language Dictionary) (Hanoi: Nha Xuat Ban Khoa Hoc, 1967), p. 927.

37. *Los Angeles Times*, November 20, 1969; *Washington Daily News*, November 25, 1969.

38. Pike, op. cit., p. 16; news articles cited above.

39. The paragraph immediately preceding Pike's mention of the document refers to a whole class of villagers being "wiped out," op. cit.

40. "15 Tieu Chuan Cuu Tap" (Fifteen Criteria for Investigation), Xerox copy obtained from U.S. Embassy, Saigon. This document is reproduced in *Viet-Nam Documents and Research Notes*, Document No. 97, August 1971, Part II.

41. "Repressing Counterrevolutionaries: The Viet Cong System of Punishment," *Viet-Nam Documents and Research Notes*, Document No. 5, October 1967.

42. *Washington Daily News*, November 5, 1969. Chuyen gave the figure of three million in the *Los Angeles Times*, November 20, 1969.

43. In the report on the interrogation of Chuyen, the interrogator pointedly put question marks after the rank and past assignments in the VPA claimed by Chuyen. U.S. State Department, Captured Documents and Interrogation Reports (1968), item no. 55, "Interrogation of Le Xuan Chuyen."

44. Ibid.

45. Speech by Tran Van Do, Troi Nam, No. 3, 1967, p. 13.

46. Vo Van Chan, The Policy of Greater Unity of the People (Saigon: Minister of Chieu Hoi, Republic of Vietnam, 1971), p. 19.

47. See Pike, op. cit., p. 18; Sir Robert Thompson, "Communist Atrocities in Vietnam," *New York Times*, June 15, 1972.

48. "Letter from Vietnam," *The New Yorker*, March 23, 1968.

49. *Washington Daily News*, March 1, 1968.

50. "Status of Refugees," official report by Office of Refugees, U.S. Agency for International Development, May 2, 1968.

51. *Saigon Post*, March 17, 1968.

52. VC Carnage in Hue, Tenth Political Warfare Battalion, 1968, p. 8.

53. Pike, op. cit., pp. 30–31.

54. *Saigon Post*, March 17, 1968.

55. Pike, op. cit., pp. 30–31.

56. "Information on the Victory in Hue."

57. Len Ackland and D. Gareth Porter, "The Bloodbath Argument," *Christian Century*, November 5, 1969. Reprinted in Paul Menzel, ed., *Moral Argument and the War in Vietnam* (Nashville: Aurora Publishers, 1971), pp. 141–46.

58. "Ban Ke Hoach Con Kich va Khoi Nghia cua Mu A" (Plan for an Offensive and General Uprising of Mui A), Xerox copy obtained from Office of Special Projects, JUSPAO, Saigon, June, 1971.

59. Len Ackland, "Resist and They Die," unpublished manuscript, 1968, pp. 5–6.

60. Ibid., pp. 15–19; *Washington Post*, December 7, 1969; and Don Oberdorfer, *Tet* (New York, Avon Books, 1971), pp. 216–53.

61. *Pike, War, Peace and the Viet Cong* (Cambridge, MIT Press, 1969).

62. Ackland, op. cit., p. 8; *Christian Science Monitor*, May 8, 1968; Vennema, op. cit., p. 10; notes from interviews in Hue by Francois Sully of *Newsweek*, March, 1968.

63. Ackland and Porter, op. cit., p. 145.

64. Agence France-Presse dispatch, March 3, 1968, in Vietnam Press Special Reports, March 5, 1968.

65. Vennema, op. cit., p. 26.

66. Vu Cuong Sat cua Viet Cong tai Co Do Hue, pp. 2, 18–21.

67. The Chinese communists faced a similar situation in 1947, when they occupied a county seat and their shadow government and officials surfaced for the first time. David Gulala tells of asking the political commissar what would happen when the Red Army had to leave the town. "They will leave, too, and resume their clandestine work," he replied. "Are you not afraid that they will lose their value now that they have revealed themselves?" Gulala asked. The commissar said, "We have secret agents in this town who did not come out when we took it. We don't even know who they are. They will still be here when we go." Galula, *Counterinsurgency Warfare: Theory and Practice* (New York: Praeger, 1964), pp. 56–57.

# Working-Class War: Mapping the Losses
## Christian G. Appy

"We all ended up going into the service about the same time—the whole crowd." I had asked Dan Shaw about himself, why *he* had joined the Marine Corps; but Dan ignored the personal thrust of the question. Military service seemed less an individual choice than a collective rite of passage, a natural phase of life for "the whole crowd" of boys in his neighborhood, so his response encompassed a circle of over twenty childhood friends who lived near the corner of Train and King streets in Dorchester, Massachusetts—a white, working-class section of Boston.

Thinking back to 1968 and his streetcorner buddies, Dan sorted them into groups, wanting to get the facts straight about each one. It did not take him long to come up with some figures. "Four of the guys didn't go into the military at all. Four got drafted by the army. Fourteen or fifteen of us went in the Marine Corps. Out of them fourteen or fifteen"—here he paused to count by naming—"Eddie, Brian, Tommy, Dennis, Steve: six of us went to Nam." They were all still teenagers. Three of the six were wounded in combat, including Dan.

His tone was calm, almost dismissive. The fact that nearly all his friends entered the military and half a dozen fought in Vietnam did not strike Dan as unusual or remarkable. In working-class neighborhoods like his, military service after high school was as commonplace among young men as college was for the youth of upper-middle-class suburbs—not welcomed by everyone but rarely questioned or avoided. In fact, when Dan thinks of the losses suffered in other parts of Dorchester, he regards his own streetcorner as relatively lucky. "Jeez, it wasn't bad. I mean some corners around here really got wiped out. Over off Norfolk street ten guys got blown away the same year."

Focusing on the world of working-class Boston, Dan has a quiet, low-key manner with few traces of bitterness. But when he speaks of the disparities in

135

military service throughout American society, his voice fills with anger, scorn, and hurt. He compares the sacrifices of poor and working-class neighborhoods with the rarity of wartime casualties in the "fancy suburbs" beyond the city limits, in places such as Milton, Lexington, and Wellesley. If three wounded veterans "wasn't bad" for a streetcorner in Dorchester, such concentrated pain was, Dan insists, unimaginable in a wealthy subdivision. "You'd be lucky to find three Vietnam veterans in one of those rich neighborhoods, never mind three who got wounded."

Dan's point is indisputable: those who fought and died in Vietnam were overwhelmingly drawn from the bottom half of the American social structure. The comparison he suggests bears out the claim. The three affluent towns of Milton, Lexington, and Wellesley had a combined wartime population of about 100,000, roughly equal to that of Dorchester. However, while those suburbs suffered a total of eleven war deaths, Dorchester lost forty-two. There was almost exactly the same disparity in casualties between Dorchester and another sample of prosperous Massachusetts towns—Andover, Lincoln, Sudbury, Weston, Dover, Amherst, and Longmeadow. These towns lost ten men from a combined population of 100,000. In other words, boys who grew up in Dorchester were four times more likely to die in Vietnam than those raised in the fancy suburbs. An extensive study of wartime casualties from Illinois reached a similar conclusion. In that state, men from neighborhoods with median family incomes under $5,000 (about $15,000 in 1990 dollars) were four times more likely to die in Vietnam than men from places with median family incomes above $15,000 ($45,000 in 1990 dollars).

Dorchester, East Los Angeles, the South side of Chicago—major urban centers such as these sent thousands of men to Vietnam. So, too, did lesser known, midsize industrial cities with large working-class populations, such as Saginaw, Michigan; Fort Wayne, Indiana; Stockton, California; Chattanooga, Tennessee; Youngstown, Ohio; Bethlehem, Pennsylvania; and Utica, New York. There was also an enormous rise in working-class suburbanization in the 1950s and 1960s. The post-World War II boom in modestly priced, uniformly designed, tract housing, along with the vast construction of new highways, allowed many workers their first opportunity to purchase homes and to live a considerable distance from their jobs. As a result, many new suburbs became predominantly working class.

Long Island, New York, became the site of numerous working-class suburbs, including the original Levittown, the first mass-produced town in American history. Built by the Levitt and Sons construction firm in the late 1940s, it was initially a middle-class town. By 1960, however, as in many other postwar suburbs, the first owners had moved on, often to larger homes in wealthier suburbs, and a majority of the newcomers were working class.

Ron Kovic, author of one of the best-known Vietnam memoirs and films, *Born on the Fourth of July*, grew up near Levittown in Massapequa. His parents, like so many others in both towns, were working people willing to make great sacrifices to own a small home with a little land and to live in a town they regarded as a safe and decent place to raise their families, in hope that their children would enjoy greater opportunity. Many commentators viewed the suburbanization of blue-collar workers as a sign that the working class was vanishing and that almost everyone was becoming middle class. In fact, however, though many workers owned more than ever before, their relative social position remained largely unchanged. The Kovics, for example, lived in the suburbs but had to raise five children on the wages of a supermarket checker and clearly did not match middle-class levels in terms of economic security, education, or social status.

Ron Kovic volunteered for the marines after graduating from high school. He was paralyzed from the chest down in a 1968 firefight during his second tour of duty in Vietnam. Upon returning home, after treatment in a decrepit, rat-infested VA hospital, Kovic was asked to be grand marshal in Massapequa's Memorial Day parade. His drivers were American Legion veterans of World War II who tried unsuccessfully to engage him in a conversation about the many local boys who had died in Vietnam:

"Remember Clasternack? . . . They got a street over in the park named after him . . . he was the first of you kids to get it . . . There was the Peters family too . . . both brothers . . . Both of them killed in the same week. And Alan Grady . . . Did you know Alan Grady? . . .

"We've lost a lot of good boys. . . . We've been hit pretty bad. The whole town's changed."

A community of only 27,000, Massapequa lost 14 men in Vietnam. In 1969, *Newsday* traced the family backgrounds of 400 men from Long Island who had been killed in Vietnam. "As a group," the newspaper concluded, "Long Island's war dead have been overwhelmingly white, working-class men. Their parents were typically blue collar or clerical workers, mailmen, factory workers, building tradesmen, and so on."

Rural and small-town America may have lost more men in Vietnam, proportionately, than did even central cities and working-class suburbs. You get a hint of this simply by flipping though the pages of the Vietnam Memorial directory. As thick as a big-city phone book, the directory lists the names and hometowns of Americans who died in Vietnam. An average page contains the names of five or six men from towns such as Alma, West Virginia (pop. 296), Lost Hills, California (pop. 200), Bryant Pond, Maine (pop. 350), Tonalea, Arizona (pop. 125), Storden, Minnesota (pop. 364), Pioneer,

Louisiana (pop. 188), Wartburg, Tennessee (pop. 541), Hillisburg, Indiana (pop. 225), Boring, Oregon (pop. 150), Racine, Missouri (pop. 274), Hygiene, Colorado (pop. 400), Clayton, Kansas (pop. 127), and Almond, Wisconsin (pop. 440). In the 1960s only about 2 percent of Americans lived in towns with fewer than 1,000 people. Among those who died in Vietnam, however, roughly four times that portion, 8 percent, came from American hamlets of that size. It is not hard to find small towns that lost more than one man in Vietnam. Empire, Alabama, for example, had four men out of a population of only 400 die in Vietnam—four men from a town in which only a few dozen boys came of draft age during the entire war.

There were also soldiers who came from neither cities, suburbs, nor small towns but from the hundreds of places in between, average towns of 15,000 to 30,000 people whose economic life, however precarious, had local roots. Some of these towns paid a high cost in Vietnam. In the foothills of eastern Alabama, for example, is the town of Talladega, with a population of approximately 17,500 (about one-quarter black), a town of small farmers and textile workers. Only one-third of Talladega's men had completed high school. Fifteen of their children died in Vietnam, a death rate three times the national average. Compare Talladega to Mountain Brook, a rich suburb outside Birmingham. Mountain Brook's population was somewhat higher than Talladega's, about 19,500 (with no black residents of draft age). More than 90 percent of its men were high school graduates. No one from Mountain Brook is listed among the Vietnam War dead.

I have described a social map of American war casualties to suggest not simply the geographic origins of U.S. soldiers but their class origins—not simply where they came from but the kinds of places as well. Class, not geography, was the crucial factor in determining which Americans fought in Vietnam. Geography reveals discrepancies in military service primarily because it often reflects class distinctions. Many men went to Vietnam from places such as Dorchester, Massapequa, Empire, and Talladega because those were the sorts of places where most poor and working-class people lived. The wealthiest youth in those towns, like those in richer communities, were far less likely either to enlist or to be drafted.

Mike Clodfelter, for example, grew up in Plainville, Kansas. In 1964 he enlisted in the army, and the following year he was sent to Vietnam. In his 1976 memoir, Clodfelter recalled, "From my own small home town . . . all but two of a dozen high school buddies would eventually serve in Vietnam and all were of working class families, while I knew of not a single middle class son of the town's businessmen, lawyers, doctors, or ranchers from my high school graduating class who experienced the Armageddon of our generation."

However, even a sketchy map of American casualties must go farther afield, beyond the conventional boundaries of the United States. Although this fact is not well known, the military took draftees and volunteers from the American territories: Puerto Rico, Guam, the U.S. Virgin Islands, American Samoa, and the Canal Zone. These territories lost a total of 436 men in Vietnam, several dozen more than the state of Nebraska. Some 48,000 Puerto Ricans served in Vietnam, many of whom could speak only a smattering of English. Of these, 345 died. This figure does not include men who were born in Puerto Rico and emigrated to the United States (or whose parents were born in Puerto Rico). We do not know these numbers because the military did not make a separate count of Hispanic-American casualties either as an inclusive category or by country of origin.

Guam drew little attention on the American mainland during the war. It was only heard of at all because American B-52s took off from there to make bombing runs over Vietnam (a twelve-hour round-trip flight requiring midair refueling) or because a conference between President Johnson and some of his top military leaders was held there in 1967. Yet the United States sent several thousand Guamanians to fight with American forces in Vietnam. Seventy of them died. Drawn from a population of only 111,000, Guam's death rate was considerably higher even than that of Dorchester, Massachusetts.

This still does not exhaust the range of places we might look for "American" casualties. There were, of course, the "Free World forces" recruited by and, in most cases, financed by the United States. These "third country forces" from South Korea, Australia, New Zealand, Thailand, and the Philippines reached a peak of about 60,000 troops (U.S. forces rose to 550,000). The U.S. government pointed to them as evidence of a united, multinational, free-world effort to resist communist aggression. But only Australia and New Zealand paid to send their troops to Vietnam. They had a force of 7,000 men and lost 469 in combat. The other nations received so much money in return for their military intervention that their forces were essentially mercenary. The Philippine government of Ferdinand Marcos, for example, received the equivalent of $26,000 for each of the 2,000 men it sent to Vietnam to carry out noncombat, civic action programs. South Korea's participation was by far the largest among the U.S.-sponsored third countries. It deployed a force of 50,000 men. In return, the Korean government enjoyed substantial increases in aid, and its soldiers were paid roughly 20 times what they earned at home. More than 4,000 of them lost their lives.

The South Vietnamese military was also essentially the product of American intervention. For twenty-one years the United States committed billions of dollars to the creation of an anticommunist government in southern Vietnam and to the recruitment, training, and arming of a military to support it. Throughout the long war against southern guerrillas and North Vietnamese regulars, about 250,000 South Vietnamese government forces were killed. The United States bears responsibility for these lives and for those of third

140 • *Vietnam and America: Readings and Documents*

country forces because their military participation was almost wholly dependent on American initiatives.

In this sense, perhaps we need to take another step. Perhaps all Vietnamese deaths, enemy and ally, civilian and combatant, should be considered American as well as Vietnamese casualties. To do so is simply to acknowledge that their fates were largely determined by American intervention. After all, without American intervention (according to almost all intelligence reports at the time and historians since), Vietnamese unification under Ho Chi Minh would have occurred with little resistance.

However one measures American responsibility for Indochinese casualties, every effort should be made to grasp the enormity of those losses. From 1961 to 1975 1.5 to 2 million Vietnamese were killed. Estimates of Cambodian and Laotian deaths are even less precise, but certainly the figure is in the hundreds of thousands. Imagine a memorial to the Indochinese who died in what they call the American, not the Vietnam, War. If similar to the Vietnam Memorial, with every name etched in granite, it would have to be forty times larger than the wall in Washington. Even such an enormous list of names would not put into perspective the scale of loss in Indochina. These are small countries with a combined wartime population of about 50 million people. Had the United States lost the same portion of its population, the Vietnam Memorial would list the names of 8 million Americans.

To insist that we recognize the disparity in casualties between the United States and Indochina is not to diminish the tragedy or significance of American losses, nor does it deflect attention from our effort to understand American soldiers. Without some awareness of the war's full destructiveness we cannot begin to understand their experience. As one veteran put it: "That's what I can't get out of my head—the bodies . . . all those bodies. Back then we didn't give a shit about the dead Vietnamese. It was like: 'Hey, they're just gooks, don't mean nothin'.' You got so cold you didn't even blink. You could even joke about it, mess around with the bodies like they was rag dolls. And after awhile we could even stack up our own KIAs [killed in action] without feeling much of anything. It's not like that now. You can't just put it out of your mind. Now I carry those bodies around every fucking day. It's a heavy load, man, a heavy fucking load."

## The Vietnam Generation's Military Minority: A Statistical Profile

Presidents Kennedy, Johnson, and Nixon sent 3 million American soldiers to South Vietnam, a country of 17 million. In the early 1960s they went by the hundreds—helicopter units, Green Beret teams, counterinsurgency hotshots, ambitious young officers, and ordinary infantrymen—all of them labeled military advisers by the American command. They fought a distant, "brushfire war" on the edge of American consciousness. Beyond the secret inner circles of government, few predicted that hundreds of thousands would follow in a massive buildup that took the American presence in Vietnam from 15,000 troops in 1964 to 550,000 in 1968. In late 1969 the gradual withdrawal of ground forces began, inching its way to the final U.S. pullout in January 1973. The bell curve of escalation and withdrawal spread the commitment of men into a decade-long chain of one-year tours of duty.

In the years of escalation, as draft calls mounted to 30,000 and 40,000 a month, many young people believed the entire generation might be mobilized for war. There were, of course, many ways to avoid the draft, and millions of men did just that. Very few, however, felt completely confident that they would never be ordered to fight. Perhaps the war would escalate to such a degree or go on so long that all exemptions and deferments would be eliminated. No one could be sure what would happen. Only in retrospect is it clear that the odds of serving in Vietnam were, for many people, really quite small. The forces that fought in Vietnam were drawn from the largest generation of young people in the nation's history. During the years 1964 to 1973, from the Gulf of Tonkin Resolution to the final withdrawal of American troops from Vietnam, 27 million men came of draft age. The 2.5 million men of that generation who went to Vietnam represent less than 10 percent of America's male baby boomers.

The parents of the Vietnam generation had an utterly different experience of war. During World War II virtually all young, able-bodied men entered the service—some 12 million. Personal connections to the military permeated society regardless of class, race, or gender. Almost every family had a close relative overseas—a husband fighting in France, a son in the South Pacific, or at least an uncle with the Seabees, a niece in the WAVES, or a cousin in the Air Corps. These connections continued well into the 1950s. Throughout the Korean War years and for several years after, roughly 70 percent of the draft-age population of men served in the military; but from the 1950s to the 1960s, military service became less and less universal. During the Vietnam years, the portion had dropped to 40 percent: 10 percent were in Vietnam, and 30 percent served in Germany, South Korea, and the dozens of other duty stations in the United States and abroad. What had been, in the 1940s, an experience shared by the vast majority gradually became the experience of a distinct minority.

What kind of minority was it? In modern American culture, *minority* usually serves as a code word for nonwhite races, especially African Americans. To speak of American forces in Vietnam as a minority invites the assumption that blacks, Hispanics, Asian Americans, and Native Americans fought and died in numbers grossly disproportionate to their percentage of the total U.S. population. It is a common assumption, but not one that has been sufficiently examined. For that matter, the whole experience of racial minorities in Vietnam has been woefully ignored by the media and academics. For Hispanics, Asian Americans, and Native Americans, even the most basic statistical information about their role in Vietnam remains either unknown or inadequately examined.

We know how many black soldiers served and died in Vietnam, but the more important task is to interpret those figures in historical context. Without that context, racial disproportions can be either exaggerated or denied. To simplify: At the beginning of the war blacks comprised more than 20 percent of American combat deaths, about twice their portion of the U.S. population. However, the portion of black casualties declined over time so that, for the war as a whole, black casualties were only slightly disproportionate (12.5 percent from a civilian population of 11 percent). The total percentage of blacks who served in Vietnam was roughly 10 percent throughout the war.

African Americans clearly faced more than their fair share of the risks in Vietnam from 1965 to 1967. That fact might well have failed to gain any public notice had the civil rights and antiwar movements not called attention to it. Martin Luther King was probably the most effective in generating concern about the number of black casualties in Vietnam. King had refrained from frequent public criticism of the war until 1967, persuaded by moderates that outspoken opposition to the war might divert energy from the cause of civil rights and alienate prowar politicians whose support the movement sought (President Johnson, for example). By early 1967, however, King believed the time had come to break his silence. As for diverting energy and resources from domestic social reform, King argued, the war itself had already done as much. More importantly, he could not in good conscience remain silent in the face of a war he believed unjust.

King's critique of the war was wide ranging, based on a historical understanding of the long struggle in Vietnam for national independence, on a commitment to nonviolence, and on outrage over the violence the United States was inflicting on the land and people of Indochina. Always central in King's criticism of the war, however, was its effect on America's poor, both black and white. "The promises of the Great Society," he said, "have been shot down on the battlefield of Vietnam." The expense of the war was taking money and support that could be spent to solve problems at home. The war on poverty was being supplanted by the war on Vietnam. Beyond that, King stressed, the poor themselves were doing much of the fighting overseas. As he put it in his famous speech at Riverside Church in New York City (April 1967), the war was not only "devastating the hopes of the poor at home," it was also "sending their sons and their brothers and their husbands to fight and to die in extraordinarily high proportions relative to the rest of the population."

While King focused attention on the economic condition of white and black soldiers, he emphasized the additional burden on blacks of fighting overseas in disproportionate numbers while being denied full citizenship at home: "We have been repeatedly faced with the cruel irony of watching Negro and white boys on TV screens as they kill and die together for a nation that has been unable to seat them together in the same schools. So we watch them in brutal solidarity burning the huts of a poor village, but we realize that they would never live on the same block in Detroit." In another speech he added, "We are willing to make the Negro 100 percent of a citizen in warfare, but reduce him to 50 percent of a citizen on American soil. Half of all Negroes live in substandard housing and he has half the income of white. There is twice as much unemployment and infant mortality among Negroes. [Yet] at the beginning of 1967 twice as many died in action—20.6 percent—in proportion to their numbers in the population as a whole."

In his postwar apologia for U.S. intervention, *America in Vietnam*, Guenter Lewy accused King of heightening racial tension by making false allegations about black casualties in Vietnam. After all, Lewy argued, black casualties for the whole war were 12.5 percent, no higher than the portion of draft-age black males in the total U.S. population. Lewy's charge falls apart, however, as soon as one points out that black casualties did not drop to the overall figure of 12.5 until well after King was assassinated. During the period King and others were articulating their criticisms of the war, the disproportions were quite significant. To attack the antiwar movement for failing to use postwar statistics is not only unfair, it is ahistorical. Moreover, King was by no means the first prominent black to criticize the war or the disproportionate loss of black soldiers. Malcolm X, Muhammad Ali, Adam Clayton Powell, Dick Gregory, John Lewis, and Julian Bond were among those who spoke out repeatedly well before 1967. In fact, had the civil rights movement not brought attention to racial disproportions in Vietnam casualties, those disproportions almost certainly would have continued. According to Commander George L. Jackson, "In response to this criticism the Department of Defense took steps to readjust force levels in order to achieve an equitable proportion and employment of Negroes in Vietnam." A detailed analysis of exactly what steps were taken has yet to be written. It is clear, however, that by late 1967, black casualties had fallen to 13 percent and then to below 10 percent in 1970–72.

Blacks were by no means united in opposition to the war or the military. For generations blacks had been struggling for equal participation in all American institutions, the military included. In World War II the struggle had focused on integration and the "right to fight." Aside from some all-black combat units, most blacks were assigned to segregated, rear-area duty. The military was officially desegregated in 1948, and most blacks served in integrated units in the Korean War. It was the Vietnam War, though, that was hailed in the mass media as America's first truly integrated war. In 1967 and 1968 several magazines and newspapers ran major stories on "the Negro in Vietnam." While disproportionate casualties were mentioned, they were not the target of criticism. Instead, these articles—including a cover story in *Ebony* (August 1968)—emphasized the contributions of black soldiers, their courageous service, and the new opportunities ostensibly provided by wartime duty in an integrated army. The point was often made that blacks had more civil rights in the military than at home. In *Harper's* magazine (June 1967) Whitney Young of the Urban League wrote, "In this war there is a degree of integration among black and white Americans far exceeding that of any other war in our history as well as any other time or place in our domestic life." As Thomas Johnson put it in *Ebony*, giving the point an ironic turn, "The Negro has found in his nation's most totalitarian society—the military—the greatest degree of functional democracy that this nation has granted to black people."

Whitney Young justified disproportionate black casualties as the result not of discrimination but of "the simple fact that a higher proportion of Negroes volunteer for hazardous duty." There was some truth to this. In airborne units—the training for which is voluntary—blacks were reported to comprise as much as 30 percent of the combat troops. Moreover, blacks had a reenlistment rate three times higher than whites. It fell dramatically as the war went on, but it was always much higher than that of white soldiers. These points surely suggest that many blacks were highly motivated, enthusiastic troops.

That enthusiasm itself does not prove that the military had equal opportunities for blacks or an absence of discrimination. After all, presumably the same blacks who volunteered for airborne (for which they received additional pay) might just as eagerly have volunteered for officer candidate school had they been offered the chance. Only 2 percent of the officers in Vietnam were black. Blacks might have taken advantage of opportunities to fill higher-paying, noncombat positions, had they been offered. The military's response was that blacks were disproportionately enlisted combat soldiers because they were simply not qualified to fill other jobs. Of course, qualifications are determined by the crudest measurement—standardized tests—and black soldiers scored significantly lower than whites. In 1965, for example, 41 percent of black soldiers scored in the lowest levels of the Armed Forces Qualification Test (categories IV and V), compared to 10 percent of the white soldiers.

These scores account for much of the disproportion. To that extent they reflect the relationship of race and class in civilian society. Poor and working-class soldiers, whether black or white, were more likely to be trained for combat than were soldiers economically and educationally more advantaged. While enlisted men of both races were primarily from the bottom half of the social structure, blacks were considerably poorer. One study found that 90 percent of black soldiers in Vietnam were from working-class and poor backgrounds. This is a large part of the reason why more blacks reenlisted. Men who reenlisted were given bonuses of $900 to $1,400, equivalent to one-third of the median family income for black families in the mid-1960s. However, the military's assignment of blacks to low-ranking positions was not simply a reflection of the economic and racial inequalities of civilian society. The military contributed its own discrimination. In the first years of American escalation, even those blacks who scored in the highest test category were placed in combat units at a level 75 percent higher than that of whites in the same category.

Though racial discrimination and racist attitudes surely persisted in the military, class was far more important than race in determining the overall social composition of American forces. Precisely when the enlisted ranks were becoming increasingly integrated by race, they were becoming ever more segregated by class. The military may never have been truly representative of the general male population, but in the 1960s it was overwhelmingly the domain of the working class.

No thorough statistical study has yet been conducted on the class origins of the men who served in Vietnam. Though the military made endless, mind-numbing efforts to quantify virtually every aspect of its venture in Vietnam, it did not make (so far as anyone has discovered) a single study of the social backgrounds of its fighting men. Quantitative evidence must be gathered from a variety of disparate studies. Probably the most ambitious effort to gather statistical information about the backgrounds of Vietnam-era soldiers was conducted just prior to the large-scale American escalation. In 1964 the National Opinion Research Center (NORC) surveyed 5 percent of all active-duty enlisted men.

### Table 1. Occupations of Fathers of Enlisted Men, by Service, 1964 (Percent)

| Father's Occupation | Army | Navy | Air Force | Marines |
|---|---|---|---|---|
| White-collar | 17.0 | 19.8 | 20.9 | 20.4 |
| Blue-collar | 52.8 | 54.5 | 52.0 | 57.2 |
| Farmer | 14.8 | 10.7 | 13.3 | 9.1 |
| Military | 1.8 | 2.1 | 1.8 | 2.0 |
| Father absent | 13.6 | 12.9 | 12.0 | 11.3 |
| (Approx. N) | (28,000) | (17,500) | (28,000) | (5,000) |

*Source:* 1964 NORC survey, in Moskos, *American Enlisted Man*, p. 195.

According to NORC's occupational survey (table 1) roughly 20 percent of American enlisted men had fathers with white-collar jobs. Among the male population as a whole more than twice that portion, 44 percent, were white-collar workers. Of course, not all white-collar jobs are necessarily middle class in the income, power, and status they confer. Many low-paying clerical and sales jobs—typically listed as white collar—are more accurately understood as working-class occupations. While the white-collar label exaggerates the size of the middle class, it nonetheless encompasses almost all privileged Americans in the labor force. Thus, the fact that only 20 percent of U.S. soldiers came from white-collar families represents a striking class difference between the military and the general population.

The high portion of farmers in the sample is a further indication of the disproportionate number of soldiers from rural small towns. In the 1960s only about 5 percent of the American labor force was engaged in agriculture. In the NORC survey, more than twice as many, 12 percent, came from farm families. Though the survey does not reveal the economic standing of this group, we should avoid an American tendency to picture all farmers as independent proprietors. At the time of the survey about two-thirds of the workers engaged in agricultural labor were wage earners (farm laborers or migrant farmworkers) with family incomes less than $1,000 per year.

There is also good reason to believe that most of the men with absent fathers grew up in hard-pressed circumstances. In 1965, almost two-thirds of the children in female-headed families lived below the census bureau's low-income level. All told, the NORC survey suggests that on the brink of the Vietnam escalation at least three-quarters of American enlisted men were working class or poor.

Although this book focuses on enlisted men, the inclusion of officers would not dramatically raise the overall class backgrounds of the Vietnam military. Officers comprised 11 percent of the total number of men in Vietnam, so even if many of them were from privileged families, the statistical impact would be limited. Furthermore, though we need further studies of the social backgrounds of the Vietnam-era officer corps, it may well have been the least privileged officer corps of the twentieth century. For example, in his study of the West Point class of 1966, Rick Atkinson found a striking historical decline in the class backgrounds of cadets. "Before World War I, the academy had drawn nearly a third of the corps from the families of doctors, lawyers, and other professionals. But by the mid 1950s, sons of professionals made up only 10 percent of the cadets, and links to the upper class had been almost severed. West Point increasingly attracted military brats and sons of the working class." Also, as the war dragged on, the officer corps was depleted of service school and ROTC graduates and had to rely increasingly on enlisted men who were given temporary field commissions or sent to officer candidate school. These officers, too, probably lowered the class background of the officer corps.

Class inequality is also strikingly revealed in the most important postwar statistical study of Vietnam veterans, *Legacies of Vietnam*. Commissioned by the Veterans' Administration in 1978, about two-thirds of the *Legacies* sample of Vietnam veterans was working class or below. That figure is remarkable because the survey used sampling techniques designed to produce the widest possible class spectrum; that is, in choosing people for the study it sought a "maximum variation in socioeconomic context." Even so, the sample of Vietnam veterans was well below the general population in its class composition. When measured against backgrounds of nonveterans of the same generation, Vietnam veterans came out on the bottom in income, occupation, and education.

The key here is disproportion. The point is not that *all* working-class men went to Vietnam while everyone better off stayed home. Given the enormous size of the generation, millions of working-class men simply were not needed by the military. Many were exempted because they failed to meet the minimum physical or mental standards of the armed forces. However, the odds of working-class men going into the military and on to Vietnam were far higher than they were for the middle class and the privileged.

The *Legacies* study also suggests an important distinction between black and white soldiers. The black veterans, at least in this sample, were significantly more representative of the entire black population than white veterans were of the white population. This reflects the fact that whites and blacks have different class distributions, with blacks having a much larger portion of poor and working people and a much smaller middle class and elite. In the *Legacies* sample, 82 percent of black nonveterans were working class and below, compared with 47 percent of the white nonveterans. In other words, while black soldiers were still, as a group, poorer than white soldiers, in relationship to the class structure of their respective races, blacks were not as disproportionately poor and working class as whites. This is, I think, one reason why black veterans seem to have less class-based resentment than white veterans toward the men of their race who did not serve in Vietnam.

Education, along with occupation and income, is a key measure of class position. Eighty percent of the men who went to Vietnam had no more than a high school education (table 2). This figure would compare well to statistics of some previous wars. After all, at the time of the Civil War and well into the twentieth century, only a small minority of Americans had high school educations. However, if considered in historical context, the low portion of college educated among American soldiers is yet another indication of the disproportionately working-class composition of the military. The 1960s was a boomtime for American education, a time when opportunities for higher education were more widespread than ever before. By 1965, 45 percent of Americans between eighteen and twenty-one had some college education. By 1970 that figure was more than 50 percent. Compared with national standards, American forces were well below average in formal education. Studies matching school enrollments to age and class show that the educational levels of American soldiers in Vietnam correspond roughly to those of draft-age, blue-collar males in the general population (table 3). Of course, many veterans took college courses after their military service. However, the *Legacies* study found that by 1981 only 22 percent of veterans had completed college compared with 46 percent of nonveterans.

The portion of soldiers with at least some college education increased significantly in the late 1960s as draft calls increased and most graduate school deferments ended. By 1970 roughly 25 percent of American forces in Vietnam had some college education. Impressive as this increase was, it still fell well below the 50 percent for the age group as a whole, and it came as American troop levels in Vietnam were beginning to drop. Moreover, college education per se was no longer so clear a mark of privilege as it had been prior to World War II. Higher education in the post-World War II era expanded enormously, especially among junior and state colleges, the kinds of schools that enrolled the greatest number of working-class students. Between 1962 and 1972, enrollments in two-year colleges tripled. College students who went to Vietnam were far more likely to come from these institutions than from elite, four-year, private colleges. A survey of Harvard's class of 1970, for example, found only two men who served in Vietnam. College students who did go to Vietnam usually secured noncombat assignments. Among soldiers in Vietnam, high school dropouts were three times more likely to experience heavy combat than were college graduates.

Young men have fought in all wars, but U.S. forces in Vietnam were probably, on average, the youngest in our history. In previous wars many men in their twenties were drafted for military service, and men of that age and older often volunteered. During the Vietnam War most of the volunteers and draftees were teenagers; the average age was nineteen. In World War II, by contrast, the average American soldier was twenty-six years old. At age eighteen young men could join or be drafted into the army. At seventeen, with the consent of a guardian, boys could enlist in the Marine Corps. Early in the war, hundreds of seventeen-year-old marines served in Vietnam. In November 1965 the Pentagon ordered that all American troops must be eighteen before being deployed in the war zone. Even so, the average age remained low. Twenty-two-year-old soldiers were often kidded about their advanced age ("hey, old man") by the younger men in their units. Most American troops were not even old enough to vote. The voting age did not drop from twenty-one to eighteen until 1971. Thus, most of the Americans who fought

**Table 2. Educational Attainment of Vietnam Veterans at Time of Separation from the Armed Forces, 1966–1971 (Percent)**

| Fiscal year | Less than 12 Years of School | 12 Years of School | 1 to 3 Years of College | 4 or More Years of College |
|---|---|---|---|---|
| 1966 | 22.9 | 62.5 | 8.3 | 6.3 |
| 1967 | 23.6 | 61.8 | 9.0 | 5.6 |
| 1968 | 19.6 | 65.5 | 9.7 | 6.2 |
| 1969 | 18.3 | 60.0 | 15.9 | 5.8 |
| 1970 | 17.5 | 56.9 | 17.0 | 8.6 |
| 1971 | 14.7 | 55.4 | 19.4 | 10.5 |
| Total, 1966–71 | 19.4 | 60.3 | 13.2 | 7.2 |

*Source:* Reports and Statistics Service, Office of Controller, Veterans' Administration, 11 April 1972, in Helmer, *Bringing the War Home*, p. 303.

**Table 3. Percentage of Males Enrolled in School, 1965–1970**

| Age | Blue-Collar | White-Collar |
|---|---|---|
| 16–17 | 80 | 92 |
| 18–19 | 49 | 73 |
| 20–24 | 20 | 43 |

*Source:* Levison, *Working-Class Majority*, p. 121.

in Vietnam were powerless, working-class teenagers sent to fight an unde-clared war by presidents for whom they were not even eligible to vote.

No statistical profile can do justice to the complexity of individual experi-ence, but without these broad outlines our understanding would be hopelessly fragmented. A class breakdown of American forces cannot be absolutely pre-cise, but I believe the following is a reasonable estimate: enlisted ranks in Viet-nam were comprised of about 25 percent poor, 55 percent working class, and 20 percent middle class, with a statistically negligible number of wealthy. Most Americans in Vietnam were nineteen-year-old high school graduates. They grew up in the white, working-class enclaves of South Boston and Cleve-land's West Side; in the black ghettos of Detroit and Birmingham; in the small rural towns of Oklahoma and Iowa; and in the housing developments of working-class suburbs. They came by the thousands from every state and every U.S. territory, but few were from places of wealth and privilege.

# The Draft and the Making of a Working-Class Military

The Selective Service System was the most important institutional mecha-nism in the creation of a working-class army. It directly inducted more than

2 million men into the military, and just as important, the threat or likelihood of the draft indirectly induced millions more to enlist. These "draft-motivated" volunteers enlisted because they had already received their induction notices or believed they soon would, and thus they enlisted in order, they hoped, to have more choice as to the nature and location of their service. Even studies conducted by the military suggest that as many as half of the men who enlisted were motivated primarily by the pressure of the draft (table 4). Draft pressure became the most important cause of enlistments as the war lengthened.

The soldiers sent to Vietnam can be divided into three categories of roughly equal size: one-third draftees, one-third draft-motivated volunteers, and one-third true volunteers. In the first years of the American buildup most of the fighting was done by men who volunteered for military service. That does not mean they volunteered to fight in Vietnam. Few did. Even among West Point's class of 1966 only one-sixth volunteered for service in Vietnam (though many more eventually ended up there). As the war continued, the number of volunteers steadily declined. From 1966 to 1969 the percentage of draftees who died in the war doubled from 21 to 40 (table 5). Almost half of the army troops were draftees, and in combat units the portion was commonly as high as two-thirds; late in the war it was even higher. The overall number of draftees was lower because the Marine Corps—the other service branch that did the bulk of fighting in Vietnam—was ordinarily limited to volunteers (though it did draft about 20,000 men during the Vietnam War).

The draft determined the social character of the armed forces by whom it exempted from service as well as by whom it actually conscripted or induced to enlist. Because the generation that came of age during the 1960s was so large, the Selective Service exempted far more men than it drafted. From 1964 to 1973, 2.2 million men were drafted, 8.7 million enlisted, and 16 million did not serve. Of course, the millions of exemptions could have been granted in a manner designed to produce a military that mirrored the social composition of society at large. A step in that direction was made with the institution of a draft lottery in late 1969, a method that can produce a

## Table 4. Percentage of Draft-Motivated Enlistments

| Year | Enlistees | Officers | Reservists |
|------|-----------|----------|------------|
| 1964 | 38 | 41 | 71 |
| 1968 | 54 | 60 | 80 |

Source: U.S. House Committee on Armed Services, 1966, 100038; 1970, 12638. Cited in Useem, *Conscription, Protest, and Social Conflict,* p. 78.

representative cross-section of draftees. However, this reform did little to democratize the forces that fought in Vietnam because student deferments were continued until 1971, troop withdrawals late in the war lowered draft calls, and physical exemptions remained relatively easy for the privileged to attain.

Prior to the draft lottery, the Selective Service did not even profess the ideal of a socially and economically balanced military. Instead, it was devoted to a form of "human resource planning" designed to serve the "national interest" by sending some men into the military and encouraging others to stay in school and seek occupational deferments. At the heart of this conscious effort at social engineering was the concept of "channeling." The basic idea was to use the threat of the draft and the lure of educational and professional deferments to channel men into nonmilitary occupations that the Selective Service believed vital to the "national health, safety and interest." The primary architect of this system was Gen. Lewis B. Hershey, director of the Selective Service from 1941 to 1968. According to his biographer, George Flynn, Hershey was at first ambivalent, if not hostile, toward student deferments, unsure of their value or fairness. However, this master bureaucrat, determined to build and maintain a permanent draft, was soon persuaded otherwise. The six advisory committees he appointed in 1948, during the creation of the first peacetime draft, all supported student deferments. They argued that virtually every academic field had contributed to victory in World War II and that the draft should protect at least the most successful college and graduate students. Many advisers were especially concerned that potential scientists be protected. As the nuclear age advanced, influential policymakers were increasingly persuaded that the outcome of future wars—whether hot or cold—might be determined not by masses of muddy combat soldiers but by

## Table 5. American Draftees Killed in the Vietnam War

| Year | Total American Deaths, All Services | Draftees (Percent) | |
| | | All Services | Army |
|---|---|---|---|
| 1965 | 1,369 | 16 | 28 |
| 1966 | 5,008 | 21 | 34 |
| 1967 | 9,378 | 34 | 57 |
| 1968 | 14,592 | 34 | 58 |
| 1969 | 9,414 | 40 | 62 |
| 1970 | 4,221 | 43 | 57 |

*Source:* Columns 1 and 2 from U.S. Bureau of the Census, 1971, 253; column 3 from U.S. House Committee on Armed Services, 1971, 172. Cited in Useem, *Conscription, Protest, and Social Conflict*, p. 107.

teams of high-powered, white-jacketed scientists and engineers. Hershey quickly embraced student deferments, and by the mid-1950s he became their most important advocate.

Most of the class-biased draft policies of the 1960s were in place by the early 1950s. Still, the Korean War was not quite as class skewed as the Vietnam War, for two reasons. First, though there were student deferments during the Korean War, college graduates enlisted in rough proportion to their numbers (they did not do so during the Vietnam War). Second, for Korea, unlike Vietnam, the reserves were mobilized. Reserve units usually have a more balanced class composition than the regular army. During the period between Korea and Vietnam, draft calls were so low the military could afford to raise its admission standards and place more draftees in electronic and technical fields. These factors raised the class level of inductees. In fact, throughout the late 1950s and early 1960s, the Selective Service System was commonly criticized not because it offered too many deferments to the privileged but because "the underprivileged were too often barred from the benefits of military service by unrealistically high mental and physical standards."

In 1963 Daniel P. Moynihan, assistant secretary of labor for policy planning, learned that one-half of the men called by their draft boards for physical and mental examinations failed one or both of the tests and were thus disqualified for military service. Moynihan was particularly disturbed that poor boys were the most likely to be rejected. They were most commonly rejected for failing the intelligence test, the Armed Forces Qualification Test. In the early 1960s almost half of the men who failed this test came from families with six or more children and annual incomes of less than $4,000. Moynihan described this high rejection rate as a form of "de facto job discrimination" against "the least mobile, least educated young men."

Moynihan organized a presidential task force to examine conscription policies and to explore proposals by which the military might take responsibility for training men who initially failed to meet the military's mental standards. The task force study, *One Third of a Nation* (1964), called for the military to lower its entrance requirements and provide special training to those with mental or social handicaps. For Moynihan, the military seemed like a vast, untapped agent of social uplift with the potential to train the unskilled, to put unemployed youth to work, and to instill confidence and pride in the psychologically defeated. More than that, he believed the military could help solve the problem he claimed was at the heart of black poverty—broken, fatherless families. The military, Moynihan argued, would serve as a surrogate black family: "Given the strains of disorganized and matrifocal family life in which so many Negro youth come of age, the armed forces are a dramatic and desperately needed change; a world away from women, a world run by strong men and unquestioned authority."

In 1964, in response to Moynihan's proposal, the military began a series of pilot programs to admit a small number of draft rejects who agreed to voluntary rehabilitation as part of their military training, but these programs had little impact on the social composition of the military. In 1965, however, as draft calls jumped to fill the troop buildup in South Vietnam, the military began to lower its admission standards quite radically. With no intention of engaging in any social uplift, the military simply accepted more and more men with terribly low scores on the mental examination. During the 1950s and early 1960s, men who had scored in the two lowest categories (IV and V) were rarely accepted into the military. Beginning in 1965, however, hundreds of thousands of category IV men were drafted. Most were from poor and broken families, 80 percent were high school dropouts, and half had IQs of less than eighty-five. Prior to American escalation in Vietnam such men were routinely rejected, but with a war on, these "new standards" men were suddenly declared fit to fight. Rejection rates plummeted. Between 1965 and 1966 the overall rejection rate fell from 50 to 34 percent, and by 1967 mental rejections were cut in half.

The new-standards men were offered no special training to raise their intellectual skills. Most were simply trained for war. Yet, in 1966 Moynihan was still calling for lower military standards. That year Secretary of Defense Robert McNamara instituted a program that promised to carry out many of Moynihan's proposals. Called Project 100,000, McNamara's program was designed to admit 100,000 men into the military each year who failed the qualifying exam even at the lower standards of 1965. This program, McNamara claimed, would offer valuable training and opportunity to America's "subterranean poor." As McNamara put it, "The poor of America . . . have not had the opportunity to earn their fair share of this nation's abundance, but they can be given an opportunity to serve in their country's defense and they can be given an opportunity to return to civilian life with skills and aptitudes which for them and their families will reverse the downward spiral of decay." Never well known, Project 100,000 has virtually disappeared from histories of the Johnson presidency. It was conceived, in fact, as a significant component of the administration's "war on poverty," part of the Great Society, a liberal effort to uplift the poor, and it was instituted with high-minded rhetoric about offering the poor an opportunity to serve. Its result, however, was to send many poor, terribly confused, and woefully uneducated boys to risk death in Vietnam. There is an important analogy here to the way American officials explained the war itself. It was not, they claimed, a unilateral military intervention to bolster a weak, corrupt, and unpopular government in South Vietnam against revolutionary nationalism, but a generous effort to help the people of South Vietnam determine their own fate. But if governments were judged by their professed intentions alone, and not by the consequences of their actions as well, every state would bask in glory. Graham Greene might have said about Project 100,000 what he said about the well-intentioned Alden Pyle in his novel *The Quiet American*: "I never knew a man who had better motives for all the trouble he caused."

The effect of Project 100,000 was dire. The promised training was never carried out. Of the 240,000 men inducted by Project 100,000 from 1966 to 1968, only 6 percent received additional training, and this amounted to little more than an effort to raise reading skills to a fifth grade level. Forty percent were trained for combat, compared with only 25 percent for all enlisted men. Also, while blacks comprised 10 percent of the entire military, they represented about 40 percent of the Project 100,000 soldiers. A 1970 Defense Department study estimates that roughly half of the almost 400,000 men who entered the military under Project 100,000 were sent to Vietnam. These men had a death rate twice as high as American forces as a whole. This was a Great Society program that was quite literally shot down on the battlefields of Vietnam.

Project 100,000 and the abandonment of all but the most minimal mental requirements for military service were crucial institutional mechanisms in lowering the class composition of the American military. Had the prewar mental standards continued, almost 3 million men would have been exempted from military service on the basis of intelligence. Under the lowered standards, 1.36 million were mentally disqualified.

Almost three times as many men, 3.5 million, were exempted because of their physical condition. One might expect men from disadvantaged backgrounds, with poorer nutrition and less access to decent health care, to receive most of these exemptions. In practice, however, most physical exemptions were assigned to men who had the knowledge and resources to claim an exemption. Poor and working-class men ordinarily allowed military doctors to determine their physical fitness. Induction center examinations were often perfunctory exercises in which all but the most obvious disabilities were overlooked. According to the best study of the subject, Baskir and Strauss's *Chance and Circumstance*, men who arrived at their induction physical with professional documentation of a disqualifying ailment had the best chance of gaining a medical exemption. Induction centers usually did not have the time or desire to challenge an outside opinion. The case of an induction center in Seattle, Washington, may be an extreme example, but it underlines the significance of this point. At that center, the registrants were divided into two groups: "Those who had letters from doctors or psychiatrists, and those who did not. Everyone with a letter received an exemption, regardless of what the letter said."

Even very minor disabilities were grounds for medical disqualification. Skin rashes, flat feet, asthma, trick knees—such ailments were easily missed or ignored by military doctors, but they were legal exemptions that were frequently granted when attested to by a family physician. Even dental braces provided a means of avoiding the military. "In the Los Angeles area alone, ten dentists willingly performed orthodontic work for anyone who could pay a $1000–2000 fee. Wearing braces was a common last-minute tactic for registrants who faced immediate call-up."

According to Baskir and Strauss, men who were knowledgeable about the system and had the means to press a claim had a 90 percent chance of receiving a physical or psychological exemption even if they were in good health. Draft lore such as Arlo Guthrie's "Alice's Restaurant" has made famous some of the more bizarre efforts at draft avoidance—loading up on drugs before the physical, fasting or gorging to get outside the weight requirements, feigning insanity or homosexuality, or aggravating an old knee injury. There is no telling how many men tried such things, but the majority who received medical exemptions through their own efforts probably did so in a far less dramatic fashion by simply finding a professional to support their claim.

That the men who were most able and likely to seek professional help in avoiding the draft were white and middle class is not surprising. On many college campuses students could find political and psychological support for draft resistance along with concrete advice on how to get an exemption. In working-class neighborhoods, the myriad ways to avoid the draft were not only less well known, they had little, if any, community support. Avoiding the draft was more likely to be viewed as an act of cowardice than as a principled unwillingness to participate in an immoral war.

The onus of responsibility for claiming exemptions fell, except in obvious cases, on the individual registrant. Even those exemptions that were especially aimed at the poor, such as those for "hardship," were often ineffectual for men who were unaware of them or lacked the wherewithal to demonstrate their claim to the Selective Service. Much depended on the discretion of local draft boards. Though the national headquarters of the Selective Service provided the general framework of guidelines and regulations, the system was designed to be highly decentralized, with authority largely delegated to the 4,000 local boards across the country.

Draft boards were comprised of volunteers who typically met only once a month. With hundreds of cases to decide, board members could give careful attention to only the most difficult. The rest were reviewed by a full-time civil service clerk whose decisions were usually rubber-stamped by the board.

One study found that the civil servant determined the outcome of 85 percent of the cases. Under this system, the advantage went to those registrants who were able to document their claims clearly and convincingly. What was persuasive to one board, however, might not be to another. There were, in fact, significant variations in the way different boards operated. Occupational deferments, for example, often depended simply on what local boards determined to be "in the national health, safety, or interest."

While local discretionary power produced a number of anomalies, most local boards administered the system in ways that reinforced the class inequalities underlying the broad national system of manpower channeling. In fact, the decentralized system probably gave an added advantage to registrants with economic clout and social connections. Draft boards were overwhelmingly controlled by conservative, white, prosperous men in their fifties or sixties. A 1966 study of the 16,638 draft board members around the nation found that only 9 percent had blue-collar occupations, while more than 70 percent were professionals, managers, proprietors, public officials, or white-collar workers over the age of fifty. Only 1.3 percent were black. Until 1967, when Congress revoked the prohibition, women were forbidden from serving on local draft boards because General Hershey "feared they would be embarrassed when a physical question emerged."

The student deferment was the most overtly class-biased feature of the Vietnam era draft system. Census records show that youth from families earning $7,500 to $10,000 were almost two and a half times more likely to attend college than those from families earning under $5,000. Also, working-class boys who did go to college were far more likely to attend part time while working. This distinction is crucial because deferments were only offered to full-time students, thus excluding those trying to earn a degree by working their way through school a few courses at a time. These students were subject to the draft.

In addition, unsuccessful students with low class ranks could lose their deferments. The grades required to keep a student deferment varied according to the practice of local draft boards, but in 1966 and 1967 the Selective Service sought to weed out poor students systematically by giving almost a million students the Selective Service Qualifying Test. Many who scored poorly were reclassified and drafted. The irony, of course, is that the draft grabbed those students who were among the least qualified according to its own test.

While unsuccessful and part-time students were "draft-bait," successful full-time students could preserve their draft immunity by going on to graduate school. Those who were trained as engineers, scientists, or teachers could then acquire occupational deferments. Though graduate students in every field received deferments, the primary intention of the inducement, according to General Hershey, was to bolster the ranks of scientists and technicians, many of whom would serve defense-related industries. In 1965 Hershey wrote, "The process of channeling manpower by deferment is entitled to much credit for the large number of graduate students in technical fields and for the fact that there is not a greater shortage of teachers, engineers and scientists working in activities which are essential to the national interest."

The campus-based antiwar and draft resistance movements deserve much of the credit for exposing the class-biased system of channeling to public scrutiny. The antiwar critique of channeling is often neglected by those who glibly accuse movement participants of hiding behind their student deferments. As one draft resistance manifesto put it: "Most of us now have deferments. . . . But all these individual outs can have no effect on the draft, the war, or the consciousness of this country. . . . To cooperate with conscription is to perpetuate its existence. . . . We will renounce all deferments." Though most young men in the antiwar movement kept their deferments or found other ways of evading the draft (a small group did accept prison sentences for resisting the draft), the major thrust of their effort was to keep *all* Americans from fighting in Vietnam. By drawing attention to the inequalities in the system, they helped generate support for the draft reforms of 1967 and the draft lottery of 1969. The 1967 reforms included the elimination of deferments for graduate school. (Those who had already begun graduate school were, however, usually allowed to keep their deferments.) This reduction in deferments was a key factor in raising the portion of college graduates who served in Vietnam from about 6 percent in 1966 to 10 percent in 1970.

Still, there were many ways to avoid Vietnam after graduating from college. In addition to seeking medical exemptions, one of the most common was to enlist in the National Guard or the reserves. In 1968, fully 80 percent of American reservists described themselves as draft-motivated enlistees (see table 4). The reserves required six years of part-time duty, but many men who joined believed correctly there was little chance they would be mobilized to fight in Vietnam. President Johnson rejected the military's frequent request for a major mobilization of the reserves and the National Guard. He feared that activating these units would draw unwanted attention to the war and exacerbate antiwar sentiment. Since these men were drawn from specific towns and urban neighborhoods, their mobilization would have a dramatic impact on concentrated populations. Johnson also realized that reservists and guardsmen were generally older than regular army troops and were, as a group, socially and economically more prominent. By relying on the draft and the active-duty military to fight the war, Johnson hoped to diffuse the impact of casualties among widely scattered, young, and powerless individuals. He wanted, as David Halberstam put it, a "silent, politically invisible war."

During the war over a million men served in the reserves and National Guard. Of these, some 37,000 were mobilized and 15,000 were sent to Vietnam. As the war continued, thousands of men tried to enlist in this relatively safe form of military service. By 1968 the National Guard alone had a waiting list of 100,000. Throughout the country the reserves and the guard were notorious for restrictive, "old-boy" admissions policies. In many places a man simply had to have connections to get in. For the poor and working class it was particularly difficult to gain admission. In the army reserves, for example, the percentage of college graduates among the enlisted men was three times higher than in the regular army.

For blacks, whatever their economic standing, to become a reservist or guardsman was nearly impossible. In 1964 only 1.45 percent of the Army National Guard was black. By 1968 this tiny percentage had actually decreased to 1.26. Exclusion of blacks was especially egregious in the South. In Mississippi, for example, where blacks comprised 42 percent of the population, only 1 black man was admitted to the National Guard of 10,365 men. In the North, the guard was only slightly more open. In Michigan, for example, only 1.34 percent of the National Guard was black, compared with 9.2 percent of the population. Thus, the safest form of military service almost entirely excluded blacks and was most open to middle-class whites.

The Selective Service System's class-biased channeling, the military's wartime slashing of admissions standards, Project 100,000, medical exemptions that favored the well-informed and privileged, student deferments, the safe haven of the National Guard and the reserves—these were the key institutional factors in the creation of a working-class military. But these are not the only factors that encouraged working-class boys to serve so disproportionately. In many respects our whole culture served to channel the working class toward the military and the middle and upper classes toward college. We can understand some of the more complex influences by exploring the consciousness of young men who fought in Vietnam—specifically, their prewar understanding of their place and purpose in American society and how they perceived the prospect of military service and war. That is the subject of chapter 2. However, before proceeding we need a brief account of common, middle-class assumptions about how working people thought about the Vietnam War, for these images and stereotypes still distort much of the thinking about our subject.

## Wartime Images of a Hawkish Working Class

That the Vietnam War was a working-class war may not be surprising news, but it has never been widely and publicly acknowledged or discussed. For that matter, class issues of any kind have rarely been a focus of common, explicit debate in American public life. Indeed, the very existence of class has been denied, diminished, or distorted by the institutions most responsible for establishing the terms of public discourse: the large corporations (including, of course, the major media), the schools, and the two major political parties.

During the war, the mass media gave little serious attention to the relationship of the working class to Vietnam. Instead, the subject was presented in an indirect and distorted way that reduced workers to a grossly misleading stereotype. Rather than documenting the class inequalities of military service and the complex feelings soldiers and their families had about their society and the war in Vietnam, the media more commonly contributed to the construction of an image of workers as the war's strongest supporters, as superpatriotic hawks whose political views could be understood simply by reading the bumper stickers on some of their cars and pickups: "America: Love it or Leave it." These "hard-hats" or "rednecks" were frequently portrayed as "Joe six-pack," a flag-waving, blue-collar, anti-intellectual who, on top of everything else, was assumed to be a bigot.

This caricature really began to crystallize in 1968 during the presidential campaign of George Wallace. The segregationist, prowar governor of Alabama surprised experts by winning 8 million votes for his third-party candidacy, many of them coming not only from white southerners, but also from white working-class voters in the North. Yet, this support was too easily taken as evidence that the working class was the most racist and prowar segment of American society. While those characteristics certainly drew many voters to Wallace, his success also reflected a deeply felt anger and disillusionment that had as much to do with class position as it did with race and war. Wallace appealed to the fear many working-class families had that their values—love of country, respect for law and order, religious faith, and hard work—were being ridiculed and threatened from above and below, by privileged campus protesters, ghetto rioters, and Great Society liberals who seemed always to talk about helping the poor without regard for the millions of working-class people just one rung up the economic ladder.

Wallace mobilized this anger, in both 1968 and 1972, by lashing out at "limousine liberals," "pointy-headed intellectuals," and "dirty hippies and protesters." Those were the people, Wallace claimed, who were running America, and who, in so doing, were always "looking down their noses at the average man on the street—the glass workers, the steel workers, the auto workers, the textile workers, the farm workers, the policeman, the beautician and the barber and the little businessman."

President Nixon courted these same "average" Americans when he called on the "forgotten Americans" to rally in support of his Vietnam policies. These people, he claimed, comprised "the great silent majority." The idea that workers formed the vanguard of this supposed majority and would break their

silence to support Nixon became a media commonplace during the tumultuous month of May 1970. The month began with Nixon's announcement
that American troops would invade Cambodia. Coming in the wake of reas-
surances that U.S. troops were being withdrawn, that the war was winding
down for America, and that the South Vietnamese were taking over the fighting, Nixon's sudden expansion of the war generated an enormous new wave of
antiwar protest. Students at more than 500 college campuses went on strike.
At one of them, Kent State, four students were killed by national guardsmen.
To Pentagon officials, Nixon described the student protesters as bums.

A few days later, on 8 May, antiwar demonstrators—most of them from
New York University and Hunter College—held a rally in the financial district of New York City. Construction workers at several large building sites in
lower Manhattan had heard about the rally a day or two in advance and
planned, as one of them put it, to stage a counterdemonstration and "bust
some heads." At noontime on the day of the rally, about 200 construction
workers, wearing their yellow hard hats, carrying American flags, and chant-
ing "All The Way USA" shoved through police lines and began beating the
antiwar demonstrators with their fists and helmets. Some used tools. At least
a few police were seen standing by as the attack continued.

From Wall Street the workers, their ranks enlarged to 500, marched to city
hall, where the American flag was flying at half-mast, on Mayor John Lindsay's
orders, in memory of the four students killed at Kent State. The workers
demanded that the flag be raised. When it was, the men cheered and sang "The
Star-Spangled Banner." Then, observing an antiwar banner at nearby Pace College, the workers broke down the glass doors of a Pace building and beat more
students. Throughout the day, dubbed "Bloody Friday" by the media, about
seventy victims were injured badly enough to require treatment.

Some workers reported that the attack was far from spontaneous and
that it had been orchestrated by union leaders in the Building and Trades
Council of Greater New York. Even so, the leaders seemed to have no trouble
finding volunteers. Two weeks later the council, perhaps hoping to offset the
violent imagery of Bloody Friday, organized a peaceful march to demonstrate
their "love of country and love and respect for our country's flag." *Time* magazine described it this way: "Callused hands gripped tiny flags. Weathered
faces shone with sweat. . . . For three hours, 100,000 members of New York's
brawniest unions marched and shouted . . . in a massive display of gleeful
patriotism and muscular pride . . . a kind of workers' Woodstock." These
events were crucial in shaping an idea that came to dominate middle-class
thought about the war—that the "hawks" were workers and the "doves" were
privileged. As the *New York Times* put it, "The typical worker—from construction craftsman to shoe clerk—has become probably the most reactionary political force in the country."

This stereotype received perhaps its most significant dramatization a few months later in the form of Archie Bunker, hero of the situation comedy "All in the Family." Archie could be counted on for mindless verbal swipes at blacks, Jews, feminists, and peace activists ("coloreds," "kikes," "libbers," and "pinkos"). But rail as he would against his long list of enemies and the liberal views of his "meathead" son-in-law, Archie's hostility was cushioned by a larger family devotion. While the nation came apart at the seams, the Bunkers kept their conflicts "all in the family." Part of the show's liberal condescension was to suggest that the working class, however retrograde in its views, does not really act out its hostilities and is therefore essentially harmless.

Of course, the image of the hawkish worker (be it Archie Bunker or the hard-hats of Bloody Friday) had enough surface familiarity to serve for many as a sufficient model of a whole class. After all, many working-class people certainly did support the war. But was the working class as a whole really more prowar than the rest of society? (Or more racist?) Not so. In fact, virtually every survey of public opinion on the war found little or no difference between the responses of the working class and those of the middle and upper classes. There were, in other words, at least as many hawks in corporate office buildings as there were in factories. Part of the problem with the hard-hat stereotype is that it made white, Christian males the symbol of the entire working class. The working class, of course, includes women, blacks, Hispanics, Jews—an enormous variety. Polls suggest that the three groups most consistently opposed to the war over time were blacks, women, and the very poor. Yet, even white, working-class men were far less conservative as a group than Archie Bunker. One survey, taken in the same year the media invented the term *hard-hats* (1970), found that 48 percent of the northern white working class was in favor of immediate withdrawal of American troops from Vietnam, while only 40 percent of the white middle class took this dove position. Moreover, while the New York construction unions continued to be prowar, members of the Teamsters and the United Auto Workers had turned against it. In 1972, a higher percentage of blue-collar workers voted for peace candidate George McGovern than did white-collar professionals.

There was, however, one very telling difference between the war-related attitudes of workers and the middle class. More workers were openly opposed to antiwar demonstrators. One study found that even one-half of those workers who favored immediate and total withdrawal from Vietnam were nevertheless opposed to antiwar demonstrators. This, I think, indicates that working-class anger at the antiwar movement—primarily a middle-class movement—often represented class conflict, not conflict over the legitimacy of the war. The union men who marched in the New York City parade carried signs that said "Support our boys in Vietnam." The sign can be read quite literally. Many of their sons were in Vietnam. Working-class people opposed college protesters largely because they saw the antiwar movement as an elitist attack on American troops by people who could avoid the war. At its best, the antiwar movement tried to correct that perception by focusing its criticism on the people in Washington who planned the war and kept it going. But class division—inflamed by the politicians and institutions that ran the war— continued to muddy the ideological water. A significant segment of the student antiwar movement explicitly denounced the unequal distribution of power and privilege in American society, but to many workers the demonstrators seemed at once to flaunt and deny their own privileges. How, they wondered, could college students possibly claim to be victims (of police brutality, of bureaucratic university administrators, of an inhuman corporate rat race that provided meaningless work) when they were so obviously better off than workers who endured far more daily indignity and mind-numbing labor? A firefighter who lost his son Ralph in Vietnam told Robert Coles:

> I'm bitter. You bet your goddamn dollar I'm bitter. It's people like us who give up our sons for the country. The business people, they run the country and make money from it. The college types, the professors, they go to Washington and tell the government what to do. . . . But their sons, they don't end up in the swamps over there, in Vietnam. No sir. They're deferred, because they're in school. Or they get sent to safe places. Or they get out with all those letters they have from their doctors. Ralph told me. He told me what went on at his physical. He said most of the kids were from average homes; and the few rich kids there were, they all had big-deal letters saying they weren't eligible. . . . Let's face it: if you have a lot of money, or if you have the right connections, you don't end up on a firing line in the jungle over there, not unless you *want* to. Ralph had no choice. He didn't want to die. He wanted to live. They just took him—to "defend democracy," that's what they keep on saying. Hell, I wonder.
>
> I think we ought to win that war or pull out. What the hell else should we do—sit and bleed ourselves to death, year after year? I hate those peace demonstrators. Why don't they go to Vietnam and demonstrate in front of the North Vietnamese? . . . The whole thing is a mess. The sooner we get the hell out of there the better. But what bothers me about the peace crowd is that you can tell from their attitude, the way they look and what they say, that they don't really love this country. Some of them almost seem *glad* to have a chance to criticize us. . . . To hell with them! Let them get out, leave, if they don't like it here! My son didn't die so they can look filthy and talk filthy and insult everything we believe in and everyone in the country—me and my wife and people here on the street, and the next street, and all over.

This man is not, by any thoughtful definition, a hawk. He wants the war ended, if not in victory, then by immediate withdrawal. He has serious doubts about the purpose of the war. As his wife says, "I think my husband and I can't help but thinking that our son gave his life for nothing, nothing at all." But they can't abide "the peace crowd." The husband believed the demonstrators cared more about the Vietnamese than they did about ordinary Americans. His wife responded:

> I told him I thought they want the war to end, so no more Ralphs will die, but he says no, they never stop and think about Ralph and his kind of people, and I'm inclined to agree. They *say* they do, but I listen to them, I watch them; since Ralph died I listen and I watch as carefully as I can. Their hearts are with other people, not their own American people, the ordinary kind of person in this country. . . . Those people, a lot of them are rich women from the suburbs, the rich suburbs. Those kids, they are in college. . . . I'm against this war, too—the way a mother is, whose sons are in the army, who has lost a son fighting in it. The world hears those demonstrators making their noise. The world doesn't hear me, and it doesn't hear a single person I know.

Since the Vietnam War, the world continues to hear very little from or about such women. In the Reagan era, however, it also stopped hearing about the experiences of people of any class who opposed the war. Lost in the silence was the awareness that a significant number of American troops themselves turned against the war in its final years. By the late 1960s, some soldiers in Vietnam began to write UUUU on their helmet liners, meaning the unwilling, led by the unqualified, doing the unnecessary for the ungrateful.

# Missing In Action: Women Warriors in Vietnam
## Carol Lynn Mithers

For years after the American military defeat in Vietnam, the war vanished below the surface of a country that wanted only to forget it. It did not go away. Nearly a decade after the last American troops left Southeast Asia, Vietnam resurfaced in a cathartic flood of memoirs, novels, poems, songs, studies, analyses, and films, all seeking to explain, understand, or in some way come to terms with what had happened there. Vietnam veterans, once reviled as "baby-killers," or feared as men of uncontrolled and unpredictable violence, reemerged as heroic Christlike figures who paid for the sins of an entire nation. Yet, even as Vietnam-related material poured out (at times threatening to turn the war into a small cottage industry), one important group of war stories remained untold. Virtually all Vietnam memoirs and novels were written by men. All war analyses and studies were written *about* men. But men were not the only ones who went to war.

About ten thousand women served with the U.S. military in Vietnam. The vast majority were nurses, low-ranking officers, but there were also enlisted women working as communications, intelligence, and language specialists, air-traffic controllers, and aerial reconnaissance photographers. As a group, they were different from the men who carried the guns, on the average several years older and more educated. They were overwhelmingly white and middle-class; idealistic, often deeply religious "good girls" for whom the admonition to "ask what you can do for your country" was not political rhetoric but a moral imperative. All had volunteered to join the military; many specifically requested assignment to Vietnam.

Like the men with whom they served, however, most knew nothing about the country of Vietnam, the politics of the war raging there, or the realities of war in general. Introduction was immediate and brutal, the first sight, for instance, of a "typical patient: a double amp. No legs, the bones and muscles and everything showing, like a piece of meat in a butcher shop."[1]

That introduction set the tone for the year to come, a time one woman later likened to "a fast forward on a tape."[2] On the one hand, Vietnam offered women the kind of intense comradeship and community that makes so many men recall war with nostalgia:

> There was no place to go . . . so you always met outside your hooches and you'd sit in the quadrangle and you'd watch the stars. And everybody was there together, there with maybe popcorn; or maybe it wouldn't be everybody, it would be just one or two people and everything would come out because there was time for you to talk about everything, and you talked about everything from the time when you were small till you were old. . . .
>
> It's hard to explain how everybody felt about everybody. We would sit around and we would just sort of be amazed at how close we all were and we knew it would never happen again. Most of us would never have this experience again.[3]

Moreover, for women raised in an era when women lived within narrow, rigidly prescribed boundaries, a year in Southeast Asia promised a rare chance for independence and adventure. For nurses, it also offered an opportunity to escape the subservient roles they had always played in civilian life. Treated by doctors as fully valued medical team members, constantly called on to master new skills and put everything they already knew into practice, Vietnam became what almost every nurse would recall as the absolute peak of her professional career.

But service in a war that had no front and was everywhere also meant fear and danger. Although women in Vietnam were classified as "noncombatants," the cities and hospital compounds where they worked received their share of mortar and rocket attacks. The red crosses on the hospitals, commented one nurse, "just gave [the enemy] something to shoot at."[4] The war's massive number of casualties—some 58,000 dead and at least 300,000 wounded—and one of the best medical evacuation systems in history (bringing men from combat to emergency room in half an hour) brought nurses an endless horror show of death and mutilation. Seventy-hour operating room shifts were spent patching bodies blown apart by mines, ripped by bullets and shrapnel and burned by napalm; helicopters came in "filled with hundreds and hundreds of body parts, arms, legs, heads. . . ."[5] Every nurse had one case she couldn't forget, one man who symbolized for her all the war's waste and carnage: the shrieking, traumatized GIs who arrived at the emergency room carrying the headless body of a friend; the man so incinerated he was "just a lump, like a burned marshmallow, and there was a tube at one end and this rasping breathing—aaaah!—like that";[6] the man carried into the

E.R., "just the trunk of a guy, no arms, no legs, not a spot on him where there's not a frag wound, blinded, but he still has his nose and mouth and he's screaming that he wants to die. . . ."[7]

Perhaps anyone who witnesses such scenes is left with indelible emotional scars. But it's one of war's central requirements, particularly for those who must deal with its casualties, that it be fought for a purpose so clear and important that people can bear sights like an armless, legless man begging to die because they are able to attach some meaning to his suffering. In Vietnam, it often seemed there was none. Not only did the reasons offered for U.S. involvement appear too flimsy to support the weight of so much pain and death, the day-to-day reality of the war itself seemed insane and out of control. There were the dead civilians and children, the atrocity stories told by both sides. There were the GIs dead from drug overdoses and from "friendly fire," and soldiers' stories of their leaders' deadly ineptitude. Nurses often treated both Vietnamese civilians and POWs, and, to their own dismay, many found themselves coming to share the GIs' open racism against the "gooks"—"we'd take some Vietnamese guy who was really injured and give him an extra hard ride over to the operating room table, really give him a hard jolt when we dropped him down. . . ."[8] And the jarring disjunction between the war as publicly reported and personally experienced suggested that either the U.S. government had no idea what was going on or was deliberately lying.

Male soldiers dealt with the war's unacceptable contradictions by using drugs, striking out against the Vietnamese and each other, and, ultimately, refusing to fight. Women drank, smoked, "partied hard," and had affairs that too often just brought more grief. Some nurses, forbidden to fraternize with enlisted men, became involved with doctors, most of whom were older and married, in relationships that ended abruptly and painfully when the men's tours of duty were up; others saw men they'd been dating brought into the emergency room in body bags. Some became cynical, some became bitter, many—like one nurse at the 27th Surgical Hospital in Chu Lai—learned to stop feeling anything at all:

> The first three months, I'd get off work and write letters home describing what I'd seen, and cry while I wrote. After three months, I realized I couldn't keep allowing myself to be open to that kind of emotional trauma or I wasn't going to make it. I pulled up the barriers around myself. I stopped crying and I stopped writing letters home. I really numbed out.
>
> What was so hard to take was a sense of tremendous helplessness about an absolutely insane situation. I almost think if I hadn't had that, I could've remained open to some degree, allowing myself to grieve, because then the grieving would have had some meaning. But this was

going on just because no one had a sane handle on it. That's what was so devastating. I saw this stupid thing happening, and there wasn't anything I could do to make it change. All I was doing was picking up the pieces.[9]

Like male GIs, women finished their tours of duty and were abruptly dropped back into civilian life. The adjustment was, at best, difficult. Women who'd been dealing nonstop with life and death had no patience for the more trivial concerns of normal American life. Nurses had "attitude problems" when it came to resuming their old "handmaiden" relationships with doctors, and missed being as needed as they had been in Vietnam. The continuing debate about the war raised conflicting emotions. Hardest of all, there was no way for a woman to come to grips with, or even acknowledge, what she had been through because it seemed that no one wanted to hear. Brush-offs, whether intentional or not, came from friends and family, from male vets who were absorbed with their own problems, and from the Veterans Administration, whose hospitals often lacked the facilities to give women the most basic health care. Isolated from each other, reluctant to identify themselves as veterans because the public image of a military woman was a lesbian, a whore, or a loser looking for a husband, the women tried to go on with their lives, and waited for the war to go away.

It didn't. Exposure to injury and death is one of the best predictors for Post Traumatic Stress Disorder (PTSD).[10] And although those beginning to acknowledge PTSD as a problem for male veterans ignored "noncombatant" women, and nurses themselves often opted for denial "because it's sort of a thing with health people never to cop to any of your own problems,"[11] still, the problems were there. Some women found themselves having olfactory hallucinations of the smell of pseudomonas, an infection common among burn patients. Others had nightmares of being shot at while running across a field or of being sought out and hurt by badly wounded men. Still others had flashbacks:

> At first it was as though I was daydreaming. What scared me to death was that I couldn't turn it off. . . . The cow grazing in the field became a water buffalo. Fields marked off and cross-sectioned became cemeteries. We flew over his tent . . . and suddenly it became the 18th Surg. . . . I started to cry, I couldn't control myself. I saw blood coming down onto the windshield and the wiper blades swishing over it. There was blood on the floor, all over the passenger area where we were sitting. The stretchers clicked into place had bodies on top of them.[12]

In 1982, the first study of women's experiences in Vietnam and their aftereffects showed what several other studies and individual accounts would later confirm: that this was a group of people seriously, often permanently, affected by their Vietnam service. Significant percentages had suffered anxiety and depression, insomnia, nightmares, war flashbacks, thoughts of suicide. Nearly half felt some emotional numbness; over half an inability to trust or become close to others. Sixty-five percent said they felt alienated from the government, and 57 percent felt they had been used by it. Included in those "symptoms" reported as still present in their lives by over half the responding women were: alienation; hypersensitivity to issues of fairness, justice, and legitimacy; cynicism and mistrust of government; and ideological changes and confusion in value systems.[13] "I don't believe anything I'm told by the government now," said one nurse who returned from a year in the busy operating room of the 12th Evacuation Hospital in Cu Chi with "an explosive temper" and the ability to hear a helicopter coming long before anyone else in the room.

> There's something all of us know who've been to Vietnam. It's not particularly how we were victimized. I guess it's being demythed. Pretty painful to go through. See, everybody else is real comfortable with their lives. We're all pretty much haunted by what happened to us, what we saw, what went on, why it happened. Maybe I could live a more peaceful life not knowing the things I found out.[14]

The experiences that women had in Vietnam were profound and painful; the stories that women Vietnam veterans have to tell are powerful, compelling, and add a new dimension to what we know about the war. In fact, once one becomes aware of them, there comes an inevitable question: why did they remain unheard for so long? To be sure, over the years, women's presence in Vietnam merited occasional notice. Two novels called *Vietnam Nurse* were published in 1966; "the view of the Vietnam war as a locale for a sort of extended prom date is certainly unusual," commented one later reviewer.[15] A third with the same title, published in 1984, was also a "romance," this one an attempt at soft-core pornography, although its descriptions of female sexual response are so strange they suggest the book was written by a male virgin.

An episode of the old "Quincy, Medical Examiner" television show dealt with a Vietnam nurse suffering from PTSD; the film "Purple Hearts" was a love story set around a Vietnam hospital. The oral histories in *Nam*, by Mark Baker (1981), and *Everything We Had*, by Al Santoli (1981), contained some women's stories. In 1982, Patricia Walsh, who worked for the U.S. Agency for International Development as a civilian nurse-anesthetist in Danang, published *Forever Sad the Hearts*, the story of a civilian nurse in Vietnam; in 1983, Lynda Van Devanter's *Home Before Morning* became the first autobiographical account of an army nurse's Vietnam experience. But such books and accounts—even the ludicrous ones—comprised but a negligible percentage of

Vietnam literature, and never really penetrated the public consciousness. As late as 1981, a chapter entitled "Women and the War," written by a respected journalist for a mainstream Vietnam book, confined itself to feminism and the antiwar movement; women who went to Vietnam were never even mentioned.[16]

This silence becomes more understandable, however, when one looks beyond Vietnam. Few women's voices have been heard in the history of *any* war. That is not because they haven't been present in those wars, haven't suffered and died. Women were found among the slain at Waterloo,[17] women served as seamstresses, spies, and soldiers during the American Revolutionary War,[18] and as nurses during the American Civil War. (Louisa May Alcott, best known for the sentimental *Little Women*, first made her reputation with *Hospital Sketches*, an account of her time as a Civil War nurse.[19] The experience was deeply traumatic—while in Fredericksburg, Alcott caught typhoid pneumonia and was sent home "hallucinating and furious much of the time, plagued by scenes from the hospital. . . . From time to time she would say, 'If you will only take that man away, I can bear the rest'.")[20]

During World War II, more than 800,000 Soviet women and girls served at the front,[21] and 100,000 Yugoslavian women fought after their country's regular army was destroyed; 25,000 died. In Italy, 25,000 women fought as partisans; 624 were killed or wounded. Fifteen—most of whom had been caught by the Germans and tortured to death—were awarded Italy's Gold Cross for Military Valor.[22] Sixty-seven Army nurses survived the defeats of Bataan and Corregidor and spent nearly three years in a Japanese POW camp in the Philippines.[23] Army nurse Genevieve de Galard spent weeks stranded in the French garrison during the battle of Dien Bien Phu, the only woman and nurse to care for the 6,000 soldiers wounded and killed.[24] Eight American women died in Vietnam; by 1968, according to the North Vietnamese government, 250,000 Vietnamese women fighters had been killed and 40,000 disabled.[25] And when women have written of their wartime experiences, as did Vera Brittain, who served as a nurse during World War I, they have been movingly eloquent:

> "The strain all along," I repeated dully, "is very great . . . very great." What exactly did those words describe? The enemy within shelling distance—refugee Sisters crowding in with nerves all awry—bright moonlight, and aeroplanes carrying machine-guns—ambulance trains jolting noisily into the siding, all day, all night—gassed men on stretchers, clawing the air—dying men, reeking with mud and foul green-stained bandages, shrieking and writhing in a grotesque travesty of manhood—dead men with fixed, empty eyes and shiny, yellow faces. . . . Yes, perhaps the strain all along *had* been very great. . . .[26]

Women's Vietnam stories remained unheard and untold for so long because what women have to say has *never* been considered a legitimate part of war's history. Women who went to Vietnam shared with men the horror, contradictions, and aftereffects specific to this particular war and, with earlier generations of women, an exclusion specific to their sex: there has always been a place for women to serve in war, but there is no place for them in its mythology.

The terrible truth about war is that for all its horror it is powerfully appealing. The visual allure of war's spectacle, the passionate feelings of comradeship engendered in those who defy danger to work towards a common goal, the intensity of coming face-to-face with death, and the opportunity to "escape [from] the cramping restrictions of an unadventurous civilian existence"[27] often seem much more exciting and meaningful than what peace can provide. The promise of transcending ordinary existence makes war mythical; within that mythology, those who've experienced the war are forever set apart and made special: they have proved themselves in a war as civilians have not, they know something civilians never will. War stories, wrote former Marine and *Newsweek* editor William Broyles, are "not meant to enlighten but exclude. . . . I suffered, I was there. You were not. Only those facts matter."[28]

War's attractions call out to women as well as to men—certainly women historically have had far more "cramping restrictions" and "unadventurous existences" from which to want escape. The physical ability to *be* in a war, to endure hardship and danger, to kill or be killed, has no gender requirements. Being admitted to the inner circle of the war's elite, however, is a very different story.

Throughout history, cultures and societies have assigned men and women very different social roles. Men, by "nature" harsh, aggressive, and violent, take as their province the dangerous "outside" world of politics and marketplace, while women, compassionate, nurturing, and fragile, are keepers of the "inner" arena of heart, hearth, and home. War not only extends those roles, with men fighting "as avatars of a nation's sanctioned violence" and women acting as "the collective 'other' to the male warrior,"[29] it becomes an arena for *proving* them. The standards for being a "real" soldier— "courage, endurance and toughness, lack of squeamishness when confronted with shocking or distasteful stimuli, avoidance of display of weakness in general, reticence about emotional or idealistic matters"[30]—are identical to those of stereotypical "real" masculinity. Going to war, then, is not simply a test of "courage" or "endurance" (or even patriotism) but of *manhood*: someone who becomes a warrior has become a "real" man.

"Real" men, of course, are the opposite of women; the imagery of sexual domination and women as inferior "other" permeates all levels of war's mythical universe. "Pussy!" the drill sergeant shouts at the recruit who isn't making it, "*Woman!*" "I didn't just screw Ho Chi Minh," Lyndon Johnson said after the passage of the Gulf of Tonkin Resolution in 1964, "I cut his pecker off."[31] Although women require the presence and attention of men to "prove" their femininity, men cannot become men except in the *absence* of women. If combat is to "make" men, women cannot be included. "War," said General Robert H. Barrow, Commander of the U.S. Marines, in 1980, "is man's work."

> Biological convergence on the battlefield would not only be dissatisfying in terms of what women could do, but it would be an enormous psychological distraction for the male who wants to think that he's fighting for that woman somewhere behind, not up there in the same foxhole with him. It tramples the male ego.[32]

War mythology does, of course, assign women a place. As civilians, points out Jean Bethke Elshtain, they stand on the sidelines as goads to action, weepers over war's tragedies, male surrogates mobilized to meet manpower needs, and witnesses to male bravery. On or near the battlefield, they may be healers, reminders of home, pure incarnations of all that men must fight to protect, or sexual objects—whores, rape victims, battle "spoils."

In Vietnam, military women might be assigned to any or all of these categories. Wearing perfume and hair ribbons to remind men of gentleness and femininity, they were sometimes idealized. "Someone wakes up on your O.R. table and says 'Oh my God, I've died and gone to heaven and you're an angel'," recalled one nurse.[33] Such "canonization" had its drawbacks.

> If the guys wanted to . . . screw ninety-seven prostitutes in a day, it was to be expected. "Boys will be boys." Every PX stocked plenty of GI issue condoms and according to the grapevine, some commanders even went so far as to bus in Vietnamese girls for hire to keep morale high. However if we wanted to have a relationship, or to occasionally be with a man we cared deeply about, we were not conducting ourselves as "ladies should." And if we might be unladylike enough to want birth control pills, which were kept in a safe and rarely dispensed, we could expect the wrath of God, or our commander, to descend upon us.[34]

As the only "round-eye women" around, they also were descended on by American men wherever they went, a deluge in which the difference between flattering popularity and sexual harassment often became blurred. Over half of the 135 former Vietnam nurses surveyed in a Northwestern State University study reported having suffered sexual harassment ranging from simple insult to rape. One nurse was offered a Bronze Star to sleep with her commander; another, who was threatened by a patient, was scolded for being "seductive."[35] One nurse who had gone with friends to a pilots' party learned that the men had plans for them.

> I said, "Hey, you know there's a room full of mattresses back there and some of the guys are getting the girls pretty drunk." There was also a lot of opium and a lot of dope. "We got to get out of here."
> We tried to put up a united front. Those of us who were reasonably sober practically carried the drunk ones to the chopper pad and tried to get someone to give us a ride home. The guys were furious. We thought it was going to be a gang rape, that's how bad it was. The GIs called the nurses "round-eye tail," and suddenly that's exactly what we were.[36]

Within such traditional categorizing, however, what women were really doing in Vietnam got lost. Certainly the gap between myth and reality was most dangerous where it concerned women's role as "noncombatants": according to one article in the military paper *Stars and Stripes*, a Harris poll found that 75 percent of women veterans had been "in or exposed" to hostile fire and combat.[37] Noncombatant status, said one nurse, simply meant that "we couldn't shoot back."[38] Added another, "I realized that [GIs] were trained to survive in a war zone but that I was not—that I could get killed. . . . The Army never taught me anything—I mean anything. Nothing. Everything I learned about surviving I learned from the men."[39]

But similar contradictions could be found everywhere. In *Home Before Morning*, Lynda Van Devanter describes a nurse's rescue of a wounded man from a flaming helicopter. Afterwards, the head nurse puts in her name for a Bronze Star with a "V" for valor. The Star comes, but without the "V"—it cannot, says the commanding officer, be awarded to a nurse.[40] And just as Vera Brittain discovered in 1918 that her devastating experiences as a combat nurse in France made her "merely the incompetent target for justifiable criticism, since a knowledge of surgical nursing did not qualify me for housekeeping,"[41] women who returned from Vietnam were told that what they had seen, felt and done did not really "count." Lynda Van Devanter described trying to join a veterans' antiwar march:

> When we moved outside to line up, I took a place near the front. However one of the leaders approached me. "This demonstration is only for vets," he said apologetically.
> "I am a vet," I said. "I was in Pleiku and Qui Nhon."
> "Pleiku!" he exclaimed. "No shit! I used to be with the 4th infantry. You must have been at the 71st Evac. . . . You folks saved my best friend's life. . . ."
> "Do you have a sign or something I can hold?" I asked.
> "Well," he said uncomfortably, "I . . . uh . . . don't think you're supposed to march."
> "But you told me it was for vets."

"It is," he said. "But you're not a vet."

"I don't understand."

"You don't look like a vet," he said. . . . "You can't be a member of our group. I'm sorry."[42]

Another nurse, who had served at Cu Chi and Danang, got the same message from different sources.

For the past twelve months I'd made decisions about whether someone was going to live or die. I got into this [county] hospital and was told I could not hang a pint of blood unless a doctor was standing there. I kept getting called in by the head nurse: "You've really got an attitude problem. You're no longer in Vietnam." Like, who do you think you are? I went through a severe depression in 1978 and I remember telling the shrink I had been in Vietnam and he just brushed that over and said "Tell me about your childhood." Just brushed it aside as if it wasn't important at all.[43]

If post-Vietnam America did not want to deal with men who symbolized a lost war, it did not know *how* to deal with women who simply could not be made to fit into any of women's traditional wartime categories. Women who'd spent a year in combat boots and mud- and blood-stained fatigues working at or near the front weren't clichéd, self-sacrificing Florence Nightingales or breathy, bouncing Hot Lips Houlihans. One name that might have suited them was "soldier"—certainly someone who'd worked around the clock in an operating room that was sometimes under fire, numbing her emotions while piecing together burned and mangled bodies had exhibited strength, courage, endurance, toughness, and lack of squeamishness in large measure.

But if being a man was the antithesis of being a woman, and if one *became* a man by becoming a soldier, how could soldiers be anything but men? If going to war was, "for those men trying to fulfill society's expectations, part and parcel of displaying their male identity and thus qualifying for the privileges it bestows,"[44] by definition, warriors simply *could not be women.* To close the gap between the myth and reality of what women do in war, writes Cynthia Enroe, "would require that military officials resolve their own ideological contradictions."[45] Instead,

women *as women* must be denied access to "the front," to "combat" so that men can claim a uniqueness and superiority that will justify their dominant position in the social order. And yet because women are in practice often exposed to frontline combat, the military has to constantly redefine "the front" and "combat" as wherever "women" are not.[46]

And if that meant that ten thousand women were left with bad dreams, problems they were told they had no right to have, and experiences they were informed did not "count," then that was something they would have to work out themselves.

During the mid 1980s, the silence surrounding women veterans seemed to break. A flurry of newspaper and news magazine articles introduced America to its "forgotten vets." The House of Representatives instructed the Veterans Administration to provide for an epidemiological study of the effect of herbicides on women who had served in Vietnam. Colonel Mary Stout, a former Vietnam nurse, was elected head of Vietnam Veterans of America. Although a movement to place the statue of a nurse next to Frederick Hart's three male soldiers at the Vietnam Memorial Wall in Washington, D.C. was thwarted by the Federal Commission on Fine Arts, three women's oral history collections (incorporating the testimonies of combat nurses, enlisted women, and civilian volunteers for organizations like the Red Cross, USO, and American Friends Service Committee) were published during that same year by the mainstream press.

Hollywood, too, which had previously shied away from Vietnam nurse features and movies-of-the-week (perhaps because multiple amputations and third-degree body burns were considered problematic in terms of entertainment value) began to discover women. Patricia Walsh's *Forever Sad the Hearts* went into development at Paramount as a feature film for Cher, and Lynda Van Devanter's *Home Before Morning* went into development as a possible CBS miniseries. Ironically both quickly became embroiled in the kind of political infighting familiar to male veterans. Walsh, claiming that Van Devanter "portrayed medical teams in an utterly disgusting fashion," formed a group called Nurses Against Misrepresentation, whose efforts were centered around preventing *Home Before Morning* from reaching the small screen.[47] (So far, neither film has been made.) And 1988 marked the premier season of "China Beach," a television series set at a large medical evacuation and R&R area, whose main characters were a combat nurse, a USO entertainer, a Red Cross "donut dolly," and a prostitute/black marketeer.

Certainly much of this burst of attention was attributable to the war's sudden emergence as a "hot" (i.e., eminently saleable) commercial and cultural topic. "China Beach," for instance, came on the heels of the series "Tour of Duty," itself spawned by the success of the feature film "Platoon."

Perhaps equally important, according to Joan Bethke Elshtain, was the *way* the War was increasingly coming to be viewed: once a reminder of national shame and defeat, Vietnam was "being reconstructed as a story of universal victimization."[48] Of course, women as victims was an image America could accept with no trouble at all.

Embracing the notion that everyone suffered and no one is to blame for what happened in Vietnam has been a way for this country to avoid facing the truth about the war and the challenges which defeat poses to our most basic assumptions about ourselves and the world. Similarly, portraying women Vietnam veterans *only* as victims (as most book and magazine articles have done), or trying to fit their wartime experiences into male war movie genre conventions, as "China Beach" almost always does, is just another way of ignoring the more complex reality of who such women were, what they did, and what it meant. Moreover, such an approach virtually guarantees that women's accounts of military service will not endure beyond a brief existence as novelty byproducts of Vietnam's currently "fashionable" status. In *The Perfect War*, James William Gibson points out that because they have regarded only high-level "official" accounts as sources of information and ignored the stories of men who actually fought, conventional assessments of what happened in Vietnam have been both skewed and incomplete. True understanding of the war, he says, requires accepting the validity of what he calls "the Warrior's knowledge."

Women's voices can complete that understanding. First, however, women must be accepted as warriors. Their knowledge of war must come to be considered legitimate. Most of all, their accounts of Vietnam must be viewed as *war stories*—stories that are *different* from those of men but no less valid, stories that, like men's, both constitute a war's history and create its mythology. "Writing women's history," points out one writer, ". . . involves much more than digging up some little-known facts; it means redefining historical categories like war."[49]

That, of course, is not easily done. One can't redefine war to legitimize women's experiences without confronting, on a number of levels, its social and sexual mythology. Feminists remain divided by conflicting beliefs about war, uncertain if women are inherently pacifist and war itself is a masculine creation or if true equality means allowing women to pick up weapons and join men on the battlefield. The belief that only war can "make" a man continues to haunt men who escaped service in Vietnam only to suffer "Viet Guilt" (or, more accurately, "Viet Envy") years later:

> Like 17 million other men who came of age during Vietnam. I did not
> serve in the armed forces. It was a blessing, then, to have escaped; it is a
> burden now. I find there is something missing in me. . . . Those like me,
> who, for one reason or another, did not serve, suffer because we chose
> not to perform a primary and expected rite of passage. We were never
> inducted, not merely into the Army, but into manhood.[50]

The old belief that war imparts some mysterious, specifically masculine, knowledge lingers in the mind of women like the writer whose short story appeared in a 1985 issue of *Mademoiselle*:

Ellen sees her brother, separated from his unit. She tries to imagine his being ambushed by the two Vietcong in the jungle, as Warren explained matter-of-factly he had been, how they had damaged his spine with his own hand grenade, attempting to set it off between his legs. She cannot, she doesn't have the words or the understanding, not a metaphor, to describe it to herself. No wonder men seldom spoke in intimacy; the things they needed to air were unspeakable.[51]

The old belief that women can't know war silences even women who should know better, women who *do* have the words and understanding and metaphor to describe a man crippled by a grenade. In a documentary aired in 1985, one nurse recalled being caught in the rain on a gunboat in Vietnam. "I was thinking," she said, "this is what *real war* [my emphasis] must be like."[52]

As long as the old war mythology holds, the experiences of women will never have legitimacy. But a male-dominated culture of war, especially one that seeks to perpetuate itself, has nothing to gain and everything to lose by acknowledging and incorporating the experiences of women Vietnam veterans. To admit that women serve and suffer in war is to destroy the claim to special male knowledge and all the privileges it brings. To admit that they have been in danger and acted heroically is to contradict the myth that they need to be protected.

Most of all, to hear the stories of women whose intimate knowledge of war is of its wreckage is to contradict the most basic myth of war's glory—to change forever a tradition in which we hear about those who have gained manhood from war, not those who've been castrated by it; in which we identify only with the victors; in which the camera quickly pans over the dead to focus on the survivors. "War," wrote William Broyles in *Esquire*, "may be for men, at some terrible level, the closest thing to what childbirth is for women: the initiation into the power of life and death."[53] Within the mythology of war, the warrior, a man who kills, who sees himself holding "the power of life and death," can imagine himself a god. The woman who has seen warriors weeping and calling "Mommy!", who knows that in the end war comes down to blood, pain, and broken bodies, can only remind him that he is not.

## Notes

1. Kathryn Marshall, *In The Combat Zone* (New York: Little, Brown, 1987), p. 214.

2. Ibid., p. 134.

3. Dan Freedman and Jacqueline Rhoads, *Nurses in Vietnam: The Forgotten Veterans* (Austin: Texas Monthly Press, 1987), pp. 129, 135.

4. Author's interview with Pamela White, 1984.

5. Author's interview with Chris McGinley-Schneider, 1984.

6. Marshall, *In The Combat Zone*, p. 133.

7. Interview with Pamela White.

8. Ibid.

9. Author's interview with Pat Miersma, 1984.

10. John P. Wilson and Gustave E. Krauss, "Predicting Post-Traumatic Stress Syndromes Among Vietnam Veterans," *Proceedings* of the twenty-fifth Neuropsychiatric Institute Conference, Veterans Mental Center, Coatesville, Pennsylvania, October 25, 1982, 37.

11. Interview with Pamela White.

12. Freedman and Rhoads, *Nurses in Vietnam,* p. 22.

13. Jenny Ann Schnaier, "Women Vietnam Veterans and Mental Health Adjustment: A Study of Their Experiences and Post-Traumatic Stress," Master's thesis, University of Maryland, 1982.

14. Interview with Pamela White.

# The Tet Offensive and Its Aftermath

## Ngo Vinh Long

### Introduction: Background and Motivation

By 1967 the American "war of attrition" and its "pacification program" had failed in Vietnam, allowing the National Liberation Front (NLF) to control most of the countryside in South Vietnam. Confronted by the deteriorating situation in the South, the United States intensified its air campaign against North Vietnam to unprecedented levels. Throughout 1967, the United States hoped that the bombing would persuade the North to end NLF attacks in exchange for a bombing halt. It was under these circumstances, in October, that the Central Committee of the Democratic Republic of Vietnam (DRV) decided to carry out a series of widespread offensive operations against urban centers in South Vietnam. The NLF leaders wanted to remind U.S. leaders that their main enemy was in the South and not in the North. They also hoped that these operations would convince the United States to end the bombing of the North and begin negotiations.

The attacks began during the Vietnamese New Year in 1968, and thus were labeled the "Tet Offensive" in the West. The offensive was composed of three phases, lasting until October of that year. During the first phase, which lasted from the end of January to the beginning of March, the NLF strike force achieved dramatic gains while receiving relatively light casualties. In my opinion, at this point the attacks should have been broken off, with military forces retreating into the countryside to consolidate their gains in newly liberated areas. Instead, Politburo members decided to mount the second and third phases of the offensive. As a result, the revolutionary units were left too long in forward positions around the urban areas, where they were subjected to horrendous air and artillery strikes. In addition, after the third phase was mounted, American and Army of the Republic of Vietnam (ARVN) troops "leapfrogged" over the revolutionary forces who were still massed around the urban areas to attack them from the rear as well as to take over liberated areas. Caught on the outskirts of these urban areas, the revolutionary units not only suffered heavy casualties in 1968, but also were unable to return to the countryside in time to provide the necessary protection to NLF political cadres and sympathetic rural supporters confronted by the Phoenix program, an accelerated pacification program, and so on.

Worse still, the Vietnamese leadership in Hanoi made one of the biggest errors in the war by ordering the remnants of the revolutionary units in the South to retreat to the border areas of Cambodia and Laos to regroup. This was tantamount to surrendering populated areas of the South to the U.S. and ARVN forces without a fight. When NLF units decided to return to the villages to help rebuild the revolutionary infrastructure, they paid a high price for their absence. In addition, northern units sent south in 1969 and 1970 could not operate effectively and suffered large casualties due to the fact that they did not have the necessary grassroots tactical input or fifth-column support which had existed before 1968.

In the views of most southern revolutionary fighters, 1969 and 1970 were the two most difficult years in the entire war. Initiative was reclaimed only after the southern revolutionaries rebuilt connections between villagers and soldiers in 1971 and 1972. This rebuilding process was done mainly through the tactic of *bam tru* or "clinging to the post (remaining close to the people)." This took place even as U.S. and ARVN troops invaded Cambodia and Laos in 1970 and 1971. In fact, these invasions and the simultaneous increase in NLF urban operations actually served to divert allied troops from the rural areas of South Vietnam and provided the Communist forces with a sufficient respite to recover from its Tet losses. This is a new point of view—one which I first presented in 1988. It is based on the most current research from both the American and Vietnamese official records, and it runs counter to previous works. These focus only on selected U.S. records to draw conclusions about Tet which in total are not borne out by my more in-depth research.

## The Current Misconceptions About Tet

With this in mind, I have written this chapter as part of my ongoing effort to combat what I perceive to be an increasing effort—in official and mainstream academic works on the war in both the United States and Vietnam since the end of the war—to claim that the North Vietnamese Army (NVA) played the decisive role in the liberation of the South not only during the final days but also for years before, starting with Tet. Officials in the DRV have even resorted to restricting debate on the conduct of the war so that the official party line would remain unchallenged. An example of this occurred in 1982, just after the publication of General Tran Van Tra's memoirs, when Communist Party officials arbitrarily banned the book even though it contained only a mild and indirect criticism of the official conduct of the war. Perhaps most surprising was the fact that Tra had been the commander of the B-2 NLF region (Saigon III and IV Corps), and deputy supreme commander of all the revolutionary forces in the South.

## *The New Communist View of Tet*

The best example of the turmoil in postwar Vietnam was the exclusion of southern political leaders and military commanders from the Defence Ministry's "Scientific Conference for an Overall Assessment of the Spring Offensive of 1968," held in Ho Chi Minh City, March 1–8, 1986, and hosted by General Hoang Van Thao, a northerner. Historically this was an insidious exclusion since the majority of the division, brigade, and regimental commanders during Tet were southerners. More than anyone they knew how the offensive unfolded and how party directives were implemented during the period from 1968 to 1972.

Of particular note, Tran Bach Dang, the planner of the attack on Saigon, and Communist Party leader in the Saigon-Giandinh-Cholon area during Tet, was not invited. When he was finally allowed to publish an article on Tet in February 1988, he pointed out that a number of powerful party leaders had prevented even a cursory analysis of the Tet policy-making process. According to Dang, almost all historical writings in Vietnam, including local party histories in the South, had to follow politically correct guidelines (*lap truong*) in order to be published. As a result, these articles did not reflect the reality of what occurred during Tet.

The fact that Dang's article was published in an official journal indicated that by early 1988 there was at least some official recognition that suppression of the debate over the Vietnamese revolution was counterproductive. Indeed, at the previously mentioned November 1988 conference held in Hanoi, (see unnumbered note at the end of this chapter) I spoke directly to this issue by introducing information gathered from interviews with NLF military personnel and political cadres from key provinces in the South.

I realized that my analysis was quite different from the official views in Vietnam at the time of the conference and might be seen as controversial. Still, I hoped that the Vietnamese might use this as an opportunity to break with the practices of the past, at least in order to promote political accommodation and integration in Vietnam. Present during my presentation were Generals Cao Pha and Hoang Phuong—associate director and director of the Military History Institute in Hanoi. General Pha followed my paper with a presentation on the Tet Offensive and General Phuong concluded with the Nixon years. Together their papers paralleled my own.

Both men repeatedly commented on the quality of my work and depth of my research, and except for disagreement on minor details, strongly seconded my conclusions. To the surprise of the Americans present General Pha even endorsed General Tra's earlier view of Tet in both his 1982 book and an article published in the February and April 1988 issues of the *Journal of Military History* (Vietnamese).

Tra's essay was spirited, but measured. It is an account which I believe cannot be fully understood without a close examination of the literature in Vietnam and a thorough understanding of the underlying political currents and political struggles during the 1980s. General Tra accused some prominent party leaders of having come close to agreeing with reactionary American Tet analysts in their effort to deny southern revolutionaries their achievements during the Tet Offensive. Tra declared that, by 1967, the Politburo had already decided that it was impossible to have a complete victory while the American and ARVN forces were nearly five times larger than the total forces of the revolutionaries.

In October 1967, Resolution 14 or the Quang Trung Resolution—after Emperor Quang Trung, who defeated the Chinese in Tet 1789—was passed by the Central Committee. It envisioned the future of the war as follows:

> 1) the "highest victory" of forcing the U.S. to enter into negotiations to end the war; 2) partial success which would nevertheless allow the U.S. and Saigon forces to retake important areas and continue the war; and 3) complete failure which would encourage the U.S. to bring in more American troops and to extend the war to North Vietnam, Laos, and Kampuchea.

However, the Politburo also ordered continuous attacks until the first objective was achieved. According to Tra the first phase of the offensive did bring about the intended success, since it forced the United States to limit bombing in the northern panhandle area and open preliminary talks. Tra, however, argues that this was only a ploy by the Johnson administration to control U.S. public opinion in preparation of a reescalation of the bombing throughout Vietnam. Realizing this, Politburo leaders ordered the second and third phases of the offensive to commence. Tra believed this was a mistake because of the subsequent carnage inflicted on the NLF in 1969–1970 and the delay in serious peace negotiations until 1972. Conversely, Tra also argues that it took the second phase of the offensive to force the United States to join the Paris peace talks. He also points out that it was not until November 1968, two months into the third phase, that President

Lyndon B. Johnson finally ordered the complete cessation of the bombing of the North and announced the beginning of a four-party peace conference. Tra went on to say,

> This was only easily understandable in wars such as a gigantic war like this last one in Vietnam. Results on the battlefields were the key and deciding elements for political and diplomatic developments. . . . There was never such a thing as snatching political victory from the jaws of military defeat or gaining diplomatic success without blood having been spilled and bones scattered on the battlefield. . . . because of the extraordinary efforts during the three phases of the Offensive by the revolutionary fighters and their supporters in the South, a decisive victory and a strategic turning was achieved.

In his aforementioned paper General Phuong noted the intensity of the American and ARVN counterattacks on all fronts during the Nixon era, declaring that 1969 and 1970 were the worst years for the revolution in the South. However, he also argued that because Nixon expanded the war into Cambodia and Laos he subjected allied forces to some of their worst defeats of the war. He implied that the success of the regular northern forces (People's Army of Vietnam/PAVN) in Cambodia and Laos were principally responsible for Communist gains in the South, and ultimately in Paris. The general also agreed with me that NLF forces recovered primarily through their use of the *bam tru* policy, which also facilitated the return of large numbers of PAVN forces. Moreover, he supported my contention that the escalating urban opposition to the Saigon regime in the South also contributed to the recovery of the NLF and brought about subsequent military and political successes.

These views have been supported by articles and books published in Vietnam during the last five years. An example of this is the lead article in the *Journal of Military History* in which Tran Vu discusses the magnitude of and the reasons for the Communist military success in 1971. He analyzes several Communist victories in South Vietnam and points out that the ARVN suffered 232,000 casualties. Vu insists that this proves that through increased NLF activities in the South

> our main force units were again able to return one by one to the battlefronts and to reinforce the base areas along the western corridor of the central provinces, in the Highlands, in the eastern provinces of the South, and in the Mekong Delta. The enemy's resolute effort to push our main force units beyond the borders [of the South] therefore had failed miserably by this time.

He goes on to say that these guerrilla activities against the pacification and Phoenix programs helped double the population in the liberated areas to nearly 3 million and expand the contested areas to 7,240 villages with over 11 million inhabitants. This not only provided revolutionaries with a contiguous area throughout the South from which to operate but also helped solve their logistics and supply problems. Vu credits the large opposition movements of women, students, workers, and intellectuals in the United States and in southern urban areas for isolating the Saigon regime and for causing doubts about the Vietnamization program among officials in Saigon and the United States. All these factors led to further defeats for the allies in 1972 which, along with timely diplomatic initiatives by Hanoi and the NLF, finally forced the Nixon administration to agree to sign the Paris peace accords.

In recent years the Vietnamese have participated in freer discussions of the war. Moreover, there has been significant reassessment of official positions regarding the war. Although there is still a lot of disagreement in Vietnamese literature on the relations between the Hanoi regime and the NLF, this is something Vietnamese historians and analysts seem determined to unravel in the future.

## The Right-Wing View, Still in Vogue in the United States

What remains a concern to me is that in the United States, with only a few exceptions, right-wing interpretations of Tet and its aftermath seem to have gained acceptance even among authors who are considered liberals by their peers. Two recent examples illustrate this point. In a book he dedicated to "the young Americans who fought in the Vietnam War . . . and those who opposed it," George Donnelson Moss reiterates the three main arguments of the American right on Tet. First, Moss asserts that Tet was a desperate act by the NLF and PAVN undertaken because the war had been going badly. He says that by the spring of 1967,

> many Vietcong units and some NVA units fighting in South Vietnam had been decimated. Others had been driven out of South Vietnam or forced to take refuge in sparsely populated . . . central highlands. The NLF infrastructure controlled fewer villages and less territory in South Vietnam than it had at the time when the Twelfth Plenum had decided to fight attrition with attrition.

Second, Moss argues that the first phase of Tet not only represented a major military defeat for the NLF, but also destroyed the NLF as a political organization in the South. He estimates that during the first three months of 1968, Viet Cong and PAVN losses totaled nearly 58,000. Thus, he declares that the VC, who had undertaken the majority of the attacks, "were largely destroyed as an effective military menace to the South Vietnamese." He also argues that in a large number of the southern provinces "the Vietcong political infrastructure, . . . painstakingly erected over the years," was destroyed during Tet. Specifically, Moss maintains that

> The VC cadres had come out into the open to organize and to lead the uprisings that were expected to follow the assaults on the towns and cities. The expected uprisings never materialized, and the VC cadres were eliminated. Nowhere in South Vietnam did risings occur. Nowhere in South Vietnam were the Vietcong welcomed by the Vietnamese people, nor did any defections from GVN [government of Vietnam] political or military ranks occur. In fact, the ARVN forces fought well despite being caught by surprise. After Tet there was no chance that the Saigon regime would be overthrown by a revolution from within South Vietnam. After the spring of 1968, the Vietnam war became, for the most part, a conventional war between the main forces units.

Finally, Moss reiterates the ultimate right-wing myth that while Tet was a military defeat for the NLF it was a psychological victory. The American military leadership both in Saigon and the United States viewed Tet as a great tactical victory. Moss goes on to say that General William C. Westmoreland, commander of MACV,

> was eager to mount a major counteroffensive and . . . win the war. But Tet-68 proved to be the great paradox. . . . Tet brought Americans defeat encased within victory. . . . The scope, scale, and intensity of the Vietcong Tet offensive shocked most Americans. Nightly, television news beamed the sights and sounds . . . of battles in Saigon and Hue into American living rooms. . . . Initial wire stories, later corrected, exaggerated the Communist successes, contributing to a widely shared sense that Tet had been an allied disaster.

The remainder of his book basically agrees with the right wing that by allowing the enemy to snatch victory from the jaws of defeat during Tet the United States not only made it possible for the eventual North Vietnamese conquest of the South but also for the rise of the so-called Vietnam syndrome.

Another variation on this theme is contained in James J. Wirtz' book *The Tet Offensive: Intelligence Failure in War*, published in 1991. The entire book is an elaboration of the author's key points made in the introduction:

> Dire consequences usually follow a disastrous defeat. Ironically, the allies defeated the communists decisively during Tet. From the communist perspective, the offensive was a gamble, even a desperate gamble, taken to offset the overwhelming resources, mobility, firepower, technological sophistication, and professionalism of their opponent. The North Vietnamese and Vietcong hoped that the attacks would foster a revolt of the southern population against the government, thereby adding tens of thousands of combat-

ants to the communist side. When the offensive failed to spark this insurrection, communist commanders lacked the resources needed to attain ambitious objectives, and the allies defeated their widely scattered forces piecemeal. . . .

If the communists failed to win the Tet offensive, what then accounts for its effect on American perceptions of the war in Vietnam? Ultimately, the shock it produced was the catalyst that led to the reevaluation of U.S. policy. The Tet attacks failed on the battlefield, but U.S. forces did not anticipate fully the scope, intensity, targets, and timing of the offensive. The allies suffered a failure of intelligence during Tet, a failure that set the stage for changes in U.S. strategy.

He concludes that "over the longer term, Tet marked the beginning of what Ronald Reagan called the 'Vietnam Syndrome': a period of public disillusionment with military intervention, defense spending, and an active anticommunist approach to foreign affairs."

The facts indicate to me that this is an entirely specious argument. Indeed, the "Vietnam syndrome" fallacy has been exposed by a long list of U.S. interventions in Third World countries since Tet and by the incredible increases in U.S. defense spending under Presidents Carter, Reagan, and Bush. To be sure, this fallacy allowed President Bush to rush headlong into the Gulf War and to announce later that the United States had "kicked the Vietnam Syndrome for good" and had "buried it in the desert sand of Saudi Arabia."

There is also no need to waste any words on an effort to discredit the argument that Tet was a decisive military defeat for the NFL/NVA and that the United States could have won the war had it not been for the psychological shock created by the military intelligence failure, exaggerated media reports, and so on. By implying that the war was lost in the United States and not in Vietnam, American writers have knowingly or unknowingly prolonged postwar recriminations within the United States. Worst still, in their treatment of Tet and its aftermath they have ignored or distorted the facts by suggesting that PAVN forces did most of the fighting in the South after the spring of 1968. They would have us believe that southerners never again played any significant role. As we shall see, this a deeply flawed argument.

## Desperate Gamble? An Analysis of What Really Happened During Tet and After

Is there any factual basis for the claim that by the spring of 1967 the NLF had largely been expelled from southern population centers to jungle hideouts along border areas? Was this really the reason Communist leaders decided to launch the desperate Tet Offensive gamble? A look at some 1967

Western news reports indicates that the revolutionaries were winning politically and militarily throughout South Vietnam.

The Associated Press reported on February 4, 1967, that during the previous month the NLF had enjoyed a series of military successes and therefore the number of American casualties was three times higher than during the same period the year before.

*Le Figaro* reported on February 15 that by the end of 1966 ARVN forces had suffered several disastrous defeats, that the number of desertions had consequently reached a monthly figure of 500 per regiment, and that Pentagon generals were obliged to admit that the pacification program had become a complete failure.

A Reuters dispatch on March 11, 1967, quoted Major John Wilson, the senior U.S. advisor in Long An Province, as saying,

> For every hectare we pacify, we have devoted to this province more men, more dollars and other means than any other province in South Vietnam. Yet, the results of these efforts are meager. . . . In reality, we can control only a very small area, according to the required norms. I would say that we control only four percent in the daytime and only one percent during the night.

The March 20, 1967, issue of *U.S. News and World Report* cited a report from the Senate Armed Services Committee saying that "at the end of the dry season, the Viet Cong still controlled 80% of South Vietnamese territory." In fact, NLF forces moved into many town and cities at will. The May 24 *New York Times* reported that

> enemy forces overran Quang Tri city, the province capital, freed 250 guerrillas from jail and successfully attacked two regimental headquarters of the South Vietnamese First Infantry Division. . . . A few days later, in a series of events that were not fully reported at that time, they moved virtually unmolested into Hue, while the army and national police fled.

On August 7, the *New York Times*, citing official U.S. statistics, stated that out of 12,537 hamlets in the South, Saigon controlled 168. On the other hand, those totally controlled by the NLF numbered 3,978. The rest of the hamlets were listed as "contested" or partially controlled by both sides. In the *Pentagon Papers*, the 1967 official U.S. "Hamlet Evaluation System" (HES) report admitted that "recent reports state that to a large extent, the VC now control the countryside."

Confronted by this deteriorating situation in the southern countryside, the Johnson administration, according to the *Pentagon Papers*, escalated the air war in the North during 1967. They hoped that the North would persuade the NLF to call off southern attacks in exchange for a bombing halt. This was what LBJ called his "peace offensive." It was later dubbed the "San Antonio Formula," since he presented it in a speech in San Antonio, Texas, on September 29, 1967. When DRV officials resisted such tactics Johnson denounced them as intransigents and stepped up the bombing.

Meanwhile, to delude the American public into believing that the Saigon regime was becoming more popular and was therefore worthy of increased support, U.S. leaders helped organize a series of "democratic elections" to legitimize General Nguyen Van Thieu as president and General Nguyen Cao Ky as vice president. The elections were a cruel farce. Thieu and Ky openly used troops and police to intimidate voters and rivals alike. They even dispatched General Nguyen Ngoc Loan, director of the National Police, to force members of the National Assembly to disqualify most serious opponents. Those who were permitted to run were constantly harassed, detained, and treated to all the worst kinds of political dirty tricks.

Even with these tactics, with the exclusion of voters in "insecure" areas as well as those dubbed sympathetic to the NLF, pacifists, or neutralists, and with rampant ballot box stuffing by soldiers and police, Thieu and Ky received 34.8 percent of the national vote. They lost outright in many larger cities such as Saigon, Danang, and Hue. The Assembly's Special Election Committee disclosed in late September that at each of 5,105 polling stations, composing nearly 90 percent of the national facilities, had each committed at least eleven violations. This was, in fact, all the violations provided for in the election laws. According to the elections laws, the National Assembly should have nullified the election if the number of voters at these polling places totaled over 800,000.

On October 1, 1967, the day before the Assembly was scheduled to vote to ratify the election, combat police blockaded all the streets to the National Assembly and General Le Nguyen Khang, commander of the 3rd Military Division, brought his army into Saigon. The following day, General Loan brought his guards into the National Assembly balcony, drew out his pistol, propped up his feet, and began drinking a beer. The implication was clear. Two hours later, Assembly members voted fifty-eight to forty-three to ratify the election. An hour later the body was dissolved. The Johnson administration immediately declared a victory for democracy in South Vietnam and vowed to do all it could to defend the new government.

It was under these circumstances that DRV Politburo members decided to initiate the Tet attacks against southern cities. This was not a desperate gamble but a calculated move designed to persuade U.S. leaders to deescalate the air war and start negotiations. According to Tran Bach Dang, who planned the 1967 attack on Saigon, the idea of a "general offensive" against urban areas in the South—especially against Saigon, which was the nerve center of the allied war effort—was to create shock waves in the South, and thus, force a turning point in the war. But this plan was not new. It had been conceived as a possible plan of action by NLF leaders as early as 1960.

In 1964, a plan of action similar to the 1968 Tet plan was introduced to the Communist Party's Central Committee. At that time there had been sufficient sappers units in the South to carry out the initial attacks. But the regular and regional forces were still not strong enough to deliver the necessary follow-up assaults. In addition, the political organizations in and around the cities and towns were considered inadequate for providing the necessary support to sustain the attacks. Moreover, in 1964 Communist leaders believed that such a general offensive would have the effect of sucking into Vietnam a huge number of American troops because the American "hawks" would be able to argue that the introduction of U.S. forces would help change the situation in the South. The plan was therefore temporarily shelved by the Central Committee. Instead, they directed southern revolutionaries to lay better groundwork for such an offensive in the future by building up their military and political forces.

By mid-1967 the Politburo and the Central Office of South Vietnam (COSVN/Trung Uong Cuc) ordered that the details of a contingency plan for attacks on Saigon and other cities be worked out. They reasoned that widespread attacks against the urban centers, which were the nerve centers of the U.S.-backed Saigon regime, would compel American leaders to pull back most U.S. forces to defend these southern centers, thereby easing their military pressure on the North. They conjectured that by that time the United States had nearly 500,000 troops in the South. They believed this was very nearly the maximum that the United States was capable of sending. Thus, they reasoned that a general offensive would demonstrate to American leaders and citizens that they had no hope of winning and hence would force them into negotiations and troop withdrawals. Representatives from the Politburo, COSVN, and B-2 Military Command, and the Saigon-Giandinh Regional Party Committee held several meetings from July to October to debate the Politburo decision and to discuss details for the offensive.

Finally, on October 25, 1967, party Central Committee members issued Resolution 14, ordering a "general offensive/general uprising" or "tong cong kich/tong khoi nghia" in the South mainly against Saigon and the upper Mekong Delta provinces. The main aims of Resolution 14 are best summarized by General Tra's aforementioned paper as follows:

> The upcoming general offensive/general uprising will be a period, a process, of intensive and complicated strategic offensives by military, political and diplomatic means. . . . The general offensive/general uprising is a process in which we will attack and advance on the enemy continuously both militarily and politically.

At this point Communist planners hypothesized that U.S./ARVN troops would counterattack savagely in order to reclaim important lost positions.

According to most southern revolutionary leaders I interviewed, they defined the offensive as a "process" involving a continuous, protracted, and varying struggle, not just military attacks. They believed that over an extended period this constant and unrelenting pressure would force the United States to enter into negotiations. At this time this concept was repeatedly emphasized in all Communist directives at all levels. Since then it has also been consistently repeated in the writings of many southern leaders and revolutionaries.

Tran Hoan, later minister of information of the Socialist Republic of Vietnam (SRVN), wrote in 1978 that before the Tet Offensive he was instructed by the secretary of the party Regional Committee of Tri Thien (northern half of Saigon's I Corps), Lieutenant General Tran Van Quang, to send out a directive to all the cadres and soldiers stressing that the

> general offensive/general uprising is a process. . . . I repeat, a process. A process of extremely arduous and complicated military combats and protracted political struggles. At present our cadres and soldiers are still quite simplistic in their thinking on this issue. . . . It is wrong and dangerous for them to think that the general offensive/general uprising is a one-blow effort.

In 1986 General Quang, then first deputy minister of defense, delivered a paper to the aforementioned Defense Ministry conference on Tet. It indicates that while no one regarded the upcoming offensive as a desperate gamble, there were considerable strategic and tactical differences of opinion between Hanoi and the people in the field. He recalled that the Ministry of Defense relayed the decision to carry out a general offensive/general uprising in October. When party Regional Committee members from the Military Command of Tri Thien met to discuss it they cited Lenin's dictum that you should not fool around with an uprising and that an uprising means that you have to carry out continuous attacks in order to assure any kind of success.

In spite of these reservations the conferees suggested to the Ministry of Defense that if a general offensive/general uprising had to be carried out, they should wait until April or May 1968 to give the local forces enough time to make the necessary preparations. As far as the Tri Thien area was concerned, the conferees requested that the Ministry supply two additional regiments of infantry, two 105mm artillery battalions, one antiaircraft battalion, and 400 tons of ammunition. The Ministry responded by saying that the party leaders and military commanders of Tri Thien should wait for further decisions to be personally delivered by Le Chuong, the political commissar of the Tri Thien Military Command, who was at the time in Hanoi. Le did not deliver the message until December 3, 1967. It stated that there should be attacks in all areas mainly through the use of local forces, and that Hue should be liberated by its own revolutionary cadres and forces. This, they asserted, would divert enemy forces from the main theater of the war, which was Saigon. Tri Thien leaders also learned that the time for the offensive had been set for sometime during the Tet New Year's celebration of 1968.

General Quang recalled that the Ministry decision was met with both fervor and trepidation by those in Tri Thien. Excitement was high since they were going to take part in a large offensive aimed at the eventual liberation of the South and peace in Vietnam. They were fearful because they were not sure that they had enough power to carry out the task ahead. Eventually they decided that since their main tasks were to cause diversion and draw enemy forces from Saigon they would try to occupy Hue for five to seven days. For this they believed they had enough resources. General Quang adds that they made this decision because they expected the Ministry to send necessary reinforcements as needed.

Quang claims that on December 25 a representative from the Politburo arrived and reminded local leaders that "the general uprising is a process," resulting in a continual series of attacks. These orders were not well executed. Instead of holding some forces in reserve for the second and third phases of the offensive local leaders threw almost all their forces into the initial attacks in direct contradiction to the scenario envisioned in Resolution 14. Another mistake was the initiation of "such a large campaign with such high objectives without having reserve forces on the spot and relying instead on reinforcements from the Ministry which never arrived while the battlefields were not yet prepared."

The careful wording in General Quang's paper glosses over some very sensitive areas that we cannot go into here, partly because the details involved would require a great deal of time to clarify. However, what emerges from his words is some clear reservation regarding Resolution 14 by the majority of southern revolutionaries. In short, it seemed that a strategy of continual attacks and a general uprising would bring more U.S. pressure, which was contradictory to the Communists' announced goal. General Hoang Van Thao addressed this issue in his summation of the 1986 conference: "On this point, almost all of our comrades agree that it is incorrect both in practice and in theory. We have all clearly seen the results of mounting one phase of general offensive/general uprising against the urban areas when favorable conditions no longer existed."

## No General Uprisings Meant No Popular Support?

Another dubious argument forwarded in the United States is the assertion by many that since there was no real general uprising during Tet there was no popular support for the NLF. However, as seen above, there was great popular support for the NLF before the Politburo issued the directive for the Tet Offensive. It is also important to define, especially to my U.S. readers, what the term "general uprising" or "tong khoi nghia" really meant to the revolutionaries at that time, and why uprisings, as understood or interpreted by Americans, did not happen.

At the 1986 Tet conference General Tran Do, the second most senior northern general in the South during the war, said that he had long analyzed the term *tong cong kich/tong khoi nghia*. *Cong kich* is the Sino-Vietnamese equivalent of the Vietnamese *tan cong*, and *khoi nghia* is a classical Chinese translation of the Vietnamese term *noi day*. This tactic of "attack and uprise, uprise and attack," or *tien cong va noi day, noi day va tan cong*, had been used by southerners throughout the war; it meant that military attacks had to involve the support of the population, and with this support there could be more attacks at a future time. The classical Sino-Vietnamese word *tong*, or "general," put in front of *cong kich* and *khoi nghia*, therefore suggested something similar to the regular NLF tactic of "simultaneous uprising" or *noi day dong loat*, which involved military attacks with logistical support by the population over a large area to avoid concentrated counterattacks by the enemy.

What was perhaps different in 1967 was that the term "termination point" or *dut diem*, used as a verb to mean "to take over a target completely," was a favorite term in the South. Hence, General Do said he and other commanders might have been thinking of this term as they began Tet. This was perhaps the reason why, of the three scenarios mentioned in Resolution 14, only the first was what those in the field were thinking about. This is especially true given the fact that by this time everyone was impatient and wanted to bring an end to the war. General Do added that had the Politburo given the campaign a less ambitious name such as "large offensive" or "strategic offensive" and had it stated clearly the campaign's limited objectives, then the people in the field would have been able to come up with better plans for the attacks and would have made better use of the forces available to them.

However, what is even more significant is General Do's explanation of the term *dut diem*. He declared that the southern commanders and population had constantly advised him and the armed forces against adopting this tactic. Their reasoning was that after taking over a target, the PAVN forces had to leave since they could not defend it. This left the local population to bear all the consequences of destructive retaliation by the enemy. Southern commanders had always worked to maintain and assure the safety of the local population in all military campaigns. In other words, the key players in the war in the South had a very different notion of uprising from the northern policy makers or American analysts.

Tran Bach Dang has written that at that juncture in the war, when the United States was dropping bombs on the towns and cities of the South in the hope of driving out the revolutionaries, "uprising" can not be understood by analyzing paradigms drawn from the Russian October Revolution, the French Revolution, or even the August 1945 revolution in Vietnam. It can only be understood in terms of the *dong khoi* or "simultaneous uprisings" in Ben Tre Province in 1959–1960, when the people there used a wide variety of methods to gain political control. Dang added,

> "Uprisings" in a war situation had to appear in different forms: the taking over of administrative power in the working-class neighborhoods, the disbanding of the puppet administrations, the patrolling of city streets, the searching out of secret police and informers, the maintaining of security and order, the organizing of the population to give direction and supplies to the soldiers, the transporting of weapons and the caring for the wounded. . . . The extent to which these were carried out differed from neighborhood to neighborhood, but in the entire city [of Saigon] this unusual atmosphere did occur.

General Quang said that before the offensive against Hue, they had already agreed that there would be no way urban inhabitants could stage any kind of uprising unless the revolutionary armed forces destroyed the various types of enemy forces and took complete control of each target. Even then, he declared, most southern leaders had envisioned an uprising in which youth groups would go around calling on enemy forces to surrender, local despots would be rooted out, and at the "highest level" armed bands would be formed to attack enemy forces along with the local fighters. The general added that during the attack and occupation of Hue NLF leaders saw their role as rallying from 530,000 to 800,000 inhabitants of Hue and the surrounding villages to participate in, and give support to, the Tet campaign.

As far as Saigon was concerned, in 1986 Tran Bach Dang disclosed that there had been a plan to have several student unions and youth organizations stage a Tet celebration on February 4–5, 1968, with several tens of thousands of people in the Tao Dan public garden situated in front of the Saigon Independence Palace. If sappers successfully penetrated the presidential palace and nearby national radio station, then the crowd would be sent to occupy these grounds. However, the Politburo, for some unexplained reason, decided to step up the date of the offensive at the very last minute and gave orders for NLF rebels in Hue to attack according to the revised Vietnamese lunar calendar date, which preceded other attacks by eighteen hours.

This was, according to Dang, a colossal mix-up. It not only destroyed the plan to get the Tet revelers to occupy the two locations, but it also left the sappers out in the cold without the support of the crack battalions that were supposed to carry out simultaneous follow-up attacks on key target areas.

These troops were, in fact, still nearly 100 kilometers away from Saigon when the sappers made their first assault. Consequently, since even the larger sapper units were composed of only a couple of dozen men—armed only with submachine guns and grenades—they were not able to defend the targets that they had occupied for a prolonged period in the face of counterattacks by the American and Saigon forces using helicopters and tanks. As a result, the population of Saigon had to use other means to show their support.

Pham Chanh Truc, later deputy mayor of Ho Chi Minh City, and secretary of the Youth League for Saigon at the time of the Tet Offensive, was the person responsible for organizing the celebration in the Tao Dan public garden and other activities for student groups in Saigon. In a 1988 article he wrote that "many comrades" had pointedly "cautioned" (*luu y*) him against saying anything on the Tet Offensive when the senior party leadership had not derived a consensus view on this issue. He says that this left him very frustrated and forced him to restrict himself to citing only a few facts in the article even though he was able to do much more. Even so, he described the profusion of activities by the Youth League in Saigon in detail. He described the daily "rehearsals" (*tap duot*) which began on December 20, 1967, the anniversary of the founding of the NLF. Students raised NLF flags at most schools and university campuses and distributed leaflets throughout the city. When the people's self-defense forces and sapper units simultaneously attacked twenty targets in the center of the city, his forces were in support.

As Tet neared, not only had Truc's group planned an unprecedented celebration known as the "Emperor Quang Trung Tet Festival" (*Hoi Tet Quang Trung*) but throughout the city people were ready to give support to the attacking troops in the target areas. However, since the attack date was pushed up at the last moment, the planned events had to be called off. Instead, each group and individual had to deal with things as they unfolded. Three of the incidents Truc mentions are worth recounting here.

The first was the seizure of the Ban Co–Vuon Chuoi area of Saigon by local inhabitants under the leadership of units of the Section II City Youth League. They chased away all the ARVN local forces and administrators and totally controlled the area until the morning of February 1. Meanwhile, Battalion 2 of the NLF main force had also penetrated the city from the southwest and seized the adjacent area of the city. These two areas were separated only by a traffic island known as Nga Bay. These two forces—the "uprising forces of the city population" and the NLF armed unit, as Truc called them—were literally within "arm's reach" (*voi tay*) of each other. If they had been able to link they would have become a formidable force for the U.S. and ARVN troops to deal with. However, for some mysterious reason which Truc says he still does not understand, these two forces did not know of the other's presence, even though each reported their situation to their respective headquarters. Strange things happen in war, but many southern leaders have told me privately that they had some evidence of betrayal which for several obvious reasons they feared to disclose.

The second example occurred when NLF Battalion 6 penetrated Saigon's twin city, Cholon. The Youth League organized the local population to aid in the capture of a huge area stretching all the way to the district of Binh Thoi. The inhabitants of the area supported the NLF soldiers with all the supplies and intelligence available, while students joined them to fight against enemy counterattacks.

Finally, on the evening of January 31, 1968, with refugees streaming into the city from the suburbs to avoid the cross fire, allied planes attacked the populated areas around the city in order to stop the advance of the NLF attacking forces as well as to preempt popular uprisings. Units of the Youth League immediately set up "support centers for war-displaced refugees" to support these war victims. As a result, the Saigon government was forced to subsidize these activities. In this way, with the support of the people, the Youth League was able to protect their own members and other revolutionary cadres as well as to expand the scope of their activities for months and years to come.

Truc contends that there was plenty of popular support both during and after the Tet Offensive and that whether an "uprising" as defined by some northern Politburo members occurred or not was besides the point. Likewise, almost all the revolutionary fighters that I have talked with over the years have defined both *khoi nghia* and *noi day* in terms of active political support and participation of the population. The southern revolutionaries have constantly reminded me that without this support they would not have been able to recover from this "darkest period" during their long struggle against the most powerful and most destructive war machine in the world. This leads us back to the American argument that the NLF was destroyed by the spring of 1968 and therefore after that the only threat to South Vietnam came from the North.

## Did the United States Destroy the NLF in the Spring of 1968?

This assertion is based on the claim that the revolutionary side suffered more than 58,000 casualties from January 29 through March 31, 1968. This is an exaggerated figure since the CIA estimated that the total number of PAVN Viet Cong (VC) participating in the Tet campaign was around 58,000. The U.S. Military Assistance Command, Vietnam (MACV) and General Earl Wheeler estimated that 60,000 enemy troops were involved in the offensive. Certainly not all the NVA and NLF soldiers were killed, and so the NLF could not have been wiped out. Besides, not all the Communist forces present in the South actually fought. This is borne out by what occurred in Saigon.

Saigon, as previously indicated, was the main target of the Tet Offensive and so NLF leaders assigned to it the largest number of attack forces. Besides, the sapper units already in place in the city—fifteen to twenty-two battalions, or 5,400 to 7,700 troops—were used for follow-up attacks on targets in the city once the sappers had breached them. In addition, three divisions of regulars were stationed just outside of Saigon's first strategic defense perimeter in case reinforcements were needed. The attack forces were divided into the Northern Vanguard Command (*bo tu lenh tien phuong Bac*) and the Southern Vanguard Command (*bo tu lenh tien phuong Nam*). The Northern Command, also known as Vanguard 1, was headed by Generals Tran Van Tra, Mai Chi To (political commissar at the time and later interior minister of the Socialist Republic of Vietnam), and Le Duc Anh (later minister of defense of the SRVN). Their forces were supposed to attack the districts of Cu Chi, Hoc Mon, Di An, Go Vap, Lai Thieu, Thu Duc, and Binh Tan and then finally to occupy the ARVN Divisional Headquarters compound at Quan Tre, a portion of Tan Son Nhut Airport, the military base in Go Vap, and the Saigon General Command Headquarters.

The Southern Command, also known as Vanguard 2, was commanded by Vo Van Kiet (later the second-ranking Politburo member and SRVN prime minister) and Tran Bach Dang. The forces under their command were supposed to attack from the south and southwest and then, in coordination with the sapper units, take over the U.S. Embassy, the Saigon presidential palace, the ARVN General Command Headquarters, the National Police Headquarters, the Nha Be petroleum storage compound, a portion of Tan Son Nhut Airport, and a number of other targets.

However, according to a classified study from Long An Province—which supplied most of the forces for the attack on Saigon from the south and southwest—a total of only eight battalions, all of them from the Southern Vanguard Command, penetrated these areas in Saigon. These battalions had brought along mainly light weapons, with only a few B40 grenade launchers, and so none of them was able to break through the heavily reinforced defense structures in the city in order to aid the sappers.

In 1987 General Huynh Cong Than (Tu Than), the commander of the Long An forces, told me that the reason this occurred was that the order for the offensive was not received by the Long An forces until 4:00 a.m. on January 20, 1968. In a period of only eight hours the Long An forces had to march a distance of thirty kilometers through rivers and marshes in order to slip through the defensive perimeter set up by the U.S. 9th and 25th Infantry Divisions and the defensive anchors set up by the ARVN to block the western and southern infiltration routes to Saigon. Had it not been for the active support and participation of several hundred thousand inhabitants of Long An and Saigon it would have been impossible to deliver the 200 metric tons of supplies needed for the attack.

Tran Bach Dang writes that the late attack order caught many of the NLF forces completely unprepared. The troops were out celebrating Tet and the battalion commanders were either still drunk or away on personal business. As a result, it required supreme efforts on the part of Huynh Cong Than and a handful of subordinate commanders to muster enough forces in time for the attack. In the face of the tremendous U.S./ARVN counterattacks with aircraft, tanks, and artillery, which delivered high explosives directly on positions within the city, Dang decided that the offensive should be called off to minimize casualties. He obtained permission from COSVN for the withdrawal of all armed forces from the city to the surrounding areas. As a result, casualties were relatively low. The worst casualties received by a battalion attacking from the outside was 100 killed. In the fiercest battle that the Southern Command engaged in, the equivalent of only one platoon were killed or wounded. Phase 1 of the Tet Offensive officially ended on February 5, the same day Dang left for HQ COSVN for an assessment of Phase 1 and planning of Phase 2. As Gabriel Kolko has documented, "A mere one thousand armed personnel in Saigon, with the aid of local political units, managed for three weeks to hold off over eleven thousand U.S. and ARVN troops and police."

Thus, it is clear that the NLF, for a variety of reasons, did not actually use that many troops during the first phase of the Tet Offensive and, therefore, could not have been depleted militarily, as many American writers have claimed. On the contrary, it actually extended its control of the rural areas after the first phase. During this phase the United States and Saigon were forced to pull back over 100 battalions to defend Saigon alone. As U.S./ARVN troops withdrew to defend Saigon and other urban areas, Saigon regional and local forces panicked and were easily driven off by local guerrillas. The villagers then razed the outposts and bases abandoned by these forces. This helped expand the NLF-controlled areas. In Long An Province, for example, this went all the way up to the doorsteps of Saigon. This situation was repeated in most areas along the Mekong Delta.

This expanded NLF control played a role in encouraging the Politburo and COSVN to decide to launch Phases 2 and 3 of the offensive. General Tran Do recalls that Le Duc Tho arrived in the South as the Politburo representative several days after the first phase ended. After reviewing the situation, Tho, with Politburo backing, ordered the offensive to continue. The initiation of the second and third phases subjected the NLF to increased casualties and hardships, and set the stage for the eventual loss of the bulk of

NLF-controlled areas in 1969–1970. But for the rest of 1968, even in areas close to Saigon the NLF was still doing very well.

Two examples illustrate this. One occurred in Ben Tre Province. Ben Tre, known as Kien Hoa under the Diem and Thieu regimes, is eighty-six kilometers southwest of Saigon. It was the birthplace of the "general uprising movement" (*phong tao dong khoi*) in 1960. By the time of Tet, the majority of the 115 provincial villages were under NLF control. For this and other reasons, it was the most bombed province in the Mekong Delta during Phase 1. Kolko notes that "the provincial capital of Ben Tre, with 140,000 inhabitants, was decimated with the justification, as an American colonel put it in one of the most quoted statements of the war, 'We had to destroy the town to save it.'"

Because it had been such a pivotal revolutionary province and because it was so strategically situated that it effectively blocked most of the routes to and from the lower Mekong Delta, Ben Tre became one of the priority provinces for massive counterattacks by ARVN/U.S. forces beginning in July 1968. The entire U.S. 9th Infantry Division was moved into the province to coordinate its attacks with the U.S. 117th Riverine Fleet and half a dozen battalions of southern marines and infantry units. In addition, there were massive B-52 raids and artillery shellings during this period. For example, 5,000 artillery shells were directed against the two villages of Luong Phu and Long My, Giong Trom District, while B-52s bombed these villages six times during the night of July 22, 1968, alone.

According to most of the people I talked with and according to documents I have obtained—the internal documents published by the Military Command of Ben Tre and the provincial party committee report—civilian and military casualties were relatively light throughout 1968. This occurred, in part, because as soon as the counterattacks began, the provincial NLF leaders decided to allow elderly people, women, children, and cadres who had not yet been exposed to move from those liberated areas which they expected to be hardest hit into the relative safety of the areas under the control of Saigon. Another important reason for light casualties was the fact that the NLF still held the initiative and was exacting a heavy toll of U.S./ARVN forces. In fact, in 1968 it managed to liberate an additional thirteen villages with a total population of 72,800, or 10 percent of the total provincial population. By the end of 1968, there were still seventy-two liberated villages which occupied two-thirds of all the land area in the province. As a party document on the province concludes,

> By the end of 1968, after more than a year of fighting, the armed forces and people of Ben Tre killed and removed from combat 28,562 enemy soldiers, overran 195 forts and base camps, downed 97 airplanes, sunk and burned 126 boats, and destroyed 96 armored vehicles. In addition,

Ben Tre also supplied the Regional Military Command and the Southern Military Command with three full infantry battalions, 10,130 volunteers and new recruits and 58 million dong.

The second example was the case of Long An Province, where, according to its own classified study, NLF forces and civilians received the highest casualties of all the provinces in the South during the three phases of the Tet Offensive. Interviews with southern military commanders and political leaders at the time have generally confirmed this fact. Yet, in late 1968, U.S. government officials still regarded the province as largely under NLF control.

## When and Why the NLF Lost Control

In order to understand when and why the NLF lost control of the countryside and what that meant for later years, it is important to understand how the NLF was able to gain and maintain control in the first place. I think that this can be achieved by focusing on only one province: Long An. Here I interviewed dozens of cadres and citizens in the summer of 1986. Since almost everyone I talked with supplied the same details, I will not quote them individually.

Long An is located immediately south of Saigon and was considered by the Saigon regime and the United States to be the gateway to the Mekong Delta or the back door to the city. They regarded this province as one of the most important military and economic centers in the South. The NLF considered Long An to be a crucial staging area for attacks on Saigon from the dangerously accessible southern and western directions. Hence, throughout the twenty-odd years of its involvement in Vietnam the United States determined to control Long An at all costs. The NLF, meanwhile, were just as determined to maintain control of Long An. This meant that the struggle there was one of the most desperate and savage of the war.

As early as late 1959 and early 1960, through a combination of "armed propaganda"—involving the use of many tactics to win over ARVN soldiers—and attacks on ARVN military outposts, the NLF had gained control of the province politically and economically. Militarily, the province already had three battalions of regular troops—Battalions D506 and D508, operating in the eastern half of the province, called Long An due to administrative redistricting by Saigon—and Battalion D504 in the western half, then called Kien Tuong. In addition, the province managed to send one platoon each to operate in the Saigon area and the Nha Be River area, respectively, as well as one squad to fight in the My Tho District of Dinh Toung Province.

The first important military factor contributing to the development and maintenance of revolutionary control in Long An was the building of strong military forces, especially the regular provincial units. In fact, the provincial regular forces were, in 1959, the first to be created and thus had to carry out all the activities that the district units and the village guerrillas were later to perform. By the end of 1961, the province had already managed to train enough district units and village guerrillas to fight on their own at the local levels as well as to coordinate their combat activities with the provincial regular troops. The provincial leadership selected some of the best from its various companies, platoons, and squads to lead the district, village, and hamlet units.

In each district there was an infantry company, a platoon of "special activities" or commando forces, and a platoon of "communication troops" (*cong binh*) specializing in attacks along the highways or waterways. They were equipped with submachine guns, machine guns, and other automatic weapons. In each village there was a platoon of about twenty-five to thirty guerrillas, and in each hamlet there was a squad of ten to fifteen guerrillas. To all these forces from 1964 on Long An added the so-called intravillage guerrilla units, whose members were picked from the various guerrilla platoons from adjacent villages. These intravillage units had specific duties assigned them by the district unit leaders. In addition, they had to coordinate their activities with all other forces. For example, during the 1964–1967 period the district of Can Giuoc had eighty hamlet guerrilla squads composed of 800 fighters, twenty village guerrilla platoons composed of 500 men, and three intravillage platoons. Intravillage Platoon 1 had thirty-five troops and had the job of cutting off enemy communications and detecting their movements along Route 5. Platoon 2 had twenty men and was assigned the job of harassing and taking the Tan Thanh military post, which protected the district town of Can Giuoc. Platoon 3 was supposed to cut all enemy communications on Route 15.

In the development of these three types of forces the emphasis was always placed on combat quality and not on the number of troops. For example, the official combat duties of these units were defined as follows: (1) The provincial forces had the duty of engaging regular U.S./ARVN troops and being capable of disabling each enemy company and battalion to force the eventual disintegration of a whole enemy regiment or division. At the same time, the provincial troops had to be able to overrun enemy forts and military bases having a battalion or more. (1a) The district forces had the job of attacking and destroying platoons and companies of mobile "security guards"—a type of ARVN regional unit—as well as overrunning forts and compounds held by a platoon of security guards. At the same time, the district forces had to coordinate with the provincial forces in attacking enemy regular troops. (1b) The village, hamlet, and intravillage guerrillas had to place under siege forts occupied by squads or platoons of ARVN "civil guards," or local forces, and to coordinate their activities with the district units in the attacks against the security guards. (2) The commando units could execute attacks against enemy bases, ammunition dumps, artillery positions, and so on. They could act independently or coordinate their activities with the provincial units. (3) The "communication troops" specialized in attacking enemy communications and movements along the highways and waterways.

This clear definition of responsibilities for the various forces contributed significantly to their effectiveness. This effectiveness, however, would not have been possible without the strong provincial troops, which were capable of engaging regular enemy forces entering the province. They provided the district and guerrilla forces with a protective umbrella under which to operate. To enable the regular provincial forces to accomplish all these tasks, supply and training had to be provided. Since the fighting was going on constantly, there was no time for rest, reinforcement, and/or rebuilding. This meant that in order to train new troops the various units had to take turns in combat activities, or training had to be carried out between battles. In order to ensure that each unit received all the supplies it needed, when and where it needed them, the population of Long An had to be organized for specific tasks. The successful accomplishment of all these tasks enabled the NLF to maintain its strength in, and control over, the province.

The second important military factor that contributed to NLF control in Long An was the ability of the NLF forces to destroy all attempts by U.S./ARVN forces to cut up the province and isolate the NLF forces. American and ARVN forces tried to accomplish this goal by stationing their troops in forts and bases along strategic highways and waterways supported by mobile forces using tanks, armored river patrol boats, helicopters, and air and artillery strikes.

The NLF in Long An thwarted these efforts with constant attacks against enemy troops to keep them off balance. In this effort their troop deployments were as follows: (1) The strongest provincial regulars were used against the main enemy forces operating in areas north of Highway 4, where they were strongest. This put the enemy on the defensive and created conditions for penetrating the most vulnerable areas south of the highway to obstruct the enemy's attempt to cut the province in half and to provide protection for their forces in the south. (2) District and guerrilla units were used to fight ARVN security and civil guards who were occupying the hundreds of forts and military compounds along the highways and waterways. This destroyed ARVN and U.S. attempts to divide the territory into smaller pieces in order to further isolate NLF forces. At the same time, these district and guerrilla units served to expand the areas of NLF control to provide it with freedom of movement. (3) Tightly coordinated attacks against main Saigon forces by NLF provincial troops and against forts and compounds were carried out in order to destroy the ability of the mobile ARVN forces and those in forts and bases to protect each other with a coordinated defensive strategy.

(4) Commando forces were deployed in all the district and village towns to attack the enemy's nerve centers, their artillery bases, and their supply bases. At the same time, the "communication troops" were used to carry out constant attacks along the highways and waterways, disrupting enemy logistical support and rear areas and thereby limiting the full use of their resources.

In order to be able to carry out the above deployment the NLF had to develop and maintain strong bases in all areas of the province, especially in the region north of Highway 4, since this would provide a staging area for attacks against Saigon. This in turn required that the NLF be able to simultaneously attack enemy forces, defend its own territories, protect the village inhabitants, create strong NLF cadres and followers among the people, and maintain the NLF spirit and political consciousness of the masses. Side by side with development of the base areas and staging areas for attacks, the NLF had to guarantee the constant movement of its various forces.

During the 1964–1967 time frame, when the NLF most tightly controlled Long An, and when there was actually no gap between the liberated areas, the provincial forces moved around constantly to execute their attacks in both regions. The district units and intravillage guerrillas were also able to move freely in their districts and between villages. This enabled the village and hamlet guerrillas to maintain their infrastructure. This was the reason why enemy forces were always off balance and on the defensive. But this situation changed after the second phase of the Tet Offensive in 1968.

## Phase 2: Threshold to Disaster

The second phase of the offensive presented the NLF in Long An with huge problems. The defense of Saigon, for example, was reorganized into three distinct and well-coordinated perimeters. The national police were responsible for the inner city, while ten paratrooper battalions, marines, and special forces occupied the infiltration routes used in the first phase of the offensive; in the outer circle U.S. troops and ARVN regulars constantly carried out their counterattacks, hoping to push the NLF forces further back into the countryside. In spite of the fact that they had to battle the constant counterattacks, the Long An forces managed to cling to the outlying area of Saigon and prepared for the second phase of the offensive against Saigon.

In general, the plan and the directions for the assault remained the same as in the first phase. The attack forces were divided into three contingents, or sections. Sections 2 and 3 from Long An were to attack from the south and southwest and Sections 1, 4, and 5 were to attack from the north and northwest. There were only slight changes in tactics, such as reliance on mortars and rockets and not sappers to attack key targets in the city. However, it was clear from the outset that the mortars and rockets used were not adequate for breaking into a heavily fortified area. In addition, there was no longer the element of surprise. In fact, when the U.S. military command and the Saigon regime learned of the impending attack they placed another brigade and hundreds of pieces of artillery on the routes to the city so that when the NLF forces advanced toward the capital they would be attacked and shelled from behind.

The attack against Saigon by the Long An contingents lasted from May 5 to June 18, 1968. The twists and turns of this six-week campaign are extremely interesting from a military point of view but are too complex to detail here. In general, the attacking forces had to fight every inch of the fifteen to twenty kilometers to Saigon. Along the way they engaged not only various ARVN forces but also the American 9th and 25th Infantry Divisions, which were something that they had managed to avoid altogether during the first phase of Tet, thanks to diversions created by local guerrillas and village inhabitants.

When the Long An contingents arrived at the city the north and northwestern contingents were still being blocked at the outer defense perimeter. Enemy forces were able to concentrate most of their forces against the Long An contingents and pushed them slowly backward. When the northern and northwestern contingents finally managed to enter the city, the Long An units were too depleted and weakened by several days of constant fighting to provide adequate support. As a result, the allies were able to concentrate their forces against Sections 1, 4, and 5. Thus, casualties during this second stage were high. After they were forced to withdraw into the outlying areas of the city, Section 2 found that it had only 775 of its 2,018 troops still in fighting condition, while Section 3 had only 640 left from its original total of 1,430.

American and ARVN forces were able to draw some valuable lessons from the second phase of the offensive. They followed the NLF units closely after the withdrawal into the outlying areas and repeatedly attacked them to prevent NLF forces from regrouping for another assault. Three additional battalions of ARVN rangers were brought in and, along with the U.S. 25th Infantry Division, launched attacks against Section 2. The ARVN 199th Brigade, reinforced by the U.S. 9th Infantry Division, struck retreating troops of Section 3. Five hundred tanks and armored vehicles were placed on Route 4. Three hundred and sixty patrol boats were stationed on the rivers so that there was one every 500 yards. Artillery strikes were increased against all the staging areas of the NLF forces and all suspected escape routes. Chemical defoliants were sprayed on vast areas that had been considered liberated zones. Most devastating of all, massive B-52 raids were conducted daily along the banks of all rivers and waterways as well as on populated areas. In fact, these raids intentionally destroyed the ecological makeup of Long An and other Delta provinces. Moreover, they terrorized the villages in order to deny the NLF sanctuary and base support. Some people have labeled this tactic "My Lai from the sky" because the aim was the same; only the tools differed.

In spite of the heavy losses the Politburo and COSVN ordered Sections 2 and 3 to remain in the outlying areas of Saigon to prepare for the third stage of the offensive. This proved dangerous since they needed to be able to resist the constant counterattacks of ARVN and U.S. forces by dispersing themselves. Instead, they had to remain at the battalion level and coordinate their maneuvers with district and village guerrillas to fight relatively big battles in a number of areas. This created a number of contradictions which had to be resolved. The first was the contradiction between combat and preparation: without fighting back, the various units would not survive; but in fighting back they would absorb heavy casualties and therefore would not have enough strength to mount a third assault on Saigon.

The second contradiction involved the question of troop concentration and dispersion. Maintaining the troops at battalion size would expose them to attrition from the bombing and shelling, but dispersing them into smaller units would not leave them enough strength to resist the mopping-up operations being carried out by the enemy forces. The solution at the time was to dig as many "combat trenches" and build as many strong tunnels as possible to minimize casualties from the shelling and bombing as well as to facilitate counterattacks against the enemy operations. Forces were concentrated quickly to counter the enemy and dispersed quickly to avoid casualties.

While the main forces of Sections 2 and 3 remained in the outlying area of Saigon and fought fierce battles with enemy forces, the guerrilla units in districts and villages, unprotected by regular troops, had to spread themselves out too thinly. Thus, they did not have the strength to attack the remaining enemy outposts in the countryside. As a result, Saigon regional forces regained their confidence, beefed up their units, and, alongside ARVN regulars, began to coordinate attacks against liberated areas. These moves, and the massive destruction of the countryside due to air strikes and chemical sprayings, served to cut off the Long An contingents fighting in the outskirts of Saigon from the rest of the rural areas. Worse still, the organizational division of the Long An forces into Sections 2 and 3 made it difficult to coordinate the activities of the units north and south of Route 4. Everyone I spoke to in Long An—from General Tu Than, Colonel Le Phai and Colonel Le Ky to the district and village leaders—said that this division was a very crucial factor affecting the ability of the Long An contingents in combat as well as the maintenance of their positions in the outlying area of Saigon. The Long An main units were able to remain and fight for half a year in the outskirts of Saigon, launching the six-week third phase of Tet in August. This was largely due to the fact that they were still able to maintain communication lines with the rural areas. But this strategy left the less experienced and more ill-equipped guerrillas in the villages and districts exposed to concerted attacks by enemy forces.

By the end of 1968 and early 1969, the United States had taken advantage of the fact that the Long An main forces were still massing in the direction of Saigon to carry out its "accelerated pacification program." The aim of this program was to move large forces quickly behind the Long An forward positions to take over the liberated areas, thereby isolating these Long An main forces in the outlying areas of Saigon. Against these Long An units Saigon used a combination of forces with the main aim of keeping them occupied and isolated in these forward positions. Meanwhile, an additional 200 patrol boats were deployed on the Vam Co East and West Rivers to facilitate further divisions on Long An to cut off NLF supply and communications lines. After successfully dividing the Long An battlefront, two brigades of the U.S. 25th Infantry Division, the ARVN 25th Division, and fifty rural pacification teams started to retake the liberated areas.

By July 1969, the pacification of the two sections on Long An was basically completed. This created increasing difficulties for the Long An forward units in the outlying areas of Saigon which lasted until the end of the year, when COSVN ordered them to withdraw to the Vietnam-Cambodian border, supposedly to rebuild. This, according to all the Long An commanders to whom I spoke, was the second-biggest mistake made by the leadership because it meant surrendering all the populated areas without a fight. It is of utmost importance in a guerrilla war to maintain contact with your support base. Even when you lose control you should try to maintain what NLF commanders called the "position of adjoining combs" (the *cai lucc*), that is to say, infiltrating the enemy's area in order to get support from the local people and to gain access to enemy territories.

## *Sticking It Out: The Rebuilding Process*

For the reason just stated, the Long An leadership decided to disobey the order from COSVN and sent the provincial forces to the district and village levels to act as local forces and to help rebuild the guerrilla military units there. Political and military cadres thus braved all kinds of sacrifices to carry out the policy of *bam tru*, or literally, "clinging onto the post." The "post" here referred to the land and the people. The NLF's main aim was to get the people to cling to the land, while the NLF cadres clung to the people so tightly that it would be difficult for the enemy, as NLF leaders declared, to "empty the countryside" or to "dry up the ocean to kill the revolutionary fish." Therefore, the NLF also developed a slogan to remind themselves and the population of their determination to stick it out at any cost: *Mot tac khong di, mot ly khong roi. Dan bam dat, can bo bam dan, bo doi bam dich ma danh* (We will not be moved, not an inch, not even a millimeter. People cling to the land, cadres cling to the people, and soldiers cling to the enemy and fight.) Hence, this policy was also known as the *ba bam*, or literally, "three clingings."

For most cadres, "clinging" meant staying close to the people to give them the necessary moral support and political guidance to help them organize into the different types of military forces mentioned earlier and to do political and propaganda work among the enemy's ranks (*binh van* and *dich van*). This often meant living most of the time in tunnels under people's houses, under roads and highways, under paddyfields, and even under the fences of the so-called new life hamlets (*ap doi moi*) and so-called camps for refugees fleeing from communism (*trai ti nan cong san*).

They had to rely on the population to sneak food and water to them. For example, children—especially kids who tended buffaloes—would pretend to go out fishing with bamboo rods and cans of earthworms which they would leave in places where the NLF cadres could pick them up. In reality, beneath the layers of earthworms was fish, meat, or rice. Likewise, the knuckles inside the bamboo canes had all been knocked out and rice, salt, and sesame seeds stuffed inside. Old people were also sneaking food to the NLF troops inside their canes. Peasants put rice and meat in plastic bags and hid them inside their manure carts, which they pushed out into the paddy fields. Fishermen, on the other hand, tied plastic bags full of food under the bottoms of their sampans or junks and rowed them to prearranged places where the NLF cadres and fighters could retrieve them.

On their part, the NLF also crept close to the villages at night to hoe the fields and till the land for the people. During the 1969–1970 period they also planted manioc in the bomb craters, especially those produced by B-52s, in order to provide for themselves and to avoid being wholly dependent on the support of the local population. By planting in the bomb craters they also would not have to prepare the soil and would, therefore, not expose themselves since the ever present enemy reconnaissance planes would be quick to detect changes on the ground. Each B-52 destroyed an area half a mile in diameter and a mile and one-half in length. Such an area was usually covered by an average of fifty to sixty huge bomb craters, each of which could support 150–200 manioc plants. Each plant produced about eight to ten pounds of manioc roots in five to six months. In bomb craters covered with water, the NLF planted bindweed (*rau muong*), which is rich in nutritional value. They also raised fish.

The NLF collected aluminum fragments from downed airplanes, copper artillery casings, and empty shells to exchange for needed supplies. A kilogram of scrap aluminum or copper could fetch enough money to buy about ten kilograms of rice or sugar, one kilogram of pork or fish, eight cans of condensed milk, or five kilograms of soap in 1969–1970.

Clinging to the people and to the enemy was very difficult. There were only a few dozen village guerrillas left in Sections 2 and 3 in 1969. That was the reason why each section in Long An had to bring its main forces back from the Cambodian border area, contrary to COSVN's orders, to rebuild the district and village guerrilla forces. In Section 3 Dong Phu Battalion and D520 Battalion returned to the districts of Can Giuoc and Can Duoc, respectively, and helped rebuild these guerrilla structures. Members of Dong Nai and Phu Loi Battalion and Battalion 1 of Regiment 320 also returned to serve as district guerrilla fighters and commanders. In Section 2 Battalion D264 returned to Duc Hoa District to help rebuild the local guerrilla forces there. This rebuilding effort had to be carried out with the utmost care, with every effort made to conceal the fact from the enemy, with total dedication on the part of many southern political cadres and with support from the population.

The people of Long An and elsewhere in the South told me again and again that the recovery of the guerrilla forces and the revolutionary structures in the South by 1971 was only made possible by the tremendous effort from the southern political and military leaders who returned in 1969–1970. During this period PAVN forces who were sent to the South to help could not function effectively and were killed in large numbers. The people of Long An told me that several thousand regular NVA troops were killed in Long An during this period. Before this period, they said, main force units operating in the South had been well integrated with both southerners and northerners so that the latter could function effectively. On the average, every northern soldier arriving in the South had to receive another year of training before he was battle ready. In addition, regional units and local guerrilla forces provided the necessary political structure and logistical support for the main forces. They also prevented concentrated attacks on main force units through widespread and simultaneous assaults on an entire province or a whole region to occupy and disperse enemy forces. Conversely, main forces had the job of drawing enemy units away from vulnerable areas as well as engaging enemy units too large for the regional and local forces to deal with. The loss of ability to coordinate the activities of these three types of forces, along with other factors, led to what southerners called the "darkest years of 1969–1970." *Bam tru* helped rebuild the regional and local forces and hence necessary structures and coordination lost during these dark days.

The recovery of the southern political and military structures, I was told, was also aided in part by the urban opposition movement which grew in the major urban areas in South Vietnam beginning in 1969. This caused both the Saigon regime and U.S. leaders to spend much attention and energy on dealing with the urban strikes and demonstrations. This was especially true after

May 1970, when over 50,000 U.S. and ARVN troops invaded Cambodia in order to "clean up the sanctuaries" and to "dismantle the Vietcong Pentagon."

The invasion of Cambodia also tied up large amounts of U.S. airpower and logistics for several years. In the long run, this helped give the southerners time and space to recover and to take the initiative in many places through coordinated deployments of the previously mentioned three types of forces. In the short run, I was told, the invasion of Cambodia actually interfered with rebuilding efforts in many of the Delta provinces because they had to send reinforcements to the border areas. In fact, both the interviewees and internal documents from Long An contend that the invasion actually caused serious damage to the rebuilding effort. This was because, in order to attack the Parrot's Beak area, where they suspected the NLF headquarters were located, Saigon's 7th, 9th, and 25th Divisions, 3rd Airborne Brigade, and an armored brigade centered their operation in Long An, with full U.S. air and artillery support. Many Long An people, especially political cadres, were killed during this operation because they were taken by surprise and because they were not able to find an effective way to counter such a huge operation at first.

But soon the NLF drew valuable lessons, reorganized themselves, and were able to mount constant counterattacks. From July to October 1970 they fought seventy-five battles, killed 1,750 ARVN soldiers, destroyed forty tanks, and downed sixteen planes and helicopters. In addition to fighting along the border areas, Long An forces also joined the main forces to liberate the entire Cambodian province of Svayrieng. After that, Long An and Kien Tuong sent five delegations of military cadres of about twenty to thirty to help the people of Svayrieng rebuild their military forces. Together they were able to form eight full companies of provincial main forces, with 300 soldiers in each. Each was equipped with weapons from Long An and Kien Tuong. In addition, each district in Svayrieng had one to two platoons of district forces, while each village had one to two full squads of guerrillas, all trained by the NLF fighters of Long An and Kien Tuong.

Because of this diversion, it was not until October 1970 that Sections 2 and 3 of Long An again merged into a unified administrative unit, known as Section 23. After this political and military cadres were sent to the district and village levels to help rebuild the administrative and military structure. Subsequently, the Military Command of Section 23 also reorganized its main forces into three special full-strength battalions (Battalions D1, D267, and D269) which incorporated a number of newly arrived northern troops. The rest of the provincial units were designated K2, K4, K7, and K9. Two battalions of sappers and one battalion of "communication troops" were also formed. The Kien Tuong Section reinforced its D504 Battalion with some northern troops and created one company of sappers, one company of urban commandos, and one mortar and rocket company. Together the above units and cadres worked among the population and coordinated their attacks against ARVN forces until the provincial NLF political and military structures recovered in late 1971 and early 1972.

The people of Long An took pains to point out to me repeatedly that one of the key things was not how the southern NLF forces were hurt or weakened, but how they recovered with help and support of the southern population, both rural and urban. In their opinion, the people were the biggest assets in any revolutionary war. Stick to the people and you can survive and gain strength. *Bam tru*, they said, was the key to survival and success during the 1969–1972 period.

Eric M. Bergerud's recent study of Hau Nghia Province—next to Long An and just southwest of Saigon—supports most of the above conclusions. He observes,

> Without doubt, 1969 was the best year for the allies both in Vietnam overall and in Hau Nghia province. Perhaps it would be more accurate to describe 1969 as the worst year for the Front because, regardless of the outward manifestations of progress, GVN again failed to win the freely given support of the rural population in Hau Nghia province. . . . The allies again failed miserably to attack the Front's political apparatus in an organized manner. This was a great disappointment for CORDS [Civil Operations and Revolutionary Development Support] because 1969 was the first year during which the attack on the enemy apparatus was given top priority in practice as well as in word.

## Conclusion

In summary, several points can be made. The Tet Offensive, though it did not overthrow the Saigon government, was successful in accomplishing its main objective of forcing the United States to de-escalate the war in North Vietnam and to begin negotiations that would eventually lead to a peace agreement based on NLF terms in January 1973. The offensive also dealt a devastating blow to the Saigon regime, making it absolutely clear that the government would never be able to survive on its own without massive U.S. aid. Significantly, the offensive set off dynamics in South Vietnam which led to the development of a vast urban peace movement and a widespread sentiment for peace throughout the South that would play a critical role in 1975.

Tet might well have had even greater results for the NLF had their troops returned to their rural bases after the first or second phase instead of trying to carry out all three phases. If the troops had returned to protect their rural bases they would probably still have achieved the original purposes of the offensive and would have emerged from it much stronger. Far fewer cadres and civilians in the countryside might have been killed in the 1969–1972 period.

Instead, the NLF forces from Long An stayed massed around Saigon; thus, enemy troops were able to inflict high casualties on both NLF and guerrilla units. Worse still, the Politburo and COSVN made the strategic mistake of ordering the NLF forces in Long An and many other provinces to leave for the border areas. As a result, 1969–1970 became the most difficult years of the war for the Communist cause.

Even so, due to popular support, the NLF was not destroyed. Instead, it managed to rebuild itself through the strategy of "three clingings." It was this recovery that led to the military successes of 1971 and 1972. It made it possible for northern forces to operate in the South again without getting into danger.

In short, the story of Tet and its aftermath demonstrates that popular support in the South allowed the NLF to rise from the ashes of defeat like the phoenix in spite of American efforts to destroy it, including the infamous Phoenix program. To claim that the NLF was defeated after the spring of 1968 never to recover again ignores or distorts the facts. In this connection, one may note that accounts of Tet and its aftermath often overemphasize the role of national leadership and directives, and fail to recognize the role of local leaders, organizations, and initiatives.

# The Vietnam War and the Limits of Military Keynesianism
## Bob Buzzanco

A t a White House meeting on 26 March 1968—just days before he withdrew from the 1968 campaign—President Lyndon Johnson met with senior military and diplomatic officials to discuss the future of the Vietnam War. Despite public claims of success in late 1967, enemy forces had conducted the widespread Tet Offensive in late January 1968 and, in response to that crisis, U.S. Commander William Westmoreland and JCS Chair Earle Wheeler had asked the president for over 200,000 more troops and the activation of nearly 300,000 reservists. Naturally, then, Johnson spent a good deal of time on 26 March agonizing over Vietnam. But there was another crisis on his mind that day as well, one that in retrospect had longer-lived and more important implications, namely the growing economic problems caused by America's deepening involvement in the war in Vietnam. The military's request for reinforcement would have cost an additional $15 billion and, as the president put it simply, that "would hurt the dollar and gold."

Such concern over the economic impact of the war had become critical by early 1968—obviously spurred on by the Tet crisis—but American leaders had been carefully monitoring the effects of military intervention in Vietnam for some time already. The war was exacerbating a deep Balance of Payments [BOP] deficit, thereby weakening the dollar and, per the Bretton Woods system, prompting foreign governments to cash in their American currency for gold, which in turn undermined the international monetary structure. The eminent business historian Louis Galambos has argued that Vietnam "was the most debilitating episode in the nation's entire history, more expensive in its own special way than World Wars I and II combined."[2] An examination of the economic legacy of Vietnam in the 1960s offers ample evidence to support such claims.

After World War II, the United States had established global hegemony based on the confluence of its military power, economic growth, and political liberalism, and for a generation afterward it maintained a dominant position in the world political economy. By the mid-1960s, however, America's role was changing, principally as participation in the Vietnam War grew and caused greater BOP deficits and shortages in American gold reserves. By 1968, the postwar system entered a crisis phase as the Tet Offensive and the so-called Gold Crisis converged to transform the international system and create new political relationships at home. The events of 1968, it is not an exaggeration to suggest, marked the evolution of America's postwar role from that of unrivaled and prosperous imperial power to "first among equals" in a system of "shared hegemony." At home, the spiraling economic growth brought on by two decades of Military Keynesianism could not be sustained in wartime and American capital began to flow overseas to the detriment of domestic workers. And politically, the 1968 Tet Offensive highlighted the failed commitment to Vietnam at the expense of developing a Great Society at home and forced a president to retreat from public life and led the public to question more intensely than before the government's priorities if not its legitimacy. By the latter months of that year, Americans were hoping to get out of Vietnam, trying to understand their place in the world, and listening attentively to the likes of Richard Nixon and George Wallace explain away the end of liberalism.

By itself, Vietnam was calling into question America's military power and world leadership. At the same time, the Bretton Woods system experienced the greatest crisis since its founding. Created near the end of World War II, the Bretton Woods system established the dollar as the world's currency, fully convertible to gold at thirty-five dollars per ounce and exchangeable with other currencies at stable rates based on the gold standard. Throughout the Vietnam War, however, the world monetary system was in disequilibrium or disarray, first as a result of the chronic and escalating BOP problem and, more critically, because of continuing runs on U.S. gold.

From the early 1950s onward, the United States experienced constant BOP deficits. Initially, they had a positive effect, exporting capital to facilitate European reconstruction and create markets. The so-called dollar gap, however, began to weaken the dollar and, by the early 1960s, politicians began to look for ways to confront and solve the growing deficits, but attempts to pare it were futile. Although reductions occurred in 1965 and 1966, "the emergence of war in Southeast Asia," as Secretary of the Treasury Henry Fowler explained, "prevented the United States from approaching equilibrium in those years." Such imbalances grew in concert with the intensified commitments to Vietnam, a war costing in the vicinity of $20–25 billion per annum by 1967–68, and thereby made it impossible to improve upon the shortfall or, because of the inflationary impact of the war, stem the outflow of gold from the United States. U.S. gold reserves, $23 billion in 1957, dropped to $16 billion in 1962 and decreased progressively thereafter. In 1965 alone, foreign central banks had redeemed dollars for $1.7 billion in gold. At the same time, European governments began to openly criticize the U.S. war in Vietnam. French officials especially complained that Vietnam–induced BOP deficits and inflation, which averaged about 5 percent during the Vietnam era, were undermining their own economy. The British government felt likewise, prompting Johnson's National Security Advisor, McGeorge Bundy, to charge that the British were "constantly trying to make narrow bargains on money while they cut back on their wider political and military responsibilities . . . [T]here is no British flag in Vietnam."

Throughout 1966 and 1967, however, the BOP deficits grew, gold continued to leave the United States, and foreign flags were still absent from Vietnam. Inflation was rising as well, with import demand up and export growth down; America's share of world trade, which approached 50 percent after World War II, was down to 25 percent in 1964 and fell to just 10 percent by 1968. The annual, publicly-stated, cost of Vietnam between 1964–67 was about $3.5–4 billion, of which over half was probably attributable to inflation. Treasury officials estimated that the BOP deficit would continue to soar due "entirely to our intensified effort in Southeast Asia" while "a further $200 million increase in [military] expenditures may occur next year [FY 67] and worsen the projected deficit by that amount."

Then, in 1967, a full-blown monetary crisis emerged. Speculators, rather than member nations of a multinational "gold pool," were absorbing virtually all the world's new gold production, leading to a run on American gold reserves—$1.2 billion in 1967 alone. President Johnson, like his predecessors, vowed to maintain full convertibility at the par value of thirty-five dollars per ounce. The French, more alarmed than ever about Vietnam-induced inflation, advocated a higher gold price and began cashing in their dollars. More critically, Britain devalued its pound sterling in November 1967.

The British devaluation—lowering the price of the pound from $2.80 to $2.40—created a monetary crisis. Speculators anticipated an increase in the official price of gold, so withdrew $641 million—60% from U.S. reserves—from the gold pool in the week of 20–27 November, and National Security Advisor Walt Rostow warned the president to "expect further heavy losses this week." DeGaulle then weighed in with a strident public attack on U.S. monetary policy. The French continued to push for a hike in the Bretton Woods price of gold to stem the *"American takeover* of our businesses" that had resulted from the "exportation of inflated dollars." The Payments deficit had to be addressed, DeGaulle insisted, so that it would not continue "to be a means of taking over European industry." In the last quarter of 1967, however, the BOP deficit soared to an annual rate of $7 billion, tripling the previous rate for the year.

Facing economic pressure abroad and at home, Johnson acted on 1 January 1968, announcing a program to reduce the BOP deficit by $3 billion in 1968 by tightening regulations on the export of capital; asking Americans to travel abroad less; and cutting back on foreign and military assistance. He did not mention Vietnam, perhaps because, as Treasury officials earlier understood, the "European monetary authorities do not accept the Vietnam War as a justification" for American economic distress. The French nonetheless responded with "shock and surprise, sour grapes, and fear of the consequences for France and Europe," while DeGaulle personally "ran through the usual routine about the overriding power of the U.S. and the necessity of opposing the U.S. in order to help restore equilibrium in the world."

At home, private sector economic experts warned of worse to come. Edward Bernstein told a Wall Street gathering that "no international monetary system can be devised under which foreign central banks can be induced to acquire unlimited amounts of dollars." The well-known economist Barbara Ward Jackson, in a memo widely circulated by Rostow, warned of "dangerous overtones of the 1929–31 disaster" in the current situation and feared that "depression and massive unemployment could occur in Europe if world trade did not stabilize." Ackley and Rostow both thought Jackson's scenario was too pessimistic, but, as Rostow put it, "the overall problem Barbara has raised is real and, in one way or another, we shall have to meet it in the weeks and months ahead."

Economic crisis, however was then put on the political backburner as Tet began and, in February and early March, the White House had to confront the breakdown of its policies in Indochina. But money and war were colliding too. The military's request for massive reinforcement, McNamara warned, would require additional appropriations of $25 billion in FY 69 and 70 alone, without the likelihood, let alone promise, of turning the corner in Vietnam. At the same time the Europeans, fearing the economic effects of another escalation in Vietnam, began cashing in their dollars for gold. During the last week of February, the gold pool sold $119 million in hard currency; on 3 and 4 March, losses totaled $141 million; and by early March new CEA Chair Arthur Okun, describing *"a bad case of the shakes"* in world financial markets, reported that the Balance of Payments deficit for the first week of March had risen to $321 million while gold losses soared to $395 million, including $179 million on 8 March alone. Should such withdrawals continue to mount, as Thomas McCormick has explained, the depletion of gold reserves could have caused a devaluation of the dollar, which could ignite a series of currency devaluations not unlike the 1930s. Then, with the absence of stable exchange rates, businesses would suffer globally.

With the crisis intensifying, the administration scrambled for a response. An Advisory Committee established by Henry Fowler, headed by Douglas Dillon and including various leaders of the Washington and Wall Street establishments, insisted that Johnson press hard for a ten percent surcharge on corporate and individual income taxes, a move Johnson had been hoping to avoid since late 1965, retain the $35 price of gold despite European calls for an increase, and, if the problems deepened, consider closing the gold pool. "My own feeling," Rostow admitted, "is that the moment of truth is close upon us." He was right. On 14 March the gold pool lost $372 million—bringing the March losses to date to $1.26 billion—and American officials anticipated that the next day's withdrawals could top $1 billion. The administration, as Rostow lamented, "can't go on as is, hoping that something will turn up." The Europeans were also pressuring the United States to act, so Johnson, on the 15th, persuaded London to close its gold market for the day, a Friday—typically the heaviest trading day of the week—and called an emergency meeting of central bankers. That weekend, Governors of the Central Banks of the United States, U.K., Germany, Italy, Belgium, the Netherlands, and Switzerland—but not France—met in Washington to deliberate world monetary conditions. The Governors, not for the first time, called on the Americans, and British, to improve their Balance of Payments positions; urged the president to retain the official price of gold; and called for a "two-tiered" system for gold in which private markets could float their rates. Perhaps the major reform emerging from the crisis was the establishment of Special Drawing Rights [SDRs]. Created by the International Monetary Fund, these international reserve units—"paper" gold—provided the world monetary system with internationally managed liquid assets to avoid future massive hard currency withdrawals.

While the Governors had stemmed the crisis with such action, LBJ was feeling more political heat than ever. The CIA warned the White House to expect more criticism from France and continued attacks on the dollar. Rostow and Economic Advisor Ernest Goldstein told the president to anticipate additional costs for Vietnam in the $6 to 8 billion range for FY 69. And, in a biting analysis, Presidential Aide Harry McPherson berated Johnson for asking Americans to keep supporting a war that was already excessively costly and had no end in sight. Lyndon Johnson, however, did not have to be told how bad the situation had turned. At a 26 March meeting he lamented the "abominable" financial situation, with rising deficits and interest rates and growing danger to the pound and dollar. Worse, Westmoreland's request for 206,000 troops would cost $15 billion, which "would hurt the dollar and gold." The United States, he went on, is "demoralized." The president thus anticipated "overwhelming disapproval in the polls and elections. I will go down the drain. I don't want the whole alliance and military pulled in with it."

The alliance and military survived much better than Johnson. In a 31 March speech to the nation, he announced limited reinforcements for Vietnam, curtailed bombing above the 20th parallel, discussed the world monetary crisis, and stressed the need for a tax surcharge. At the end of his address he stunned the nation by withdrawing from the 1968 campaign. Although the war in Vietnam would continue for five more years, Johnson was admitting failure in early 1968. The United States could no longer use its military and economic power in the same, often unrestrained, fashion that it had in the generation after World War II. The BOP deficit continued to grow. Without a tax bill, the administration faced back-to-back budget deficits of over $20 billion. And, as Okun emphasized, unless the world financial community regained confidence in the dollar, the *"consequences for prosperity at home are incalculable."*

The American financial community likewise understood just how serious the war was affecting the economy. Walter Wriston, the president of Citibank, told a group of European financial leaders in January that it would be possible to overcome the monetary crisis without changing the gold standard, but "the chances would be greater if the Vietnamese war ended." Roy Reierson, senior vice-president and chief economist at the Bankers Trust Company on Wall Street, complained in March that Vietnam had caused domestic inflation and had unduly burdened the BOP position. In an address amid the Tet and Gold crises, a partner at Saloman Brothers, Sidney Homer, observed that "military setbacks in Southeast Asia will surely intensify attacks on the dollar." Vietnam had not alone caused the economic crises of the 1960s, Homer went on, but it had "aggravated our problems and in a sense frozen them." In a report to investors, Goldman, Sachs economists simply explained that reduced spending in Vietnam "could contribute significantly to the solution of many of the problems currently plaguing the U.S. economy."

Most strikingly, the venerable chair of the Federal Reserve System, William McChesney Martin, offered an alarming public analysis of America's economic future. Speaking to financial leaders amid the March crisis, he admonished that "it's time that we stopped talking about 'guns and butter,' it's time that we stopped assuming that we are in a 'little war' in Vietnam, and face up to the fact that we are in a wartime economy." Because of "an intolerable budget deficit and an intolerable deficit in our balance of payments," Martin predicted "either an uncontrollable recession or an uncontrollable inflation." The combination of Vietnam and BOP deficits had put the United States, Martin feared, "in the midst . . . of the worst financial crisis since 1931." The Fed Chair, by Spring 1968, had become increasingly frustrated with Johnson's attempts to pay for Vietnam and the Great Society without a tax increase. Writing to a relative shortly after the uproar over his public pronouncements, he complained that "I have been trying for the past two years to make the point on 'guns and butter' and the cost of the Vietnam war, economically, without too much success but I think in due course the chickens will come home to roost." By late 1968, Martin could only lament that the surtax was "18 months late . . . guns and butter [are] not attainable in wartime." The Bretton Woods system and Military Keynesianism—which had driven economic growth in the Cold War—had been dealt a serious blow by the Vietnam War, and the United States would henceforth have to negotiate its hegemony and economic influence with Western Europe and Japan.

At the same time, the political underpinning of the American empire, economic and social Liberalism, came unglued. The traditional Democratic electoral coalition of labor, Blacks and others identified as liberals were put on the defensive in 1968, never to regain their former position. Joseph Califano, the president's trusted aide on domestic matters, described attitudes on Capitol Hill in March as "one of almost anarchistic willingness to pull down the temple around their ears" due to the intensifying economic crisis. In meetings with the media in February and March, LBJ constantly lamented the breakdown of the political order in Washington. By early summer, he was bemoaning that he had "failed to communicate with the public on the Vietnam War and social program accomplishments." Communication, however, was not the president's principal problem. The United States was in turmoil in 1968, with Johnson's decision against reelection, the King and Kennedy assassinations, urban riots and college protests, the failure of the Poor People's Campaign, and the debacle at the Democratic convention in Chicago all intensifying the backlash against the old, Liberal, order. Harry McPherson, unwittingly but perhaps better than anyone else, conveyed the Liberals' lamentations—or, more accurately, hypocrisy—about the breakdown of their world as he wrote to LBJ that "the Negro . . . showed himself to be, not only ungrateful, but sullen, full of hate and the potential for violence." By Autumn, Americans were listening attentively as Richard Nixon and George Wallace, among others, were cataloguing the sins of the Liberal state. With Vietnam, economic distress, and "disorder" rampant, Liberals, it seemed, no longer deserved to be loved.

The world the Liberals made after World War II was being transformed and America's leadership in the world political economy had to take on new forms. In Indochina, the United States, under the direction of new commander Creighton Abrams, began the process of "Vietnamization" that would lead to the withdrawal of troops but parallel intensification of the war from the air—"changing the color of the corpses" as George McGovern charged—in order to temper political opposition to the war. Though U.S. troops would continue fighting until 1973, the establishment understood that it would not conclude the war successfully. As former President Dwight Eisenhower observed in mid-1968, the United States "should not expect to attain more at the conference table than we could attain on the battlefield." Economically, two decades of "growth liberalism"—to use Robert Collins's apt term—stalled. The "dollar gap," so essential to European recovery after the war, had become the "dollar glut," with Vietnam exacerbating it and causing unbearable BOP deficits.

Europeans, feeling the effects of American inflation and handcuffed by fixed exchange rates and the gold standard, began to question and attack the Bretton Woods system in late 1967 and 1968, cashing in their dollars for American gold until LBJ could tolerate it no more. Just three years later, Richard Nixon officially ended the Bretton Woods system by taking the United States off the gold standard and devaluing the dollar. The American economy, as business writer Hobart Rowan put it, "continued to show the effects of the deep distortions of the Vietnam War, which had drained the nation's wealth, triggered the inflation, and exacerbated the balance of payments and trade deficits. The dollar's devaluation . . . was a confession of the failure of economic policy." General Michael Davison, who had served as the Chief of Staff and Deputy Commander in Chief of the Army's Pacific Command during the Vietnam War, likewise scored the cost of intervention. National leaders, he contended, "should have had their nose pressed to the fiscal wall. . . . And we could have saved billions of dollars, and those billions that we wasted out there were contributory to the later *inflation* and *recession* in my view, and they were contributory to the political ferment when the American people saw the billions of dollars flowing out there and for what purpose?"

Tet, Gold and the crisis of Liberalism also—maybe most importantly—eroded faith in the established order. Allies sought changes in the American-dominated world political economy and, at home, citizens began to mistrust their government with new intensity and criticized the utility of the Liberal state and big government. It was a crisis of confidence of such magnitude that American leaders had to respond and create a new order. To be sure, the United States still had military superiority and the biggest economy, but the Tet Offensive had undermined the American attempt to impose its will militarily on Vietnam, and the Gold Crisis had shown that other nations would no longer accept the financial burden for the American empire. Since the late 1960s the world has changed markedly: the United States, as in the Gulf War and Bosnia, seeks to intervene in league with other powers; the yen and mark now rank with the dollar as vital world currencies; business is now far more concerned with the transnational nature of capital, and the production and export of money and services now match, at least, the creation and trade of goods in importance; and, at home, the dreams of the Great Society are a distant memory as national legislators conduct a political war against the poor and minorities.

Perhaps most importantly, the American economy and investment strategies have taken on a far more transnational character. Capital knows no nationality and dollars, often literally, went south in increasing amounts in the following decades. The number of U.S. banks with branches overseas rose tenfold between 1965 and 1974 and their assets increased by 1400%. At the same time the number of foreign banks with Wall Street branches doubled, with their assets increasing by 600%. The so-called Eurodollar market, unregulated by the state and not restrained by domestic currency markets, flourished, rising from $36 to $80 billion between 1967 and 1969 alone. Multinational financial institutions sensed that a domestically-based manufacturing economy was losing steam and emphasized global capital investment in areas where lower labor costs and hospitable climates for foreign investment offered a better return than the home market. Where LBJ and his advisors were trying to maintain American hegemony based on traditional strategies of military power and economic growth, businesses understood that governments and national economies were giving way to a truly global financial and monetary system.

Ultimately, world economic equilibrium was restored, but at a cost. Development and rising standards of living stalled in much of the world. And at home, the attack against Cold War liberalism continues to this day.

The legacy of 1968, as LBJ himself, writing after he left office, poignantly observed, was powerful and compelling. "The American people recoiled in anguish in 1968," he lamented, "as violence again struck down national leaders and lit flames in the skies above a dozen cities. We confronted the perils of inflation at home and the danger of the dollar's decline abroad. The agony of an odious war, forced upon us so cruelly for so long, cut deep divisions across our national life. These, with all their shock and sorrow, are forever part of the fabric of that turbulent period."

# Tet, Gold, and the Transformation of American Hegemony

## Bob Buzzanco

After World War II, the United States established world hegemony based on the confluence of its military power, economic growth, and political liberalism, and for a generation afterward maintained a dominant position in the world political economy. By the mid-1960s, however, America's role was changing, principally as U.S. participation in the Vietnam War grew. By 1968, the postwar system entered a crisis phase as the Tet Offensive, the so-called Gold Crisis, and a political backlash against liberalism converged to transform the international system and create new political relationships at home. The events of 1968, it is not an exaggeration to suggest, marked the evolution of America's postwar role from that of unrivaled and prosperous imperial power to "first among equals" in a system of "shared hegemony." At home, the spiraling economic growth brought on by two decades of Military Keynesianism could not be sustained in wartime and American capital began to flow overseas to the detriment of domestic workers. And politically, the Tet Offensive—highlighting the failed commitment to Vietnam at the expense of developing a Great Society at home—forced a president to retreat from public life and led the public to question more intensely than before the government's priorities and, indeed, virtue. By the latter months of that year, Americans were hoping to get out of Vietnam, trying to understand their place in the world, and listening attentively to the likes of Richard Nixon and George Wallace explain away the end of liberalism.

Though a good number of scholars have analysed these episodes in part, fewer have woven them together in a holistic examination of the Cold War, grand strategy, or the nature of American hegemony. Among those who have, Lloyd Gardner, Gabriel Kolko, Burton Kaufman, Herbert Schandler, David

Calleo, and, recently, Louis Galambos and, especially, Robert Collins, stand out. Still, a thorough and integrated appraisal of the shocks of 1968 is needed.

Events in Vietnam provided the first, and most intense, crisis of 1968. At the end of January the enemy Viet Cong [VC] and northern People's Army of Vietnam [PAVN]—taking advantage of the traditional cease fire to mark the lunar new year of Tet—conducted a countrywide offensive, attacking virtually every political and military center of importance and even invading the grounds of the American embassy in Saigon. Coming just months after a White House-orchestrated public relations campaign had promised "light at the end of the tunnel," Tet deeply unnerved the White House and stunned the nation at large. The United States, it had become clear, would not soon or successfully conclude its role in Vietnam.

Since 1968, Tet has had a critical place in discussions of Vietnam, with almost all scholarship agreeing that the offensive amounted to a great military victory but psychological defeat for American forces. Such interpretations, however, are based mostly on the public pronouncements of administration and service officials and neglect the actual reports coming out of Vietnam. The Tet Offensive, U.S. military officials in Vietnam conceded, had taken the United States and southern Vietnamese Army—the ARVN—by surprise, undermined previous claims of initiative and progress, seriously set back the American pacification program, prompted large scale desertion among Vietnamese forces, let loose a flood of refugees, and unleashed a torrent of criticism at home, including among mainstream supporters of the war in the political arena and the media, most notably Walter Cronkite.

At the outset of Tet, Hanoi was boasting that "for months, Johnson and Westmoreland have been repeating that the 'Viet Cong,' decimated by blows from U.S. forces, are panting for breath, that the South Viet Nam people are gradually rallying around the 'elected' government of Saigon, that the four-stage war plan of the U.S. command is progressing as predicted by the Pentagon's electronic brains. And yet, the whole of South Viet Nam is now ablaze." Though of course not employing such revolutionary jargon, American military officials implicitly corroborated such analysis. General John Chaisson, director of the Combat Operations Center in Saigon, admitted at the outset of the offensive—while President Lyndon Johnson and Commander William Westmoreland were proclaiming great success—that "we have been faced with a real battle, there is no sense in ducking it; there is no sense in hiding it." Chaisson thus had to give the enemy "credit for having engineered and planned a very successful offensive in its initial phases." Barely a week later, Westmoreland, expecting another series of attacks in the northern RVN, asked for reinforcements—"which I desperately need"—and conceded that "we are now in a new ballgame where we face a determined, highly disciplined enemy, fully mobilized to achieve a quick victory."

With such appraisals regularly flowing out of Vietnam, and facing severe and increasing pressure at home, LBJ sent JCS Chair Earle Wheeler to Saigon in late February. The general brought back a fairly grim evaluation of the situation. "There is no doubt that the enemy launched a major, powerful nationwide assault," he observed. "This offensive has by no means run its course." Pacification "had been brought to a halt," he added. "To a large extent, the VC now control the countryside." America's margin of survival, he found, had been "very small indeed," while the enemy's "determination appears to be unshaken." Using euphemism to convey his distress, Wheeler concluded that Tet "was a very near thing." Army Chief Harold K. Johnson was more direct: "we suffered a loss, there can be no doubt about it," he cabled to Westmoreland.

Although both civilian and military officials would continue to assert, and often still do, that Tet was in reality a U.S. victory because of the great number of enemy losses—a point sharply disputed by Ngo Vinh Long—it was clear that the United States could not maintain its commitment to and policies in Vietnam along the shopworn and inadequate lines that it had for the previous several years. A new commander, Creighton Abrams, assumed control of military operations in Saigon and began to put into place the strategy of "Vietnamization" that would ultimately lead to American de-escalation. Clearly, Tet had proven that American military strategy in Vietnam had failed. Politically, however, the armed forces—fearing blame for defeat in Indochina—performed much better. In late February, recycling a request they had made earlier and often, Wheeler and Westmoreland requested a reinforcement of 206,000 troops and the activation of almost 300,000 reservists. LBJ had repeatedly turned down such escalation and, it was clear, would reject it again. But by forcing the president's hand and making him refuse the reinforcement plans, the military successfully deferred blame onto the White House for making the troops fight "with one hand tied behind their back."

While the events of February and March marked the nadir of the U.S. role in Vietnam in 1968, the situation there—again contrary to most established scholarship—remained troubled throughout the year. Though the enemy's "mini-Tet" offensives of May and August lacked the scope and impact of the January-February attacks, they did pose significant problems for and kept American forces off balance. The enemy, U.S. officials continued to recognize, was replacing its losses and retaining the military initiative. Between March and May, military officials admitted, the Communists had infiltrated over 60,000 new troops into the south, bringing the total for 1968 up to nearly 200,000. Accordingly Wheeler reported that the American position in southern Vietnam was "relatively" better in June, but the enemy position in the north was "sharply" improved, and he "expect[ed] the rapidly recuperating North Vietnam[ese] to make substantial impacts on us in late summer and fall." In the northernmost provinces, Marine officials reported in June, such "impacts" occurred and Communist forces "were considered to have recuperated most quickly from losses suffered during May." The August attacks, they observed later, were "widespread and well co-ordinated" and ground contacts had "increased sharply" throughout the entire 1st Corp Tactical Zone. At the same time, Commander Abrams lamented the long-term political problems plaguing the RVN, conceding that the "most serious—and telling—flaw in the [Vietnamese and American] effort has been the conspicuous shortage of good Vietnamese leadership (both civilian and military) at all levels of command."

By itself, Tet was a military crisis of great magnitude that forced national leaders to appraise the war seriously at last and conclude, haltingly, that success would not be forthcoming. At the same time, the Bretton Woods system experienced the greatest crisis since its founding. Created near the end of World War II, the Bretton Woods system established the dollar as the world's currency, fully convertible to gold at thirty-five dollars per ounce and exchangeable with other currencies at stable rates based on the gold standard. Throughout the Vietnam War, however, the world monetary system was in disequilibrium or disarray, first as a result of America's chronic and escalating Balance of Payments problem and, more critically, because of a run on U.S. gold in early 1968. Vietnam, as Burton Kaufman has explained, exacerbated the BOP problem, thereby weakening the dollar, which in turn undermined the international monetary structure.

From the early 1950s onward, the United States experienced constant BOP deficits. Initially, they had a positive effect, exporting capital to facilitate European reconstruction and create markets. The so-called dollar gap, however, began to weaken the dollar and, by the early 1960s, politicians began to look for ways to confront and solve the growing deficits, but attempts to pare it were futile. Although reductions occurred in 1965 and 1966, "the emergence of war in Southeast Asia," as Secretary of the Treasury Henry Fowler explained, "prevented the United States from approaching equilibrium in those years." Such imbalances grew in concert with the intensified commitments to Vietnam, a war costing in the vicinity of $20–25 billion per annum by 1967–68, and thereby made it impossible to improve upon the Balance of Payments shortfall or, because of the inflationary impact of the war, stem the outflow of gold from the United States. Then, in 1967, a full-blown monetary crisis emerged. Speculators, rather than member nations of a multinational "gold pool," were absorbing virtually all the world's new gold production, leading to a run on American gold reserves—$1.2 billion in 1967 alone. President Johnson, like his predecessors, vowed to maintain full convertibility at the par value of thirty-five dollars per ounce. The French, charging that the United States was exporting its Vietnam-induced inflation overseas, advocated a higher gold price and began cashing in their dollars. More critically, Britain devalued its pound sterling in November 1967.

The British devaluation—lowering the price of the pound from $2.80 to $2.40—created a monetary crisis. Speculators anticipated an increase in the official price of gold, so withdrew $641 million—60% from U.S. reserves—from the gold pool in the week of 20-27 November and National Security Advisor Walt Rostow warned the president to "expect further heavy losses this week." DeGaulle then weighed in with a strident public attack on U.S. monetary policy. The French continued to push for a hike in the Bretton Woods price of gold to stem the "*American takeover* of our businesses" that had resulted from the "exportation of inflated dollars." The Payments deficit had to be addressed, DeGaulle insisted, so that it would not continue "to be a means of taking over European industry." In the last quarter of 1967, however, the BOP deficit soared to an annual rate of $7 billion, tripling the previous rate for the year.

Facing economic pressure abroad and at home, Johnson acted on 1 January 1968, announcing a program to reduce the BOP deficit by $3 billion in 1968 by tightening regulations on the export of capital; asking Americans to travel abroad less; and cutting back on foreign and military assistance. He did not mention Vietnam, perhaps because, as Treasury officials earlier understood, the "European monetary authorities do not accept the Vietnam War as a justification" for American economic distress. The French nonetheless responded with "shock and surprise, sour grapes, and fear of the consequences for France and Europe," while DeGaulle personally "ran through the usual routine about the overriding power of the U.S. and the necessity of opposing the U.S. in order to help restore equilibrium in the world."

At home, private sector economic experts warned of worse to come. Edward Bernstein told a Wall Street gathering that "no international monetary system can be devised under which foreign central banks can be induced to acquire unlimited amounts of dollars." Barbara Ward Jackson, in a memo widely circulated by Rostow, warned of "dangerous overtones of the 1929–31 disaster" in the current situation and feared that "depression and massive unemployment could occur in Europe if world trade did not stabilize." Ackley and Rostow both thought Jackson's scenario was too pessimistic, but, as Rostow put it, "the overall problem Barbara has raised is real and, in one way or another, we shall have to meet it in the weeks and months ahead."

Economic crisis, however was then put on the political backburner as Tet began and, in February and early March, the White House had to confront the breakdown of its policies in Indochina. But money and war were colliding too. The military's request for massive reinforcement, McNamara warned, would require additional appropriations of $25 billion in FY 69 and 70 alone, without the likelihood, let alone promise, of turning the corner in Vietnam. At the same time the Europeans, fearing the economic effects of another escalation in Vietnam, began cashing in their dollars for gold. During the last week of February, the gold pool sold $119 million in hard currency; on 3 and 4 March, losses totaled $141 million; and by early March new CEA Chair Arthur Okun, describing "*a bad case of the shakes*" in world financial markets, reported that the Balance of Payments deficit for the first week of March had risen to $321 million while gold losses soared to $395 million, including $179 million on 8 March alone. Should such withdrawals continue to mount, as Thomas McCormick has explained, the depletion of gold reserves could have caused a devaluation of the dollar, which could ignite a series of currency devaluations not unlike the 1930s. Then, with the absence of stable exchange rates, businesses would suffer globally.

With the crisis intensifying, the administration scrambled for a response. An Advisory Committee established by Henry Fowler, headed by Douglas Dillon and including various leaders of the Washington and Wall Street establishments, insisted that Johnson press hard for a ten percent surcharge on corporate and individual income taxes, a move Johnson had been hoping to avoid since late 1965, retain the $35 price of gold despite European calls for an increase, and, if the problems deepened, consider closing the gold pool. "My own feeling," Rostow admitted, "is that the moment of truth is close upon us." He was right. On 14 March the gold pool lost $372 million—bringing the March losses to date to $1.26 billion—and American officials anticipated that the next day's withdrawals could top $1 billion. The administration, as Rostow lamented, "can't go on as is, hoping that something will turn up."

The Europeans were also pressuring the United States to act, so Johnson, on the 15th, closed the London gold market for the day, a Friday—typically the heaviest trading day of the week—and called an emergency meeting of central bankers. That weekend, Governors of the Central Banks of the United States, U.K., Germany, Italy, Belgium, the Netherlands, and Switzerland—but not France—met in Washington to deliberate world monetary conditions. The Governors, not for the first time, called on the Americans, and British, to improve their Balance of Payments positions; urged the president to retain the official price of gold; and called for a "two-tiered" system for gold in which private markets could float their rates. Perhaps the major reform emerging from the crisis was the establishment of Special Drawing Rights [SDRs]. Created by the International Monetary Fund, these international reserve units—"paper" gold—provided the world monetary system with internationally managed liquid assets to avoid future massive hard currency withdrawals.

While the Governors had stemmed the crisis with such action, LBJ was feeling more political heat than ever. The CIA warned the White House to expect more criticism from France and continued attacks on the dollar. Rostow and Economic Advisor Ernest Goldstein told the president to anticipate additional costs for Vietnam in the $6 to 8 billion range for FY 69. And, in a biting analysis, Presidential Aide Harry McPherson berated Johnson for asking Americans to keep supporting a war that was already excessively costly and had no end in sight. Lyndon Johnson, however, did not have to be told how bad the situation had turned. At a 26 March meeting he lamented the "abominable" financial situation, with rising deficits and interest rates and growing danger to the pound and dollar. Worse, Westmoreland's request for 206,000 troops would cost $15 billion, which "would hurt the dollar and gold." The United States, he went on, is "demoralized." The president thus anticipated "overwhelming disapproval in the polls and elections. I will go down the drain. I don't want the whole alliance and military pulled in with it."

The alliance and military survived much better than Johnson. In a 31 March speech to the nation, he announced limited reinforcements for Vietnam, curtailed bombing above the 20th parallel, discussed the world monetary crisis, and stressed the need for a tax surcharge. At the end of his address he stunned the nation by withdrawing from the 1968 campaign. Although the war in Vietnam would continue for five more years, Johnson was admitting failure in early 1968. The United States could no longer use its military and economic power in the same, often unrestrained, fashion that it had in the generation after World War II. The BOP deficit continued to grow. Without a tax bill, the administration faced back-to-back budget deficits of over $20 billion. And, as Okun emphasized, unless the world financial community regained confidence in the dollar, the *"consequences for prosperity at home are incalculable."*

The American financial community likewise understood just how seriously the war was affecting the economy. Walter Wriston, the president of Citibank, told a group of European financial leaders in January that it would be possible to overcome the monetary crisis without changing the gold standard, but "the chances would be greater if the Vietnamese war ended." Roy Reierson, senior vice-president and chief economist at the Bankers Trust Company on Wall Street, complained in March that Vietnam had caused domestic inflation and had unduly burdened the BOP position. In an address amid the Tet and Gold crises, a partner at Saloman Brothers, Sidney Homer, observed that "military setbacks in Southeast Asia will surely intensify attacks on the dollar." Vietnam had not alone caused the economic crises of the 1960s, Homer went on, but it had "aggravated our problems and in a sense frozen them." In a report to investors, Goldman, Sachs economists simply explained that reduced spending in Vietnam "could contribute significantly to the solution of many of the problems currently plaguing the U.S. economy." And the venerable chair of the Federal Reserve System, William McChesney Martin, lamented in late 1968 that the surtax was "18 months late . . . guns and butter [are] not attainable in wartime." The Bretton Woods system and Military Keynesianism—which had driven economic growth in the Cold War—had been dealt a serious blow by the Vietnam War, and the United States would henceforth have to negotiate its hegemony and economic influence with Western Europe and Japan.

At the same time, the political underpinning of the American empire, economic and social Liberalism, came unglued. The traditional Democratic electoral coalition of labor, Blacks and others identified as liberals were put on the defensive in 1968, never to regain their former position. Joseph Califano, the president's trusted aide on domestic matters, described attitudes on Capitol Hill in March as "one of almost anarchistic willingness to pull down the temple around their ears" due to the intensifying economic crisis. In meetings with the media in February and March, LBJ constantly lamented the breakdown of the political order in Washington. By early summer, he was bemoaning that he had "failed to communicate with the public on the Vietnam War and social program accomplishments." Communication, however, was not the president's principal problem. The United States was in turmoil in 1968, with Johnson's decision against reelection, the King and Kennedy assassinations, urban riots and college protests, the failure of the Poor People's Campaign, and the debacle at the Democratic convention in Chicago all intensifying the backlash against the old, Liberal, order. Harry McPherson, unwittingly but perhaps better than anyone else, conveyed the Liberals' lamentations—or, more accurately, hypocrisy—about the breakdown of their world as he wrote to LBJ that "the Negro . . . showed himself to be, not only ungrateful, but sullen, full of hate and the potential for violence." By Autumn, Americans were listening attentively as Richard Nixon and George Wallace, among others, were cataloguing the sins of the Liberal state. With Vietnam, economic distress, and "disorder" rampant, Liberals, it seemed, no longer deserved to be loved.

The world the Liberals made after World War II was being transformed and America's leadership in the world political economy had to take on new forms. In Indochina, the United States, under the direction of new commander Creighton Abrams, began the process of "Vietnamization" that would lead to the withdrawal of troops but parallel intensification of the war from the air—"changing the color of the corpses" as George McGovern charged—in order to temper political opposition to the war. Though U.S. troops would continue fighting until 1973, the establishment understood that it would not conclude the war successfully. As former President Dwight Eisenhower observed in mid-1968, the United States "should not expect to attain more at the conference table than we could attain on the battlefield." Economically, two decades of "growth liberalism"—to use Robert Collins's apt term— stalled. The "dollar gap," so essential to European recovery after the war, had become the "dollar glut," with Vietnam exacerbating it and causing unbearable BOP deficits.

Europeans, feeling the effects of American inflation and handcuffed by fixed exchange rates and the gold standard, began to question and attack the Bretton Woods system in late 1967 and 1968, cashing in their dollars for American gold until LBJ could tolerate it no more. Just three years later, Richard Nixon officially ended the Bretton Woods system by taking the United States off the gold standard and devaluing the dollar. The American economy, as business writer Hobart Rowan put it, "continued to show the effects of the deep distortions of the Vietnam War, which had drained the nation's wealth, triggered the inflation, and exacerbated the balance of payments and trade deficits. The dollar's devaluation . . . was a confession of the failure of economic policy." General Michael Davison, who had served as the Chief of Staff and Deputy Commander in Chief of the Army's Pacific Command during the Vietnam War, likewise scored the cost of intervention. National leaders, he contended, "should have had their nose pressed to the fiscal wall. . . . And we could have saved billions of dollars, and those billions that we wasted out there were contributory to the later *inflation* and *recession* in my view, and they were contributory to the political ferment when the American people saw the billions of dollars flowing out there and for what purpose?"

Tet, Gold and the crisis of Liberalism also—maybe most importantly— eroded faith in the established order. Allies sought changes in the American-dominated world political economy and, at home, citizens began to mistrust their government with new intensity and criticized the utility of the Liberal state and big government. It was a crisis of confidence of such magnitude that American leaders had to respond and create a new order. To be sure, the United States still had military superiority and the biggest economy, but the Tet Offensive had undermined the American attempt to impose its will militarily on Vietnam, and the Gold Crisis had shown that other nations would no longer accept the financial burden for the American empire. Since the late 1960s the world has changed markedly: the United States, as in the Gulf War and Bosnia, seeks to intervene in league with other powers; the yen and mark now rank with the dollar as vital world currencies; business is now far more concerned with the transnational nature of capital, and the production and export of money and services now match, at least, the creation and trade of goods in importance; and, at home, the dreams of the Great Society are a distant memory as national legislators conduct a political war against the poor and minorities.

Perhaps most importantly, the American economy and investment strategies have taken on a far more transnational character. Capital knows no nationality and dollars, often literally, went south in increasing amounts in the following decades. The number of U.S. banks with branches overseas rose tenfold between 1965 and 1974 and their assets increased by 1400%. At the same time the number of foreign banks with Wall Street branches doubled, with their assets increasing by 600%. The so-called Eurodollar market, unregulated by the state and not restrained by domestic currency markets, flourished, rising from $36 to $80 billion between 1967 and 1969 alone. Multinational financial institutions sensed that a domestically-based manufacturing economy was losing steam and emphasized global capital investment in areas where lower labor costs and hospitable climates for foreign investment offered a better return than the home market. Where LBJ and his advisors were trying to maintain American hegemony based on traditional strategies of military power and economic growth, businesses understood that governments and national economies were giving way to a truly global financial and monetary system.

Ultimately, world economic equilibrium was restored, but at a cost. Development and rising standards of living stalled in much of the world. And at home, the attack against Cold War liberalism continues to this day.

The legacy of 1968, as LBJ himself, writing after he left office, poignantly observed, was powerful and compelling. "The American people recoiled in anguish in 1968," he lamented, "as violence again struck down national leaders and lit flames in the skies above a dozen cities. We confronted the perils of inflation at home and the danger of the dollar's decline abroad. The agony of an odious war, forced upon us so cruelly for so long, cut deep divisions across our national life. These, with all their shock and sorrow, are forever part of the fabric of that turbulent period."

# The Collapse of the Armed Forces
## Col. Robert D. Heinl, Jr.

The morale, discipline and battleworthiness of the U.S. Armed Forces are, with a few salient exceptions, lower and worse than at anytime in this century and possibly in the history of the United States.

By every conceivable indicator, our army that now remains in Vietnam is in a state approaching collapse, with individual units avoiding or having *refused* combat, murdering their officers and non commissioned officers, drug-ridden, and dispirited where not near mutinous.

Elsewhere than Vietnam, the situation is nearly as serious.

Intolerably clobbered and buffeted from without and within by social turbulence, pandemic drug addiction, race war, sedition, civilian scapegoatise, draftee recalcitrance and malevolence, barracks theft and common crime, unsupported in their travail by the general government, in Congress as well as the executive branch, distrusted, disliked, and often reviled by the public, the uniformed services today are places of agony for the loyal, silent professionals who doggedly hang on and try to keep the ship afloat.

The responses of the services to these unheard-of conditions, forces and new public attitudes, are confused, resentful, occasional pollyanna-ish, and in some cases even calculated to worsen the malaise that is wracking. While no senior officer (especially one on active duty) can openly voice any such assessment, the foregoing conclusions find virtually unanimous support in numerous non-attributable interviews with responsible senior and mid-level officers, as well as career noncommissioned officers and petty officers in all services.

Historical precedents do not exist for some of the services' problems, such as desertion, mutiny, unpopularity, seditious attacks, and racial troubles. Others, such as drugs, pose difficulties that are wholly NEW. Nowhere, however, in the history of the Armed Forces have comparable past troubles presented themselves in such general magnitude, acuteness, or concentrated focus as today.

By several orders of magnitude, the Army seems to be in worse trouble. But the Navy has serious and unprecedented problems, while the Air Force, on the surface at least still clear of the quicksands in which the Army is sinking, is itself facing disquieting difficulties.

Only the Marines—who have made news this year by their hard line against indiscipline and general permissiveness—seem with their expected staunchness and tough tradition, to be weathering the storm.

## Back to the Campus

To understand the military consequences of what is happening to the U.S. Armed Forces, Vietnam is a good place to start. It is in Vietnam that the rearguard of a 500,000 man army, in its day and in the observation of the writer the best army the United States ever put into the field, is numbly extricating itself from a nightmare war the Armed Forces feel they had foisted on them by bright civilians who are now back on campus writing books about the folly of it all.

"They have set up separate companies," writes an American soldier from Cu Chi, quoted in the *New York Times*, "for men who refuse to go into the field. Is no big thing to refuse to go. If a man is ordered to go to such and such a place he no longer goes through the hassle of refusing; he just packs his shirt and goes to visit some buddies at another base camp. Operations have become incredibly ragtag. Many guys don't even put on their uniforms any more . . . The American garrison on the larger bases are virtually disarmed. The lifers have taken our weapons from us and put them under lock and key . . . There have also been quite a few frag incidents in the battalion."

Can all this really be typical or even truthful?

Unfortunately the answer is yes.

"Frag incidents" or just "fragging" is current soldier slang in Vietnam for the murder or attempted murder of strict, unpopular, or just aggressive officers and NCOs. With extreme reluctance (after a young West Pointer from Senator Mike Mansfield's Montana was fragged in his sleep) the Pentagon has now disclosed that fraggings in 1970 (109) have more than doubled those of the previous year (96).

Word of the deaths of officers will bring cheers at troop movies or in bivouacs of certain units.

In one such division—the morale plagued Americal—fraggings during 1971 have been authoritatively estimated to be running about one a week.

Yet fraggings, though hard to document, form part of the ugly lore of every war. The first such verified incident known to have taken place occurred 190 years ago when Pennsylvania soldiers in the Continental Army killed one of their captains during the night of 1 January 1781.

## Bounties and Evasions

Bounties, raised by common subscription in amounts running anywhere from $50 to $1,000, have been widely reported put on the heads of leaders whom the privates and Sp4s want to rub out.

Shortly after the costly assault on Hamburger Hill in mid-1969, the GI underground newspaper in Vietnam, "G.I. Says," publicly offered a $10,000 bounty on Lt. Col. Weldon Honeycutt, the officer who ordered (and led) the attack. Despite several attempts, however, Honeycutt managed to live out his tour and return Stateside.

"Another Hamburger Hill," (i.e., toughly contested assault), conceded a veteran major, "is definitely out."

The issue of "combat refusal," an official euphemism for disobedience of orders to fight—the soldier's gravest crime—has only recently been again precipitated on the frontier of Laos by Troop B, 1st Cavalry's mass refusal to recapture their captain's command vehicle containing communication gear, codes and other secret operation orders.

As early as mid-1969, however, an entire company of the 196th Light Infantry Brigade publicly sat down on the battlefield. Later that year, another rifle company, from the famed 1st Air Cavalry Division, flatly refused—on CBS-TV—to advance down a dangerous trail.

(Yet combat refusals have been heard of before: as early as 1813, a corps of 4,000 Kentucky soldiers declined to engage British Indians who just sacked and massacred Ft. Dearborn (later Chicago).)

While denying further unit refusals the Air Cav has admitted some 35 individual refusals in 1970 alone. By comparison, only two years earlier in 1968, the entire number of officially recorded refusals for our whole army in Vietnam—from over seven divisions—was 68.

"Search and evade" (meaning tacit avoidance of combat by units in the field) is now virtually a principle of war, vividly expressed by the GI phrase, "CYA (cover your ass) and get home!"

That "search-and-evade" has not gone unnoticed by the enemy is underscored by the Viet Cong delegation's recent statement at the Paris Peace Talks that communist units in Indochina have been ordered not to engage American units which do not molest them. The same statement boasted—not without foundation in fact—that American defectors are in the VC ranks.

Symbolic anti-war fasts (such as the one at Pleiku where an entire medical unit, led by its officers, refused Thanksgiving turkey), peace symbols, "V"-signs not for victory but for peace, booing and cursing of officers and even of hapless entertainers such as Bob Hope, are unhappily commonplace.

As for drugs and race, Vietnam's problems today not only reflect but reinforce those of the Armed Forces as a whole. In April, for example, members of a Congressional investigating subcommittee reported that 12% to 15% of our troops in Vietnam are now using high-grade heroin, and that drug addiction there is "of epidemic proportions."

Only last year an Air Force major and command pilot for Ambassador Bunker was apprehended at Ton Son Nhut air base outside Saigon with $8 million worth of heroin in his aircraft. The major is now in Leavenworth.

Early this year, an Air Force regular colonel was court-martialed and cashiered for leading his squadron in pot parties, while, at Cam Ranh Air Force Base, 43 members of the base security police squadron were recently swept up in dragnet narcotics raids.

All the foregoing facts—and many more dire indicators of the worse kind of military trouble—point to widespread conditions among American forces in Vietnam that have only been exceeded in this century by the French Army's Nivelle mutinies of 1917 and the collapse of the Tsarist armies in 1916 and 1917.

## Society Notes

It is a truism that national armies closely reflect societies from which they have been raised. It would be strange indeed if the Armed Forces did not today mirror the agonizing divisions and social traumas of American society, and of course they do.

For this very reason, our Armed Forces outside Vietnam not only reflect these conditions but disclose the depths of their troubles in an awful litany of sedition, disaffection, desertion, race, drugs, breakdowns of authority, abandonment of discipline, and, as a cumulative result, the lowest state of military morale in the history of the country.

Sedition—coupled with disaffection within the ranks, and externally fomented with an audacity and intensity previously inconceivable—infests the Armed Services:

At best count, there appear to be some 144 underground newspapers published on or aimed at U.S. military bases in this country and overseas. Since 1970 the number of such sheets has increased 40% (up from 103 last fall). These journals are not mere gripe-sheets that poke soldier fun in the "Beetle Bailey" tradition, at the brass and the sergeants. "In Vietnam," writes the Ft. Lewis-McChord Free Press, "the Lifers, the Brass, are the true Enemy, not the enemy." Another West Coast sheet advises readers: "Don't desert. Go to Vietnam and kill your commanding officer."

At least 14 GI dissent organizations (including two made up exclusively of officers) now operate more or less openly. Ancillary to these are at least six antiwar veterans' groups which strive to influence GIs.

Three well-established lawyer groups specialize in support of GI dissent. Two (GI Civil Liberties Defense Committee and New York Draft and Military Law Panel) operate in the open. A third is a semi-underground network of lawyers who can only be contacted through the GI Alliance, a Washington, D.C., group which tries to coordinate seditious antimilitary activities throughout the country.

One antimilitary legal effort operates right in the theater of war. A three-man law office, backed by the Lawyers' Military Defense Committee, of Cambridge, Mass., was set up last fall in Saigon to provide free civilian legal services for dissident soldiers being court-martialed in Vietnam.

Besides these lawyers' fronts, the Pacific Counseling Service (an umbrella organization with Unitarian backing for a prolifery of antimilitary activities) provides legal help and incitement to dissident GIs through not one but seven branches (Tacoma, Oakland, Los Angeles, San Diego, Monterey, Tokyo, and Okinawa).

Another of Pacific Counseling's activities is to air-drop planeloads of sedition literature into Oakland's sprawling Army Base, our major West Coast staging point for Vietnam.

On the religious front, a community of turbulent priests and clergymen, some unfrocked, calls itself the Order of Maximilian. Maximilian is a saint said to have been martyred by the Romans for refusing military service as un-Christian. Maximilian's present-day followers visit military posts, infiltrate brigs and stockades in the guise of spiritual counseling, work to recruit military chaplains, and hold services of "consecrations" of post chapels in the name of their saintly draft-dodger.

By present count at least 11 (some go as high as 26) off-base antiwar "coffee houses" ply GIs with rock music, lukewarm coffee, antiwar literature, how-to-do-it tips on desertion, and similar disruptive counsels. Among the best-known coffee houses are: The Shelter Half (Ft. Lewis, Wash.); The Home Front (Ft. Carson, Colo.); and The Oleo Strut (Ft. Hood, Tex.).

Virtually all the coffee houses are or have been supported by the U.S. Serviceman's Fund, whose offices are in New York City's Bronx. Until May 1970 the Fund was recognized as a tax-exempt "charitable corporation," a determination which changed when IRS agents found that its main function was sowing dissention among GIs and that it was a satellite of "The New Mobilization Committee," a communist-front organization aimed at disruption of the Armed Forces.

Another "New Mobe" satellite is the G.I. Press Service, based in Washington, which calls itself the Associated Press of military underground newspapers. Robert Wilkinson, G.I. Press's editor, is well known to military intelligence and has been barred from South Vietnam.

While refusing to divulge names, IRS sources say that the Serviceman's Fund has been largely bankrolled by well-to-do liberals. One example of this kind of liberal support for sedition which did surface identifiably last year was the $8,500 nut channeled from the Philip Stern Family Foundation to underwrite Seaman Roger Priest's underground paper OM, which, among other writings, ran do-it-yourself advice for desertion to Canada and advocated assassination of President Nixon.

The nation-wide campus-radical offensive against ROTC and college officer-training is well known. Events last year at Stanford University, however, demonstrate the extremes to which this campaign (which peaked after Cambodia) has gone. After the Stanford faculty voted to accept a modified, specially restructured ROTC program, the university was subjected to a cyclone of continuing violence which included at least $200,000 in ultimate damage to buildings (highlighted by systematic destruction of 40 twenty-foot stained glass windows in the library). In the end, led by university president Richard W. Lyman, the faculty reversed itself. Lyman was quoted at the time that "ROTC is costing Stanford too much."

"Entertainment Industry for Peace and Justice," the antiwar show-biz front organized by Jane Fonda, Dick Gregory, and Dalton Trumbo, now claims over 800 film, TV, and music names. This organization is backing Miss Fonda's antimilitary road-show that opened outside the gates of Ft. Bragg, N.C., in mid-March.

Describing her performances (scripted by Jules Pfeiffer) as the soldiers' alternative to Bob Hope, Miss Fonda says her cast will repeat the Ft. Bragg show at or outside 19 more major bases. Although her project reportedly received financial backing from the ubiquitous Serviceman's Fund, Miss Fonda insisted on $1.50 admission from each of her GI audience at Bragg, a factor which, according to soldiers, somewhat limited attendance.

Freshman Representative Ronald V. Dellums (D-Calif.) runs a somewhat different kind of antimilitary production. As a Congressman, Dellums cannot be barred from military posts and has been taking full advantage of the fact. At Ft. Meade, Md., last month, Dellums led a soldier audience as they booed and cursed their commanding officer who was present on-stage in the post theater which the Army had to make available.

Dellums has also used Capitol Hill facilities for his "Ad Hoc hearings" on alleged war crimes in Vietnam, much of which involves repetition of unfounded and often unprovable charges first surfaced in the Detroit "Winter Soldiers" hearings earlier this year. As in the case of the latter, ex-soldier witnesses appearing before Dellums have not always been willing to cooperate with Army war-crimes investigators or even to disclose sufficient evidence to permit independent verification of their charges. Yet the fact that five West

Point graduates willingly testified for Dellums suggests the extent to which officer solidarity and traditions against politics have been shattered in today's Armed Forces.

## The Action Groups

Not unsurprisingly, the end-product of the atmosphere of incitement of unpunished sedition, and of recalcitrant antimilitary malevolence which pervades the world of the draftee (and to an extent the low-ranking men in "volunteer" services, too) is overt action.

One militant West Coast Group, Movement for a Democratic Military (MDM), has specialized in weapons theft from military bases in California. During 1970, large armory thefts were successfully perpetrated against Oakland Army Base, Vets Cronkhite and Ord, and even the Marine Corps Base at Camp Pendleton, where a team wearing Marine uniforms got away with nine M-16 rifles and an M-79 grenade launcher.

Operating in the Middle West, three soldiers from Ft Carson, Colo., home of the Army's permissive experimental unit, the 4th Mechanized Division, were recently indicted by a federal grand jury for dynamiting the telephone exchange, power plant and water works of another Army installation, Camp McCoy, Wis., on 26 July 1970.

The Navy, particularly on the West Coast, has also experienced disturbing cases of sabotage in the past two years, mainly directed at ships' engineering and electrical machinery.

It will be surprising, according to informed officers, if further such tangible evidence of disaffection within the ranks does not continue to come to light. Their view is that the situation could become considerably worse before it gets better.

## Tough Laws, Weak Courts

A frequent reaction when people learn the extent and intensity of the subversion which has been beamed at the Armed forces for the past three or more years is to ask whether such activities aren't banned by law. The answer is that indeed they are.

Federal law (181USC 2387) prohibits all manner of activities (including incitements, counseling, distribution or preparation of literature, and related conspiracies) intended to subvert the loyalty, morale or discipline of the Armed services. The penalty for violating this statute is up to ten years in prison, a $10,000 fine, or both.

Despite this tough law, on the books for many years, neither the Johnson, nor so far, the Nixon administration has brought a single prosecution against any of the wide range of individuals and groups, some mentioned here, whose avowed aims are to nullify the discipline and seduce the allegiance of the Armed Forces.

Government lawyers (who asked not to be named) suggested two reasons for failure to prosecute. Under President Johnson, two liberal Attorneys General, Messers. Ramsey Clark and Nicholas deB. Katzenbach, were reportedly unsympathetic to military pleas for help and in general to prosecutions for sedition of any kind. Besides, the lawyers said, the courts have now gone so far in extending First Amendment shelter to any form of utterance, that there is doubt whether cases brought under this law would hold.

Whatever the reason—and it appears mainly to be disinclination to prosecute or even test existing law—the services are today being denied legal protection they previously enjoyed without question and at a time when they need it worse than ever before. Continuing failure to invoke these sanctions prompted one senior commander to comment bitterly, "We simply can't turn this thing around until we get some support from our elected and appointed civilian officials."

One area of the U.S. government in which the Armed Forces are encountering noticeable lack of support is the federal judiciary.

Until a very few years ago, the processes of military justice were regarded as a nearly untouchable preserve which the civil courts entered with reluctance and diffidence.

Plagued by a new breed of litigious soldier (and some litigious officers, too), the courts have responded by unprecedented rulings, mostly libertarian in thrust, which both specifically and generally have hampered and impeded the traditional operations of military justice and dealt body blows to discipline.

Andrew Stapp, the seditious soldier who founded the American Serviceman's Union, an organization aimed at undermining the disciplinary structure of the Armed Forces, last year had his well earned undesirable discharge reversed by a U.S. judge who said Stapp's right to unionize and try to overthrow the Army was an "off-duty" activity which the Army had no right to penalize in discharging him.

Libertarian Supreme Court Justice W. O. Douglas has impeded the Army in mobilizing and moving reservists, while his O'Callaghan decision not only released a convicted rapist but threw a wrench into military jurisdiction and court-martial precedents going back in some cases nearly two centuries.

In Oakland, Cal., last year, a federal court yanked some 37 soldiers from the gangplank of a transport for Vietnam (where all 37 had suddenly discovered conscientious objections to war) and still has them stalled on the West Coast some 18 months later.

The long-standing federal law against wearing of Armed Forces uniforms by persons intending to discredit the services was struck down in 1969 by the

Supreme Court, which reversed the conviction of a uniformed actor who put on an antimilitary "guerrilla theater" skit on the street in Houston, Tex. As a result the Armed Forces are now no longer able to control subversive exploitation of the uniform for seditious purposes.

## Tactics of Harassment

Part of the defense establishment's problem with the judiciary is the now widely pursued practice of taking commanding officers into civil courts by dissident soldiers either to harass or annul normal discipline or administrative procedures of the services.

Only a short time ago, for example, a dissident group of active-duty officers, members of the Concerned Officers' Movement (COM), filed a sweeping lawsuit against Defense Secretary Laird himself, as well as all three service secretaries, demanding official recognition of their "right" to oppose the Vietnam war, accusing the secretaries of "harassing" them, and calling for court injunction to ban disciplinary "retaliation" against COM members.

Such nuisance suits from the inside (usually, like the Laird suit, on constitutional grounds) by people still in uniform, let alone by officers, were unheard-of until two or three years ago. Now, according to one Army general, the practice has become so common that, in his words, "I can't even give a directive without getting permission from my staff judge advocate."

## Racial Incidents

Sedition and subversion and legal harassment, rank near the top of what might be called the unprecedented external problems that elements in American society are inflicting on the Armed Forces.

Internally speaking, racial conflicts and drugs—also previously insignificant—are tearing the services apart today.

Racial trouble is no new thing for the Army. In 1906, after considerable provocation, three companies of the 25th Infantry (a colored regular regiment) attacked white troops and townspeople of Brownsville, Texas, and had to be disbanded. Among the few pre-World War II War Department records still heavily classified and thus unavailable to scholars are Army documents on racial troubles.

Racial conflicts (most but not all sparked by young black enlisted men) are erupting murderously in all services.

At a recent high commanders' conference, General Westmoreland and other senior generals heard the report from Germany that in many units white soldiers are now afraid to enter barracks alone at night for fear of "head-hunting" ambushes by blacks.

In the quoted words of one soldier on duty in West Germany, "I'm much more afraid of getting mugged on the post than I am of getting attacked by the Russians."

Other reports tell of jail-delivery attacks on Army stockades and military police to release black prisoners, and of officers being struck in public by black soldiers. Augsburg, Krailsheim, and Hohenfels are said to be rife with racial trouble. Hohenfels was the scene of a racial fragging last year—one of the few so recorded outside Vietnam.

In Ulm, last fall, a white noncommissioned officer killed a black soldier who was holding a loaded .45 on two unarmed white officers.

Elsewhere, according to *Fortune* magazine, junior officers are now being attacked at night when inspecting barracks containing numbers of black soldiers.

Kelley Hill, a Ft. Benning, Ga., barracks area, has been the scene of repeated nighttime assaults on white soldiers. One such soldier bitterly remarked, "Kelley Hill may belong to the commander in the daytime but it belongs to the blacks after dark."

Even the cloistered quarters of WACs have been hit by racial hair-pulling. In one West Coast WAC detachment this year, black women on duty as charge-o-quarters took advantage of their trust to vandalize unlocked rooms occupied by white WACS. On this rampage, they destroyed clothing, emptied drawers, and overturned furniture of their white sisters.

But the Army has no monopoly on racial troubles.

As early as July 1969 the Marines (who had previously enjoyed a highly praised record on race) made headlines at Camp Lejeune, N.C., when a mass affray launched by 30–50 black Marines ended fatally with a white corporal's skull smashed in and 145 other white Marines in the sick bay.

That same year, at Newport, R.I., naval station, blacks killed a white petty officer, while in March 1971 the National Naval Medical Center in Bethesda, Md., outside Washington, was beset by racial fighting so severe that the base enlisted men's club had to be closed.

All services are today striving energetically to cool and control this ugly violence which in the words of one noncommissioned officer, has made his once tough unit divide up "like two street gangs."

MGen Orwin C. Talbott, at Ft. Benning, has instituted what he calls "race relations, coordinating groups" which work to defuse the resentments of young black troopers at a Georgia base.

MGen John C. Bennett, commanding the 4th Mechanized Division at Ft. Carson, Colo., has a highly successful "racial relations committee" which has kept Carson cool for over a year.

At once-troubled Camp Lejeune, MGen Michael P. Ryan, the Tarawa hero who commands the 2nd Marine Division, appears to have turned off the race war that two years ago was clawing at the vitals of his division.

Yet even the encouraging results attained by these commanders do not bespeak general containment of the service-wide race problem any more than the near-desperate attack being mounted on drug abuse has brought the narcotics epidemic under control within the military.

## Drugs and the Military

The drug problem—like the civilian situation from which it directly derives—is running away with the services. In March, Navy Secretary John H. Chafee, speaking for the two sea services, said bluntly that drug abuse in both Navy and Marines is out of control.

In 1966, the Navy discharged 170 drug offenders. Three years later (1969), 3,800 were discharged. Last year in 1970, the total jumped to over 5,000.

Drug abuse in the Pacific Fleet—with Asia on one side, and kinky California on the other—gives the Navy its worst headaches. To cite one example, a destroyer due to sail from the West Coast last year for the Far East nearly had to postpone deployment when, five days before departure, a ring of some 30 drug users (over 10 percent of the crew) was uncovered.

Only last week, eight midshipmen were dismissed from the Naval Academy following disclosure of an alleged drug ring. While the Navy emphatically denies allegations in a copyrighted article by the *Annapolis Capitol* that up to 12,000 midshipmen now use marijuana, midshipman sources confirm that pot is anything but unknown at Annapolis.

Yet the Navy is somewhat ahead in the drug game because of the difficulty in concealing addiction at close quarters aboard ship, and because fixes are unobtainable during long deployments at sea.

The Air Force, despite 2,715 drug investigations in 1970, is in even better shape: its rate of 3 cases per thousand airmen is the lowest in the services.

By contrast, the Army had 17,742 drug investigations the same year. According to Col. Thomas B. Hauschild, of the Medical Command of our Army forces in Europe, some 46 percent of the roughly 200,000 soldiers there had used illegal drugs at least once. In one battalion surveyed in West Germany, over 50 percent of the men smoked marijuana regularly (some on duty), while roughly half of those were using hard drugs of some type.

What these statistics say is that the Armed Forces (like their parent society) are in the grip of a drug pandemic—a conclusion underscored by the one fact that, just since 1968, the total number of verified drug addiction cases throughout the Armed Forces has nearly doubled. One other yardstick:

according to military medical sources, needle hepatitis now poses as great a problem among young soldiers as VD.

At Ft. Bragg, the Army's third largest post, adjacent to Fayetteville, N.C. (a garrison town whose conditions one official likened to New York's "East Village" and San Francisco's "Haight-Ashbury") a recent survey disclosed that 4% (or over 1,400) of the 36,000 soldiers there are hard-drug (mainly heroin and LSD) addicts. In the 82nd Airborne Division, the strategic-reserve unit that boasts its title of "America's Honor Guard," approximately 450 soldier drug abusers were being treated when this reporter visited the post in April. About a hundred were under intensive treatment in special drug wards.

Yet Bragg is the scene of one of the most imaginative and hopeful drug programs in the Armed Forces. The post commander, LGen John J. Tolson, and the 82nd Airborne's commander, MGen George S. Blanchard, are pushing "Operation Awareness," a broad post-wide program focused on hard drugs, prevention, and enforcement.

Spearheading Operation Awareness is a tough yet deeply humane Army chaplain and onetime Brooklyn longshoreman, LCol John P. McCullagh. Father McCullagh has made himself one of the Army's top experts on drugs, and was last year called as an expert witness by Harold Hughes's Senate Subcommittee on Alcohol and Narcotics.

## No Street Is Safe

One side-effect of the narcotics flood throughout the services is a concurrent epidemic of barracks theft and common criminality inside military or naval bases which once had the safest streets in America.

According to the personnel chief of one of the Army's major units, unauthorized absence, historically the services' top disciplinary problem, is now being crowded by the thefts. Barracks theft destroys trust and mutual loyalty among men who ought to be comrades and who must rely absolutely on each other in combat. It corrodes morale and is itself an indicator of impossible conditions in a fighting unit.

At Ft. Bragg, primarily because of addict thieves, soldiers in many units cannot even keep bedding on their bunks in barracks. After what used to be reveille, they strip their bunks of bedding and cram it away under lock and key with whatever valuables they dare keep on hand.

Radios, sports gear, tape decks, and cameras—let alone individual equipment—are stolen on sight. Unlocked cars, on the manicured streets of this fine old post, are more likely to be stolen than not. Fayetteville, according to soldiers, abounds with off-post fences who will pay pennies for Army blankets and higher amounts for just about anything else.

Unhappily, conditions at Ft. Bragg are not unusual.

Soldier muggings and holdups are on the rise everywhere. Ft. Dix, N.J., has a higher rate of on-post crime than any base on the East Coast. Soldier muggings are reported to average one a night, with a big upsurge every payday. Despite 450 MP's (one for every 55 soldiers stationed there—one of the highest such ratios in the country) no solution appears in sight.

Crimes are so intense and violent in the vicinity of an open-gate "honor system" detention facility at Ft. Dix that, according to press reports, units on the base are unwilling to detail armed sentinels to man posts nearby, for fear of assault and robbery.

## Desertions and Disasters

With conditions what they are in the Armed Forces, and with intense efforts on the part of elements in our society to disrupt discipline and destroy morale the consequences can be clearly measured in two ultimate indicators: man-power retention (reenlistments and their antithesis, desertions); and the state of discipline.

In both respects the picture is anything but encouraging.

Desertion, to be sure, has often been a serious problem in the past. In 1826, for example, desertions exceeded 50% of the total enlistments in the Army. During the Civil War, in 1864, Jefferson Davis reported to the Confederate Congress: "Two thirds of our men are absent, most absent without leave."

Desertion rates are going straight up in Army, Marines, and Air Force. Curiously, however, during the period since 1968 when desertion has nearly doubled for all three other services, the Navy's rate has risen by less than 20 percent.

In 1970, the Army had 65,643 deserters, or roughly the equivalent of four infantry divisions. This desertion rate (52.3 soldiers per thousand) is well over twice the peak rate for Korea (22.5 per thousand). It is more than quadruple the 1966 desertion-rate (14.7 per thousand) of the then well-trained, high-spirited professional Army.

If desertions continue to rise (as they are still doing this year), they will attain or surpass the WWII peak of 63 per thousand, which, incidentally, occurred in the same year (1945) when more soldiers were actually being discharged from the Army for psychoneurosis than were drafted.

The Air Force,—relatively uninvolved in the Vietnam war, all-volunteer, management-oriented rather than disciplinary and hierarchic—enjoys a numerical rate of less that one deserter per thousand men, but even this is double what it was three years ago.

The Marines in 1970 had the highest desertion index in the modern history of the Corps and, for that year at least, slightly higher than the Army's. As the Marines now phase out of Vietnam (and haven't taken a draftee in nearly two years), their desertions are expected to decrease sharply. Meanwhile, grimly remarked one officer, "let the bastards go. We're all the better without them."

Letting the bastards go is something the Marines can probably afford. "The Marine Corps Isn't Looking for a Lot of Recruits," reads a current recruiting poster, "We Just Need a Few Good Men." This is the happy situation of a Corps slimming down to an elite force again composed of true volunteers who want to be professionals.

But letting the bastards go doesn't work at all for the Army and the Navy, who do need a lot of recruits and whose reenlistment problems are dire.

Admiral Elmo R. Zumwalt, Jr., chief of Naval Operations, minces no words. "We have a personnel crisis," he recently said, "that borders on disaster."

The Navy's crisis, as Zumwalt accurately describes it, is that of a highly technical, material oriented service that finds itself unable to retain the expensively-trained technicians needed to operate warships, which are the largest, most complex items of machinery that man makes and uses.

## Non-Volunteer Force?

If 45% of his sailors shipped over after their first enlistment, Admiral Zumwalt would be all smiles. With only 13% doing so, he is growing sideburns to enhance the Navy's appeal to youth.

Among the Army's volunteer (non-draftee) soldiers on their first hitch, the figures are much the same: less than 14% re-up.

The Air Force is slightly, but not much, better off: 16% of its first-termers stay on.

Moreover—and this is the heart of the Army's dilemma—only 4 % of the voluntary enlistees now choose service in combat arms (infantry, armor, artillery) and of those only 2.5% opt for infantry. Today's soldiers, it seems, volunteer readily enough for the tail of the Army, but not for its teeth.

For all services, the combined retention rate this past year is about half what it was in 1966, and the lowest since the bad times of similar low morale and national disenchantment after Korea.

Both Army and Navy are responding to their manpower problems in measures intended to seduce recruits and reenlistees: disciplinary permissiveness, abolition of reveille and KP, fewer inspections, longer haircuts—essentially cosmetic changes aimed at softening (and blurring) traditional military and naval images.

Amid such changes (not unlike the Army's 1946 Doolittle Board coincidences intended in their similar postwar day to sweeten life for the privates), those which are not cosmetic at all may well exert profound and deleterious effects on the leadership, command authority and discipline of the services.

## Soulbone Connected to the Backbone

"Discipline," George Washington once remarked, "is the soul of an army."

Washington should know. In January 1781, all the Pennsylvania and New Jersey troops in the Continental Army mutinied. Washington only quelled the outbreaks by disarming the Jersey mutineers and having their leaders shot in hollow square—by a firing squad made up of fellow mutineers.

(The navy's only mutiny, aboard USS *Somers* in 1842, was quelled when the captain hanged the mutineers from the yardarm while still at sea.)

If Washington was correct (and almost any professional soldier, whether officer or NCO, will agree), then the Armed Forces today are in deep trouble.

What enhances this trouble, by exponential dimensions, is the kind of manpower with which the Armed Forces now have to work. As early as three years ago, *U.S. News and World Report* reported that the services were already plagued with "... a new breed of man, who thinks he is his own Secretary of State, Secretary of Defense, and Attorney General. He considers himself superior to any officer alive. And he is smart enough to go by the book. He walks a tightrope between the regulations and sedition."

Yet the problem is not just one of trouble-makers and how to cope with them.

The trouble of the services—produced by and also in turn producing the dismaying conditions described in this article—is above all a crisis of soul and backbone. It entails—the word is not too strong—something very near a collapse of the command authority and leadership George Washington saw as the soul of military forces. This collapse results, at least in part, from a concurrent collapse of public confidence in the military establishment.

General Matthew B. Ridgway, one of the Army's finest leaders in this century (who revitalized the shaken Eighth Army in Korea after its headlong rout by the Chinese in 1950) recently said, "Not before in my lifetime . . . has the Army's public image fallen to such low esteem . . . "

But the fall in public esteem of all three major services—not just the Army—is exceeded by the fall or at least the enfeeblement of the hierarchic and disciplinary system by which they exist and, when ordered to do so, fight and sometimes die.

Take the case of the noncommissioned and petty officers.

In Rudyard Kipling's lines, "the backbone o' the Army is the noncommissioned man!"

Today, the NCOs—the lifers—have been made strangers in their own home, the regular service, by the collective malevolence, recalcitrance, and cleverness of college-educated draftees who have outflanked the traditional NCO hierarchy and created a privates' power structure with more influence on the Army of today than its sergeants major.

## No Office for the Ombudsman

In the 4th Mechanized Division at Ft. Carson, Sp 4 David Gyongyos, on his second year in the Army, enjoys an office across the hall from the division commander, a full-time secretary, and staff car and driver also assigned full time. He has the home phone numbers of the general and chief of staff and doesn't hesitate to use them out of working hours when he feels like it.

Gyongyos (with a bachelor's degree in theology and two years' law school) is chairman of the division's Enlisted Men's Councils, a system of elected soviets made up of privates and Sp 4s (NCOs aren't allowed) which sits at the elbow of every unit commander down to the companies. "I represent, electively," Gyongyos expansively told this reporter, "the 17,000 men on this post."

The division sergeant major, with a quarter-century in the Army, who is supposed to be the division's first soldier and—non-electively—father and ombudsman of every soldier, has an office which is not even on the same floor with the general (or Sp 4 Gyongyos either). He gets his transportation, as needed, from the motor pool. He does not "rap" freely over the phone to the general's quarters.

The very most that Gyongyos will concede to the sergeant major, the first sergeants, the platoon sergeants—the historic enlisted leadership of armies—is that they are "combat technicians." They are not, he coldly adds, "highly skilled in the social sciences."

The soldiers' soviets of the 4th Division represent an experiment in what the Army calls "better communications," Conditions throughout the rest of the Army do not quite duplicate those at Carson, but the same spirit is abroad. And experienced NCOs everywhere feel threatened or at least puzzled.

Most major units of the Army, Navy, and Air Force have some form of enlisted men's councils, as well as junior officer councils. Even the trainee companies at Ft. Ord, Calif. have councils, made up of recruits, who take questions and complaints past their DIs to company commanders and hold weekly meetings and post minutes on bulletin-boards. General Pershing, who once said, "All a soldier needs to know is how to shoot and salute," would be surprised.

## The Vocalists

As for the officers, said a four-star admiral, "We have lost our voice."

The foregoing may be true as far as admirals are concerned, but hasn't hampered short-term junior officers (including several West Pointers) from banding together into highly vocal antiwar and antimilitary organizations, such as the Concerned Officers' Movement (COM). At Norfolk, the local

COM chapter has a peace billboard outside gate 2, Norfolk Naval Station, where every sailor can profit by the example of his officers.

Inspection—one of the most important and traditionally visible tools of command—is being widely soft-pedaled because it is looked on as "chicken" by young soldiers, sailors, and airmen.

In a move "to eliminate irritants to Air Force life" all major Air Force commands got orders last year to cut back on inspection of people and facilities.

"You just damn near don't inspect barracks any more," said one Air Force colonel, "this is considered an irritant." Besides, he added, (partly to prevent barracks theft and partly for privacy), airmen keep the keys to their own rooms, anyway.

Aboard ships of the Navy, where every inch of metal and flake of paint partakes in the seaworthiness and battle readiness of the vessel, inspection is still a vital and nearly constant process, but even here, Admiral Zumwalt has discouraged "unnecessary" inspections.

If officers have lost their voices, their ears have in many commands been opened if not burnt in an unprecedented fashion via direct "hot lines" or "action lines" whereby any enlisted man can ring up his CO and voice a gripe or an obscenity, or just tell him what he thinks about something or, for that matter, someone.

Starting last year at Naval Air Station, Miramar, Cal., sailors have been able to dial "C-A-P-T" and get their captain on the line. The system so impressed Admiral Zumwalt that he ordered all other shore stations to follow suit, even permitting anonymous calls.

At Ft. Lewis, Wash., soldiers dial "B-O-S-S-" for the privilege of giving the general an earful.

At the Air Force Academy, cadets receive early indoctrination in the new order of things: here, too, a cadet (anonymously, if he wishes) can phone the Superintendent, record his message and, also by recording receive the general's personal thanks for having called.

## Word to the Whys

"Discipline," wrote Sir John Jervis, one of England's greatest admirals, "is summed up in the one word, obedience."

Robert E. Lee later said, "Men must be habituated to obey or they cannot be controlled in battle."

In the Armed forces today, obedience appears to be a sometime thing.

"You can't give them an order and expect them to obey immediately," says an infantry officer in Vietnam. "They ask why, and you have to tell them."

Command authority, i.e., the unquestioned ability of an officer or NCO to give an order and expect it to be complied with, is at an all-time low. It is so low that, in many units, officers give the impression of having lost their nerve in issuing, let alone enforcing orders.

In the words of an Air Force officer to this reporter, "If a captain went down on the line and gave an order and expected it to be obeyed because 'I said so!'—there'd be a rebellion."

Other officers unhesitatingly confirmed the foregoing.

What all this amounts to—conspicuously in Vietnam and only less so elsewhere—is that today's junior enlisted man, not the lifer, but the educated draftee or draft-motivated "volunteer"—now demands that orders be simplistically justified on his own terms before he feels any obligation to obey.

Yet the young soldiers, sailors and airmen might obey more willingly if they had more confidence in their leaders. And there are ample indications that Armed Forces junior (and NCO) leadership has been soft, inexperienced, and sometimes plain incompetent.

In the 82nd Airborne Division today, the average length of service of the company commanders is only 3 1/2 years.

In the Navy, a man makes petty officer 2d class in about 2 1/2 years after he first enlists. By contrast, in the taut and professional pre-WWII fleet, a man required 2 1/2 years just to make himself a really first-class seaman.

The grade of corporal has practically been superseded in the Army: Sp 4s hold most of the corporals' billets. Where the corporal once commanded a squad, today's Army gives the job to a staff sergeant, two ranks higher. Within the squad, it now takes a sergeant to command three other soldiers in the lowly fire-team.

"This never would have happened," somberly said a veteran artillery sergeant major, "if the NCOs had done their jobs . . . The NCOs are our weak point." Sp 4 Gyongyos at Ft. Carson agrees: "It is the shared perception of the privates that the NCOs have not looked out for the soldiers."

When B Troop, 1st Cavalry, mutinied during the Laos operation, and refused to fight, not an officer or NCO raised his hand (or his pistol) or stepped forward. Fifty-three privates and Sp 4s cowed all the lifers of their units.

"Officers," says a recently retired senior admiral, "do not stand up for what they believe. The older enlisted men are really horrified."

Lieutenant William L. Calley, Jr., an ex-company clerk, was a platoon leader who never even learned to read a map. His credentials for a commission were derisory; he was no more officer-material than any Pfc. in his platoon. Yet the Army had to take him because no one else was available. Commenting on the Calley conviction, a colonel at Ft. Benning said, "We have at least two or three thousand more Calleys in the Army just waiting for the next calamity."

Albert Johnson, the tough Master Chief Petty Officer of the Atlantic Fleet, shakes his head and says: "You used to hear it all the time—people would say, 'The Chiefs run the Navy.' But you don't hear it much any more, especially from the Chiefs."

## A Hard Lot at Best

But the lot of even the best, most forceful leader is a hard one in today's military.

In the words of a West Point lieutenant colonel commanding an airborne battalion, "There are so many ways nowadays for a soldier that is smart and bad to get back at you." The colonel should know: recently he reduced a sergeant for gross public insubordination and now he is having to prepare a lengthy apologia, through channels to the Secretary of The Army, in order to satisfy the offending sergeant's congressman.

"How do we enforce discipline?" asks a senior general. Then he answers himself: "Sweep it under the rug. Keep them happy. Keep it out of the press. Do things the easy way: no court-martials, but strong discipline."

Towards the end of the eighteenth century, after years of costly, frustrating and considerably less than successful war, Britain's armed forces were swept by disaffection culminating in the widespread mutinies in most of the ships and fleets that constituted England's "wooden walls" against France.

Writing to a friend in 1779, Britain's First Lord of the Admiralty said, "The Channel Fleet is now lost to the country as much as if it was at the bottom of the sea."

Have things gone that far in the United States today?

The most optimistic answer is—probably not. Or at least not yet.

But many a thoughtful officer would be quick to echo the words of BGen Donn A. Starry, who recently wrote, "The Army can defend the nation against anything but the nation itself."

Or—in the wry words of Pogo—we have met the enemy, and they are us.

# Rifle, Dope & Camera: The "Grunt" Filmmaker

"I *hate* this movie."
—*Dispatches*, Michael Herr

## Maggie Jaffe

This essay is comprised of three parts. Part one investigates drug use or "abuse" during the Vietnam War (1961–75), since drugs and the Vietnam War are inextricably linked, and drugs themselves are inseparable from ideology. For example, "strung-out" veterans, in part, and not the government, were routinely held accountable for failure in winning the Vietnam War, at least until the mid-to-late 80s. For the Vietnam vet, particularly, accusations of drug abuse was, and often still is, leveled against him as a visible display of "moral weakness." Although overwhelming evidence points to the United States' "shadow government" as complicit in the drug trade in Southeast Asia, as well as in Latin America, Richard Nixon's 1973 "War on Drugs" program incarcerated numerous nonviolent drug users, many veterans among them. Finally, drug warfare has replaced the long-standing war on communism to a considerable extent.

Drug taking by Vietnam veterans was also perceived as a rebellion against the war. However, as Jonathan Shay, psychiatrist and author of *Achilles in Vietnam*, suggests, drugs or alcohol are often times used as "self-medication" and this demands closer analysis: "The use of drugs/alcohol [officially prescribed, unofficially encouraged, or covert/illegal] to suppress grief in Vietnam strikes me as *very* important" (email post to VWAR—l@ubvm.cc.buffalo.edu 5 February, 1995).

Part two, *Self-Portrait As Mars: Otto Dix and Art Against War*, is perhaps the most problematic-seeming aspect of this essay. Why Dix? For a few reasons. His strongest anti-war paintings were executed during the 1920s, a period marked by Germany's increased militarism, culminating in the Nazi election in 1933—and there are important affinities between his art and the filmic anti-war "art" of the American "grunt," or front-line, director-screenwriters.

Both cultures produced powerful anti-war art during growing right-wing militarism, paramilitarism and xenophobia. Both countries suffered economic loss (particularly severe in Germany), and pulled back social services, especially for their vets, to bolster their respective militaries. And both countries suffered the psychological traumas associated with losing a war. Just as Dix and other German artists produced anti-war art during Germany's increased militarization, so too movies by Vietnam veterans came of age during the hawkish Reagan-Bush era. Under Reagan, for example, defense spending went from 144 billion dollars in 1980 to a grossly disproportionate 293 billion dollars in 1988.

Arguably, all wars, hence all war movies, resemble each other to a considerable extent. Nevertheless, the Vietnam war movie is singular in that drug taking played a significant role in the filmic representation of the Vietnam veteran. Typically, in a World War Two flick GIs share a pack of smokes in a foxhole. But in Vietnam war movies, grass, hash, speed, and acid take precedence over tobacco, and drugs, death and Vietnam are unfailingly yoked. For the Vietnam vet, who was transformed from a drug-crazed "baby killer" into a victim of the callous State, the examination of grunt-directors' art is additionally important.

Part three, "We Don't Do Dew When We Do Business": A Drug Filmography, examines the movies of filmmakers who served in Vietnam, specifically, Oliver Stone, Jim Carabatsos, Gustav Hasford, Patrick Duncan and Michael Herr. Herr is included because he was in Vietnam as a journalist for *Esquire* magazine: his critically acclaimed *Dispatches* (1977) details the war's devastating impact on the soldiers with whom he lived. He also co-wrote screenplays for two of the best known Vietnam War movies: *Apocalypse Now* (1979) and *Full Metal Jacket* (1987). Adrian Lyne's *Jacob's Ladder* (1990) is also included, although Lyne is not a veteran, because the subject of his movie is involuntary drug experimentation by the military.

Paradoxically, the veteran filmmaker emerged more than ten years after the fall of Saigon, and at the height of the Reagan-Bush conservative "revolution." Perhaps time was needed to transform traumatic memories into art. Whatever the reasons, by the late 1980s Hollywood would at long last explicitly film the war. During the "conflict" itself, John Wayne's *The Green Berets* (1968) was the sole *mainstream* movie about Vietnam, although Jean-Jacques Malo insists that over 30 films about the war were made by 1968 (See his review of *From Hanoi to Hollywood: The Vietnam War in American Film. Viet Nam Generation* v4, n1-2 April 1992). With the demise of communism and the renewed militarism of the Reagan-Bush regimes, as well as the construction of the Vietnam Veterans Memorial in 1982, the "psychopathic" and "drug-crazed" Vietnam vet was rehabilitated with the help of the culture industry "in conjunction with the rehabilitation of U.S. military power" (Miller 185).

Concurrent with Washington's bombing of Tripoli and Benghazi, Libya, *Platoon* and *Heartbreak Ridge* were released in 1986. Similarly, the United States conducted midnight bombing raids on Panama City, arrested Manuel Noriega (the reputed drug "kingpin"), and imprisoned him for life within the U.S., while *Born on the Fourth of July* and *84 Charlie MoPic* had their 1989 premieres. That same year, Oliver North, a highly decorated Vietnam veteran, was the first person convicted in connection with the Iran-*Contra* "affair." Instead of doing prison time, North received a three-year suspended sentence. Meanwhile, the "radical" left presses reported on the CIA-*Contra*-Cocaine Connection, whereas the mainstream media barely touched it. Interestingly, Stone wanted to film a political satire about Noriega, but the project fell through because he could not get sufficient backing. (See "A Talk With Manuel Noriega: Drugs, *Contras*, Invasion & More." *The Nation* 24 January 1994: 80–90). With considerable pragmatism as well as cynicism, General Maxwell D. Thurman, who planned the Panama Invasion, summed up the U.S.'s foreign policy this way: "the Latin American drug war is the only war we've got" (Gibson 291).

Incongruously enough, Stone's *The Doors* explored the Sixties drug subculture through the complex characterization of Jim Morrison, and this film coincided with the 1991 Persian Gulf War. According to James Gibson, "with Communism in rapid decline and Noriega out of commission in a Miami jail, American political culture needed a new demon against which to mobilize" (292). What better demon than Saddam [Adolf Hitler] Hussein on one front, the "War on Drugs" on the other.

In Ronald Siegel's *Intoxication: Life in Pursuit of Artificial Paradise*, he suggests that "throughout our entire history as a species, intoxication functioned like the basic drives of hunger, thirst or sex, sometimes overshadowing all other activities in life. *Intoxication is the fourth drive*" (10). About heroin use, especially, during the Vietnam War, Siegel has this to say:

> Approximately one out of every three soldiers tried heroin while in Vietnam and half of them became addicted. The point is not whether they were good or bad soldiers, but that heroin use did not necessarily result in dysfunction and life-long enslavement to the habit. When the men returned to the United States, and were removed from the social setting of the war, their craving was minimal. Although heroin was less accessible and more expensive in the States, half the returnees who had been addicted in Vietnam used heroin again at home. Surprisingly, only 12 percent became readdicted—a remarkably low recidivism rate. Many

soldiers found they could use heroin, even at the rate of more than once a week, without readdicton (305).

Siegel credits low recidivism on "chipping," or sporadic substance use, to control addiction. Curiously, though, he does not mention the enormous capital that was made from heroin by top-brass South Vietnamese and U.S. officials. During 1970, particularly, heroin use, both domestically and among GIs, had almost reached "epidemic" proportions (according to the media), and the period is in fact referred to as the "Heroin Epidemic of 1970."

Robert Jay Lifton, who acknowledges addiction as a problem for the vet, also looks at the ideology of drug use, and in this way differs from Siegel on a few crucial points:

> There has to be no doubt about the actuality during the early 1970s of widespread heroin addiction in Vietnam—probably related to such factors as easy, low-cost availability of the virtually pure drug, the drying up (at least temporarily) of marihuana supplies, the death-linked corruption of the environment, and the related apathy of those who were (in one journalist's words) 'at the butt end of a bad war.'
>
> Yet despite the actuality, the drug epidemic takes on near mythic quality. The men are sent to war and encounter evil; they take on the taint of sickness of that evil in the form of the 'heroin plague' (the mass media term); the society that sent them becomes terrified of them, lest they carry the 'plague' back home; a system of forced 'testing' and 'decontamination' is set up before the men can be permitted to reenter the society . . . but the system does not always work, the fear of contagion remains acute, as images of the infected men returning to spread their plague throughout the mother country. Now the addicts, instead of the war itself and the way we are fighting it, become the locus of evil. (125)

Lifton cites Alfred W. McCoy's *The Politics of Heroin: CIA Complicity in the Global Drug Trade,* which is an in-depth analysis of U.S. involvement in the heroin drug trade, to corroborate his ideological position on drug use in Vietnam.

McCoy's expanded and updated reworking of his 1972 *The Politics of Heroin* includes information on the lucrative cocaine industry in Latin America of the 1980s, as well as his earlier investigations into heroin trafficking from the "Golden Triangle" (where Burma, Thailand and Laos converge) before and during the Vietnam War. This rigorously researched work historically traces the cultivation of the poppy: the Greek physician Hippocrates (466–377 B.C.) described it as a great boon for healing, and Homer mentioned opium in *The Odyssey* which "lulls all pain and anger, and brings forgetfulness of every sorrow" (3). Much of McCoy's focus, though, is on "the rise of large-scale heroin production in Southeast Asia [as] the culmination of four hundred years of Western intervention" (77).

In 1971 the CIA published its own version of the "The GI Heroin Epidemic," allegedly in response to a "need" for top-grade heroin in South Vietnam. But McCoy's take on the "epidemic" is vastly different than the CIA's—in fact, he closely documents the CIA's role in the Laotian heroin trade. According to McCoy, South Vietnamese officials benefited most by the "plague"—amassing an 88 million dollar profit on the sale of heroin—which ironically jeopardized the GI's ability to fight for South Vietnam:

> By 1968 the emotional malaise of the Vietnam GI was already well developed; the race riot in Long Binh stockade and the My Lai massacre were only the most obvious signs of the problem. But there was no serious heroin use until the spring of 1970, when large quantities were being sold everywhere in Vietnam. And the simple fact is that there would have been no epidemic without this well-organized, comprehensive sales campaign. The roots of the problem lay not with the GI victim or the army's marijuana crackdown, but with those Vietnamese officials who organized and protected heroin traffic. (224)

How did U.S. military officials "face the twin liabilities of the Vietnam drug problem—the heroin epidemic among the GIs and the growing exports to the United States"? With a mixture of "embarrassment, apathy and complicity," insists McCoy (254).

Larry Ingraham's "The Nam and The World" tries to clarify the most common misconceptions that people back in "the world" had about drug abuse, namely that heroin was mostly used by injection, led to criminal behavior, meant a loss of job proficiency, was a sign of mental illness, was used to relieve combat stress as well as to relieve boredom, and was counter cultural. Before 1969, 60 men were polled about drug use in the army, but material on heroin was difficult to obtain, although the men described marijuana or other drug use. By polling 78 enlisted men who tested positive for opiates *after* 1969, his findings indicate that heroin use was much more widespread. Still, injection of heroin was frowned upon—the preferred method was mixing it with tobacco—and that those men who only smoked marijuana, rather than used heroin, speed, or LSD, were given the "highest status," since grass users rarely fought, nodded out, displayed erratic behavior, or jeopardized any of the other men. Although "heads" and "juicers" worked together by day, at night they were mostly segregated. Participation in the "head" society meant acceptance and sharing of each other's drugs, food and music:

> You really got into each other. We were all really tight in a way really different from juicers. There were no fights, no need to brag about your girl, no need to argue. Everyone was equal, honest and 'real,' if you know what I mean. (126)

Black and Chicano soldiers who shared "J's" with others "stated that before Vietnam they would never have believed that 'whites would willingly eat from the same spoon or drink from the same can of soda as blacks'" (126). Although the "heads" would use counter-cultural phrases—"fascist pigs" for police, the "green machine" for Army bureaucracy—Ingraham suggests that this "did not reflect a 'radical-left' political ideology, and did not represent a rejection of conventional values and living patterns" (123). Overall, his findings indicate that drug use was important for a sense of community while in Vietnam, but that the majority of soldiers did not use illicit drugs.

In contrast to Ingraham, John Steinbeck, the son of the famous author, claimed that 75% of soldiers smoked marijuana while in Vietnam, and "that use of the drug did not seriously affect the soldier's fighting ability, but made the horrors of combat easier to endure" ("U.S. Denies" 10).

Although the Pentagon refuted Steinbeck's findings, not surprisingly, in an attempt to demonize marijuana use, the Criminal Investigation Division (C.I.D.) of the Army interrogated the soldiers of Charlie Company about the use of the drug before and during the My Lai Massacre:

> The C.I.D. interviewed more than seventy-five witnesses by November 26, 1969. Many of them recalled being asked about the use of marijuana in Charlie Company; that question seemed of special interest to the investigators. The GIs all acknowledged that many members of the company smoked or otherwise made use of marijuana, which is plentiful in South Vietnam, but none believed it was in any way a significant factor in what happened at My Lai 4. (Hersh 121)

## II: Self-Portrait As Mars: *Otto Dix and Art Against War*

In the early years of World War One, the German artist-soldier, Otto Dix, executed two powerful drawings: *Self-Portrait as Soldier* (1914) and *Self-Portrait as Mars* (1915). In the former, the brooding boyish delicacy of his pre-war work *(Self-Portrait with Carnation,* for example) is transformed into brutishness. His head is shaved, his neck grossly thickened, his mouth painted dark red and curved downward in a scowl. His name and the date—Dix 14—are scrawled on the right side of his head in thick black paint. In *Self-Portrait as Mars* Dix employs a highly mannered cubist style: the same scowling face of the first self-portrait is transformed into intersecting lines and angles. Mars, the God of War, wears an elaborate helmet with metallic-like searchlights. Surrounding the figure are Dix's private symbols of war: splotches of blood, teeth biting down into blood, a terrified runaway horse, and half-ruined buildings, which might be an image from his recurring dream of crawling through a devastated cityscape: "I must crawl through ruined houses, through corridors where I don't get through. The ruins were constantly in my dreams" (McGreevy 47). More importantly, after four years in the trenches, Dix would "turn away from the fragmented planes of Cubism and Futurism to his first love, Realism—and tinge it with a critical message" (McGreevy 34). In other words, war compelled Dix to re-think the function of art, to utilize it as instruction and critique, rather than as investigation into the formal qualities associated with Cubism and Futurism. In the end, Dix insisted on "'see[ing] the thing entirely naked—clearly—almost without art'" (McGreevy 34).

By 1924, Dix finished his great anti-war cycle, *War (Der Krieg)*, which was published in book form, comprising of 50 paintings. Besides *War,* he painted the triptych *War* (1929–32); and the triptych *Trench Warfare* (1932), which was destroyed by the Nazis, along with more than two hundred of his other paintings. In fact, Dix specifically painted *Trench Warfare* as a warning against the increased bellicosity of the National Socialist German Worker's Party. In 1933 he also painted *The Seven Deadly Sins* which detailed Envy as a grotesque child who wears a mask with Hitler's unmistakable features.

After Hitler's 1933 election, Dix was stripped of his position as art teacher and was labeled "degenerate" in Hitler's staged Degenerate Art Exhibit, along with Max Beckmann, Marc Chagall, Max Ernst, Lyonel Feininger, George Grosz, John Heartfield, Wassily Kandinsky, Paul Klee, El Lissitzky, Franz Marc, Piet Mondrian, Emil Nolde, and many others. In the Degenerate Art catalogue, Dix's *War Cripples* was cited as "sabotage of national defense by the painter Otto Dix" (Barron 373). In total, 16,000 paintings by 1,400 artists were destroyed by the Nazis.

Under Nazi occupation, Dix painted only still lifes, or *nature morte,* as he jokingly said, instead of his usual depiction of the war, portraits of shattered vets, or of Berlin's *demi-monde.* Because he was unable or unwilling to emigrate, he practiced what other outcast artists, especially in the Soviet Union or satellite nations, would later refer to as "internal immigration."

As it turned out, his service as a soldier was far from over. In 1945, when he was 54 years of age, Dix was drafted into the newly formed *Volkssturm,* the "home defense unit." He was then separated from his unit and taken as a POW by the French, where he was rescued from semi-starvation by a French officer who recognized his name from an artistic publication. He then painted endless posters of Charles de Gaulle for food (Fickert 8). One of his most moving paintings from this period was called *Self-Portrait as a Prisoner of War* (1947) where his gray, grizzled, and deeply lined face fronts a thick tangle of barbed wire. Here Dix uses blues, greens and grays to indicate melancholia, defeat, and cold, instead of his predominant red.

Dix spent nearly 30 years of his artistic career detailing the horrors of war, which perhaps was the only way he could exorcise the four years spent in the trenches, where either 8 million (Forgacs) or 15 million men (McGreevy) died in four years. Mostly, his anti-war paintings were in response to the renewed militarism of the German culture. Judging from his self-portraits as a soldier, Dix was also interested in humans' capacity for violence as well. For Dix, like Friedrich Nietzsche whose *The Joyful Wisdom* he took with him into battle (along with a bible, pencil and a sketch pad), war was as powerful as birth, which was why Dix insisted that, "ultimately, all wars are fought over and for the sake of the vulva" (Eberle 41). As Maria Tatar puts it:

> Dix's equation of Mother Earth with human mothers, his focus on the regenerative powers of earth and the procreative capabilities of women, becomes especially significant in the context of myths about male combat as a virile form of reproduction. The gulf between maternal and military service . . . is not as great as it might first seem. But the parallels go beyond the Gnostic conundrum and its answer: 'How long will men make war? As long as women have children,' though the answer has an interesting double meaning in implying that men compete with women's procreative powers by making war. (78)

For most of Dix's contemporary artists, though, capital was perceived as the driving force behind the war.

World War One was praised as "a miracle," as "great," and as "constructive as well as destructive" (Karcher 29). The majority of young European men were either conscripted, or they enlisted for adventure as well as honor for their countries, fueled by the writings of Ernst Jünger in Germany ("War, the father of all things, is also our father. War is not only our father but also our son. We created him and he created us"); along with Guillaume Apollinaire in France; and Filippo Marinetti in Italy. Marinetti, in fact, seems to anticipate our present-day fetishizing of the "bionic" body, when he proclaimed: "War is beautiful because it initiates the dreamt-of metalization of the human body."

After the terror of the trenches, soldier-artists and poets were part of the growing anti-war movement. Tragically, a disproportionate number of poets died in battle, including Wilfred Owen, Isaac Rosenberg, Rupert Brooke, Julian Grenfell, John McCrae, Charles Sorley, Edward Thomas, T. E. Hulme, Georg Trakl, Ernst Stadler, August Stramm, and even Apollinaire himself. The literature and even the newly developed art form, the cinema, dealt quite explicitly with the devastating losses suffered during World War One. And many fiercely anti-war films, novels, and resistance writing joined the ranks of poets protesting the war: Erich Maria Remarch's *All Quiet on the Western Front* (1928), which was directed by Lewis Milestone in 1930;[1] Jean Renoir's *Grand Illusion* (1937); Humphrey Cobb's novel *Paths of Glory* (1935); Ford Maddox Ford's *Parade's End* (1924); John Dos Passos's *Three Soldiers* (1921); and Ernst Friedrich's *War Against War!* (1924).

Friedrich (1894–1967), a life-long socialist and pacifist, published *War Against War!* in German, English, Dutch and French with hundreds of grisly photographs of World War One casualties, particularly of mortared soldiers' faces. His accompanying text details the connection between capital, the church, and war. When World War One was declared, he refused to fight and was institutionalized for "insanity." He was imprisoned during the Weimar Republic and later by the Nazis, and his Anti-War Museum in Berlin, which the Nazis destroyed, became a gathering place for storm-troopers (Kellner 15). For the remainder of the war, he was exiled in France. Friederich's logo of two hands breaking a rifle in half became the symbol for the War Resisters League in the U.S. and the War Resisters International in the U.K. (Kellner 12).

Even the "horror" classic *The Cabinet of Dr. Caligari* (1919) was intended as an anti-war movie, inspired by the war experiences of a Czech soldier, Hans Janowitz, and Carl Mayer, an Austrian. The army forced Mayer to undergo repeated mental examinations, and Dr. Caligiri himself was modeled after a high-ranking military psychiatrist. In the film, his somnambulist, Cesare is representative of the common man who "under the pressure of compulsive military service, is drilled to kill and to be killed" (Rigby 21). Much to the authors' dismay, the producers framed the story so that all references to war and to the military's brutality were excised, and Caligari himself seemed somewhat benevolent (Rigby 21–23).

After Kaiser Wilhelm abdicated in 1918, and a socialist government headed by Philipp Schneidemann came to power, many German artists supported these socialist or revolutionary politics. "For a time the coincidence of radical aesthetics and radical politics was simply assumed. Artists and writers declared themselves revolutionaries, and the term radical was used interchangeably in its political and aesthetic senses" (Rigby 2). Almost all artists were fiercely antiwar, even though some like Otto Dix, George Grosz, and Franz Marc had initially enlisted. Perhaps Emil Nolde best summed up his and other artists' feelings about the war: "money was the lubricant of the whole murdering war machine" and "the share-holders in the steel works and oil and poisonous gas companies were safely out of danger celebrating dark, devilish triumphs" (Rigby 1).

Clearly, the Versailles Treaty of 1918 imposed many hardships on Germany, including curfew, censorship, and occupation by allied forces. Furthermore, the unprecedented inflation of 1923 plunged Germany into economic chaos. Prostitution, drugs (cocaine and heroin), and alcohol abuse marked this period, and as the saying went, "more money for more sin" (de Jonge 75). Many demobbed soldiers also joined the fascist *Freikorps,* which was responsible for the murders of Rosa Luxemburg and Karl Liebknecht, who were perceived as "Soviet dupes" (de Jonge 42). Hitler's trump card was in fact the harsh conditions forced on Germany by the Versailles Treaty, and he appealed especially to defeated soldiers who saw in the Nazis an opportunity to oust foreign elements from Germany—the Bosheviks, Jews, and Gypsies—whom they perceived as being responsible for the war's loss.

Although Germany and the United States both suffered the defeats of war, war made a vastly different impact on Germans than on Americans—arguably, except for front-line veterans. In fact, Dix's paintings included a number of legless veterans who were reduced to begging on the streets of Berlin but were mostly ignored by the civilian population. As George Grosz, whose own art bitterly satired the military and the Ruling Classes, recalled: "after the war thousands of quivering and quaking, real and fake cripples peopled the street corners of Berlin. Some feigned war injuries, others were hideously deformed. As a result, Germans became 'inured to the strange, unusual and repulsive'" (Rigby 27).

In the United States, also, the government's neglect of vets in terms of psychiatric and physical care is well documented, including 250,000 cases of exposure to agent orange as well as 64,000 of their children who were born with birth defects or disorders *(Jacknife)*. Lawsuits against Agent Orange are *still* being argued in the Supreme Court, 25 years or more after the fact. Furthermore, more than 110,000 Vietnam veterans have died since the war's end, and thirty percent of these deaths were from suicide (Golub 285). James Gibson suggests that the psychological defeat of losing the war is partly responsible for the growing interest in paramilitary groups in the United States. Unlike their German counterparts who joined repressive auxiliary armies, the Vietnam veteran rarely involved himself in paramilitary "war games," although Robert K. Brown, a former captain in the U.S. Army Special Forces during the Vietnam War, was the founding editor of *Soldier of Fortune* in 1975. "SOF's position was explicit from the start: the independent warrior must step in to fill the dangerous void created by the American failure in Vietnam" *(Warrior,* 7). According to Gibson, though, men in their 20s to 40s, and not particularly the Vietnam-era soldiers, largely comprised the paramilitary organizations of the 1980s.

While the post-World War One era's prevailing zeitgeist was anti-war, the growing threat of European and Japanese fascism to the United States made an ideological shift toward war essential. How, then, to sell war to its battle-weary citizens? By creating an alliance between the film industry and the military:

> Of the 1,700 full—length feature films made from 1941 to 1945, more than one-third were war-related. . . . In the words of Elmer Davis, director of the Office of War Information (whose Hollywood branch guided scriptwriters so that films would receive official approval), 'the easiest way to inject propaganda ideas into most people's minds is to let it go in through the medium of an entertainment picture when they do not real-

ize that they are being propagandized.' An estimated 85 million people went to the movies each week during those years, and the war films they saw told essentially the same story again and again. *(Warrior,* 21)

Several Hollywood directors served in the military during World War Two as well: William Wyler, John Huston, John Ford, Darryl Zanuck, and Samuel Fuller. They almost always presented the war nobly, often times employing John Wayne, who ironically never saw combat, as the hero. Fuller, though, made many public statements against war and even cites the World War One classic *All Quiet on the Western Front* "as one of the most honest movies because it is against war" *(American Cinema).*

Even during the peaceful post-World War Two years, Hollywood churned out a disproportionately high number of pro-war films: "These genre conventions outlived the war they portrayed. From 1948 to 1968, under the shadow of the Cold War . . . war movies and Westerns continued to be America's most popular entertainment" (Gibson, *Warrior,* 22). Gibson estimates that "5000 war movies were made between 1945 and 1965, and 1200 received major assistance from the Defense Department" ("American Paramilitary," 17).

Although the post-Vietnam War era is more closely linked to the sensibility of post-World War One, most Vietnam War movies use the World War Two movie as its paradigm. However, Hollywood's convention did not match the Vietnam soldier's, nor the veteran directors' reality. As Thomas Dogherty puts it: "The Vietnam film is impossible to understand unless you have all this other background about World War Two combat films and the post-war celebrations . . . When Hollywood comes to make the Vietnam cycle, they have to say, 'forget everything we told you in those previous 30 years of war films: war is really something that is horrible, and deadly, and it can have no moral meaning'" *(American Cinema).*

## III: "We Don't Do Dew When We Do Business": A Drug Filmography

Oliver Stone's connection with the Vietnam War is well documented: he came from a prominent family, dropped out of Yale in 1965, and ended up in Vietnam teaching Chinese students in a Catholic school. On the day of his arrival he witnessed a VC attack on a Saigon restaurant. He then volunteered for the infantry in 1967 because he "believed in the John Wayne image of America" (Devine 243). He also admitted to smoking a lot of pot in Vietnam because he "didn't want to know what was going on anymore. All notions of romanticism had vanished" (Devine 244). Shortly after his return to the States, he went to Mexico, got busted for possession of marijuana, had his father bail him out, and ended up in New York University on a GI bill.

There, Martin Scorsese, his professor, encouraged his student project, *Last Year in Vietnam*.

*Platoon*, known as the first grunt's movie, was written and directed by Stone, and it delineates Chris (Christ?) as the "fucking new guy" torn between the good-bad sergeants, Elias and Barnes. Where Elias is encoded as "brotherly," Barnes is like the Monster in the Village whose scarred and sutured body symbolizes our losses in the Vietnam War. Unintentionally humorous, Barnes's exaggerated wounds are reminiscent of a 1966 David Levine caricature that was printed in *The New York Review of Books*. In Levine's drawing Johnson pulls up his shirt to show journalists his appendix scar. Instead of a scar, though, he points to a map of Vietnam.

You won't find the standard drug-crazed grunt in *Platoon*. In fact, the dope-smokers are antiwar and communal rather than competitive. The juicers are militaristic, racist and crudely sexist ("I still like a piece of pussy. . . . Ain't nothin' like a piece of pussy, except maybe the Indy 500," says Bunny). And this reductive dichotomy between heads and juicers mirrors the representations of Elias and Barnes. In one scene Chris and Elias end up in a hooch with a group of Brothers and a few hip whites. There, they smoke grass (using an M16 as a kind of peace pipe) and dance to Smokey Robinson's "The Tracks of My Tears." Meanwhile, Barnes hangs out with the "crackers" drinking booze, listening to country & western music, and usurping the authority of the "Jew" lieutenant while maintaining loyalty to the military. Bunny insists that the VC are putting chemicals in the grass to make the soldiers not want to fight. And under battle stress, one of the black soldiers becomes addicted to heroin. When Chris tries to enlist the other "heads" into fragging Barnes for the murder of Elias, Barnes overhears them and says: "why do you smoke this shit, to escape from reality? Me, I don't need this shit. I am reality."

Stone's and Ron Kovic's collaboration on *Born on the Fourth of July* produced a powerful antiwar movie mostly because of the "unheroic" nature of watching Kovic's mangled body in a hospital bed, with his uptight family, with his unconsummated desire for women. Employing the genre known as *Bildungsroman*—the evolution of a young school boy into a man—Kovic changes from a gungho, God-fearing Marine, into a bitterly wounded vet, who this time fights against the system which sent him to war.

Although Kovic himself does not get high, *Born* details drug use in the veterans hospital where the aides over-tranquilize the patients; two men are shown shooting heroin, and other less wounded soldiers smoke hash. Timmy, a vet who is Kovic's first contact in "the world," describes how he controls his excruciating headaches with drugs. When Kovic joins an anti-war rally, marijuana is the catalyst for social change, since "hard core" draft resisters smoked grass as a way to goad the "pigs." Nevertheless, alcohol, and not drugs, is the drug of choice for Kovic and for the other severely maimed veterans.

Stone's *The Doors* treats the Vietnam War tangentially, but its ubiquitous shadow is in contrast with sun-drenched southern California and its alienated youth. As a child, Jim Morrison witnessed a car accident and the death of a Navajo elder-shaman. Later, during Morrison's acid dreams, this shaman metaphorically stands as testimony to the United States' subjugation of its indigenous people. But the old man is mute, since he is merely the catalyst for Morrison's transformation into a shaman of sorts.

In the film, Morrison (the son of a Navy admiral who was involved in the Gulf of Tonkien incident), as well as The Doors—named for Aldous Huxley's *The Doors of Perception*—use drugs and music as a way to break through the complacency, "warmongering bullshit," and materialism of American life. Morrison's sexuality *(Eros)* wars against war *(Thanatos)*, as he urges his followers to drop acid, get naked, and "fuck, fuck, fuck." One of the funniest lines in the movie is when a Miami cop yells out after Morrison supposedly whipped it out at a concert: "Who's the guy with the penis. Where's that son-of-a-bitch!" The movie also chronicles the "bi-coastal" drug scene: when The Doors are in New York, they are invited to Andy Warhol's "factory" where they meet up with the Velvet Underground whose music is a paean to heroin: *"When I put a spike into my vein, then I tell you things aren't quite the same."* Morrison draws the line at heroin use however: when his girlfriend Pam is caught shooting up, he locks her in a closet and sets fire to it. She narrowly escapes.

The war is writ small in *The Doors,* with glimpses of it on the "boob tube": the My Lai massacre, a young napalmed child, wounded soldiers screaming in agony. Stone uses the television as a commentary on Morrison's dissolution; after all, his fascination with death has its corroboration in our fascination with war. (In Stone's recent *Natural Born Killers* (1994) the TV images surrealistically fill the screen and attempt to explain how gratuitous violence breeds natural born killers.) In spite of the claim that the Vietnam War was the first "television war," however, "content analyses of network news program reveal that American audiences rarely saw the suffering of soldiers in the field. Most often, audiences saw the movement of soldiers as they jumped off helicopters in secured landing zones" (Haines 92).

Jim Carabatsos served with the First Air Cavalry Division and wanted to write "the real story about what it was like to be 19 years old and in Vietnam . . . but nobody wanted to listen" (Devine 266). Yet he wrote the screenplay for *Hamburger Hill* (1987) based on his participation in the devastating ten-day assault on the A Shau Valley in 1969. John Irvin, the director, was a 1969 documentary filmmaker for BBC in Vietnam, and the producer's son served there as well. *Hamburger Hill* is action-oriented as well as politically conservative, a sure-fire success for the "new" mood of the late 80s. Self-consciously imitative of *Pork Chop Hill* (1959), one of the few movies about the Korean War (1950–53), *Hamburger Hill* does not hint at strained race relations, nor disgust with the military-industrial complex for supporting the longest war in American history.

In truth, by the early 1960s, the war was consistently opposed to by high-ranking military commanders: "several powerful and respected military leaders of the postwar era—especially Generals Matthew B. Ridgeway, James Gavin, and David Monroe Shoup—rejected outright the notion that the United States could play a constructive military role in Indochina and so opposed entry into Vietnam from within the defense establishment in the 1950s and then publicly criticized the war in the 1960s (Buzzanco 9). According to Carabatsos, though, hippies, the liberal media, and incompetent politicians should be held accountable for our losses in Vietnam. When a highly decorated sergeant rotates back to the world for medical reasons, he relates to the men on Hamburger Hill how "longhairs" threw dog shit on him. Worse, he goes home to find a "hairhead" pissing in his toilet, having moved in with his wife and children. *Hamburger Hill*, then, is in ideological lockstep with President Reagan's belligerent foreign policies, as well as with his much-touted "Just Say No" anti-drug domestic program. No wonder the film had overwhelming support from the U.S. Department of Defense which provided F-4 fighters and CH-46 helicopters, as well as the Philippine Defense Department which offered personnel support (Devine 267).

Carabatsos also wrote the screenplay for Clint Eastwood's *Heartbreak Ridge* (1986), which takes its name from the controversial Korean War battle, where the battle was won but at the cost of an extremely high number of casualties. Unlike the stalemate in Korea, *Heartbreak Ridge* depicts a "win" in Grenada, a Caribbean island eight by eighteen miles, with 100,000 inhabitants. But the military withdrew support from Carabatsos's film project because of his "obscene dialogue."

In the "real" invasion led by "Stormin'" Norman Schwarzkopf, military incompetence will jeopardize the lives of many of the American soldiers. Scott Custer, paratrooper with the 82nd airborne, reports:

> They handed us out tourist maps when we got there—and no grid coordinates. When you have to make indirect fire calls for mortar fire or aircraft fire, you need to have grid coordinates, otherwise there's a chance of making us the casualties of our own actions. We had no way to direct anything from these maps. They had points of interests, which was fine if I was on a seven-day vacation and wanted to see Grand Anse Harbor or go visit the Windsor Nutmeg Plantation, [the maps] would be just great. ("Operation Urgent Fury")

Francis Ford Coppola's *Apocalypse Now* is a reworking of Joseph Conrad's colonialist novella, *Heart of Darkness* (1899). In the film, Captain Willard, a CIA operative, is ordered on a secret mission into Cambodia to "terminate with extreme prejudice" Colonel Kurtz who overstepped his bounds by adopting a genocidal policy toward the "natives." Although Coppola is not a veteran, he enlisted Michael Herr as one of the screenwriters, and Herr is credited with Willard's voice over.

On board the naval patrol boat which takes them up the Mekong River are "rock 'n' rollers with one foot in the grave," who smoke grass and drop acid during highly inappropriate times. The bottom line is that real men drink bourbon while plotting assassination for the military, but dopers— white or black—basically fuck up by getting themselves shot and even beheaded. Clean and Chef smoke too much grass. Lance B. Johnson, or LBJ, a surfer from southern California, drops acid, but Willard takes him along to scout out the terrain even if he is acting "weird." And Dennis Hopper as the photojournalist admitted to being so "fucked up during the shooting," he couldn't remember many of his lines. Why else would he call Kurtz's inarticulate recital of T. S. Eliot's "The Hollow Men" the work of a genius? The war, then, is not a planned action by an imperial power but part of the American psychosis, fueled in part by drugs and technology.

In spite of its acclaim, *Apocalypse Now* does not answer the fundamental question of why we were in Vietnam in the first place.

Part of the problem is modeling the film on Conrad's *Heart of Darkness*. Since "darkness" is at our heart's core, neither film nor novella are obliged to critique European or American imperialism. Between 1890 and 1910, under the auspices of the Belgian King, Leopold II, 15 to 40 million Africans died in the Congo, either by starvation or by murder. Unlike Conrad who excused colonialism by positing it as "natural" human behavior, Roger Casement, Conrad's acquaintance in the Congo, wrote specifically about Leopold's genocidal policy. Casement was hanged for Sedition for the crime of gun-running in the Irish Rebellion of 1916. After his death, he was severely discredited by the British press as being "addicted to the grossest sodomitical practices" (Taussig 14).

Additionally problematic is Col. Kurtz as the "Great White Father" to the primitive Montaganards which describes United States' racism without really interrogating it, nor does Coppola interrogate Willard as a CIA operative. But it is difficult to read Coppola's intention. When they attack a Viet Cong village, Col. Kilgore orders Richard Wagner's "The Flight of the Valkyries" to be played over loud speakers, an overture closely associated with Fascism. "We use Wagner. It scares the shit out of the slopes," says Kilgore. Still, as Frank Tomasulo claims: "Francis Coppola was no stranger to the concept of an ambivalent war. He was the screen writer of *Patton*" (147). He also hired John Milius as *Apocalypse Now's* co-writer, who is best known for his ideologically right-wing movies like *Dirty Harry, Magnum Force,* and *Conan the Barbarian.* Even in the scene where Kilgore plays Wagner, Coppola uses a "point-of-view camera angle [which] inscribes the viewer in the helicopter looking down on the Vietnamese villagers, making them faceless and tiny in the frame as they are gunned down. [B]ut the camera moves in to isolate the agony of one wounded American soldier. The audience is thus cinematically implicated in the exhilarating superiority of the American attack" (147). Finally, in the provocative documentary, *Hearts of Darkness* (1991), which depicts the filming of *Apocalypse Now,* Eleanor Coppola tellingly calls the war "thrilling": Coppola himself seems to share this feeling.

Stanley Kubrick's *Full Metal Jacket* is based on Gustav Hasford's *The Short-Timers* (1979), a stunning novel about the Marines at Hue during the Tet offensive, in which a sniper is a fifteen-year-old-Eurasian girl with the "eyes of a grunt." In spite of Herr's and Hasford's work on the screenplay, the film and novel take divergent paths. In writing Hasford's eulogy Kali Tal insists:

> It was easy to sensationalize the female sniper, easy to 'disappear' Black Alice and his bag of gook feet, easy to kill off Cowboy. Easy, easy, easy. But what made Hasford great was his refusal to take the easy way out—his novels are about refusing to take the easy way out. *The Short-Timers* brings you to a place where the logical and rational thing, the hardest thing and the *right* thing to do is to shoot your best friend in the head. (7)

The occasional drug use in *The Short-Timers* is entirely dropped in the movie—almost as if the war itself is enough of a high—which is odd, since Herr wrote intimately about his personal drug use in Vietnam, and in the novel Joker and Cowboy occasionally get high. Besides that, Kubrick, whose *Paths Of Glory* (1957) is known for its powerful anti-war statement, seems to substitute aesthetics for politics in *Full Metal Jacket* by using a "slow motion technique to show the killing of American soldiers." Furthermore, *Full Metal Jacket,* like *Hamburger Hill* and *Platoon,* "use a familiar plot device from World War II combat films: characters, developed as members of a platoon on a mission, are killed in pursuit of their objective" (Haines 93).

Patrick Duncan directed and wrote the screenplay for *84 Charlie MoPic* which, among other things, interrogates war by connecting it with capital, through the characterization of LT as the "corporate" officer. In fact, all of the men in this recon unit are poor. Paradoxically, Duncan views the military as a stepping stone out of his own poverty: "'If it hadn't been for the army and, possibly, for Vietnam, I might still be picking fruit, a migrant worker'" (Jaehne 12). But his anti-corporate stance and innovative directing style cost him financial backing and support both from mainstream Hollywood and from the military itself.

The plot is relatively straight forward. A battle-tested five-man team of the 82nd airborne are sent out on long-range reconnaissance patrol (LRRP). Only this time, two FNGs accompany them: LT, who would like to build his career in "The Nam," and MoPic, a cameraman, who is making a [mo]tion [pic]ture for the army to use in future training sessions. The movie-within-the-movie is called *Project Daspo: Lessons Learned,* August, 1969, Central Highlands, Vietnam.

Easy, who is "short" ("how short?" "I'm so short you have to dig a hole to kick my ass"), is the doper and the joker. When the men enter the jungle, Easy bends to an exotic white flower, looks up at the camera with a grin, and says "Flower Power." The flower is actually *Datura wrightii,* commonly known as jimson weed, or thorn apple, a hallucinogen indigenous to the old and new world. Next, Easy offers to "hold" MoPic's dew, but OD, the sergeant (olive drab? over dose?), scatters it in the dust. "We don't do dew when we do business," OD says. Easy replies that he's coming back to harvest in six months. But he would rather have hash because grass makes him paranoid. But of course it's "The Nam" which is making everyone's "shit flaky." Hammer admits that he volunteered for the bush because he was doing too much acid back at the "green line." And Easy gets *beaucoup* paranoid when he takes some uppers. As usual, OD talks him through it.

Traditionally, the cameraman is invisible and invincible, but MoPic's shaking hand-held camera during combat evokes a kind of claustrophobic terror in the viewer. But this is Duncan's point. He insists that for the film to convey the sense of the soldier's experience in Vietnam, he had to use "a sustained, first-person camera approach" and not Cinema Scope (Cohn 260). Duncan contends that the war scenes in *Platoon,* for example, "still made war look like fun. . . . In reality a dead body's a very ugly thing, and it's hard to carry. Life isn't cheap and I wanted to rub that in the audience's face" (Devine 295).

The lack of a soundtrack is also purposely realistic as well as anti-aesthetic: we hear the men grunt, someone pissing, static radio calls for help as well as unnerving screams, and the beautiful but ominous jungle sounds (although the film was shot in southern California, one bird call seems imitative of *dien cai dau,* which is Vietnamese for "going crazy"). MoPic also describes how he would receive canisters of film from the field: sometimes the film was blank, other times filled with indescribable horror. And this self-consciousness about filming and "shooting" resonates throughout the film. The accouterments of survival are also closely detailed by MoPic's camera: Easy's radio that one night picks up an incongruously tender rendition of Donovan's "Try and Catch the Wind" that fades in the thick jungle air, still-damp socks, dry rations, flak jacket, and weapons.

On July 21,1995, the Los Angeles Public Broadcasting Station premiered *84 Charlie MoPic* on Saturday, at midnight. I taped the show, hoping that an interview with Patrick Duncan would follow. Instead, PBS's version of *MoPic* was far more sanitized and less "offensive" for the viewing public. For example, when Easy "sounds off," he says that soon he will be a PFC, a "private fucking civilian," but in PBS's version he calls himself a "private freaking civilian." "Jingle bells, mortar shells, VC in the grass, you can take your Merry Christmas, and stick it up your ass," metamorphoses into "stick it up your nose." And the scene where OD makes Easy throw a lid of grass into the dust is entirely excised from this version as well. If drug use is perceived as anti-war and anti-state, then PBS's "liberal slant" is not borne-out by their "revision" of *Charlie Mopic*.

Involuntary drug taking is the central premise of Adrian Lyne's *Jacob's Ladder* (1990), a complex and haunting film about the difficulties of coping with the war's aftermath. Years after the war ends, Jake (Jacob), a professor-turned mail carrier, lives in Brooklyn with Jezzie (Jezebel), an emotionally volatile co-worker. Through a series of jagged flashbacks to "The Nam," we piece together fragments of his pained and nightmarish memories, especially of one day in the Mekong Delta, 1971, when Jake was bayoneted. We also learn that he has family in another "reality": a wife, Sarah, and three sons, including Gabriel, who might have died in a freakish bicycle accident.

Interspersed with gripping scenes of the war are hallucinatory subway sequences (note the negative references to drugs on the subway posters—"hell is drug addiction"; the one word "Ecstasy" appears juxtaposed with the subway's grime). Finally, a mysterious character who was shadowing Jake explains what happened that crucial day in Nam. Michael Newman identifies himself as a chemist who made "dynamite" LSD until the military blackmailed him into working for them or he would face a stiff prison sentence. He tells Jake that the men in his platoon were given a powerful hallucinogenic, called the Ladder because it takes the user down to the indescribable hell of berserk rage. Not only that, the drug was first tested on jungle monkeys and then on Vietnamese POWs, and they "tore each other to pieces." Knowing this, the drug was then administered to the Americans by their own commanders. Evidently, Jake escaped the Ladder's effects because he had "beaucoup shits" that day and most likely expelled much of the drug's harmful properties.

At the film's end, this coda appears on a darkened screen: "It was reported that the hallucinogenic drug BZ was used in experiments on soldiers during the Vietnam War. The Pentagon denied the story."

But that *it* needs further explanation to support the film's courageous allegations. One wishes *Jacob's Ladder* went farther in its contention that the military was using human guinea pigs to test mind-altering drugs. As is, the film is best remembered for its Ambrose-Bierce-like ending in "An Occurrence at Owl Creek" as well as the little known short story by Conrad Aiken entitled "Mr. Arcularis." Mr. Arcularis imagines he's on a sea voyage where he meets a young woman to whom he is attracted. At the story's end, we learn that Mr. Arcularis is really in an operating room, and that he is dying.

On one level, *Ladder* seems to accurately describe PTSD, and Tim Robbins turns in a gripping performance as the deeply-suffering vet. The rendition of "Mr. Postman" by the "sisters" is one of the film's highlights. Still, the self-conscious use of Old and New Testament names is not fully developed. In fact, the dichotomy between the good blonde wife, Sarah, and the somewhat sinister Latina, Jezzie, seems racist in this otherwise sensitive movie. The depoliticized representation of poverty is equally troubling. Jake lives in the "hellish" ghetto of downtown Brooklyn with Jezzie, while Sarah and family inhabit a middle-class house in a predominately white neighborhood.

In Edward Zwick's recent *Courage Under Fire* (1996), the first film about the Gulf War, the war itself is not interrogated, which is surprising since the screenplay was written by Patrick Duncan, director of *84 Charlie MoPic*. The film does critique casualties caused by "friendly fire," but most of the story's focus is the betrayal of the female captain by her men, including men of color. *Courage Under Fire,* then, proposes gender warfare as the singular culprit rather than underscoring the economic causes of war in the Persian Gulf. In *Courage,* drugs are largely invisible except when a pharmacist is caught with "works" in his bunker. His habit, most likely heroin, is undetected because he shoots up between his toes.

Altogether, drug representation seems to align itself with the ideological beliefs of the director screenwriters. Carabastos's *Hamburger Hill* blames, in part, the war's loss on "hairheads," or potheads. Stone sees dope smoking as community and as an anti-war statement as well as potential for self-destruction. Coppola perceives drug taking as a sign of American psychosis and the Vietnam War itself is a bad acid trip. But Duncan's representation might be the most realistic: when the men are on a dangerous mission, they throw away their drugs.

Quite rightly, none of the filmmakers explicitly represent heroin use in their films, since these are "true-life" experiences of directors or screen-writers who served in Vietnam *before* 1970, the year associated with the "GI Heroin Epidemic." Nevertheless, the film *Who'll Stop the Rain* (1979), based on Robert Stone's novel *Dog Soldiers* (1973), as well as Stephen Wright's novel, *Meditations in Green* (1983), use heroin as a metaphor for the corrupt war. The army produced its own filmic version of heroin addiction in *Narcotic Deaths* (1970), "the ultimate in shock and gore," and ABC's *Heroes and Heroin* (1971) documented heroin use in soldiers returning from Vietnam (Starks 195).

For the Vietnam-era soldier, World War Two actors—John Wayne, Audie Murphy, Dana Andrews, Aldo Ray—were models for appropriate conduct in battle. Obviously, for future soldiers, the representation of the Vietnam vet is more problematic. Nevertheless, the Vietnam veteran changed from a stoned psychopath, into Rambo, and finally into a human being. This metamorphosis happened to coincide with the rebuilding of the U.S. military might and with the collapse of its old nemesis, the Soviet Union.

Fast forward to 1991: once again the United States prepares for war. Only this time we wear desert camo, try out our unsurpassed "smart" weapons, have the government spend a billion dollars a day on war, and bury thousands of charred bodies in mass graves, which will not be shown on TV screens. More significantly, this time we win. President Bush assured the American public that our "victory" in the Persian Gulf assumes that, "by God, we kicked the Vietnam Syndrome once and for all." (For Bush, the "Vietnam Syndrome" is another form of addiction). So far, Gulf War veterans have almost no media visibility, except for dire reports about their unusual health problems, euphemistically called the "Gulf War Syndrome." However Hollywood depicts Gulf War veterans, one thing is certain, they will not be shown getting stoned, since drug testing was and very likely will be standard procedure for the 90s soldier, nor will they be shown protesting the war.

Even in the best-intentioned anti-war movie, the filmic fascination with war, both in American city streets and abroad, is "normalized" by our extraordinary technological "advances," so that the defeat in Vietnam might be perceived as merely a "technical glitch." Since the Vietnam War movie uses the "unproblematic" World War Two movie as its paradigm and not the more problematic art from World War One, the above-mentioned films present wars as inevitable and necessary. Still, like Walt Whitman, wound dresser and poet, the grunt director-screenwriter can honestly say, "I was the man, I suffered, I was there." Nevertheless, even the most grueling veteran anti-war movie still does not clarify the reasons for the Vietnam War, or for any other wars that follow. Where grunt Vietnam war movies are almost always against war, none consistently address the underpinnings of the Vietnam War: capitalism and imperialism.

## Works Cited

*American Cinema: The Combat Movie.* Narr. Matthew Modine. PBS. 1994.

Barron, Stephanie. *"Degenerate Art": The Fate of the Avant-Garde in Nazi Germany.* New York: Harry Abrams, 1991.

Buzzanco, Robert. *Masters of War: Military Dissent & Politics in the Vietnam Era.* New York: Cambridge UP, 1996.

Cohn, Lawrence. "The Long Road for '84 Charlie MoPic'; Vietnam Pic Hits N.Y. After 5 Years." *Variety* 22–28 March, 1989: 22.

Devine, Jeremy M. *Vietnam at 24 Frames a Second: A Critical and Thematic Analysis of over 400 Films about the Vietnam War.* Jefferson, North Carolina: McFarland & Company, 1995.

Eberle, Matthias. *World War I and the Weimar Artists: Dix, Grosz, Beckmann, Schlemmer,* New Haven: Yale UP, 1985.

Fickert Kurt, J. Introduction. *Der Krieg: 24 Offsetdrucke nach Originalen aus dem Radierwerk.* By Otto Dix. New York: Garland, 1972: 5–9.

Forgacs, David. "Fascism, Violence and Modernity." *The Violent Muse: Violence and the Artistic Imagination in Europe, 1910–1939.* Ed. Jana Howlett and Rod Mengham. Manchester: Manchester UP, 1994.

Gibson, James William. *Warrior Dreams: Violence and Manhood in Post-Vietnam America.* New York: Hill and Wang, 1994.

_____. "American Paramilitary Culture." *Vietnam Images,* ed. Jeffrey Walsh (London: Macmillan Press, 1989)10–42.

Golub, Deborah. "Symbolic Expression in Post-Traumatic Stress Disorder: Vietnam Combat Veterans in Art Therapy." *The Arts in Psychotherapy* 12 (4) 1985: 285–296.

Haines, Harry W. "'They Were Called and They Went': The Political Rehabilitation of the Vietnam Veteran." *From Hanoi to Hollywood. The Vietnam War in American Film.* Ed. Linda Dittmar and Gene Michaud. Rutgers, NJ: Rutgers UP, 1990: 80–97.

Hersh, Seymour. *My Lai 4: A Report on the Massacre and its Aftermath.* New York: Random House, 1970.

Ingraham, Larry H. "'The Nam' and 'The World'. Heroin Use by U.S. Enlisted Men Serving in Vietnam." *Psychiatry* 37 (May 74): 114–28.

*Jacknife.* Dir. David Jones. Cineplex Odeon, 1989.

Jaehne, Karen. "Company Man." *Film Comment* March–April 1989: 11–15.

Jonge, Alex, de. *The Weimar Chronicle: Prelude to Hitler.* New York: New American Library, 1978.

Karcher, Eva. *Otto Dix.* Köln, Germany: Benedikt Taschen, 1992.

Kellner, Douglas. Introduction. *War Against War!* By Ernst Friedrich. Seattle: The Real Comet Press, 1987. Originally published in German in 1924 under the title *Krieg dem Kriege!*

Lifton, Robert Jay. *Home From the War: Vietnam Veterans Neither Victims Nor Executioners.* New York: Simon and Schuster, 1973.

McCoy, Alfred, W. *The Politics of Heroin: CIA Complicity in the Global Drug Trade.* Brooklyn, New York: Lawrence Hill Books, 1991.

McGreevy, Linda, F. *The Life and Works of Otto Dix: German Critical Realist.* Ann Arbor, MI: UMI Press, 1981.

Miller, Daniel. "Primetime Television's Tour of Duty." *Inventing Vietnam: The War in Film and Television.* Ed. Michael Anderegg. Philadelphia: Temple UP, 1991. 166–89.

"Operation Urgent Fury: Grenada." *Frontline.* PBS. Narr. Seymour Hersh. 29 January, 1991.

Rigby, Ida Katherine. *An Alle Künstler! [To All Artists!] War—Revolution—Weimar.* San Diego: San Diego State UP, 1983.

Siegel, Ronald K. *Intoxication: Life in Pursuit of Artificial Paradise.* New York: E.P. Dutton, 1989.

Starks, Michael. *Cocaine Fiends and Reefer Madness: An Illustrated History of Drugs in the Movies,* New Brunswick, NJ: Cornwall Books, 1982.

Ta, Kalí. "Gustav Hasford 1947–1993". *Nobody Gets Off the Bus. Viet Nam Generation* Spring 1994: 7.

Tatar, Maria. "Fighting for Life; Figurations of War, Women, and the City in the Work of Otto Dix." *Lustmord: Sexual Murder in Weimar Germany.* Princeton: Princeton UP, 1995.

Taussig, Michael. *Shamanism, Colonialism and the Wild Man: A Study in Terror and Healing.* Chicago: University of Chicago Press, 1987.

Tomasulo, Frank, P. "The Politics of Ambivalence: *Apocalypse Now* as Prowar and Antiwar Film." *From Hanoi to Hollywood: The Vietnam War in American Film.* Ed. Linda Dittmar and Gene Michaud. Rutgers, NJ: Rutgers UP, 1990: 145–58.

"U.S Denies 75% of GIs in Vietnam Use Marijuana." *New York Times* 28 December 1967:10.

## Note

1. Lewis Milestone, a Romanian Jew, emigrated to the United States in 1913. He joined the US Signal Corps for four years and was the cameraman for Army training films. Similarly, the World War Two veteran, Samuel Fuller, shot his first film during the liberation of Buchenwald.

# Reflections on the Vietnam War: The Views of a Vietnamese on Vietnamese-American Misconceptions

## Bui Diem

### Introduction

During the past few years, we have been exposed to a myriad of discussions and reevaluations of Vietnam in dozens of magazines, newspapers, and television programs. In colleges and universities around the country there are hundreds of courses dealing with the American experience in the Vietnam War. It appears as if, after a long period of recoil and amnesia during which nobody wanted to hear or think about the divisive war, the citizens of the United States are now catching up with the study of this tragic event. Thus has begun the earnest process of making a serious and objective assessment of the lessons of Vietnam.

There is no longer any doubt that the war in Vietnam was a watershed in American history. Based on the available abundance of materials on Vietnam, there is clear evidence that the war is still much in the subconscious of the American people and that, denial notwithstanding, the Vietnam syndrome remains like a ghost, lurking in their minds. This is true whether or not time has tempered our judgments on the war and the way it was conducted.

History may never render a clear and final verdict as to what went wrong during the war and why American and South Vietnamese forces failed to prevent North Vietnam from achieving its conquest of South Vietnam. Many of the so-called "doves" who opposed the war at that time continue to condemn U.S. intervention as wrong and immoral. Many maintain that for these reasons alone it was doomed to failure from the very beginning. By the same token, many of those we dubbed "hawks" who supported the war, continue to believe that it could have been won if only the United States had had the stomach to see it through to the end. Historian Robert Schulzinger of the University of Colorado noted in this respect that: "As the war itself was divisive, its memory is divisive." So the arguments will probably continue as long as there are different views, opinions, and perspectives, not only on Vietnam but also on larger issues such as those pertaining to the U.S. role in the world, the use of U.S. military forces overseas or, in general terms, the advisability of U.S. intervention abroad on any level or in any fashion.

It would be futile in this chapter to attempt to address all of these issues. As a Vietnamese who happened, by the hazards of his assignment in Saigon and Washington, to be an eyewitness watching American and Vietnamese leaders at work during the peak of the U.S. intervention in the midsixties as well as at the end in 1975, I simply offer a few of my personal reflections on the war. It is my sincere hope that these reflections will contribute to "the quest for wisdom" that, according to Henry Kissinger, "America owed to itself if Vietnam is to leave any useful legacy."

## One Man's View of the Two Vietnams

The Geneva Agreements of 1954 divided Vietnam into two states at the 17th parallel: The Democratic Republic of Vietnam (North Vietnam) and the State of Vietnam (South Vietnam), later changed to the Republic of Vietnam. For the great majority of those in South Vietnam all they asked for was to be left alone so they could devote their energies to rebuilding their homes and families after the destruction of eight years of war. They did not take pleasure in the partition of the country imposed upon them by the big powers but, while protesting against it, they saw in it their only real opportunity for getting rid of the French.

South Vietnamese citizens also hoped to regain their national independence as well as peace, albeit a temporary one, and the chance to carve out a prosperous territory from the richer half of Vietnam, one without Communist influence. As to the unity of the country, an ultimate goal for all Vietnamese, it would have to be a matter for future generations to decide. These later generations would have to decide when the moment was right for a *peaceful* solution to this problem.

Southerners willingly waited for the reunification of their country. Vietnam had been occupied and divided many times throughout its long history, and all Vietnamese accepted the de facto and temporary partition of the country as a partial solution comparable to the situations in Germany and Korea. In a sense, ours was basically a defensive posture, a passive attitude, and our wish to be left alone contrasted vividly with the North Vietnamese

Communists' aggressive determination to try to reunify the country immediately and at any cost. This was best demonstrated by Hanoi's decision in 1959 to support the creation of the National Liberation Front of South Vietnam and begin a war of subversion to take the South.

## American Involvement: The Vietnamese View

The United States became deeply involved in the Vietnam War in the midsixties but, as everyone knows, the roots of the involvement can be traced back to the midfifties when, following the French defeat at Dien Bien Phu and the resultant Geneva Peace Agreement of 1954, the United States decided to shore up the government of Ngo Dinh Diem and transform South Vietnam into an anti-Communist bastion.

Counting the years from the 1950s to the fall of Saigon, it was no less than two full decades that America was immersed in the Indochina conflict. In terms of coexistence and joint efforts between two peoples who shared the same goal of defeating communism, this was indeed a long period of time. Yet, strangely enough, the way I saw it, the degree of understanding between the two sides was such that at times, for many Americans and South Vietnamese, it looked as if there were two separate wars—one fought by the Americans and another fought by the South Vietnamese. In my opinion, that was one of the main reasons for the tragic outcome in Vietnam.

In looking back at this period one cannot help being impressed by the fact that, at the onset, the United States and Vietnam had nothing in common and that if it were not for the fortuitous geopolitical events and international circumstances of the post–World War II era these two peoples would never have come together. Indeed, two nationalities, quite apart in terms of geographical location, international status, civilization, culture, and conceptualization, were thrown together at a time when the Vietnamese knew almost nothing about America and Americans knew even less about Vietnam.

I still remember those days in the fifties and the early sixties. The few vague notions that we had about the United States involved the generous Marshall Plan in Europe, the prestigious Gen. Douglas MacArthur in the war in Korea, the decisive and moralistic anti-Communist stands of John Foster Dulles, and especially the idealistic inaugural address of John F. Kennedy: "We shall pay any price, bear any burden, meet any hardship, support any friend, oppose any foe, in order to assure the survival and the success of liberty."

Vietnamese knowledge and understanding of the United States was, to be sure, limited, but the attraction to what America represented in the world was irresistible and that was the reason why, in their fight for freedom against both the French and the Communists, the South Vietnamese looked on the Americans as their natural friends and allies. They did not even question the virtue, or the right and wrong, of the American intervention. They considered it a logical continuation of the American salvation of South Korea. South Vietnamese faith in the United States was unshakable simply because, in the trusting, and perhaps naive, minds of the masses of South Vietnamese citizens they believed that such a powerful and seemingly omnipotent nation as the United States of America could not be wrong. Besides, they reasoned, the United States had never lost a war in its illustrious history.

But if the faith of the South Vietnamese in American power was total, their ignorance about America's people, culture, and politics, was equally profound. The great majority of the Vietnamese—including the southern leadership and intellectual elites—did not understand the American political process or the power of American public opinion. Having lived too long under one authoritarian regime or another, southern Vietnamese could not evaluate the influence of public opinion on the U.S. Congress, or understand the influence that the Congress could have over a president and his administration in terms of budget and foreign policy. In fact, during my tenure in Washington, I spent a great deal of time dealing with this matter. Each time I was called home for consultations or my colleagues came to the United States on their fact-finding tours, I briefed these South Vietnamese legislators, military men, journalists, professors, and dozens of others. I tried to describe to them what I saw from my observation post in Washington. I tried to convey to them the changing mood of Americans during the tumultuous days of the late 1960s, the spreading antiwar feelings, the emerging conflict between the executive and legislative branches of the U.S. government which made access to foreign aid more and more difficult.

With their fixed ideas about the United States, they nevertheless regarded as inconceivable the possibility of a reduced American role in international affairs, and particularly in Vietnam, since they themselves had witnessed the huge U.S. investment and involvement in the midsixties. This inflexible vision was even more deeply rooted in the minds of the South Vietnamese military leaders who practically ruled the country during the last ten years of South Vietnam's existence. These leaders, having had close contacts for many years with their U.S. military counterparts and, to a large degree, having been conditioned by the generally conservative ideas of the U.S. military establishment, could not and would not believe that America would be compelled to withdraw in 1973. In fact, many South Vietnamese generals believed until the final days before the collapse of Saigon that the U.S. B-52s would return and wipe out the Communist offensive.

The innocence and naivete of the South Vietnamese can perhaps best be illustrated by my own experiences. In 1964, as a journalist, I made an initiation trip of three months to the United States. After that trip, I wrote some articles about life in the United States and what I had seen in San Francisco at the Republican National Convention of 1964. From that time forward, I was seen by those in South Vietnam as somewhat of an expert on American affairs. Thinking of it now, I cannot help but be a little embarrassed because there is a mountain of differences between even the little that I know now about America—American policies and politics, after three decades of painful and costly lessons—and what I knew then in the 1960s.

In politics, perception quite often counts more than facts. In this respect, the Americans were perceived by the Vietnamese as having a contingency plan for every situation, and of course the CIA was believed to be behind every move by the United States Embassy in Saigon. These misconceptions gradually led to an abdication of judgments on the part of South Vietnamese leaders and to increased reliance on the Americans. The American buildup in 1965 reinforced these beliefs among the South Vietnamese. Many in fact, were awestruck by scenes such as American helicopters ferrying, in some cases, hot meals to U.S. troops—even during the fighting. The Vietnamese marveled at the scores of gadgets piled high in huge post exchanges (PXs) for the use of the American GIs. Many Vietnamese whispered among themselves that "the men of the affluent society have brought here a new sort of war," an "affluent war" that they had never seen or even thought of before. They witnessed the generous, perhaps excessive, use of bombs and strafings by American aircraft which lasted for hours and hours. In many cases these attacks were undertaken where U.S. forces had only encountered enemy sniper fire. Of course, the South Vietnamese were not then aware of the fact that hundreds of millions and even billions of U.S. taxpayers dollars were being spent to pay for the hot meals, PXs, and bombs. When protests later began in the United States most people in South Vietnam attributed America's growing desire to withdraw to the antiwar critics who believed, unfairly and wrongly, that all the billions of dollars being spent in Vietnam were on the South Vietnamese. Indeed, both sides misunderstood each other.

The South Vietnamese, in fact, failed to understand the real nature of the U.S. intervention, making erroneous assumptions about the staying power of America and, in the process, abdicated their own role in the war. This resignation which, in retrospect appears to be one of the most fatal mistakes made by my countrymen, was somewhat facilitated by their partners, the Americans, who either out of impatience or overconfidence, tried to do everything themselves. In the end, North Vietnam's control of their own destiny contrasted to South Vietnam's failure to create viable local leadership and was one of the most fundamental and important differences between the two factions. It may well have been why the South lost the war.

## American Misconceptions

These are only a few examples which illustrate the innocence or, to put it more accurately, the ignorance of the South Vietnamese about America, and South Vietnam's basically defensive sociopolitical posture and military objectives during the war. The Americans, for their part, did not have any better understanding of Vietnam, its culture, or its people. To quote Allan E. Goodman, of the School of Foreign Service at Georgetown University:

> A basic point must be made about the American ignorance of the Vietnamese. U.S. policy planners never had the kind of anthropological and sociological analyses of South Vietnamese behavior and customs that the French had of the North Vietnamese, for example. The classic work from the French era—Paul Mus's *Sociologie d'une Guerre* (1952)—was never translated into English. . . . In the years during which our commitment to Vietnam was in the process of gathering momentum, there were no academic programs of language study research in Vietnamese available in any U.S. university. Between 1965 and 1970 only twenty Ph.D. theses were done on Vietnam, out of some five thousand in the field of modern history and international relations. Throughout this period, moreover, Vietnamese studies were orphans in American academia. And when, in early 1970, AID [Agency for International Development] offered $1 million to create a Vietnamese Study Center there was only one taker.

The Americans came to Vietnam with good intentions, and at least in the midsixties the power of U.S. military forces was so overwhelming that for many Americans it seemed not to matter much whether or not they should understand the Vietnamese. It was believed that there was no problem that could not be solved if America set its mind to do it, so the mood was "let's do it." Unfortunately, the war dragged on inconclusively, and in the end the contradictions were precisely those that stemmed from the American failure to understand not only the nature of the war, but also the mentality of both their friends and enemies.

Together these mutual misunderstandings added fuel to the fire of Communist insurrection. For example, after encouraging the overthrow of South Vietnam's authoritarian leader Ngo Dinh Diem and putting ashore more than a half-million men and bombing targets in the country from north to south, the United States continued to claim that "it is not proper for the United States to intervene into the internal affairs of South Vietnam." After repeating over and over again President Kennedy's last public words about Vietnam, "In the final analysis it is their war and they are the ones who have to win or lose it," the United States *took over the war* and tried to do everything the American way with almost no consideration as to whether or not such a strategy would meet the complexities or local conditions of the war.

Undoubtedly, Americans and Vietnamese had different habits and different ways of thinking; therefore, it was not easy for Americans to understand and evaluate the South Vietnamese. But the Americans made things all the more difficult for themselves by the rotation system under which they came into South Vietnam for a short period of time and then went home, making room for others to follow. With such a system, millions of Americans came to Vietnam, at a cost of billions of dollars, but few had the time, or the desire, to really get acquainted with the people they came to help, and especially with the very special nature of this war.

One of the many difficulties of the war in Vietnam that the Americans had to cope with was its complex nature. The good, the bad, and the ugly— you could find it all in Vietnam, depending on where you chose to look. Stereotype images and misperceptions characterized many Americans' judgments. To be sure, American misunderstanding of the South Vietnamese was one thing, but misunderstanding of the North Vietnamese Communists was another, and that was what hurt the most.

The whole concept of gradual escalation was, in this context, a vivid example of misunderstanding. It was based on the assumption that at some point the Communists would have to accept a compromise because the cost would be too high for them to go on fighting. The truth of the matter was, after having been assured publicly that their territory would never be invaded, the Communists found that if they could extend the war indefinitely they could win simply by not losing. Their own heartland, despite massive, but often sporadic air attacks, would not be invaded. By the same token, the search and destroy operations in the South ultimately became a hide and seek war game in which the Communists controlled not only the place, but also the tempo of the fighting when and where they were strong. In turn, when they were not strong they could hide in their sanctuaries in North Vietnam, Laos, and Cambodia. Thus, they only had to survive, no matter what the cost, and wait for America to tire of the war, no matter how long that might take.

## Conclusion

The list of mistakes and oversights by both allies is a long one, but the more I have reflected on the Vietnam War, the more I come to the conclusion that a very powerful explanation for what went wrong in Vietnam can be found in the lack of understanding between the United States and South Vietnam. American military and diplomatic strategy was shaped by a profound misunderstanding of the Vietnamese—both friends and foes—of their culture as well as their view of the fundamental issues of war and peace. The tragedy did not come in one day, but was an accumulation of years of errors and mistakes the biggest of all, it seems to me, being the lack of effort from Americans and South Vietnamese to better understand each other.

It has been said that America lost its innocence and arrogance in Vietnam. As a Vietnamese, I would complete the remark by saying that South Vietnam had no arrogance to lose but instead lost its innocence and, ultimately, its existence as a free nation.

# *Documents*

# From *When the Light's Put Out*
## Ngo Tat To

When the Light's Put Out, *which was first published in 1939, speaks of the multiple problems thrust upon the Vietnamese peasants during the French colonial era: the behavior of officialdom and the landlords, and the various forms of taxes, of which the worst was the head tax, or, as translated literally from the Vietnamese, the "body tax" (thue than) or "man tax" (thue dinh), which was applied to adult males from the age of eighteen. More specifically, it describes the plight of a woman named Mrs. Dau, whose husband was arrested because he could not pay his body tax on time. She was consequently forced to sell her dogs, her provisions, and even her own child in order to meet the official bail set for her husband's release. She went on to experience a multitude of other misfortunes. Of the book's thirty-six chapters, two short chapters (Chapters 12 and 13) are presented here. Although the Foreign Languages Publishing House in Hanoi has already published a full translation of this work, the present translation, done independently, is included here for the reader's comparison.*

*The author, Mr. Ngo Tat To (1892–1954), was a Confucian scholar turned modern writer and is best known for his "reportage and documentary fiction" (*phong su va tieu thuyet phong su*).*

## Chapter 12

The afternoon sunlight printed its yellow rays on the tops of the bamboo. A flock of sparrows twittered among the branches of a carambola, and a few thrushes chattered to each other in the upper reaches of the areca nut tree.

Representative Que, his bearded chin thrust upward, stood in his brick-paved yard looking on as a pair of pigeons cooed to each other in front of their roost holes. When he saw Mrs. Dau and her daughter poking their heads into the yard, he addressed them curtly; "What took you so long getting here—making other people wait for hours like this? Getting involved with you people is just a big nuisance. None of your kind will ever learn how to keep an appointment!"

The mother and daughter bowed their heads politely. "Venerable sir, my husband is tied up at the communal house. It took me forever just to persuade the officials to untie him long enough to sign the contract here. Moreover, it is quite a long way, so I couldn't help being late. Please forgive me!"

"Madame is in the guest house. Take yourselves over there and speak with her!" Then he called across the yard, "One of you guys in there, come out and keep the dogs out of their way."

Like a clown waiting for his cue, the cook drawled out a long "ye-e-es," took up a rod to hold back the household dogs, and led Mrs. Dau and her daughter, together with their bitch and her puppies, up to the house.

Madame Representative commenced in a petulant voice, "I told you to bring something along to cover up the puppies with, so they wouldn't be exposed to the sun. So why did you cover them like that with only a bamboo strainer?"

Embarrassed, Mrs. Dau could only answer with these words: "I beg you, Madame."

Asking the cook to tie the mother dog by her leash to the house post, Mrs. Dau took the basket of puppies and slowly placed it on the threshold.

Madame Representative glanced over at Ty, the daughter, then chided Mrs. Dau in a shrill voice, "How dare the two of you—you and your husband—tell me that your daughter is seven years old already? How come seven and still so puny? I should have known! How can one ever expect to get one word of truth out of your kind!"

"Venerable madame, we do not dare to lie. She is indeed seven. Her brother is five, and there is another daughter who is two. I have three children in all."

Representative Que came in from the yard just then and shook a finger in Mrs. Dau's face, showing that his temper had been ruffled. "Shut your mouth! Don't start in on any of your impertinences around here! However many children you have, that's your business! The more you give birth to, the more you've got to dispose of. So what? Open that basket, let me see the puppies!"

Madame Representative seconded her husband's words. "You see! How can one listen to nonsense like that!"

Then, looking around at Mrs. Dau, she said, "Mind yourself now, hear! Otherwise I'm going to kick you all out and won't bother with any more business. Do you think maybe I'm on the same level with you, eh? Even before I began to speak, you started to talk back! Vulgar woman! The little girl there is no bigger than that, and you dare insist that she is seven. Do you think you're talking to the dogs or something?"

The little girl, Ty, had shrunk back behind the house post, with a listless expression. It was as if she were worrying that maybe at some point she had lost a year of her life. Mrs. Dau continued to sit in the same spot, numb and motionless. Her eyelashes glinted with teardrops.

Purplish veins appeared on both sides of Representative Que's forehead, a foreshadowing of angry words. "So she still won't open her basket to let the puppies out, huh? If she's so reluctant about it, then she can just take them back and raise them herself."

Her tears falling slowly one by one on the brick threshold, Mrs. Dau painstakingly undid the knots at the basket rim and removed the bamboo sieve. Representative Que quickly seated himself next to the basket. The four pups, one by one, were taken up by the nape of the neck, and the ears, eyes, tongues, paws, stomachs, tails, and chests were carefully inspected, each young hair getting its due attention. The Representative next admired the mother dog. A moment later, with a somewhat softer appearance, he came inside the room and settled himself on the plank bed, crossing his legs in the shape of the Chinese character for the number five.[1]

Looking down on Mrs. Dau he said, "Where is the contract? Hand it here."

Mrs. Dau fumbled for the document, which had been tied to her bodice strap. Cringing, she placed it on the plank bed.

Holding the contract, Representative Que repeatedly examined the place that bore the stamp of the village chief administrator. After a long pause, he turned and ordered a boy attendant, "Go and bring several bowls of rice leftovers. Bring enough for me to feed the pups, and we'll see if they eat it."

The boy responded instantly and "on three feet and four legs" was off to the servants' quarters.

Mrs. Dau and her daughter were crouched next to the house post, each peering into the tearful face of the other.

The four puppies swarmed over to the edge of the threshold, each assuming its place at the mother dog's breasts.

Representative Que good-naturedly commanded his spouse, "Check to see that they are all indeed without spots on their tails." "I too am looking. It seems none of them has."

## Chapter 13

The boy returned with a small basket full of leftover rice. Representative Que ordered Mrs. Dau and her daughter to move the pups over to the other side of the threshold. Hastily, he himself ran out, took the basket, and scooped out a bowlful of rice for each puppy. As Mrs. Dau had truthfully informed him, all four pups already knew how to eat. The mother dog, on the other hand, seemed tired and anxious and only nibbled a few bites, then stopped.

Appearing calm and easy, Representative Que looked at Mrs. Dau, "Where did you buy the female dog?"

"My mother bought it, sir, in Lau Cai, and gave it to me."

"Hm, how about that! It may very well be of Mongolian descent then. You can't get dogs like that in the countryside!"

Madame Representative was quick to direct praise to herself. "Since I'd heard from several different people that she had this very intelligent bitch, I spared no effort in trying to get it. And finally this morning I was successful. Ordinarily, though, who would be so stupid as to buy up a whole litter of puppies that had just barely opened their eyes? And so, what do you think of the four of them?"

Representative Que nodded and mumbled, "Beautiful all of them. Each with its own special characteristic—one with an extra toe, one with a tiger skin, an all-black one, and one with all four cherry-blossom paws. All with floppy ears and short faces, spotted tongues, and eyes in the shape of banyan leaves. Really handsome."

While still talking, he strutted back to the plank bed. Then once again he settled himself with his legs crossed in the form of the Chinese character for the number five, then briskly pulled over a water pipe, and began smoking, slapping his thighs in self-congratulation.

"The more one knows, the harder one has to work! Province Chief Dang, Representative Bui, Judge Tien, and District Chief Xung at the province capital all know how skilled I am at choosing dogs, and that's why they all insist on having me buy dogs for them. I have decided that when these four are fairly well grown, I'll give one to each of them. But I'd be hesitant to give away the all-black one and would rather keep it myself, since it's supposed to be the kind that will bring profit to its owner. With such a dog in the house one is sure to be prosperous."

Madame Representative interrupted in a half-serious, half-playful voice: "Nobody gives things away free. Whoever wants a good breed will have to hand me the money. Otherwise I'll just keep the whole bunch of them myself."

"In all, we have fourteen dogs as it is. Why should you want to keep all of these, too, and have to feed them all?"

"I'd like to keep them as watchdogs. It's better to raise dogs than to raise servants. This house is so large; ten or more watchdogs wouldn't be too many, would they?"

Then laughing heartily and shaking her finger at Mrs. Dau; she said, "The dog food in my home is worth much more than your kind of 'human food.'"

Mrs. Dau, visibly hurt, lowered her head and silently wiped her tears, not knowing what to say.

The pups had stopped eating, and one by one they went back to their mother, leaving several heaps of unfinished rice. Representative Que ordered the boy attendant to gather it all into a basket and give it to Ty. In a mock-humane voice, that representative of the people addressed the miserable little girl: "You, little girl! Take that basket of rice and eat it. Don't waste heaven's resources. You can eat it with your fingers; you don't have to have a bowl and chopsticks."

With tears rolling like drops of rain, Ty squeamishly eyed the basket of leftover rice but felt no desire to stretch out her hands to receive it.

The representative of the people was furious. "Are you not going to eat up that leftover dog food?"

Madame Representative completely blew her top. "Did your mother teach you that, you little devil? You keep up that kind of haughty attitude around here, and I'll have every last one of your bones splintered. Here now, let me just tell you this: you don't *deserve* my family's dog food. My dogs cost several dozen piasters each, but your kind of people—as you can see, I was able to buy one of you for a single piaster. Don't you be haughty to me, now!"

Representative Que told Mrs. Dau, cruelly, "You disgusting woman! Are you just going to sit there and stare? Don't you know how to make your daughter behave? Are you perhaps afraid that if she should eat dog food you'll be shamed?"

Apparently because she could not bear to see her mother scolded this way, Ty quickly took the rice. Timidly, she took up a handful and stuffed it into her mouth, then languidly chewed on it like an ox chewing rice chaff.

Madame Representative gritted her teeth and shook her finger in the little girl's face; "I'm telling you once and for all—you've got to finish that basket of rice before tomorrow, and only then will you get anything else to eat!"

Mrs. Dau leaned her head against the house post and sobbed silently. Representative Que shouted out; "Hey you, are you going to take your money or aren't you? Or maybe you're still wanting to hold on to your child and the dogs?"

Mrs. Dau quickly wiped away the tears and stood up. "Venerable sir..."

Not letting her finish the sentence, Representative Que turned to prod his wife. "Pay her and make her go home. Letting her sit here forever like this, I just can't put up with it any longer."

Madame Representative went to open the trunk to get the money. The bells fastened to the lid [as a sort of burglar alarm] clinked and clanked a few times, and then Madame Representative threw two strings of coins out onto the threshold. "There! There's the money!"

Mrs. Dau cautiously picked up the coins and was about to untie the strings to recount them. Madame's voice was high and rasping. "Nobody would think of shortchanging you! There is no need to count them!"

Mrs. Dau tucked the coins down behind her back, then, sobbing, she said to Ty, "Child, stay here and attend the venerable sir and madame. Mother has to go."

Ty embraced her mother and cried like the wind and the rain. "Mama, don't go too quickly! Please stay here with me a little while longer."

Representative Que arose abruptly, extended his giant hand, and slapped the girl on the face. He then roared out like a stage general, "You, boy, haul her out to the kitchen."

At once, Ty was separated from her mother and was made to follow the Representative's attendant out the doorway. She turned back to look at her mother. Her lips were trembling, and she was sobbing.

"Mama, please bring brother Dan over tomorrow to play with me, because I miss him very much."

Mrs. Dau's breasts were round with milk, and it had begun to drip out, getting her bodice wet. Mrs. Dau was uneasy about it and worried about the baby girl at home since, according to the experience of mothers with babies, should they be away from their children and should their milk begin to drip out in such a way, it was a sign that the babies were hungry and crying for milk. She did not dare to think any more about her daughter Ty but gathered up the basket, the bamboo sieve, and also the tattered conical hat and hurried out through the gate of Doai hamlet.

The sun had already sunk below the horizon. Flocks of crows flew down onto the graveyards. The buffalo boys, hastening the cattle back to their resting places, were sounding their coconut-leaf horns. By the time she reached Dong Xa village, night had fallen.

The communal house was empty. Inside, a band of mosquito bats whirred. A lamp flickering on the altar strained to spit out its weak yellow rays, to give light to a few tablets of black incense smoldering below the altar door.

In the various rooms of the communal house there remained only darkness to emphasize the eerie atmosphere of the place. Some time ago, the people had removed their noise and activity to the house of the village chief administrator.

As if she had guessed that this was the case, Mrs. Dau started off alone for the place where the noise of the prisoners could be heard. Finally she went inside.

Under the brightness of the two-wick lamps, the scene within the chief administrator's house was at that time just like the earlier scene in the communal house. Mr. Dau and the other men who had not paid the required amount of tax sat with their elbows roped to the supporting room pillars. Men and women waiting to pay their taxes were still crowded at one of the doorways.

As before, guards and their deputies reclined on the floor near the opium pipe, in attendance on the canton chief. The treasurer, the council chairman, the vice-chairman, and other village notables sat and sprawled beside a clutter of books and notebooks.

When Mrs. Dau's sweaty, tearful countenance appeared at the doorway, she was at once met with a chorus of yells from these notables.

"So you managed to sell your child, did you. Bring the money on up now, quickly!"

"Yes."

Saying this, she pulled out the two strings of one-cent coins that had been tucked under her waist strap and also the eight dimes—the money for which she had sold her potatoes—that had been securely fastened at the bodice strap. She put back one dime out of it, then tiptoed up to lay the two piasters and seven dimes before the village chief administrator.

"Please, sir, I did not have the time to change it to paper money, so please accept it from me!"

"Then for each piaster you must pay a three-cent surcharge. Hand it here and I will accept it. But why only two piasters and seven dimes?"

Uncomprehending, Mrs. Dau gave over the remaining dime to pay for the currency exchange and answered in a trembling voice; "Sir, I thought that each body tax for this year was only that much."

"That's correct. The amount of each body tax is only two piasters and seven dimes this year. But your family must pay two accounts, don't you see? One is for your husband and one is for Hoi."

"Sir, but my brother-in-law has been dead since January! Is it possible that my husband has not registered his death?"

The village chief administrator became annoyed. "Even if his death has been registered, he still has to pay his body tax. Why didn't he die in October of last year?"

She was more confused than ever, and sensed that they were deliberately doing all they could to bully her. "But, Sir, he has been dead for nearly five months. Why must he still pay body tax?"

The village chief administrator shouted; "Go and ask Mr. Frenchman, I don't know."

The secretary solemnly explained, "Even in death one cannot always avoid paying taxes to the government! It is because, even though your brother-in-law died in the Annamese month of January, the 'death registration' record of the village was compiled at the beginning of the Western year, that is, the Annamese eleventh month of last year. Hoi's name appeared in that record since he was still living at that time. When the list is sent to the province capital, the administration there, in order to form the list for the Treasury, goes only according to the number of men given therein. When it is tax-collecting time, the Treasury goes by the amount of taxes given on this list and must collect it. Your brother died in January, but even if he had died in December, it would still have been the same story. After the record is once completed, it can never be altered. Whether the dead are registered or not makes no difference! Therefore, this year our village cannot deduct the body tax for your Hoi. As he is dead, without wife or children, the village chief administrator has to collect it from his relatives. If your husband does not pay for him, who will?"

Half-speaking, half-whining, Mrs. Dau replied, "I am a woman, and don't know about this sort of official business. . . . How unlucky that my brother-in-law should pass away, for it's just like losing the right hand of our family! With him alive, surely we would not be so miserable. But unfortunately he died, and now of course his body tax has to be paid by my husband. But I beg you to let it be delayed until tomorrow. Today I will pay for one account, but first, please free my husband, since he's already weak from illness and has been tied up all day. Otherwise he may die too."

The village chief administrator, his eyes distended, snarled, "If he dies, I will bury him myself! You think *I'd* be scared if your husband died? If you don't want your husband tied up, then bring two more piasters and seven dimes. Otherwise I will keep him tied up, tied up until all the tax money is paid."

Mrs. Dau, as though at her wit's end, squatted down at her husband's side and wailed, "Heaven, oh heaven! I have sold my daughter together with my dogs and four baskets of potatoes in order to raise two piasters and seven dimes, thinking I had enough to pay my husband's body tax so that he would not be beaten tonight. But whoever thought of having to pay a body tax for the dead? What an awful thing to happen to me! Oh heaven, my brother-in-law is dead, and still he has to pay his tax—heaven, is such a thing possible? What can I smash my head against to raise two piasters and seven dimes now?"

The guard foreman sat up quickly, the veins showing on his neck, and shouted, "Is this the place for you to cry, eh, woman? If you want to live, shut up—or else I am going to give you another beating!"[2]

Trembling, Mr. Dau advised his wife; "Please go back home to the children. They will be out of breath from crying. Just leave me here; I won't die from having to be tied up for another night! Don't say anything more, or they will beat you, and you will only suffer the more for it!"

Still Mrs. Dau could not calm herself.

The treasurer, who had just finished recounting the two strings of coins, called to Mrs. Dau, saying, "Hey woman, stop your crying, and come over here and take a look: for each piaster, four cents are missing! From the dime that you paid for exchange fees, eight cents must be deducted for this, so that means you still owe us four more cents."

Mrs. Dau again wailed, "What a terrible fate! I had thought all the time that there would be a dime left to buy rice for my children. Now everything is gone, and still there is not enough! That Madame Representative is so rich—heaven only knows—and still she cheats!" Dejectedly, she sat down and cried.

Mr. Dau insisted, "Please listen to me, dear! If you love me, then please go home to the children. Don't sit here crying, it just makes me get all churned up inside!"

Friends, who were tied up alongside Mr. Dau, asked, trying to express their compassion, "If you have sold your eldest daughter, then who are the two younger children at home staying with?"

Sobbing, she replied, "They are staying at home all alone. Who else is there, gentlemen?"

The men looked uneasy. "What a pity! A five-year-old boy having to take care of a two-year-old girl! What a pity!"

"According to what those officials just said, even the dead have to pay taxes. That means your family still owes them another payment. If you do not have the money to give them, then even if you stayed here until tomorrow morning, you still wouldn't be able to plead for his release. The more you say, the more worn out you will be, and none of them will take pity on you. It's better that you go home so the children won't have to suffer."

"Right, he's right! Please take heart and leave your husband here, and go back to your children to rest. It will just be all the more painful for you to stay around here, so what's the use of it? And if you are not able to control yourself, your mouth may itch to say a few things that could only end in getting your husband beaten."

Those speeches, though full of kindness, could not really help Mrs. Dau, and in any case she already thought as they did. Sadly she murmured in her husband's ear, "Ty saved a dish of potatoes for you. I will bring it over for you; is that all right?"

Mr. Dau shook his head, "My mouth is very bitter. I don't feel like eating anything just now. You just go on home to the children. Don't worry about my eating."

Saying good-bye to her husband with tears streaming from her eyes, Mrs. Dau stumbled out with the basket, the bamboo sieve, and the torn hat.

## Notes

1. That is, with one foot resting on the other knee.
2. She had been beaten at the communal house that morning.

# Ho Chi Minh: A Profile
## Bernard B. Fall

Certain great political figures in history are remembered for their talents both as writers and as leaders of men. The names of Julius Caesar, Napoleon I, Winston Churchill, and Charles de Gaulle come readily to mind. There are others whose impact on history is likely to be no less great and, for ill or for good, may be even longer lasting than that of the men in the first category. These are men who have the ability to organize, to work with a wide variety of people, and to achieve results through personal contact rather than through the persuasiveness of their writings or their thinking. Louis XIV, Marshal Tito, and, of course, Lyndon B. Johnson fall into this category of men whose deeds will endure but whose writings are unlikely material for literary anthologies.

Ho Chi Minh, as the following pages will amply show, also falls into the latter group. He has been too much the doer, the organizer, the conspirator, and, finally, the father of his own country to engage in the contemplation that serious writing generally requires. Hitler used the enforced leisure of his stay at Landsberg prison to write his *Mein Kampf*. Lenin had years of comfortable and safe exile in Switzerland to do his writing. Even Mao Tse-tung, though a guerrilla leader, had long periods of time in his Yenan redoubt, and, in later years, the protection offered by his enormous country, to produce his philosophy of revolution.

Ho Chi Minh seldom had any such leisure.[1] Born on May 19, 1890, in the village of Kim-Lien in Nghé-An province of Central Viet-Nam, he has been on the run since the age of thirteen, when he was expelled from the French *lycée* at Vinh for anti-French nationalist activities (the French side of the story says, for failing grades), and he has never stopped since. Lenin and Marx were revolutionaries, but they lived the life of the middle class of their times. Mao Tse-tung was a peasant guerrilla for two decades, but he at least benefited from the fact that he operated within a large organization; he went hungry only when everyone else went hungry and he certainly never had to worry about paying his rent. Ho Chi Minh, on the other hand, had to eke out a meager living in a completely hostile as well as alien environment. In the early days of the colonial regime, a young Vietnamese could better his status only by going abroad and either furthering his education or making money. But to go abroad in itself required funds which a poor Vietnamese could not dream of acquiring. So, in 1911, Ho Chi Minh went to sea as a mess boy on a French liner. His association with equally destitute French sailors must have been an eye-opener to him, as were his travels throughout the world—he navigated mostly on the Africa runs, but eventually landed in the major ports on the American East Coast (and perhaps also in San Francisco). The life of a mess boy aboard a ship is not one that permits much time for philosophizing, but it left some indelible impressions on Ho Chi Minh, which are clearly reflected in his early writings.

More than most other colonial revolutionaries, Ho Chi Minh understood that Viet-Nam's case as a colonial country was not exceptional but rather was typical of the whole colonial system. In his writings, Ho was to show a constant concern for other colonial struggles in Africa, the Middle East, and Latin America. His early writings also clearly reflect the personal humiliations he must have suffered at the hands of the colonial masters—not because they hated him as a person, but simply because, as a "colored" colonial, he *did not count as a human being.* This intense personalization of the whole anticolonial struggle shines clearly throughout Ho's writings. He was not interested in debating general political theories. He was far more interested in demonstrating that such-and-such French colonial official, fully named, was a sadist who enjoyed harassing his colonial charges than in patiently whittling away at the colonial structure in the hope that it would, in its own time and on its own conditions, yield a small measure of self-government to the subject nation. In fact, Ho's most important work, *French Colonization On Trial,* originally written in French, is in reality a series of highly emotional pamphlets denouncing the various abuses of the French colonial system.

Before Ho reached that stage, however, much else was to happen to him that would explain his sense of disillusionment and bitterness toward the West. At the outset of World War I, after years at sea, Ho took a job in London. It was again a menial job, as a kitchen helper, and he supplemented his meager earnings by shoveling snow in the winter for the London school system. In England, Ho made his first politically significant contact, with the Chinese Overseas Workers' Association. Yet at age twenty-four he was little more than a naïve young Asian desperately trying to make a living, like thousands of West Indians and Pakistanis in London today. At some point, the maturation process must have suddenly accelerated, but the available evidence does not throw much light on this. Toward the end of 1917, Ho moved to war-torn France, where 80,000 Vietnamese (they were still known as Annamites) were either fighting for the French Army or working in French war factories side by side with French women. Vietnamese military police units had fired into mutineering French troops in 1917, and tens of thousands of Vietnamese workers could see for themselves that the myth of the all-powerful and all-knowing white master, so assiduously fostered overseas by the colonial administration, was exactly that: a myth.

In the Europe of the last days of World War I, politics were in ferment. In Russia, Communism was moving from theory to practice—from an abstract philosophy to a system of government; Imperial Germany was cracking behind its thin layer of front-line troops, and Red banners had been flying from German warships at their base in Kiel. There was a good chance that the next German government would be Socialist, and the same was true in many areas of the collapsing Austro-Hungarian state. The latter, in fact, must have provided to a man like Ho Chi Minh an interesting case of a colonial empire losing its grip on its subjects. In French politics there was also a move to the left. The French Socialist Party had been anxiously watching events in Russia. As early as 1917, a split had occurred within its ranks between those who still believed in a slow evolutionary process and the minority who believed that the time for a Marxist revolution had come.

In all Western Socialist parties, with their equalitarian theories, the "colonials" (in the sense that the word is understood in Britain and France—i.e., the indigenous nationals of the colonies) had always loomed as politically important. This was truer in France than in Britain, since the French were propagating an assimilation theory whose goal was the eventual complete merger of all French colonies into a permanent unit. The term "Overseas France," which the French used in referring to their empire until the late 1940's, is an example of that particular delusion. All French political parties supported this policy, although only the Socialists were willing to recognize its logical implication—i.e., in effect, to give full political rights to the natives. The best way for French political parties to show their commitment to the ideal of assimilation (while at the same time acquiring a useful following in the colonies) was to grant a great deal of importance to those colonials residing in metropolitan France—as long as they were willing to play the game. (That was also the case, of course, in Britain, where such Indian nationalists as Nehru and Krishna Menon were not only the darlings of the Labour Party but, in the case of Menon, actually ran for office.) Thus a young and enthusiastic man like Ho Chi Minh was given an opportunity out of all proportion to his educational background or following at home to influence politics in the colonial mainland. By the end of World War I, he was a fully accepted member of the French Socialist hierarchy and met on a basis of equality some of the men who would hold office in France almost until Charles de Gaulle's return to power in 1958.

Yet there was one important difference between Ho Chi Minh and the many other Westernized colonials who were active in European politics, and particularly between Ho and those who eventually turned toward Communism: Ho constantly kept alive his own identification with Vietnamese national objectives. This was true even at a time when "internationalism" was the order of the day among both the Socialists and those who were eventually to become the Communists. This can be seen particularly clearly in the aliases used by Ho Chi Minh in the 1920's. The name he used the most was Nguyen Ai Quoc. "Nguyen" is the most common Vietnamese family name, like "Smith" in English, and was designed to emphasize Ho's association with the common man. It also happens to have been his real family name, since his name at birth was Nguyen That Thanh (Ho Chi Minh being merely another alias). But "Ai Quoc" reveals his clear feelings, for it means "Loves His Country," or "the Patriot." Another name Ho used in France in the 1920's, and which finally earned him a rebuke by the French Communist Party specialist on colonial affairs, Jacques Doriot,[2] was Nguyen O Phap ("Nguyen Who Hates the French").

For a man who was to spend twenty full years in the service of the Communist International, this ethnocentrism was remarkable. It clearly shines through all his writings, even when they deal with the creation of the Indochinese Communist Party (ICP). Throughout his whole life, Ho has never quite reconciled within himself the at times conflicting demands of over-all Communist strategy and his own love for his country. It would be quite inaccurate to say, as have some Western scholars recently, that Ho has let his Communist allegiances override his Vietnamese patriotism. The contrary, in fact, is true. Thus, recently published sources show that when international Communist tactics demanded that the anticolonial struggle in overseas areas be subordinated to a "united front" struggle against the rising fascist threat in Germany, Italy, and Japan (as at the Seventh Comintern Congress of July-August, 1935), Ho had a great deal of trouble getting this line accepted in the ICP; obviously, his heart was not in it.[3] This is clearly reflected in the truncated version of his 1939 report to the Comintern printed in this volume.[4] In fact, throughout the 1920's and 1930's, Ho makes anticolonialism such a central issue of all his public statements at Communist Party congresses, to the almost total exclusion of any other consideration (particularly those of Soviet diplomatic requirements), that one can well wonder where he would have stood politically had any strong nationalist Vietnamese party existed in Viet-Nam, or had any French political party other than the Communist Party espoused a deliberate policy of eventual independence for the colonies.

This writer has unfortunately been unable to obtain a copy of what was probably Ho Chi Minh's earliest signed public document, his appeal on behalf of Viet-Nam to the heads of state of the victorious Allied powers assembled at Versailles in 1919. An original of this one-page flyer (with the touching misspelling of the signature as Nguyen Ai *Quac*) can be seen in the Revolutionary Museum in Hanoi.[5] Yet, surprisingly, the document does not appear in the four-volume *Selected Works of Ho Chi Minh*, published in Hanoi between 1960 and 1962, on which this present volume is in part based.[6] Perhaps it was omitted because Ho's demands in 1919 were so very modest in relation to what he eventually obtained. His eight-point program did not even include full independence, but sought equality between rulers and ruled, basic civic rights, more schools, abolishment of administrative arbitrariness and its replacement by duly enacted laws, and appointment of a Vietnamese delegation to advise the French Government on Vietnamese affairs. This hardheaded practicality—the ability to perceive what is feasible at one particular point in history and what is not—is what sets off Ho Chi Minh not only from some of his more ebullient associates in North Viet-Nam but also from most of the hopelessly unrealistic non-Communist Vietnamese politicians. Many of them, particularly former North Vietnamese nationalists who are refugees in Saigon, have reproached Ho for having accepted the division of the country at the 17th parallel in 1954, apparently forgetting that the alternative might well have been an American entry into the Indochina War right there and then in support of the French, and at the same time the commitment of a *united* Sino-Soviet bloc on the side of Ho Chi Minh. Whatever has happened in Viet-Nam between 1954 and the time of this writing, it would seem preferable to this alternative, which might have led to another world war in 1954.

One of North Viet-Nam's severest scholarly critics, Professor P. J. Honey, a lecturer at the University of London, made the point in a television interview early in 1966 that "one of the things which has impressed [him] enormously about Ho Chi Minh is how much he learned from Gandhi." There are very few Communist leaders in the world who can evoke such a comparison and even fewer to whom it would actually be applicable. Here also, it could be argued that this Gandhi-like deportment is nothing but an "act." But if so, Ho has played one and the same act successfully for audiences ranging from Western Communists to Vietnamese peasants to American OSS officers for over forty years—and without ever making a slip. In fact, Ho Chi Minh, like everyone else, no doubt play-acts part of the time, and as chief executive of his part of the country he is a captive of his mythology. But it is also true that he *means* to be exactly what he is.

There are, after all, enough writers of ability (or, for that matter, Party hacks) in North Viet-Nam who could have concocted a whole synthetic body of "collected works" of far greater importance—or at least greater volume—than those which are officially attributed to him. Yet Ho's writings, which now cover almost five decades, show little change in style, making allowance for the fact that his early writings were almost all in French (the English versions published in Hanoi represent a double translation: from original Vietnamese thoughts into French, and then into English) while his most recent ones are almost exclusively in Vietnamese. The interviews are generally conducted in French, although Ho does not object to using some English at times. His style has perhaps lost some of its erstwhile *ad hominem* virulence; for example, President Johnson is not the object of the personal invective with which French colonial governors were treated in the 1920s.

There is a quality of candor in Ho, which again is Gandhi-like—a certain deceptive simplicity not often found in Communist leaders, which has permitted him time and again to avoid paying the price in decreasing popularity for mistakes made by the regime he heads. Most bureaucracies are unwilling to admit mistakes, as becomes amply clear to anyone who looks at the Western record in Viet-Nam over the past twenty years. Yet, on August 18, 1956, three months before the farmers of his own native province rose in rebellion over the botched land reform which Hanoi had thoughtlessly rammed through, Ho Chi Minh went on the radio to admit that "the leadership of the Party Central Committee and of the Government is sometimes lacking in concreteness, and control and encouragement is disregarded. All this has caused us to commit errors and meet with shortcomings in carrying out land reform."

The same candor made him state ten years later, on July 17, 1966, that the United States would eventually destroy most of North Viet-Nam's major cities—a prospect which could hardly have heartened his fellow citizens but which, under the circumstances, he felt they must face up to. In the same speech, he also promised his people the possibility of war for perhaps another five, ten, or twenty years.

In compiling any selection of a writer's works, the editor must make the difficult choice between pieces that are most representative of the author's style and those that best reflect the times in which he lived. The process was complicated in this case by the fact that even the edition of Ho's works published in Hanoi represents a selection from a larger body of writings that has never been assembled in its entirety—including pieces that have appeared under pseudonyms to which Ho Chi Minh has thus far not admitted.[7] We do not know why certain pieces were omitted from the edition. In addition to the 1919 appeal to the Great Powers, already mentioned, this writer recalls a brochure on the plight of the American Negro, published by Ho Chi Minh in Moscow in the 1920's, which did not find its way into the Hanoi edition; nor did his haunting poems, written while he was imprisoned by Nationalist

Chinese authorities from August 28, 1942, until September 16, 1943.[8] Perhaps his editors did not feel that the at times sentimental poetry fitted in too well with the image of a strong father-like leader. I have included a few of these poems because they show us another aspect of the man and another step in his historical development. Following the practice of the Hanoi editors, I have also included personal interviews granted by Ho Chi Minh in the materials I have added covering the 1960–66 period.

At the time of this writing, it was impossible to predict how long the Second Indochina War would continue and for how long Ho Chi Minh would be the leader of those Vietnamese forces which oppose the United States in Viet-Nam. Perhaps the logical ending to such a book, and perhaps the crowning achievement of two such doers as Lyndon B. Johnson and Ho Chi Minh, would be their signatures, along with those of other interested parties, on a treaty ensuring a lasting and just peace for the Vietnamese people, both North and South. The chances are, unfortunately, that Ho's grim appeal to his people to fight on in the ruins of their country for twenty years, and President Johnson's admonition of October, 1966, to the American troops in Viet-Nam "to bring back that coon skin on the wall," are a more accurate reflection of the prevailing moods.

*Saigon, South Viet-Nam*
*Christmas Day, 1966*

## Footnotes

1. For a more extensive biography of Ho, see Fall, *The Two Viet-Nams* (2d rev. ed.; New York: Frederick A. Praeger, 1967).

2. Jacques Doriot will eventually receive the full biographic treatment he deserves. A very able and highly regarded senior member of the Communist Party hierarchy, and its leading expert on colonial questions, Doriot broke with the party in the 1930's and formed a French fascist party, known as the Parti Populaire Français, whose admiration for the German Nazis was a matter of record even in pre-war days. After France was occupied by the Germans, the PPF built up an unsavory reputation as a military strong-arm squad for the Vichy Government. Doriot himself eventually joined the infamous Waffen-SS as a lieutenant, and for a while fought with the Germans on the Eastern Front against the Russians. Having fled France in August, 1944, he was subsequently killed by an American fighter-bomber on a road in Italy.

3. See Charles B. McLane, *Soviet Strategies in Southeast Asia: An Exploration of Eastern Policy Under Lenin and Stalin* (Princeton, N.J.: Princeton University Press, 1966), pp. 214–20.

4. See pp. 130–31.

5. Unfortunately, a photograph of the text taken by the editor in 1962 failed to be completely legible.

6. With the exception of the poetry and the last nine articles included in Part Five, all the selections in this volume are from the four-volume edition *The Selected Works of Ho Chi Minh* (Hanoi: Foreign Languages Publishing House, 1960, 1961, 1962) and are reprinted here with only minor stylistic changes. Some footnotes giving factual information have been reprinted from the Hanoi edition; italicized notes have been added by the editor.

7. According to McLane, *op. cit.,* some of the most incisive reports on Indochinese Communism, written in the 1930's were signed with the name "Orgwald"; in the view of the knowledgeable McLane, "Orgwald" may well have been still another alias for Ho Chi Minh.

8. *Prison Diary* (Hanoi: Foreign Languages Publishing House, 1959).

# Appeal Made on the Occasion of the Founding of the Communist Party of Indochina[1]
## (February 18, 1930)

Workers, peasants, soldiers, youth, and pupils!
Oppressed and exploited compatriots!
Sisters and brothers! Comrades!

Imperialist contradictions were the cause of the 1914–18 World War. After this horrible slaughter, the world was divided into two camps: One is the revolutionary camp including the oppressed colonies and the exploited working class throughout the world. The vanguard force of this camp is the Soviet Union. The other is the counterrevolutionary camp of international capitalism and imperialism whose general staff is the League of Nations.

During this World War, various nations suffered untold losses in property and human lives. The French imperialists were the hardest hit. Therefore, in order to restore the capitalist forces in France, the French imperialists have resorted to every underhand scheme to intensify their capitalist exploitation in Indochina. They set up new factories to exploit the workers with low wages. They plundered the peasants' land to establish plantations and drive them to utter poverty. They levied many heavy taxes. They imposed public loans upon our people. In short, they reduced us to wretchedness. They increased their military forces, firstly to strangle the Vietnamese revolution, secondly to prepare for a new imperialist war in the Pacific aimed at capturing new colonies, thirdly to suppress the Chinese revolution, fourthly to attack the Soviet Union because the latter helps the revolution of the oppressed nations and the exploited working class. World War II will break out. When it breaks, the French imperialists will certainly drive our people to a more horrible slaughter. If we give them a free hand to prepare for this war, suppress the Chinese revolution, and attack the Soviet

301

Union, if we give them a free hand to stifle the Vietnamese revolution, it is tantamount to giving them a free hand to wipe our race off the earth and drown our nation in the Pacific.

However the French imperialists' barbarous oppression and ruthless exploitation have awakened our compatriots, who have all realized that revolution is the only road to life, without it they will die out piecemeal. This is the reason why the Vietnamese revolutionary movement has grown even stronger with each passing day. The workers refuse to work, the peasants demand land, the pupils strike, the traders boycott. Everywhere the masses have risen to oppose the French imperialists.

The Vietnamese revolution has made the French imperialists tremble with fear. On the one hand, they utilize the feudalists and comprador bourgeois in our country to oppress and exploit our people. On the other, they terrorize, arrest, jail, deport, and kill a great number of Vietnamese revolutionaries. If the French imperialists think that they can suppress the Vietnamese revolution by means of terrorist acts, they are utterly mistaken. Firstly, it is because the Vietnamese revolution is not isolated but enjoys the assistance of the world proletarian class in general and of the French working class in particular. Secondly, while the French imperialists are frenziedly carrying out terrorist acts, the Vietnamese Communists, formerly working separately, have now united into a single party, the Communist Party of Indochina, to lead our entire people in their revolution.

Workers, peasants, soldiers, youth, pupils!

Oppressed and exploited compatriots!

The Communist Party of Indochina is founded. It is the party of the working class. It will help the proletarian class to lead the revolution in order to struggle for all the oppressed and exploited people. From now on we must join the Party, help it and follow it in order to implement the following slogans:

1. To overthrow French imperialism, feudalism, and the reactionary Vietnamese capitalist class.
2. To make Indochina completely independent.
3. To establish a worker-peasant and soldier government.
4. To confiscate the banks and other enterprises belonging to the imperialists and put them under the control of the worker-peasant and soldier government.
5. To confiscate the whole of the plantations and property belonging to the imperialists and the Vietnamese reactionary capitalist class and distribute them to poor peasants.
6. To implement the eight-hour working day.

7. To abolish public loans and poll tax. To waive unjust taxes hitting the poor people.

8. To bring back all freedoms to the masses.

9. To carry out universal education.

10. To implement equality between man and woman.

## Note

1. The Communist Party of Indochina, founded on February 3, 1930, was the outcome of the conference convened in Hong Kong by the Communist International. This historic conference merged the three Communist groups in the three parts of Viet-Nam (North, Center, and South) into a single Communist Party. Comrade Nguyen Ai Quoc was charged by the Communist International to attend the conference. Basing itself on Nguyen Ai Quoc's proposals, the conference approved of the general political thesis on the revolutionary line in Viet-Nam at that stage and decided to unify the Party under the name of the Communist Party of Indochina, to draft the Party's political program, its constitution, and the statutes of various mass organizations, and to appoint the Party's Provisional Central Committee.

# Declaration of Independence of the Democratic Republic of Viet-Nam[1]

## (September 2, 1945)

A ll men are created equal; they are endowed by their Creator with certain unalienable Rights; among these are Life, Liberty, and the pursuit of Happiness.

This immortal statement was made in the Declaration of Independence of the United States of America in 1776. In a broader sense, this means: All the peoples on the earth are equal from birth, all the peoples have a right to live, to be happy and free.

The Declaration of the French Revolution made in 1791 on the Rights of Man and the Citizen also states: "All men are born free and with equal rights, and must always remain free and have equal rights."

Those are undeniable truths.

Nevertheless, for more than eighty years, the French imperialists, abusing the standard of Liberty, Equality, and Fraternity, have violated our Fatherland and oppressed our fellow citizens. They have acted contrary to the ideals of humanity and justice.

In the field of politics, they have deprived our people of every democratic liberty.

They have enforced inhuman laws; they have set up three distinct political regimes in the North, the Center, and the South of Viet-Nam in order to wreck our national unity and prevent our people from being united.

They have built more prisons than schools. They have mercilessly slain our patriots; they have drowned our uprisings in rivers of blood.

They have fettered public opinion; they have practiced obscurantism against our people.

To weaken our race they have forced us to use opium and alcohol.

In the field of economics, they have fleeced us to the backbone, impoverished our people and devastated our land.

They have robbed us of our rice fields, our mines, our forests, and our raw materials. They have monopolized the issuing of bank notes and the export trade.

They have invented numerous unjustifiable taxes and reduced our people, especially our peasantry, to a state of extreme poverty.

They have hampered the prospering of our national bourgeoisie; they have mercilessly exploited our workers.

In the autumn of 1940, when the Japanese fascists violated Indochina's territory to establish new bases in their fight against the Allies, the French imperialists went down on their bended knees and handed over our country to them.

Thus, from that date, our people were subjected to the double yoke of the French and the Japanese. Their sufferings and miseries increased. The result was that, from the end of last year to the beginning of this year, from Quang Tri Province to the North of Viet-Nam, more than two million of our fellow citizens died from starvation. On March 9, [1945], the French troops were disarmed by the Japanese. The French colonialists either fled or surrendered, showing that not only were they incapable of "protecting" us, but that, in the span of five years, they had twice sold our country to the Japanese.

On several occasions before March 9, the Viet Minh League urged the French to ally themselves with it against the Japanese. Instead of agreeing to this proposal, the French colonialists so intensified their terrorist activities against the Viet Minh members that before fleeing they massacred a great number of our political prisoners detained at Yen Bay and Cao Bang.

Notwithstanding all this, our fellow citizens have always manifested toward the French a tolerant and humane attitude. Even after the Japanese *Putsch* of March, 1945, the Viet Minh League helped many Frenchmen to cross the frontier, rescued some of them from Japanese jails, and protected French lives and property.

From the autumn of 1940, our country had in fact ceased to be a French colony and had become a Japanese possession.

After the Japanese had surrendered to the Allies, our whole people rose to regain our national sovereignty and to found the Democratic Republic of Viet-Nam.

The truth is that we have wrested our independence from the Japanese and not from the French.

The French have fled, the Japanese have capitulated, Emperor Bao Dai has abdicated. Our people have broken the chains which for nearly a century have fettered them and have won independence for the Fatherland. Our people at the same time have overthrown the monarchic regime that has reigned supreme for dozens of centuries. In its place has been established the present Democratic Republic.

For these reasons, we, members of the Provisional Government, representing the whole Vietnamese people, declare that from now on we break off all relations of a colonial character with France; we repeal all the international obligation that France has so far subscribed to on behalf of Viet-Nam, and we abolish all the special rights the French have unlawfully acquired in our Fatherland.

The whole Vietnamese people, animated by a common purpose, are determined to fight to the bitter end against any attempt by the French colonialists to reconquer their country.

We are convinced that the Allied nations, which at Teheran and San Francisco have acknowledged the principles of self-determination and equality of nations, will not refuse to acknowledge the independence of Viet-Nam.

A people who have courageously opposed French domination for more than eighty years, a people who have fought side by side with the Allies against the fascists during these last years, such a people must be free and independent.

For these reasons, we, members of the Provisional Government of the Democratic Republic of Viet-Nam, solemnly declare to the world that Viet-Nam has the right to be free and independent country—and in fact it is so already. The entire Vietnamese people are determined to mobilize all their physical and mental strength, to sacrifice their lives and property in order to safeguard their independence and liberty.

## Note

1. *The borrowing from the United States Declaration of Independence was open and intended. American members of the OSS mission parachuted to Ho in the summer of 1945 recall several of Ho's attempts to obtain a copy of the Declaration, or, failing this, a close approximation of its essential passages.*—Ed.

# Congratulatory Letter to Armymen, War Service Workers, Shock Youth, and People in the Northwest Area Who Have Won Brilliant Victory at Dien Bien Phu[1]
## (May 8, 1954)

O ur army has liberated Dien Bien Phu. The Government and I convey our cordial greetings to you, cadres, fighters, war service workers, shock youth, and local people who have gloriously fulfilled your tasks. This victory is big, but it is only the beginning. We must not be self-complacent and subjective and underestimate the enemy. We are determined to fight for independence, national unity, democracy, and peace. A struggle, whether military or diplomatic, must be long and hard before complete victory can be achieved.

The Government and I will reward the officers, soldiers, patriotic workers, shock youth, and local people who have performed brilliant deeds.

## Appeal Made After the Successful Conclusion of the Geneva Agreements (July 22, 1954)

The Geneva Conference has come to an end. It is a great victory for our diplomacy.

On behalf of the Government, I cordially make the following appeal:

1. For the sake of peace, unity, independence, and democracy of the Fatherland, our people, armymen, cadres, and Government have, during these eight years or so, joined in a monolithic bloc, endured hardship, and resolutely overcome all difficulties to carry out the Resistance; we have won many brilliant victories. On this occasion, on behalf of the Government, I cordially congratulate you, from North to South. I respectfully bow to the memory of the armymen and people who have sacrificed their lives for the Fatherland, and send my homages of comfort to the wounded and sick armymen.

This great victory is also due to the support given us in our just struggle by the peoples of our brother countries, by the French people, and by the peace-loving people of the world.

Thanks to these victories and the efforts made by the delegation of the Soviet Union at the Berlin Conference, negotiations were opened between our country and France at the Geneva Conference. At this conference, the struggle of our delegation and the assistance given by the delegations of the Soviet Union and China have ended in a great victory for us. The French Government has recognized the independence, sovereignty, unity, and territorial integrity of our country; it has agreed to withdraw French troops from our country, etc.

From now on, we must make every effort to consolidate peace and achieve reunification, independence, and democracy throughout our country.

2. In order to re-establish peace, the first step to take is that the armed forces of both parties should cease fire.

The regroupment in two regions is a temporary measure; it is a transitional step for the implementation of the armistice and restoration of peace, and paves the way for national reunification through general elections. Regroupment in regions is in no way a partition of our country, neither is it an administrative division.

During the armistice, our army is regrouped in the North; the French troops are regrouped in the South, that is to say, there is a change of regions. A number of regions which were formerly occupied by the French now become our free zones. Vice versa, a number of regions formerly liberated by us will now be temporarily occupied by the French troops before they leave for France.

This is a necessity; North, Central, and South Viet-Nam are territories of ours. Our country will certainly be unified, our entire people will surely be liberated.

Our compatriots in the South were the first to wage the war of Resistance. They possess a high political consciousness. I am confident that they will place national interests above local interests, permanent interests above temporary interests, and join their efforts with the entire people in strengthening peace, achieving unity, independence, and democracy all over the country. The Party, Government, and I always follow the efforts of our people and we are sure that our compatriots will be victorious.

3. The struggle to consolidate peace and achieve reunification, independence, and democracy is also a long and hard struggle. In order to carry the day, our people, armymen, and cadres from North to South must unite closely. They must be at one in thought and deed.

We are resolved to abide by the agreements entered into with the French Government. At the same time, we demand that the French Government correctly implement the agreements they have signed with us.

We must do our utmost to strengthen peace and be vigilant to check the maneuvers of peace wreckers.

We must endeavor to struggle for the holding of free general elections throughout the country to reunify our territory.

We must exert all our efforts to restore, build, strengthen, and develop our forces in every field so as to attain complete independence.

We must do our utmost to carry out social reforms in order to improve our people's livelihood and realize genuine democracy.

We further tighten our fraternal relations with Cambodia and Laos.

We strengthen the great friendship between us and the Soviet Union, China, and other brother countries. To maintain peace, we enhance our solidarity with the French people, and people all over the world.

4. I call on all our compatriots, armymen, and cadres to follow strictly the lines and policies laid down by the Party and Government, to struggle for the consolidation of peace and the achievement of national reunification, independence, and democracy throughout the country.

I eagerly appeal to all genuine patriots, irrespective of their social class, creed, political stand, and former affiliation, to cooperate sincerely with us and fight for the sake of our country and our people so as to bring about peace and achieve reunification, independence, and democracy for our beloved Viet-Nam.

If our people are as one, if thousands of men are like one, victory will certainly be ours.

Long live a peaceful, unified, independent, and democratic Viet-Nam.

## Note

1. *There exists another version of this proclamation, dated May 13, 1954, and addressed to Ho's "nephews and nieces," to whom he awards the insignia "Combattant of Dien Bien Phu."*—Ed.

# First Appeal to the United States
## (June 18, 1919)*

## Ho Chi Minh

*D*uring the Versailles Peace Conference in Paris, where a treaty was signed on June 28, 1919 between the Allies and Germany to end World War I, Ho Chi Minh wrote this polite appeal to the principles of Wilsonian self-determination. He avoids insisting on immediate independence for Vietnam but instead claims legal and political rights for which France presumably stands. At the same time, he is careful to hold full independence as the ultimate goal ("While waiting for the principle of national self-determination to pass from ideal to reality"). From the end of World War I through World War II and its aftermath, Ho Chi Minh would repeatedly call upon the Western democracies to live up to their announced principles. Reading 9 presents one of his appeals to President Truman in the fall of 1945.

## A. Letter of Nguyen Ai Quoc to the American Secretary of State

Paris, 18 June, 1919

To his Excellency, the Secretary of State of the Republic of the United States, Delegate to the Peace Conference[1]

Excellency,

We take the liberty of submitting to you the accompanying memorandum setting forth the claims of the Annamite people on the occasion of the Allied victory.

We count on your great kindness to honor our appeal by your support whenever the opportunity arises.

---

*Translations of the French originals in the National Archives, Washington, D.C.

We beg your Excellency graciously to accept the expression of our profound respect.

FOR THE GROUP OF ANNAMITE PATRIOTS
[signed] Nguyen Ai Quoc[2]
56, rue Monsieur le Prince—Paris

## B. *Revendications du Peuple Annamite*  *[Claims of the Annamite People]*

Since the victory of the Allies, all the subject peoples are frantic with hope at the prospect of an era of right and justice which should begin for them by virtue of the formal and solemn engagements, made before the whole world by the various powers of the *entente*[3] in the struggle of civilization against barbarism.

While waiting for the principle of national self-determination to pass from ideal to reality through the effective recognition of the sacred right of all peoples to decide their own destiny, the inhabitants of the ancient Empire of Annam, at the present time French Indochina, present to the noble Governments of the *entente* in general and in particular to the honorable French Government the following humble claims:

(1) General amnesty for all the native people who have been condemned for political activity.

(2) Reform of Indochinese justice by granting to the native population the same judicial guarantees as the Europeans have, and the total suppression of the special courts which are the instruments of terrorization and oppression against the most responsible elements of the Annamite people.

(3) Freedom of press and speech.

(4) Freedom of association and assembly.

(5) Freedom to emigrate and to travel abroad.

(6) Freedom of education, and creation in every province of technical and professional schools for the native population.

(7) Replacement of the regime of arbitrary decrees by a regime of law.

(8) A permanent delegation of native people elected to attend the French parliament in order to keep the latter informed of their needs.

The Annamite people, in presenting these claims, count on the worldwide justice of all the Powers, and rely in particular on the goodwill of the noble French people who hold our destiny in their hands and who, as France is a republic, have taken us under their protection. In requesting the protection of the French people, the people of Annam, far from feeling humiliated, on the contrary consider themselves honored, because they know that the French people stand for liberty and justice and will never renounce their sublime ideal of universal brotherhood. Consequently, in giving heed to the voice of the oppressed, the French people will be doing their duty to France and to humanity.

IN THE NAME OF THE GROUP OF ANNAMITE PATRIOTS:
*Nguyen Ai Quoc*

## Notes

1. The U.S. Secretary of State at the time was Robert Lansing.—eds.
2. Ho Chi Minh's pseudonym at the time.
3. The *entente*, or Allied powers during World War I, included France, England, and after 1917, the United States.—eds.

# *Washington's Man in Saigon: American Commitment to South Vietnam (1961)*[1]

## Vice-President Lyndon B. Johnson, President Ngo Dinh Diem, and President John F. Kennedy

*W*hen John F. Kennedy defeated the Republican contender, Richard Nixon, in the presidential election of 1960, he inherited, and then deepened and extended, an ambiguous commitment to an anti-communist regime in South Vietnam. The backing given to the regime of Ngo Dinh Diem had supposedly been conditional on that government's undertaking what President Dwight D. Eisenhower in 1954 called "needed reforms" (Reading 21). Seven years later, as the letter presented here shows, the emphasis placed on internal reform had been overshadowed by global Cold War considerations. In the view of President Kennedy and many of his advisers, "South Vietnam would become a test case of America's determination to uphold its commitments in a menacing world and of its capacity to meet the new challenges posed by guerrilla warfare in the emerging nations."[1]

Seeing the situation as a conflict with "communism" to be won by militarily defeating "guerrilla warfare" consistently deflected attention from the problems of the southern Vietnamese countryside, where the war would be won or lost. As Reading 26 shows, the insurgents who were fighting against Diem and his American supporters never allowed their attention to be so diverted.

## A. *Joint Declaration by U.S. Vice-President Johnson and Ngo Dinh Diem (May 13, 1961)*

[Saigon]

... The United States ... is conscious of the determination, energy, and sacrifices which the Vietnamese people, under the dedicated leadership of President Ngo Dinh Diem, have brought to the defense of freedom in their land.

The United States is also conscious of its responsibility and duty, in its own self-interest as well as in the interest of other free peoples, to assist a brave country in the defense of its liberties against unprovoked subversion and Communist terror. It has no other motive than the defense of freedom.

The United States recognizes that the President of the Republic of Vietnam, Ngo Dinh Diem, who was recently reelected to office by an overwhelming majority of his countrymen despite bitter Communist opposition, is in the vanguard of those leaders who stand for freedom on the periphery of the Communist empire in Asia.

Free Vietnam cannot alone withstand the pressure which this Communist empire is exerting against it. Under these circumstances—the need of free Vietnam for increased and accelerated emergency assistance and the will and determination of the United States to provide such assistance to those willing to fight for their liberties—it is natural that a large measure of agreement on the means to accomplish the joint purpose was found in high-level conversations between the two Governments.

Both Governments recognize that under the circumstances of guerrilla warfare now existing in free Vietnam, it is necessary to give high priority to the restoration of a sense of security to the people of free Vietnam. This priority, however, in no way diminishes the necessity, in policies and programs of both Governments, to pursue vigorously appropriate measures in other fields to achieve a prosperous and happy society. ...

## B. *President Diem to President Kennedy*

December 7, 1961

Dear Mr. President:

Since its birth, more than six years ago, the Republic of Vietnam has enjoyed the close friendship and cooperation of the United States of America.

Like the United States, the Republic of Vietnam has always been devoted to the preservation of peace. My people know only too well the sorrows of war. We have honored the 1954 Geneva Agreements even though they resulted in the partition of our country and the enslavement of more than half of our people by Communist tyranny. We have never considered the reunification of our nation by force. On the contrary, we have publicly pledged that we will not violate the demarcation line and the demilitarized zone set up by the Agreements. We have always been prepared and have on many occasions stated our willingness to reunify Vietnam on the basis of democratic and truly free elections.

The record of the Communist authorities in the northern part of our country is quite otherwise. They not only consented to the division of Vietnam, but were eager for it. They pledged themselves to observe the Geneva Agreements and during the seven years since have never ceased to violate them. They call for free elections but are ignorant of the very meaning of the words. They talk of "peaceful reunification" and wage war against us.

From the beginning, the Communists resorted to terror in their efforts to subvert our people, destroy our government, and impose a Communist regime upon us. They have attacked defenseless teachers, closed schools, killed members of our anti-malarial program, and looted hospitals. This is coldly calculated to destroy our government's humanitarian efforts to serve our people.

We have long sought to check the Communist attack from the North on our people by appeals to the International Control Commission. Over the years, we have repeatedly published to the world the evidence of the Communist plot to overthrow our government and seize control of all of Vietnam by illegal intrusions from outside our country. . . .

. . . the Vietnamese nation now faces what is perhaps the gravest crisis in its long history. For more than 2,000 years my people have lived and built, fought and died in this land. We have not always been free. Indeed, much of our history and many of its proudest moments have arisen from conquest by foreign powers and our struggle against great odds to regain or defend our precious independence. But it is not only our freedom which is at stake today, it is our national identity. For, if we lose this war, our people will be swallowed by the Communist bloc, all our proud heritage will be blotted out by the "Socialist society" and Vietnam will leave the pages of history. We will lose our national soul.

Mr. President, my people and I are mindful of the great assistance which the United States has given us. Your help has not been lightly received, for the Vietnamese are proud people, and we are determined to do our part in the defense of the free world. It is clear to all of us that the defeat of the Vietcong demands the total mobilization of our government and our people, and you may be sure that we will devote all of our resources of money, minds, and men to this great task.

But Vietnam is not a great power and the forces of international Communism now arrayed against us are more than we can meet with the resources at hand. We must have further assistance from the United States if we are to win the war now being waged against us.

We can certainly assure mankind that our action is purely defensive. Much as we regret the subjugation of more than half of our people in North Vietnam we have no intention, and indeed no means, to free them by use of force.

I have said that Vietnam is at war. War means many things, but most of all it means the death of brave people for a cause they believe in. Vietnam has suffered many wars, and through the centuries we have always had patriots and heroes who were willing to shed their blood for Vietnam. We will keep faith with them.

When Communism has long ebbed away into the past, my people will still be here, a free united nation growing from the deep roots of our Vietnamese heritage. They will remember your help in our time of need. This struggle will then be a part of our common history. And your help, your friendship, and the strong bonds between our two peoples will be a part of Vietnam, then as now.

## C. President Kennedy to President Diem

December 14, 1961

Dear Mr. President:

I have received your recent letter in which you described so cogently the dangerous condition caused by North Vietnam's efforts to take over your country. The situation in your embattled country is well known to me and to the American people. We have been deeply disturbed by the assault on your country. Our indignation has mounted as the deliberate savagery of the Communist program of assassination, kidnapping, and wanton violence became clear.

Your letter underlines what our own information has convincingly shown—that the campaign of force and terror now being waged against your people and your Government is supported and directed from the outside by the authorities at Hanoi. They have thus violated the provisions of the Geneva Accords designed to ensure peace in Vietnam and to which they bound themselves in 1954.

At that time, the United States, although not a party to the Accords, declared that it "would view any renewal of the aggression in violation of the Agreements with grave concern and as seriously threatening international peace and security." We continue to maintain that view.

In accordance with that declaration, and in response to your request, we are prepared to help the Republic of Vietnam to protect its people and to pre-serve its independence. We shall promptly increase our assistance to your defense effort as well as help relieve the destruction of the floods which you describe. I have already given the orders to get these programs underway.

The United States, like the Republic of Vietnam, remains devoted to the cause of peace and our primary purpose is to help your people maintain their independence. If the Communist authorities in North Vietnam will stop their campaign to destroy the Republic of Vietnam, the measures we are taking to assist your defense efforts will no longer be necessary. We shall seek to persuade the Communists to give up their attempts of force and subversion. In any case, we are confident that the Vietnamese people will preserve their independence and gain the peace and prosperity for which they have sought so hard and so long.

## Notes

1. *Department of State Bulletins,* 36 (June 19, 1961), pp. 956–957; 37 (January 1, 1962), pp. 13–14.
2. George C. Herring, making good use of *The Pentagon Papers,* accurately captures the perspective of the Kennedy crisis managers, in *America's Longest War: The United States and Vietnam, 1950–1975* (New York: John Wiley & Sons, 1979), p. 75.

# Heroin and Politics in Saigon
## Alfred W. McCoy

*France may have lost the war, but French influence remained strong. The United States had yet to establish primacy in any part of Vietnam. In the following selection, Alfred McCoy describes the intricate interweaving of politics and underworld activities in Saigon. Originally, the Binh Xuyen were river pirates who first appeared in Saigon in the early 1920s. Flourishing on their organization of the opium trade, prostitution, and extortion, they represented, by the 1940s, a significant political force whose allegiance was sought by the Viet Minh, among others. For a time, the Binh Xuyen participated in a nationalist coalition with the Viet Minh, only to break away over an issue of discipline.*

*If Diem was to truly rule in Saigon, the power of the Binh Xuyen had to be broken. To break it would mean, as well, to break the continuing influence and control of the French secret police. The CIA enthusiastically welcomed this task. And just as the French secret police had used the opium trade to fund counterinsurgency in their war against the Viet Minh, so the CIA, in its struggle against the National Liberation Front, soon embraced the drug traffic as well. Saigon governments selected and supported by the United States, from Diem through Ky and Thieu, were deeply engaged in a trade that fed the heroin habits of Americans at home and abroad.*

Ngo Dinh Diem was a political unknown who had acceded to the premiership largely because Washington was convinced that his strong anti-Communist, anti-French beliefs best suited American interests. But the immediate problem for Diem and the Americans was control of Saigon. If Diem were to be of any use to the Americans in blocking the unification of Vietnam, he would have to wrest control of the streets from the Binh Xuyen. For whoever controlled the streets controlled Saigon, and whoever controlled Saigon held the key to Vietnam's rice-rich Mekong Delta.

While the French and American governments disavowed any self-interest and tried to make even their most partisan suggestions seem a pragmatic response to the changing situation in Saigon, both gave their intelligence agencies a free hand to see if Saigon's reality could be molded in their favor. Behind the diplomatic amity, the CIA, led by Colonel Lansdale,[1] and the

French 2$^{eme}$ Bureau, under Captain Savani, engaged in a savage clandestine battle for Saigon.

In the movie version of Graham Greene's novel about this period, *The Quiet American*, Colonel Lansdale was played by the World War II combat hero Audie Murphy, whose previous roles as the white-hat hero in dozens of westerns allowed him to project the evangelistic anti-communism so characteristic of Lansdale. What Murphy did not portray was Lansdale's mastery of the CIA's repertoire of covert action techniques, including sabotage, psychological warfare, and counter-terrorism. When Lansdale arrived in Saigon in May 1954 he was fresh from engineering President Ramón Magsaysay's successful counterinsurgency campaign against the Philippine Communist party. As the prophet of a new counterinsurgency doctrine and representative of a wealthy government, Lansdale was a formidable opponent.

In seeking to depose Bay Vien,[2] Lansdale was not just challenging the 2$^{eme}$ Bureau, he was taking on Saigon's Corsican community—Corsican businessmen, Corsican colonists, and the Corsican underworld. From the late nineteenth century onward, Corsicans had dominated the Indochina civil service.[3] At the end of World War II, Corsican resistance fighters, some of them gangsters, had joined the regular army and come to Indochina with the Expeditionary Corps. Many remained in Saigon after their enlistment to go into legitimate business or to reap profits from the black market that flourished in wartime. Those with strong underworld connections in Marseille were able to engage in currency smuggling between the two ports. The Marseille gangster Barthélemy Guerini worked closely with contacts in Indochina to smuggle Swiss gold to Asia immediately after World War II.[4] Moreover, Corsican gangsters close to Corsican officers in Saigon's 2$^{eme}$ Bureau purchased surplus opium and shipped it to Marseille, where it made a small contribution to the city's growing heroin industry.[5]

The unchallenged leader of Saigon's Corsican underworld was the eminently respectable Mathieu Franchini. Owner of the exclusive Continental Palace Hotel, Franchini made a fortune playing the piaster-gold circuit between Saigon and Marseille during the First Indochina War.[6] He became the Binh Xuyen's investment counselor and managed a good deal of their opium and gambling profits. When Bay Vien's fortune reached monumental proportions, Franchini sent him to Paris where "new found Corsican friends gave him good advice about investing his surplus millions.[7] According to reliable Vietnamese sources, it was Franchini who controlled most of Saigon's opium exports to Marseille. Neither he nor his associates could view with equanimity the prospect of an American takeover.

Many people within the 2$^{eme}$ Bureau had worked as much as eight years building up sect armies like the Binh Xuyen; many Corsicans outside the military had businesses, positions, rackets, and power that would be threatened by a decline in French influence. While they certainly did not share Premier Mendès-France's ideas of cooperation with the Viet Minh, they were even more hostile to the idea of turning things over to the Americans.

When Lansdale arrived in Saigon he faced the task of building an alternative to the mosaic of religious armies and criminal gangs that had ruled South Vietnam in the latter years of the war. Ngo Dinh Diem's appointment as premier in July 1954 gave Lansdale the lever he needed. Although he was handpicked by the Americans, Diem had spent most of the previous decade in exile and had few political supporters and almost no armed forces. Prime minister in name only, Diem controlled merely the few blocks of downtown Saigon surrounding the presidential palace. The French and their clients— ARVN, the Binh Xuyen, and the armed religious sects, Cao Dai and Hoa Hao—could easily mount an anti-Diem coup if he threatened their interests. Lansdale proceeded to fragment his opposition's solid front and to build Diem an effective military apparatus. French control over the army was broken and Colonel Duong Van Minh ("Big Minh"), an American sympathizer, was recruited to lead the attacks on the Binh Xuyen. By manipulating payments to the armed religious sects, Lansdale was able to neutralize most of them, leaving the Binh Xuyen as the only French pawn. The Binh Xuyen financed themselves largely from their vice rackets, and their loyalty could not be manipulated through financial pressures. But, deserted by ARVN and the religious sects, the Binh Xuyen were soon crushed.

Lansdale's victory did not come easily. Soon after he arrived he began sizing up his opponent's financial and military strength. Knowing something of the opium trade's importance as a source of income for French clandestine services, he now began to look more closely at Operation X[8] with the help of a respected Cholon Chinese banker. But the banker was abruptly murdered and Lansdale dropped the inquiry. There was reason to believe that the banker had gotten too close to the Corsicans involved, and they killed him to prevent the information from getting any further.[9]

An attempted anti-Diem coup in late 1954 led to Lansdale's replacing the palace guard. After the embassy approved secret funding (later estimated at $2 million, Lansdale convinced a Cao Dai dissident named Trinh Minh Thé to offer *maquis* near the Cambodian border as a refuge in case Diem was ever forced to Saigon.[10] When the impending crisis between the French and the Americans threatened Diem's security in the capital, Thé moved his forces into the city as a permanent security force in February 1955 and paraded 2,500 of his barefoot soldiers through downtown Saigon to demonstrate his loyalty to the prime minister. The 2[eme] Bureau was outraged at Lansdale's support for Thé. Practicing what Lansdale jocularly referred to as the "unorthodox doctrine of zapping a commander,"[12] Thé had murdered French General Chanson in 1951 and had further incensed the French when he blew up a car in 1953 in downtown Saigon, killing a number of passersby. Officers from the 2ᵉᵐᵉ Bureau personally visited Lansdale to warn him that they would kill Thé, and they "usually added the pious one that I would be standing next to him when he was gunned down."[13]

On February 11, 1955, the French army abdicated its financial controls and responsibilities for ARVN to the United States, losing not only ARVN but control of the Hoa Hao and Cao Dai religious sects as well. Approximately 20,000 of them had served as supplementary forces to the French and Vietnamese armies,[14] and had been paid directly by the 2ᵉᵐᵉ Bureau. Now, with their stipends cut and their numbers reduced, they were to be integrated into ARVN, where they would be controlled by Diem and his American advisers.

Lansdale was given $8.6 million to pay back salaries and "bonuses" to sect commanders who cooperated by "integrating" into ARVN.[15] Needless to say, this act aroused enormous hostility from the French. When Lansdale met with General Gambiez of the French army to discuss the sect problem, the tensions were obvious:

> We sat at a small table in his office. . . . A huge Alsatian dog crouched under it. Gambiez informed me that at one word from him, the dog would attack me, being a trained killer. I asked Gambiez to please note that my hands were in my pockets as I sat at the table; I had a small .25 automatic pointing at his stomach which would tickle him fatally. Gambiez called off his dog and I put my hands on the table. We found we could work together.[16]

By February the 2ᵉᵐᵉ Bureau realized that they were gradually losing to Lansdale's team, so they tried to discredit him as an irresponsible adventurer in the eyes of his own government by convening an unprecedented secret agents' tribunal. But the session was unsuccessful, and the 2ᵉᵐᵉ Bureau officers were humiliated; their animosity toward Lansdale was, no doubt, intensified.[17]

But the French were not yet defeated, and late in February they mounted a successful counteroffensive. When Diem refused to meet the sects' demands for financial support and integration into ARVN, the French seized the opportunity and brought all the sect leaders together in Tay Ninh on February 22, where they formed the United Front and agreed to work for Diem's overthrow. Money was to be provided by the Binh Xuyen. When a month of fruitless negotiations failed to bring any concessions from Diem, the United Front sent a five-day ultimatum to Diem demanding economic and political reforms.[18] Suddenly the lethargic quadrille of political intrigue was over and the time for confrontation was at hand.

Lansdale was now working feverishly to break up the United Front and was meeting with Diem regularly.[19] With the help of the CIA station chief, Lansdale put together a special team to tackle the Binh Xuyen, the financial linchpin of the United Front. Lansdale recruited a former Saigon police chief named Mai Huu Xuan, who had formed the Military Security Service (MSS) with two hundred to three hundred of his best detectives when the Binh Xuyen took over the police force in 1954. Embittered by four years of losing to the Binh Xuyen, the MSS began a year-long battle with the Binh Xuyen's action committees. Many of these covert cells had been eliminated by April 1955, a factor that Xuan felt was critical in the Binh Xuyen's defeat.[20] Another of Lansdale's recruits was Colonel Duong Van Minh, the ARVN commander for Saigon-Cholon. Lansdale made ample discretionary funds available to Minh, whom he incorporated in his plans to assault the Binh Xuyen.[21]

The fighting began on March 28 when a pro-Diem paratroop company attacked the Binh Xuyen-occupied police headquarters. The Binh Xuyen counterattacked the following night, beginning with a mortar attack on the presidential palace at midnight. When French tanks rolled into the city several hours later to impose a cease-fire agreed to by the United States, Lansdale protested bitterly to Ambassador Collins, "explaining that only the Binh Xuyen would gain by a cease-fire."[22]

For almost a month French tanks and troops kept the Binh Xuyen and ARVN alert. Then on April 27 Ambassador Collins met with Secretary of State Dulles in Washington and told him that Diem's obstinacy was the reason for the violent confrontation in Saigon. Dismayed, Dulles cabled Saigon that the United States was no longer supporting Diem.[23] A few hours after this telegram arrived, Diem's troops attacked Binh Xuyen units and drove them out of downtown Saigon into neighboring Cholon. Elated by Diem's easy victory, Dulles cabled Saigon his full support for Diem. The embassy burned his earlier telegram.[24]

During the fighting of April 28 Lansdale remained in constant communication with the presidential palace, while his rival Captain Savani moved into the Binh Xuyen headquarters at the Y Bridge in Cholon, where he took command of the bandit battalions and assigned his officers to accompany Binh Xuyen troops in the house-to-house fighting.[25] The Binh Xuyen radio offered a reward to anyone who could bring Lansdale to their headquarters where, Bay Vien promised, his stomach would be cut open and his entrails stuffed with mud.[26]

On May 2 the fighting resumed as ARVN units penetrated Cholon, leveling whole city blocks and pushing the Binh Xuyen steadily backward. Softened by years of corruption, the Binh Xuyen bandits were no longer the tough guerrillas of a decade before. Within a week most of them had retreated into the depths of the Rung Sat swamp.

Although the war between Diem and Bay Vien was over, the struggle between Lansdale and the Corsicans was not quite finished. True to the

Corsican tradition, the defeated French launched a vendetta against the entire American community. As Lansdale describes it:

> A group of soreheads among the French in Saigon undertook a spite-ful terror campaign against American residents. Grenades were tossed at night into the yards of houses where Americans lived. American owned automobiles were blown up or booby-trapped. French security officials blandly informed nervous American officials that the terrorist activity was the work of the Viet Minh.[27]

A sniper put a bullet through Lansdale's car window as he was driving through Saigon, and a Frenchman who resembled him was machine-gunned to death in front of Lansdale's house by a passing car. When Lansdale was finally able to determine that the ringleaders were French intelligence officers, grenades started going off in front of their houses in the evenings.[28]

During his May 8–11, 1955, meeting with French Premier Edgar Faure in Paris, Dulles announced his continuing support for Diem, and both agreed that France and the United States would pursue independent policies in Indochina. The partnership was over; France would leave, and the United States would remain in Vietnam to back Diem.[29]

## Notes

1. For more on Lansdale, see Readings 17 and 22.—eds.
2. Elected head of the Binh Xuyen in February 1946. For more on his career, see McCoy, *The Politics of Heroin*, p. 148.—eds.
3. Pierre Brocheux, "L'Economie et la société dans l'ouest de la Cochinchine pendant la période coloniale (1890–1940)" (Ph.D. diss., University of Paris, 1969), p. 298.
4. Eugène Saccomano, *Bandits à Marseille* (Paris: Julliard, 1968), p. 44.
5. In 1958 a U.S. narcotics agent told a Senate subcommittee, "When French Indochina existed, there were quantities of opium that were shipped to the labs . . . around Marseille, France, to the Corsican underworld there, and then transshipped to the United States" (U.S. Congress, Senate Select Committee on Improper Activities in the Labor Management Field, *Hearings*, 85th Cong., 2nd sess., 1959, 1225, cited in *Earth*, March 1972, pp. 93–94).
6. Lucien Bodard, *L'Humiliation* (Paris: Gallimard, 1965), pp. 80–81.
7. Lucien Bodard, *The Quicksand War: Prelude to Vietnam* (Boston: Little, Brown, 1967), pp. 121, 124.
8. The clandestine opium trade conducted by the French secret service that financed counterinsurgency efforts in Vietnam under the French and, in a different form, the United States. See McCoy, *The Politics of Heroin*, pp. 131f.—eds.
9. Interview with Gen. Edward G. Lansdale, Alexandria, Virginia, June 17, 1971.

10. Bernard B. Fall, *The Two Viet-Nams: A Political and Military Analysis* (New York: Praeger, 1967), p. 246; New York Times, *The Pentagon Papers* (New York: Quadrangle Books, 1971), p. 60. Hereafter *The Pentagon Papers* (New York Times ed.).

11. Edward G. Lansdale, "Subject: The Cao Dai," memo to Ambassador Bunker and members, U.S. Council, May 1968, p. 14.

12. Lansdale, memo to Ambassador Bunker et al., May 1968, p. 2.

13. Lansdale, memo to Ambassador Bunker et al., May 1968, p. 11.

14. Lt. Col. Grimaldi, Inspecteur des Forces Supplétives, "Inspection des forces supplétives du Sud Vietnam," *Notions de case sur les forces supplétives du Sud Vietnam* (S.P. 50.295, May 15, 1954), p. 24.

15. Fall, pp. 245–246.

16. Lansdale, memo to Ambassador Bunker et al., May 1968, pp. 15–16.

17. Interview with Gen. Edward G. Lansdale, Alexandria, Virginia, June 17, 1971; Edward G. Lansdale, *In the Midst of Wars* (New York: Harper & Row, 1972), pp. 221–224.

18. Lansdale, *In the Midst of Wars*, pp. 245–247; *The Pentagon Papers* (Gravel ed.), 1:230.

19. *The Pentagon Papers* (New York Times ed.), p. 21.

20. Interview with Gen. Mai Huu Xuan, Saigon, July 19, 1971.

21. Lansdale, *In the Midst of Wars*, p. 270.

22. *The Pentagon Papers* (Gravel ed.), 1:231.

23. *The Pentagon Papers* (Gravel ed.), 1:233.

24. *The Pentagon Papers* (New York Times ed.), p. 22.

25. Interview with Lt. Col. Lucien Conein, McLean, Virginia, June 18, 1971. [For more on the role of Conein, see Reading 17.—eds.]

26. Lansdale, memo to Ambassador Bunker et al., May 1968, p. 17.

27. Lansdale, *In the Midst of Wars*, pp. 316–317.

28. Lansdale, *In the Midst of Wars*, p. 318.

29. *The Pentagon Papers* (Gravel ed.), 1:238–239.

# Founding Program of the National Liberation Front of South Vietnam*

*D*uring the Vietnam War, information about the insurgents, whom the US government called the enemy, was not easy to come by. For most American readers, the only accessible accounts were those written by people either in the direct employ of the US government (including the CIA)[1] or on leave from government service to publish interpretations that generally coincided with official Washington views. Preeminent among this group of "court scholars" is former US Information Agency official Douglas Pike, whose 1966 book Viet Cong attempted to prove that the program of the National Liberation Front (NLF) was a pipe dream; that the social changes carried out in liberated zones were "more apparent than real"; that NLF administrative techniques were "more manipulated than participational," as its cadres were unable to overcome the crippling localism and parochialism of the Vietnamese villagers.[2] In a later work, Pike predicted that the Vietnamese revolutionaries would reluctantly concede failure in the South and reconcile themselves to an indefinitely divided country.[3]

It would be an exaggeration to argue that the United States was beaten in Vietnam because it relied on such flawed interpretations, but the absence of reliable data about Asia had much to do with the events of a generation earlier that go by the name McCarthyism.[4] Far wider than the anti-communist inquisition presided over by Wisconsin Senator Joseph McCarthy, the attack on radicalism during the late 1940s and 1950s decimated the corps of American Asia specialists and reinforced an anti-intellectual bias against scholarship that might be sympathetic to the revolutionary side.[5]

Thus, the book by one of the few Western journalists actually to travel in National Liberation Front zones in South Vietnam, Wilfred G. Burchett's Vietnam: Inside Story of the Guerrilla War (New York: International Publishers, 1965), was either ignored or dismissed as "pro-communist." McCarthyism, the

---

*Liberation Radio/South Vietnam, February 13–14, 1961, Foreign Broadcast Information Service Daily Reports.

*pathological intolerance of radicalism, thus sentenced Americans to interpretations, like those of Douglas Pike, that supported the previously set assumptions of Washington policy makers.*

*Here, in their own words, is what the people in the National Liberation Front thought they were and what they were fighting for.*

## I. Overthrow the camouflaged colonial regime of the American imperialists and the dictatorial power of Ngo Dinh Diem, servant of the Americans, and institute a government of national democratic union.

The present South Vietnamese regime is a camouflaged colonial regime dominated by the Yankees, and the South Vietnamese Government is a servile government, implementing faithfully all the policies of the American imperialists. Therefore, this regime must be overthrown and a government of national and democratic union put in its place composed of representatives of all social classes, of all nationalities, of the various political parties, of all religions; patriotic, eminent citizens must take over for the people the control of economic, political, social, and cultural interests and thus bring about independence, democracy, well-being, peace, neutrality, and efforts toward the peaceful unification of the country.

## II. Institute a largely liberal and democratic regime.

1. Abolish the present constitution of the dictatorial powers of Ngo Dinh Diem, servant of the Americans. Elect a new National Assembly through universal suffrage. 2. Implement essential democratic liberties: freedom of opinion, of press, of assembly, of movement, of trade-unionism; freedom of religion without any discrimination; and the right of all patriotic organizations of whatever political tendency to carry on normal activities. 3. Proclaim a general amnesty for all political prisoners and the dissolution of concentration camps of all sorts; abolish fascist law 10/59 [see Reading 24—eds.] and all the other antidemocratic laws; authorize the return to the country of all persons persecuted by the American-Diem regime who are now refugees abroad. 4. Interdict all illegal arrests and detentions; prohibit torture; and punish all the Diem bullies who have not repented and who have committed crimes against the people.

## III. Establish an independent and sovereign economy, and improve the living conditions of the people.

1. Suppress the monopolies imposed by American imperialists and their servants; establish an independent and sovereign economy and finances in accordance with the national interests; confiscate to the profit of the nation

the properties of the American imperialists and their servants. 2. Support the national bourgeoisie in the reconstruction and development of crafts and industry; provide active protection for national products through the suppression of production taxes and the limitation or prohibition of imports that the national economy is capable of producing: reduce customs fees on raw materials and machines. 3. Revitalize agriculture; modernize production, fishing, and cattle raising; help the farmers in putting to the plow unused land and in developing production; protect the crops and guarantee their disposal. 4. Encourage and reinforce economic relations between the city and country, the plain and the mountain regions; develop commercial exchanges with foreign countries, regardless of their political regime, on the basis of equality and mutual interests. 5. Institute a just and rational system of taxation; eliminate harassing penalties. 6. Implement the labor code; prohibition of discharges, of penalties, of ill-treatment of wage earners; improvement of the living conditions of workers and civil servants; imposition of wage scales and protective measures for young apprentices. 7. Organize social welfare: find work for jobless persons; assume the support and protection of orphans, old people, invalids; come to the help of the victims of the Americans and Diemists; organize help for areas hit by bad crops, fires, or natural calamities. 8. Come to help of displaced persons desiring to return to their native areas and to those who wish to remain permanently in the South; improve their working and living conditions. 9. Prohibit expulsions, spoliation, and compulsory concentration of the population; guarantee job security for the urban and rural working populations.

## IV. Reduce land rent; implement agrarian reform with the aim of providing land to the tillers.

1. Reduce land rent; guarantee to the farmers the right to till the soil; guarantee the property right of accession to fallow lands to those who have cultivated them; guarantee property rights to those farmers who have already received land. 2. Dissolve "prosperity zones," and put an end to recruitment for the camps that are called "agricultural development centers." Allow those compatriots who already have been forced into "prosperity zones" and "agricultural development centers" to return freely to their own lands. 3. Confiscate the land owned by American imperialists and their servants, and distribute it to poor peasants without any land or with insufficient land; redistribute the communal lands on a just and rational basis. 4. By negotiation and on the basis of fair prices, repurchase for distribution to landless peasants or peasants with insufficient land those surplus lands that the owners of large estates will be made to relinquish if their domain exceeds a certain limit, to be determined in accordance with regional particularities. The farmers who benefit from such

land distribution will not be compelled to make any payment or to submit to any other conditions.

### V. Develop a national and democratic culture and education.

1. Combat all forms of culture and education enslaved to Yankee fashions; develop a culture and education that is national, progressive, and at the service of the Fatherland and people. 2. Liquidate illiteracy; increase the number of schools in the fields of general education as well as in those of technical and professional education, in advanced study as well as in other fields; adopt Vietnamese as the vernacular language; reduce the expenses of education and exempt from payment students who are without means; resume the examination system. 3. Promote science and technology and the national letters and arts; encourage and support the intellectuals and artists so as to permit them to develop their talents in the service of national reconstruction. 4. Watch over public health; develop sports and physical education.

### VI. Create a national army devoted to the defense of the Fatherland and the people.

1. Establish a national army devoted to the defense of the Fatherland and the people; abolish the system of American military advisers. 2. Abolish the draft system; improve the living conditions of the simple soldiers and guarantee their political rights; put an end to ill-treatment of the military; pay particular attention to the dependents of soldiers without means. 3. Reward officers and soldiers having participated in the struggle against the domination by the Americans and their servants; adopt a policy of clemency toward the former collaborators of the Americans and Diemists guilty of crimes against the people but who have finally repented and are ready to serve the people. 4. Abolish all foreign military bases established on the territory of Vietnam.

### VII. Guarantee equality between the various minorities and between the two sexes; protect the legitimate interests of foreign citizens established in Vietnam and of Vietnamese citizens residing abroad.

1. Implement the right to autonomy of the national minorities: found autonomous zones in the areas with minority population, those zones to be an integral part of the Vietnamese nation. Guarantee equality between the various nationalities: each nationality has the right to use and develop its language and writing system, to maintain or to modify freely its *mores* and customs; abolish the policy of the Americans and Diemists of racial discrimination and forced assimilation. Create conditions permitting the national minorities to reach the general level of progress of the population: development of their economy and culture; formation of cadres of minority

nationalities. 2. Establish equality between the two sexes; women shall have equal rights with men from all viewpoints (political, economic, cultural, social, etc.). 3. Protect the legitimate interests of foreign citizens established in Vietnam. 4. Defend and take care of the interests of Vietnamese citizens residing abroad.

### VIII. *Promote a foreign policy of peace and neutrality.*

1. Cancel all unequal treaties that infringe upon the sovereignty of the people and that were concluded with other countries by the servants of the Americans. 2. Establish diplomatic relations with all countries, regardless of their political regime, in accordance with the principles of peaceful coexistence adopted at the Bandung Conference. 3. Develop close solidarity with peace-loving nations and neutral countries; develop free relations with the nations of Southeast Asia, in particular with Cambodia and Laos. 4. Stay out of any military bloc; refuse any military alliance with another country. 5. Accept economic aid from any country willing to help us without attaching any conditions to such help.

### IX. *Re-establish normal relations between the two zones, and prepare for the peaceful reunification of the country.*

The peaceful reunification of the country constitutes the dearest desire of all our compatriots throughout the country. The National Liberation Front of South Vietnam advocates the peaceful reunification by stages on the basis of negotiations and through the seeking of ways and means in conformity with the interests of the Vietnamese nation. While awaiting this reunification, the governments of the two zones will, on the basis of negotiations, promise to banish all separatist and warmongering propaganda and not to use force to settle differences between the zones. Commercial and cultural exchanges between the two zones will be implemented: the inhabitants of the two zones will be free to move about throughout the country as their family and business interests indicate. The freedom of postal exchanges will be guaranteed.

### X. *Struggle against all aggressive war; actively defend universal peace.*

1. Struggle against all aggressive war and against all forms of imperialist domination; support the national emancipation movements of the various peoples. 2. Banish all war-mongering propaganda; demand general disarmament and the prohibition of nuclear weapons; and advocate the utilization of atomic energy for peaceful purposes. 3. Support all movements of struggle for peace, democracy, and social progress throughout the world; contribute actively to the defense of peace in South-east Asia and in the world.

# Notes

1. See the article by CIA agent George Carver, "The Faceless Viet Cong," *Foreign Affairs*, April 1966. for Carver's CIA affiliation, see Frank Snepp, *Decent Interval: An Insider's Account of Saigon's Indecent End Told by the CIA's Chief Strategist in Vietnam* (New York: Random House, 1977), p. 237. (Snepp also worked for the CIA.)

2. Douglas Pike, *Viet Cong: The Organization and Techniques of the National Liberation Front of South Vietnam* (Cambridge, MA: MIT Press, 1966), p. 382.

3. Douglas Pike, *War, Peace, and the Viet Cong* (Cambridge, MA: MIT Press, 1969), Chap. 5.

4. McCarthyism still awaits a convincing overall study. Until that time, David Caute's encyclopedic *The Great Fear: The Anti-Communist Purge Under Truman and Eisenhower* (New York: Simon & Schuster, 1978) is serviceable. Ellen Schrecker's *No Ivory Tower: McCarthyism and the Universities* (New York: Oxford University Press, 1986) clarifies much about the intellectual purges of the McCarthy era.

5. For an insightful account, see Ross Y. Koen, *The China Lobby in American Politics*, edited and with an introduction by Richard C. Kagan (New York: Harper & Row, 1974; first published—and suppressed—in 1960).

# Declaration of Independence from the War in Vietnam
## (April 1967)

## The Reverend Martin Luther King, Jr.

*I*n the two years after he received the Nobel Prize for Peace in 1964, the Reverend Martin Luther King made occasional public statements about his growing concern over the Vietnam War. But until early 1967, Dr. King maintained a moderate position on the issue as he attempted to stay in the middle of the surging forces of the black movement. On one side, militant groups such as the Student Nonviolent Coordinating Committee (SNCC) and the Black Panther Party, as well as various nationalist organizations, were denouncing the war as an imperialist attack on another non-white people. On the other, such conservative older groups as the NAACP and the Urban League were attempting to fence off what they still called the "civil rights movement" both from the spontaneous urban rebellions and from the politically conscious younger activists who saw the war as a principal cause of the increasing desperation that was fueling these rebellions.

On April 4, 1967, Dr. King implemented a fateful decision when he went to the pulpit of Manhattan's Riverside Church to deliver the sermon here reprinted. The 3,000 people who packed the church rose in a tumultuous ovation at the end of what they may have sensed to be one of the most profound statements of this historical period.

The significance of this "Declaration of Independence from the War in Vietnam" was obvious at once to all the contending forces. Dr. King was denounced by The New York Times, black syndicated columnist Carl Rowan, many leaders of the black establishment, and of course by voices from the right shouting such epithets as "traitor" and "treason." The antiwar movement enthusiastically welcomed this powerful new recruit to its ranks. On April 15, in New York, Dr. King made a similar address to the hundreds of thousands who marched against the war from Central Park to the United Nations.

*Martin Luther King's "Declaration" had a profound influence, strengthening antiwar consciousness and activity everywhere, from churches and colleges to the streets of the ghettos and the ranks of GIs in Vietnam (see Reading 48 for its influence within the military).*

Over the past two years, as I have moved to break the betrayal of my own silences and to speak from the burnings of my own heart, as I have called for radical departures from the destruction of Vietnam, many persons have questioned me about the wisdom of my path. At the heart of their concerns this query has often loomed large and loud: Why are you speaking about the war, Dr. King? Why are you joining the voices of dissent? Peace and civil rights don't mix, they say. Aren't you hurting the cause of your people, they ask. And when I hear them, though I often understand the source of their concern, I am nevertheless greatly saddened, for such questions mean that the inquirers have not really known me, my commitment or my calling. Indeed, their questions suggest that they do not know the world in which they live.

In the light of such tragic misunderstanding, I deem it of signal importance to try to state clearly why I believe that the path from Dexter Avenue Baptist Church—the church in Montgomery, Alabama, where I began my pastorage—leads clearly to this sanctuary tonight.

I come to this platform to make a passionate plea to my beloved nation. This speech is not addressed to Hanoi or to the National Liberation Front. It is not addressed to China or to Russia.

Nor is it an attempt to overlook the ambiguity of the total situation and the need for a collective solution to the tragedy of Vietnam. Neither is it an attempt to make North Vietnam or the National Liberation Front paragons of virtue, nor to overlook the role they can play in a successful resolution of the problem. While they both may have justifiable reasons to be suspicious of the good faith of the United States, life and history give eloquent testimony to the fact that conflicts are never resolved without trustful give and take on both sides.

Tonight, however, I wish not to speak with Hanoi and the NLF, but rather to my fellow Americans who, with me, bear the greatest responsibility in ending a conflict that has exacted a heavy price on both continents.

Since I am a preacher by trade, I suppose it is not surprising that I have seven major reasons for bringing Vietnam into the field of my moral vision. There is at the outset a very obvious and almost facile connection between the war in Vietnam and the struggle I, and others, have been waging in America. A few years ago there was a shining moment in that struggle. It seemed as if there was a real promise of hope for the poor—both black and white—through the Poverty Program. Then came the build-up in Vietnam, and I watched the program broken and eviscerated as if it were some idle political plaything of a society gone mad on war, and I knew that America would never invest the necessary funds or energies in rehabilitation of its poor so long as Vietnam continued to draw men and skills and money like some demonic, destructive suction tube. So I was increasingly compelled to see the war as an enemy of the poor and to attack it as such.

Perhaps the more tragic recognition of reality took place when it became clear to me that the war was doing far more than devastating the hopes of the poor at home. It was sending their sons and their brothers and their husbands to fight and to die in extraordinarily high proportions relative to the rest of the population. We were taking the young black men who had been crippled by our society and sending them 8000 miles away to guarantee liberties in Southeast Asia which they had not found in Southwest Georgia and East Harlem. So we have been repeatedly faced with the cruel irony of watching Negro and white boys on TV screens as they kill and die together for a nation that has been unable to seat them together in the same schools. So we watch them in brutal solidarity burning the huts of a poor village, but we realize that they would never live on the same block in Detroit. I could not be silent in the face of such cruel manipulation of the poor.

My third reason grows out of my experience in the ghettos of the North over the last three years—especially the last three summers. As I have walked among the desperate, rejected and angry young men, I have told them that Molotov cocktails and rifles would not solve their problems. I have tried to offer them my deepest compassion while maintaining my conviction that social change comes most meaningfully through non-violent action. But, they asked, what about Vietnam? They asked if our own nation wasn't using massive doses of violence to solve its problems, to bring about the changes it wanted. Their questions hit home, and I knew that I could never again raise my voice against the violence of the oppressed in the ghettos without having first spoken clearly to the greatest purveyor of violence in the world today— my own government.

For those who ask the question, "Aren't you a Civil Rights leader?" and thereby mean to exclude me from the movement for peace, I have this further answer. In 1957 when a group of us formed the Southern Christian Leadership Conference, we chose as our motto: "To save the soul of America." We were convinced that we could not limit our vision to certain rights for black people, but instead affirmed the conviction that America would never be free or saved from itself unless the descendants of its slaves were loosed from the shackles they still wear.

Now, it should be incandescently clear that no one who has any concern for the integrity and life of America today can ignore the present war. If America's soul becomes totally poisoned, part of the autopsy must read

"Vietnam." It can never be saved so long as it destroys the deepest hopes of men the world over.

As if the weight of such a commitment to the life and health of America were not enough, another burden of responsibility was placed upon me in 1964; and I cannot forget that the Nobel Prize for Peace was also a commission—a commission to work harder than I had ever worked before for the "brotherhood of man." This is a calling that takes me beyond national allegiances, but even if it were not present I would yet have to live with the meaning of my commitment to the ministry of Jesus Christ. To me the relationship of this ministry to the making of peace is so obvious that I sometimes marvel at those who ask me why I am speaking against the war. Could it be that they do not know that the good news was meant for all men—for communist and capitalist, for their children and ours, for black and white, for revolutionary and conservative? Have they forgotten that my ministry is in obedience to the One who loved His enemies so fully that He died for them? What then can I say to the Viet Cong or to Castro or to Mao as a faithful minister of this One? Can I threaten them with death, or must I not share with them my life?

And as I ponder the madness of Vietnam, my mind goes constantly to the people of that peninsula. I speak now not of the soldiers of each side, not of the junta in Saigon, but simply of the people who have been living under the curse of war for almost three continuous decades. I think of them, too, because it is clear to me that there will be no meaningful solution there until some attempt is made to know them and their broken cries.

They must see Americans as strange liberators. The Vietnamese proclaimed their own independence in 1945 after a combined French and Japanese occupation and before the communist revolution in China. Even though they quoted the American Declaration of Independence in their own document of freedom, we refused to recognize them. Instead, we decided to support France in its reconquest of her former colony.

Our government felt then that the Vietnamese people were not "ready" for independence, and we again fell victim to the deadly Western arrogance that has poisoned the international atmosphere for so long. With that tragic decision, we rejected a revolutionary government seeking self-determination, and a government that had been established not by China (for whom the Vietnamese have no great love) but by clearly indigenous forces that included some communists. For the peasants, this new government meant real land reform, one of the most important needs in their lives.

For nine years following 1945 we denied the people of Vietnam the right of independence. For nine years we vigorously supported the French in their abortive effort to re-colonize Vietnam.

Before the end of the war we were meeting 80 per cent of the French war costs. Even before the French were defeated at Dien Bien Phu, they began to despair of their reckless action, but we did not. We encouraged them with our huge financial and military supplies to continue the war even after they had lost the will to do so.

After the French were defeated it looked as if independence and land reform would come again through the Geneva agreements. But instead there came the United States, determined that Ho should not unify the temporarily divided nation, and the peasants watched again as we supported one of the most vicious modern dictators—our chosen man, Premier Diem. The peasants watched and cringed as Diem ruthlessly routed out all opposition, supported their extortionist landlords and refused even to discuss reunification with the North. The peasants watched as all this was presided over by U.S. influence and then by increasing numbers of U.S. troops who came to help quell the insurgency that Diem's methods had aroused. When Diem was overthrown they may have been happy, but the long line of military dictatorships seemed to offer no real change—especially in terms of their need for land and peace.

The only change came from America as we increased our troop commitments in support of governments which were singularly corrupt, inept and without popular support. All the while, the people read our leaflets and received regular promises of peace and democracy—and land reform. Now they languish under our bombs and consider us—not their fellow Vietnamese—the real enemy. They move sadly and apathetically as we herd them off the land of their fathers into concentration camps where minimal social needs are rarely met. They know they must move or be destroyed by our bombs. So they go.

They watch as we poison their water, as we kill a million acres of their crops. They must weep as the bulldozers destroy their precious trees. They wander into the hospitals, with at least 20 casualties from American firepower for each Viet Cong-inflicted injury. So far we may have killed a million of them—mostly children.

What do the peasants think as we ally ourselves with the landlords and as we refuse to put any action into our many words concerning land reform? What do they think as we test out our latest weapons on them, just as the Germans tested out new medicine and new tortures in the concentration camps of Europe? Where are the roots of the independent Vietnam we claim to be building?

Now there is little left to build on—save bitterness. Soon the only solid physical foundations remaining will be found at our military bases and in the concrete of the concentration camps we call "fortified hamlets." The peasants may well wonder if we plan to build our new Vietnam on such grounds as these. Could we blame them for such thoughts? We must speak for them and raise the questions they cannot raise. These too are our brothers.

Perhaps the more difficult but no less necessary task is to speak for those who have been designated as our enemies. What of the NLF—that strangely anonymous group we call VC or communists? What must they think of us in America when they realize that we permitted the repression and cruelty of Diem which helped to bring them into being as a resistance group in the South? How can they believe in our integrity when now we speak of "aggression from the North" as if there were nothing more essential to the war? How can they trust us when now we charge *them* with violence after the murderous reign of Diem, and charge *them* with violence while we pour new weapons of death into their land?

How do they judge us when our officials know that their membership is less than 25 per cent communist and yet insist on giving them the blanket name? What must they be thinking when they know that we are aware of their control of major sections of Vietnam and yet we appear ready to allow national elections in which this highly organized political parallel government will have no part? They ask how we can speak of free elections when the Saigon press is censored and controlled by the military junta. And they are surely right to wonder what kind of new government we plan to help form without them—the only party in real touch with the peasants. They question our political goals and they deny the reality of a peace settlement from which they will be excluded. Their questions are frighteningly relevant.

Here is the true meaning and value of compassion and non-violence—when it helps us to see the enemy's point of view, to hear his questions, to know of his assessment of ourselves. For from his view we may indeed see the basic weaknesses of our own condition, and if we are mature, we may learn and grow and profit from the wisdom of the brothers who are called the opposition.

So, too, with Hanoi. In the North, where our bombs now pummel the land, and our mines endanger the waterways, we are met by a deep but understandable mistrust. In Hanoi are the men who led the nation to independence against the Japanese and the French, the men who sought membership in the French commonwealth and were betrayed by the weakness of Paris and the willfulness of the colonial armies. It was they who led a second struggle against French domination at tremendous costs, and then were persuaded at Geneva to give up, as a temporary measure, the land they controlled between the 13th and 17th parallels. After 1954 they watched us conspire with Diem to prevent elections which would have surely brought Ho Chi Minh to power over a united Vietnam, and they realized they had been betrayed again.

When we ask why they do not leap to negotiate, these things must be remembered. Also, it must be clear that the leaders of Hanoi considered the presence of American troops in support of the Diem regime to have been the initial military breach of the Geneva Agreements concerning foreign troops, and they remind us that they did not begin to send in any large number of supplies or men until American forces had moved into the tens of thousands.

Hanoi remembers how our leaders refused to tell us the truth about the earlier North Vietnamese overtures for peace, how the President claimed that none existed when they had clearly been made. Ho Chi Minh has watched as America has spoken of peace and built up its forces, and now he has surely heard the increasing international rumors of American plans for an invasion of the North. Perhaps only his sense of humor and irony can save him when he hears the most powerful nation of the world speaking of aggression as it drops thousands of bombs on a poor, weak nation more than 8000 miles from its shores.

At this point, I should make it clear that while I have tried here to give a voice to the voiceless of Vietnam and to understand the arguments of those who are called enemy, I am as deeply concerned about our own troops there as anything else. For it occurs to me that what we are submitting them to in Vietnam is not simply the brutalizing process that goes on in any war where armies face each other and seek to destroy. We are adding cynicism to the process of death, for our troops must know after a short period there that none of the things we claim to be fighting for are really involved. Before long they must know that their government has sent them into a struggle among Vietnamese, and the more sophisticated surely realize that we are on the side of the wealthy and the secure while we create a hell for the poor.

Somehow this madness must cease. I speak as a child of God and brother to the suffering poor of Vietnam and the poor of America who are paying the double price of smashed hopes at home and death and corruption in Vietnam. I speak as a citizen of the world, for the world as it stands aghast at the path we have taken. I speak as an American to the leaders of my own nation. The great initiative in this war is ours. The initiative to stop must be ours.

This is the message of the great Buddhist leaders of Vietnam. Recently, one of them wrote these words: "Each day the war goes on the hatred increases in the hearts of the Vietnamese and in the hearts of those of humanitarian instinct. The Americans are forcing even their friends into becoming their enemies. It is curious that the Americans, who calculate so carefully on the possibilities of military victory, do not realize that in the process they are incurring deep psychological and political defeat. The image of America will never again be the image of revolution, freedom and democracy, but the image of violence and militarism."

If we continue, there will be no doubt in my mind and in the mind of the world that we have no honorable intentions in Vietnam. It will become clear that our minimal expectation is to occupy it as an American colony, and men will not refrain from thinking that our maximum hope is to goad China into a war so that we may bomb her nuclear installations.

The world now demands a maturity of America that we may not be able to achieve. It demands that we admit that we have been wrong from the beginning of our adventure in Vietnam, that we have been detrimental to the life of her people.

In order to atone for our sins and errors in Vietnam, we should take the initiative in bringing the war to a halt. I would like to suggest five concrete things that our government should do immediately to begin the long and difficult process of extricating ourselves from this nightmare:

1. End all bombing in North and South Vietnam.
2. Declare a unilateral cease-fire in the hope that such action will create the atmosphere for negotiation.
3. Take immediate steps to prevent other battlegrounds in Southeast Asia by curtailing our military build-up in Thailand and our interference in Laos.
4. Realistically accept the fact that the National Liberation Front has substantial support in South Vietnam and must thereby play a role in any meaningful negotiations and in any future Vietnam government.
5. Set a date on which we will remove all foreign troops from Vietnam in accordance with the 1954 Geneva Agreement.

Part of our ongoing commitment might well express itself in an offer to grant asylum to any Vietnamese who fears for his life under a new regime which included the NLF. Then we must make what reparations we can for the damage we have done. We must provide the medical aid that is badly needed, in this country if necessary.

Meanwhile, we in the churches and synagogues have a continuing task while we urge our government to disengage itself from a disgraceful commitment. We must be prepared to match actions with words by seeking out every creative means of protest possible.

As we counsel young men concerning military service we must clarify for them our nation's role in Vietnam and challenge them with the alternative of conscientious objection. I am pleased to say that this is the path now being chosen by more than 70 students at my own Alma Mater, Morehouse College, and I recommend it to all who find the American course in Vietnam a dishonorable and unjust one. Moreover, I would encourage all ministers of draft age to give up their ministerial exemptions and seek status as conscientious objectors. Every man of humane convictions must decide on the protest that best suits his convictions, but we must *all* protest.

There is something seductively tempting about stopping there and sending us all off on what in some circles has become a popular crusade against the war in Vietnam. I say we must enter that struggle, but I wish to go on now to say something even more disturbing. The war in Vietnam is but a symptom of a far deeper malady within the American spirit, and if we ignore this sobering reality we will find ourselves organizing clergy- and laymen-concerned committees for the next generation. We will be marching and attending rallies without end unless there is a significant and profound change in American life and policy.

In 1957 a sensitive American official overseas said that it seemed to him that our nation was on the wrong side of a world revolution. During the past ten years we have seen emerge a pattern of suppression which now has justified the presence of U.S. military "advisors" in Venezuela. The need to maintain social stability for our investments accounts for the counterrevolutionary action of American forces in Guatemala. It tells why American helicopters are being used against guerrillas in Colombia and why American napalm and green beret forces have already been active against rebels in Peru. With such activity in mind, the words of John F. Kennedy come back to haunt us. Five years ago he said, "Those who make peaceful revolution impossible will make violent revolution inevitable."

Increasingly, by choice or by accident, this is the role our nation has taken—by refusing to give up the privileges and the pleasures that come from the immense profits of overseas investment.

I am convinced that if we are to get on the right side of the world revolution, we as a nation must undergo a radical revolution of values. When machines and computers, profit and property rights are considered more important than people, the giant triplets of racism, materialism, and militarism are incapable of being conquered.

A true revolution of values will soon cause us to question the fairness and justice of many of our past and present policies. True compassion is more than flinging a coin to a beggar; it is not haphazard and superficial. It comes to see that an edifice which produces beggars needs re-structuring. A true revolution of values will soon look easily on the glaring contrast of poverty and wealth. With righteous indignation, it will look across the seas and see individual capitalists of the West investing huge sums of money in Asia, Africa and South America, only to take the profits out with no concern for the social betterment of the countries, and say: "This is not just." It will look at our alliance with the landed gentry of Latin America and say: "This is not just." The Western arrogance of feeling that it has everything to teach others and nothing to learn from them is not just. A true revolution of values will lay hands on the world order and say of war: "This way of settling differences is not just." This business of burning human beings with napalm, of filling our nation's homes with orphans and widows, of injecting poisonous drugs of hate into the veins of peoples normally humane, of sending men home from dark and bloody battlefields physically handicapped and psychologically deranged, cannot be reconciled with wisdom, justice, and love. A nation that continues year after year to spend more money on military defense than on programs of social uplift is approaching spiritual death.

America, the richest and most powerful nation in the world, can well lead the way in this revolution of values. There is nothing, except a tragic death wish, to prevent us from re-ordering our priorities, so that the pursuit of peace will take precedence over the pursuit of war. There is nothing to keep us from molding a recalcitrant status quo until we have fashioned it into a brotherhood.

This kind of positive revolution of values is our best defense against communism. War is not the answer. Communism will never be defeated by the use of atomic bombs or nuclear weapons. Let us not join those who shout war and through their misguided passions urge the United States to relinquish its participation in the United Nations. These are the days which demand wise restraint and calm reasonableness. We must not call everyone a communist or an appeaser who advocates the seating of Red China in the United Nations and who recognizes that hate and hysteria are not the final answers to the problem of these turbulent days. We must not engage in a negative anti-communism, but rather in a positive thrust for democracy, realizing that our greatest defense against communism is to take offensive action in behalf of justice. We must with positive action seek to remove those conditions of poverty, insecurity and injustice which are the fertile soil in which the seed of communism grows and develops.

These are revolutionary times. All over the globe men are revolting against old systems of exploitation and oppression, and out of the wombs of a frail world, new systems of justice and equality are being born. The shirtless and barefoot people of the land are rising up as never before. "The people who sat in darkness have seen a great light." We in the West must support these revolutions. It is a sad fact that, because of comfort, complacency, a morbid fear of communism, and our proneness to adjust to injustice, the Western nations that initiated so much of the revolutionary spirit of the modern world have now become the arch anti-revolutionaries. This has driven many to feel that only Marxism has the revolutionary spirit. Therefore, communism is a judgment against our failure to make democracy real and follow through on the revolutions that we initiated. Our only hope today lies in our ability to recapture the revolutionary spirit and go out into a sometimes hostile world declaring eternal hostility to poverty, racism, and militarism.

We must move past indecision to action. We must find new ways to speak for peace in Vietnam and justice throughout the developing world—a world that borders on our doors. If we do not act we shall surely be dragged down the long, dark and shameful corridors of time reserved for those who possess power without compassion, might without morality, and strength without sight.

Now let us begin. Now let us re-dedicate ourselves to the long and bitter—but beautiful—struggle for a new world. This is the calling of the sons of God, and our brothers wait eagerly for our response. Shall we say the odds are too great? Shall we tell them the struggle is too hard? Will our message be that the forces of American life militate against their arrival as full men, and we send our deepest regrets? Or will there be another message, of longing, of hope, of solidarity with their yearnings, of commitment to their cause, whatever the cost? The choice is ours and though we might prefer it otherwise we *must* choose in this crucial moment of human history.

# The Ecological Impact of the Air War

## Paul Feeny with Jim Allaway

D uring all of World War II, the United States dropped about 2 million tons of bombs in all theaters, including the strategic bombing of Europe and Japan and the tactical bombing in all campaigns throughout the Pacific and European theaters. By the end of 1971, the United States had dropped 6.3 million tons of bombs on Indochina.[1] In just two years, 1968–1969, the United States dropped over one and a half times more tonnage on South Vietnam alone than all the Allies dropped on Germany throughout World War II.[2] By 1969, North Vietnam was being hit each month with the explosive force of two atomic bombs. The 1972 Christmas bombing alone ravaged Hanoi and Haiphong with more tonnage than Germany dropped on Great Britain from 1940 through 1945. The total firepower used by the United States on Vietnam probably exceeded the amount used in all previous wars combined. Bombs dropped on Vietnam between 1965 and 1969 equaled "500 pounds . . . for every man, woman, and child in Vietnam."[3] Even these statistics do not convey the vast ecological disaster caused by just the immediate after-effects of the high explosives, such as the 21 million bomb craters created in South Vietnam alone, not to mention the prolonged effects of chemical warfare.[4]

The US air war in Indochina employed unprecedented technological sophistication. The incendiary bombs of World War II and Korea were refined into new napalm and phosphorus bombs with the capacity for creating far greater areas of burning, more intense heat, and improved ability to stick to human skin. The gargantuan "Daisy Cutter," weighing 7.5 tons, was dropped by parachute and detonated above the ground, flattening all trees and structures in an area with a diameter equal to ten football fields. "Smart bombs" were guided by laser. The major university laboratories worked to perfect a whole arsenal of fragmentation bombs, including cluster bombs carried in a "mother bomb" and "flechette

349

*bombs" designed to maximize internal body wounds. When Vietnamese surgeons became adept at removing the metal flechettes imbedded deeply in the victims' bodies, US scientists redesigned the bombs to use plastic flechettes that could not be detected by X-rays.*

*The essence of air war is terror. Planes appear suddenly, and nobody in their path knows their intended target. In the South, this terror was aimed at the rural population, seeking to drive them into government-controlled areas, punishing them for supporting the guerrillas and trying to isolate the guerrilla army from its base among the people. This strategic theory tends to ignore the possibility that the terror may translate into anger and hatred. Indeed, many analysts have concluded that the terror bombing of the countryside in Vietnam probably created more opponents than it destroyed.*

*Against the North, the terror was first called "retaliatory" and a means to "punish" those supporting the insurrection in the South. But even before the admitted bombing began, another possible aim of the air war had been suggested by CIA analyst William Kaye: "Unless major military operations sap a substantial proportion of North Viet Nam's national effort, a degree of industrial progress is likely to be achieved that may well become a more effective means of political penetration in neighboring countries than direct military intervention."[5] When the "retaliatory" raids commenced, their very first targets—announced as military bases—were North Vietnam's most advanced industrial centers. For example, the air raids in "retaliation" for the Gulf of Tonkin incidents (Reading 34) were officially described as PT bases. But, as journalist Bernard Fall pointed out in the Washington Post, "none of the targets attacked was previously known as a regular port or base area. Hon-gay, for example, was one of the largest open-pit mining operations in Asia, if not the world."[6] By 1967, the secret study conducted by the Jason Division of the Institute for Defense Analysis reached this conclusion:*

> The bombing of North Vietnam has inflicted heavy costs not so much to North Vietnam's military capability or its infiltration system as to the North Vietnam economy as a whole. . . . Virtually all of the military and economic targets in North Vietnam that can be considered even remotely significant have been struck, except for a few targets in Hanoi and Haiphong. Almost all modern industrial output has been halted. . . .[7]

*During the first year of the bombing of the North, the destruction of hospitals, schools, and churches seemed to be too systematic to be explained as accidental. Between August 5, 1964, and July 11, 1965, nearly thirty medical establishments of the DRV, including internationally acclaimed hospitals, were destroyed. The bombing of the Quynh Lap leper sanatorium seemed particularly difficult to accept as an "accident"—the explanation offered by US Ambassador to Japan Edwin O. Reischauer after footage of the actual raids taken by Japanese journalists was played on Japanese television. This was the world's most famous facility for the treatment of leprosy; it was located on an isolated coastal spot far removed from other habitations; its 160 buildings displayed prominent Red Crosses on the roofs. After the first attack, on June 12, 1965, by several waves of US planes, the Japanese journalists witnessed and photographed thirteen more low-level strafing and bombing attacks in the next ten days. After the Peace Accords, the Senate Armed Services Committee heard testimony about this kind of raid. For example, Alan Stevenson, by then a stockbroker, testified that, as an Army intelligence specialist, he had routinely listed hospitals among targets: "The bigger the hospital the better it was."[8] In fact, the classified US Air Force bombing manual (in Chapter 6) defined hospitals, schools, and churches as "psychosocial targets," useful for the destruction of civilian order and morale.*

*This reading focuses on yet another form of the air war: chemical warfare. In 1961, President Kennedy authorized a massive campaign of chemical warfare, Operation Hades, later renamed Operation Ranch Hand.[9] This poisoning and defoliation of Vietnamese cropland and forests lasted for at least ten years, from 1961 to 1971.[10] At first it was secret; the spray crews were listed as members of the US Embassy in Saigon.[11] Of course, it was no secret to those being sprayed:*

> . . . At first they felt sick and had some diarrhea, then they began to feel it hard to breathe and they had low blood pressure; some serious cases had trouble with their optic nerves and were blind. Pregnant women gave birth to stillborn or premature children. Most of the affected cattle died from serious diarrhea, and the river fish floated on the surface of the water belly up, soon after the chemicals were spread.[12]

*In South Vietnam alone, US planes sprayed 18 million gallons of poisonous chemicals.[13]*

*One of the defoliants, Agent Orange, contained TCDD-dioxin, the most toxic known substance,[14] which is also "100,000 times more potent than thalidomide as a cause of birth defects in some species."[15] The Indochinese were not the only people who came into contact with dioxin; so did Americans involved in Operation Ranch Hand and GIs on the ground. Some of these veterans now have many of the same symptoms, including children with birth defects, as the Vietnamese. After over a decade of protest and litigation, the House of Representatives approved legislation in January 1984, providing benefits to veterans suffering health problems as a result of exposure to Agent Orange. Then in May 1984, seven chemical companies agreed to pay $180 million to settle a class action suit brought on behalf of tens of thousands of Vietnam veterans, many of whom denounced this settlement as a sell-out designed to prevent full disclosure of the health disorders caused by this particular form of chemical warfare.*

ONLY WE CAN PREVENT FORESTS
—*Motto over the door to headquarters,*
*Operation Ranch Hand, Saigon*

## A. Defoliants and Herbicides

Use of defoliants in South Vietnam began on an experimental basis in 1961 and became fully operational the following year.[16] This program had two major objectives. The first was *defoliation* (operation RANCH HAND), in which forests, roadsides, base perimeters, etc., were sprayed in order to remove the foliage cover which had afforded concealment to the enemy. At low concentrations these chemicals do indeed act merely as defoliants; at the concentrations used in Vietnam, however, they normally act also as herbicides, killing a significant fraction of the plants in addition to defoliating them. The second major objective was the *destruction of crops,* mostly rice, carried out in the hope of denying food to the enemy.[17] Crop destruction was largely confined to the mountainous areas of northern and western South Vietnam, where the impact was felt most severely by the small population of about one million, mostly Montagnards. Crop destruction may also have had the objective of driving South Vietnamese civilians into the "strategic hamlets" set up for them by the South Vietnamese Government.[18]

Though some spraying in Vietnam has been done with helicopters or ground equipment, the principal means of application has been the twin-engine C-123 cargo plane. In the years 1962 through 1968 these aircraft made more than 19,000 individual spray flights. Each plane is fitted with a 950-gallon tank from which the herbicide is pumped to spray booms under each wing and at the tail. When the herbicide hits the airstream it is dispersed into fine droplets. One aircraft flying at about 150 feet above the tree tops produces a swath of affected vegetation about 300 feet wide and ten miles long.[19] Precautions must be taken that the sprayed chemical does not drift into adjacent, non-target areas. Occasional incidents occur in which an aircraft is forced to dump its herbicide quickly; it can pump out the entire 950 gallons in about 30 seconds.[20]

Three formulations account for almost all the herbicides used in Indochina: agents Orange, White, and Blue. The composition and mode of action of these agents are discussed in greater detail in Appendix E [not reprinted here—eds.], which also contains a listing of appropriate references; a summary of the main facts is given below.

> *Orange:* Composition, 2,4-D and 2,4,5-T; an oily liquid insoluble in water. Mainly used against broad-leaved and woody vegetation. One application defoliates hardwoods and kills some canopy trees; two applications produce a heavy kill of all woody vegetation; the resulting invasion by bamboo and grasses may arrest forest regeneration indefinitely. On mangrove forests Orange kills almost all trees in a single application; mangrove areas sprayed in 1961 have still shown no significant signs of

regeneration. The chemical itself persists for only a few weeks, except in stagnant water or poorly aerated ground, where high concentrations could conceivably accumulate. 2,4,5-T or an associated impurity (dioxin) is thought to be a teratogen (causing serious birth deformities, like thalidomide); its use in the U.S. has been restricted since late 1969. Orange accounts for about 60 percent of the herbicide used in Vietnam; it was being sprayed at least until August 1970.

*White:* Composition, butyl esters of 2,4-D and picloram; a solution in water. Used much like Orange, but less volatile and therefore less subject to wind drift; it is preferred near populated areas. Picloram is one of the most potent herbicides known; it is remarkably persistent, like the insecticide DDT; its use on agricultural land in the U.S. is prohibited. Since White is water soluble, it can easily be washed by rainfall into adjacent areas.

*Blue:* Composition, organic arsenates including cacodylic acid; a solution in water. Its prime use is for crop destruction, especially rice. It is more effective against grasses than are Orange or White, and acts more rapidly (within a few days).

Herbicides are sprayed at a rate of about three gallons per acre, the stock solution of each agent being formulated to obtain the desired coverage. In the case of Orange, the rate of application is about 26 pounds per acre, almost ten times the rate recommended for use in the U.S.[21] It is estimated that more than 100 million pounds of herbicides have by now been sprayed on Vietnam, covering a total of almost six million acres. . . .[22]

The greatest impact has been on tropical hardwood forests. About 35 percent of South Vietnam's 14 million acres of dense forest have been sprayed one or more times, resulting in the destruction of enough merchantable timber (six billion board feet) to supply the country's domestic needs for about 30 years; this also represents a loss of about $500 million in taxes that would otherwise have accrued to the South Vietnamese Government. Of the three-quarter million acres of coastal mangrove forests, mostly in the Delta area, about one-half have been totally destroyed.

## B. Bombing and Spraying: The Potential Consequences

Forests are first to go. Then the animals—some, like the elephant, are killed deliberately since they could be used to transport supplies; others just happen to be in the wrong place at the wrong time. Finally, the land itself is destroyed: farms, rice paddies, and village sites in many regions are bomb-pocked and barren.

In the brief discussion that follows, only the most obvious environmental effects of the air war will be mentioned, but even such a superficial enumeration conveys an idea of the pervasiveness of the damage. The very fact that data on the present extent of this damage are scant, combined with the virtual impossibility of predicting future consequences, is in itself one of the most ominous signs of danger.

The air war has been a severe shock to all the natural ecosystems of Indochina. Such damage would be of concern wherever it occurred since it affects an intricate web of relationships; but Indochina is especially sensitive because tropical ecosystems are thought to be less resilient than those of temperate regions. Tropical systems are characterized by many more species per unit area; each is finely adapted and food webs are complex and intricate. In a northern forest a major calamity has relatively short-term consequences, since most of the species are already adapted to surviving frosts and unseasonal floods. The rates of reproduction and recolonization are usually high. In tropical regions, where the climatic conditions are much more predictable and favorable, species tend to be less well adapted to rapid change.

*Flora.* The direct attack on the flora by defoliation and the use of herbicides has been described above. In addition to the very extensive damage done by this chemical warfare, fires—many undoubtedly caused by bombing and napalm—have consumed or defoliated large areas of forest. Revegetation of soils in severely defoliated forests may be retarded by rapid loss of plant nutrients following defoliation and by invasion of bamboo and other grasses. Tropical forests carry most of their nutrients in the vegetation itself, rather than in the soil; hence, following decomposition of the plants, most of the nutrients are lost directly, with the remainder being subject to leaching from the soils.[23]

Mangrove forests have suffered particularly severe damage from defoliation—about half have been totally destroyed in South Vietnam—and so far there is no evidence of regeneration. These forests play an important part in the natural process of delta formation, and stabilize the coastline and river banks. They also provide essential cover and food during the life cycles of many fish and other animals.

*Fauna.* The weapons of air warfare affect animals directly by killing them, and indirectly by changing their environment, with the result that populations are changed and the diversity of species is reduced. Natural checks and balances to pests and disease vectors may be upset, particularly as predatory fauna are killed. The invasion of destroyed areas by other plant groups may result in larger populations of undesired animals favoring this new habitat—rats, for example, often thrive in bamboo, which is a predominant regrowth species in defoliated forest areas. The population of the tiger has apparently increased as its natural food supply has been augmented by battlefield casualties.

There are contradictory claims about the toxicity of herbicides to animals. Though some authorities claim there is little danger, evidence indicates that 2,4-D in moderate doses may be toxic to some fish, that plants treated with 2,4-D may accumulate toxic quantities of nitrates (which could affect domestic stock as well as wild fauna), and that dioxin, a contaminant of some 2,4,5-T solutions used, is toxic and concentrates in the food chain since it does not break down with time. Finally, domestic livestock are affected by herbicides, both directly and indirectly, as they eat plants that have been contaminated.

*Agriculture.* Agriculture, and land utilization in general, are affected not only by chemical warfare but also directly by bombing. One may estimate that at least 12,000,000 craters have been produced in the Indochina air war so far, covering an area of at least 200,000 acres and excavating about 1.5 billion cubic yards of soil.[24] (Roughly two-thirds of the bomb tonnage was deployed within South Vietnam, whose total area is 42 million acres.) Some areas in Indochina have been likened to moonscapes. The long-term effects of this cratering are hard to assess, but the fact that craters do not naturally fill in is evidenced by craters from World War II which are still found in the jungles of New Guinea. A bomb crater destroys the surface organic layer and throws up subsoil; it creates severe local relief and erosion in the soil and may disrupt drainage patterns. Usually it fills with water and becomes very difficult to drain, making heavily bombed areas virtually unsuitable for cultivation.

*Flooding.* The control of water flow is a vital problem in many areas of Indochina. Defoliation and laterization lead to more rapid runoff of rain water; the destruction of many man-made control structures compounds the problem. The destructiveness of the floods in central South Vietnam in November 1970 was blamed in part on defoliation and bomb damage. People were driven by the floods out of refugee camps to which they had come, in the first place, because of crop destruction or bombing in their native highlands.

*Malnutrition.* It is generally recognized that crop destruction has had its chief impact on the civilian population rather than on enemy soldiers, who are in the best position to obtain food in times of scarcity. The Herbicides Assessment Commission has concluded that the food destroyed would have been enough to feed 600,000 persons for a year, and that nearly all of it would have been consumed by civilians. Although the amount destroyed is less than two percent of the national crop of South Vietnam in any one year, the most extensive crop destruction has been carried out in the central highlands, a food-scarce area with a population of about one million, mainly Montagnards. It is among these people that problems of malnutrition and starvation are most severe.

*Birth abnormalities.* According to a report released by the National Institutes of Health in the fall of 1969, 2,4,5-T (or an associated impurity, dioxin) was shown to produce significant increases in the incidence of fetus malformation in animals as early as 1965. Moreover, the Herbicide Assessment Commission team in Vietnam has found a suggestive correlation between years of peak defoliation in Tay Ninh province and an increase in stillbirths and birth deformities.

*Malaria.* Of the endemic diseases in Indochina, malaria is probably the most widespread; in the past it has been far more common in the upland regions than in the lowlands. Now, large numbers of bomb craters have filled with water. This stagnant water, present throughout Vietnam and parts of Laos and Cambodia, is an ideal breeding habitat for various species of mosquito, including those which are malaria vectors. . . .

Americans have begun to become aware of the vast complexity of their environment, and of the unpredictable consequences that go with disturbing it. In Indochina, the environment has not merely been disturbed—there has been a deliberate and unprecedented onslaught on it, with chemicals, with explosives, and with fire. The short listing just given, incomplete and inconclusive as it is, by its very open-endedness points up the ominous results which may have been, and which may continue to be, provoked in Indochina.

## Notes

1. Littauer and Uphoff, p. 9. This volume, prepared by the Air War Study Group of Cornell University, is the essential text on the air war through mid-1971, giving rich bibliographic material and statistics.
2. Littauer and Uphoff, pp. 10 and 203.
3. Noam Chomsky, *At War with Asia* (New York: Pantheon Books, 1970), pp. 290–291.
4. "The Legacy of the Vietnam War," *Indochina Newsletter,* 18 (November–December, 1982), p. 12.
5. In *China Quarterly,* January–March, 1962, as quoted in Carol Brightman's invaluable article, "The Discriminating Air War: The Real Targets in North Vietnam," *Viet Report,* 3 (April–May 1967), p. 21.
6. *Washington Post,* August 9, 1964.
7. As quoted in Littauer and Uphoff, p. 47.
8. *San Francisco Chronicle,* August 9, 1973.
9. For the official report, see Major William A. Buckingham, Jr., *Operation Ranch Hand: The Air Force and Herbicides in Southeast Asia, 1961–1971* (Washington, D.C.: Office of Air Force History, US Air Force, 1982). A pioneering source of information about chemical and biological warfare in Southeast Asia was *Viet Report,* particularly the issue of June–July 1966, with data about bacteriological weapons and official Cambodian charges that the United States was spraying a "deadly yellow powder" within its border. Other excellent sources include Thomas Whiteside, *The Withering Rain: America's*

*Herbicidal Folly* (New York: Dutton, 1971); J. B. Neilands, Gordon H. Orians, E. W. Pfeiffer, Alje Vennema, and Arthur H. Westing, eds., *Harvest of Death: Chemical Warfare in Vietnam and Cambodia* (New York: Free Press, 1972); John Lewallen, *Ecology of Devastation: Indochina* (Baltimore: Penguin, 1971); E. W. Pfeiffer, "Operation Ranch Hand: The U.S. Herbicide Program," *Bulletin of the Atomic Scientists,* May 1982, pp. 20–24.

10. Defoliation was also employed in Laos (1965–1969) and Cambodia (1969).

11. Michael Uhl and Tod Ensign, *GI Guinea Pigs: How the Pentagon Exposed Our Troops to Dangers More Deadly Than War—Agent Orange and Atomic Radiation* (New York: Playboy Press, 1980), p. 117.

12. Report of Cao Van Nguyen, M.D., after chemical attack near Saigon, October 3, 1964, as quoted in Committee of Concerned Asian Scholars, *The Indochina Story: A Fully Documented Account* (New York: Bantam, 1970).

13. "The Legacy of the Vietnam War," p. 12.

14. *New York Times,* February 1, 1984.

15. Dr. Jacqueline Verrett of the Food and Drug Administration, as quoted in Fred A. Wilcox, *Waiting for an Army to Die: The Tragedy of Agent Orange* (New York: Random House, Vintage, 1983), p. xi.

16. Herbicide Assessment Commission for the American Association for the Advancement of Science, *Background Material Relevant to the Presentations at the 1970 Annual Meeting of the AAAS,* Chicago, Ill., December 29, 1970, p. 14.

17. Stanford Biology Study Group, "The Destruction of Indochina," *Bulletin of the Atomic Scientists,* 27 (1971), pp. 36–40; A. H. Westing, "Agent Blue in Vietnam," *New York Times,* July 12, 1971.

18. Ngo Vinh Long, "Leaf Abscission?" *Bulletin of Concerned Asian Scholars,* October 1969, p. 54.

19. The C-123 cruises at 230 miles per hour; at this low speed and at minimal altitude, it becomes vulnerable to ground fire from any weapons, even small-caliber. Hence in all areas where hostile elements may be present, even if they have no conventional anti-aircraft capability, the spraying missions are preceded by fighter-bomber sweeps providing maximum-intensity ground-fire suppression. The effects of this support activity must be reckoned as a contingent cost of the herbicide program.

20. Gordon H. Orians and E. W. Pfeiffer, "Ecological Effects of the War in Vietnam," *Science,* 168 (1970), pp. 544–554.

21. Statement of A. W. Galston before the Subcommittee on National Security Policy and Scientific Developments, U.S. House of Representatives, December 1969; reprinted in Thomas Whiteside, *Defoliation* (New York: Ballantine, 1970), p. 107.

22. *Impact of the Vietnam War,* a report prepared for the Committee on Foreign Relations, U.S. Senate, by the Congressional Research Service of the Library of Congress (Washington, D.C.: U.S. Government Printing Office, June 30, 1971). The figures which follow are abstracted from the excellent summary presented in this report, pp. 10ff.

358 Vietnam and America: Readings and Documents

23. In temperate zones, by contrast, most of the nutrients reside in the soil rather than in the flora of the forest. L. E. Rodin and N. I. Bazilevich, *Production and Mineral Cycling in Terrestrial Vegetation* (Edinburgh and London: Oliver & Boyd, 1967), p. 246. (Translated from Russian edition, 1965.)

24. Total expenditure of aerial munitions through 1971 is about 6,300,000 tons. If half of this is crater-producing, in the form of 500-pound bombs, there will be about 12,000,000 craters. Taking each to be 30 feet in diameter, conical in shape and with a maximum depth of 15 feet, the quoted figures for area and volume can be derived. [We are indebted to Professor A. H. Westing for discussion of this point. . . .]

# U.S. Promise of Postwar Reconstruction: Letter to DRV Prime Minister Pham Van Dong

## (February 1, 1973)

## President Richard M. Nixon

*V*ietnamese officials repeatedly claimed that President Nixon pledged postwar aid amounting to over $4 billion to the DRV. US officials maintained that the only mention of aid was in Article 21 of the Peace Accords (Reading 61), which they did not consider binding. Secretary of State Rogers testified before the House International Relations Committee on February, 8, 1973: "We have not made any commitment for any reconstruction or rehabilitation effort" in North Vietnam.[1] Henry Kissinger testified to the same committee on March 29, 1973, but apparently no record was kept of what he said. The State Department steadily maintained it had no copy of a reported letter from President Nixon promising aid. But on May 19, 1977, over four years after it was written, the letter was declassified by the State Department and released to Congress and the media. The release of the letter came in response to a threat by Congressman Lester Wolff, Democrat of New York and chairman of the House International Relations Subcommittee on Asian and Pacific Affairs, to subpoena former President Nixon to testify about the Vietnamese claim that there was indeed a promise by the President. The text of the letter mentions a "range of $3.25 billion" over five years, and one of the two addenda mentions $1 billion to $1.5 billion in other forms of aid, amounting to well over $4 billion. Kissinger and Le Duc Tho had negotiated the terms of the letter during the peace talks. It was addressed to Prime Minister Pham Van Dong of the DRV and signed by President Richard Nixon on February 1, 1973.

The President wishes to inform the Democratic Republic of Vietnam of the principles which will govern United States participation in the postwar reconstruction of North Vietnam. As indicated in Article 21 of the Agreement on Ending the War and Restoring Peace in Vietnam signed in Paris on Jan. 27, 1973, the United States undertakes this participation in accordance with its traditional policies. These principles are as follows:

1. The Government of the United States of America will contribute to postwar reconstruction in North Vietnam without any political conditions.

2. Preliminary United States studies indicate that the appropriate programs for the United States contribution to postwar reconstruction will fall in the range of $3.25 billion of grant aid over five years. Other forms of aid will be agreed upon between the two parties. This estimate is subject to revision and to detailed discussion between the Government of the United States and the Government of the Democratic Republic [of] Vietnam.

3. The United States will propose to the Democratic Republic of Vietnam the establishment of a United States–North Vietnamese Joint Economic Commission within 30 days from the date of this message.

4. The function of the commission will be to develop programs for the United States contribution to reconstruction of North Vietnam. This United States contribution will be based upon such factors as:

   (a) the needs of North Vietnam arising from the dislocation of war;

   (b) the requirements for postwar reconstruction in the agricultural and industrial sectors of North Vietnam's economy.

5. The Joint Economic Commission will have an equal number of representatives from each side. It will agree upon a mechanism to administer the program which will constitute the United States contribution to the reconstruction of North Vietnam. The commission will attempt to complete this agreement within 60 days after its establishment.

6. The two members of the commission will function on the principle of respect for each other's sovereignty, noninterference in each other's internal affairs, equality and mutual benefit. The offices of the commission will be located at a place to be agreed upon by the United States and the Democratic Republic of Vietnam.

7. The United States considers that the implementation of the foregoing principles will prompt economic, trade and other relations between the United States of America and the Democratic Republic of Vietnam and will contribute to insuring a stable and lasting peace

in Indochina. These principles accord with the spirit of Chapter VIII of the Agreement on Ending the War and Restoring Peace in Vietnam which was signed in Paris on Jan. 27, 1973.

## *Understanding Regarding Economic Reconstruction Program*

It is understood that the recommendations of the Joint Economic Commission mentioned in the President's note to the Prime Minister will be implemented by each member in accordance with its own constitutional provisions.

## *Note Regarding Other Forms of Aid*

In regard to other forms of aid, United States studies indicate that the appropriate programs could fall in the range of $1 billion to $1.5 billion, depending on food and other commodity needs of the Democratic Republic of Vietnam.

## *Note*

1. *The New York Times*, May 20, 1977.

# The Great Spring Victory: An Account of the Liberation of South Vietnam

## General Van Tien Dung

*T*he last US troops were pulled out of Vietnam on March 29, 1973, as North Vietnam released its last US prisoners of war. Thieu still hoped for US reintervention. In a news conference on March 15, Nixon threatened to take some action, but once the Paris Peace Accords had been signed, the mood in Congress was to get out. On July 1, Congress passed a law prohibiting expending any funds for US combat activities "in or over or from off the shores of North Vietnam, South Vietnam, Laos or Cambodia" as of August 15, 1973. That law ended the bombing of Cambodia (Reading 58) and prevented Nixon and his successor, Gerald Ford, from reintroducing troops. It did not, however, end US military and economic aid to the Thieu regime, although the amounts approved by Congress were reduced. The bombing of the South continued with US-supplied equipment. In late 1973, Thieu declared the Third Indochina War and went on the offensive, only to be routed by the DRV-PRG counterattack. In the United States, media attention was focused primarily on the Watergate scandal as the nation watched Nixon avoid impeachment proceedings by resigning from office on August 9, 1974.

General Van Tien Dung, General Vo Nguyen Giap's chief of staff at Dien Bien Phu, was the only military person besides Giap among the eleven-member Politburo after Ho Chi Minh's death. He had the responsibility of leading the final offensive in South Vietnam. Our Great Spring Victory, the book from which this reading is selected, is his account of that offensive. In the introduction, he says the army and the people of Vietnam were determined "to fulfill the testament of President Ho Chi Minh" and won the final offensive in only fifty-five days, with three major campaigns: the campaign to liberate Tay Nguyen (the

*Central Highlands), which began with the attack on Ban Me Thuot; the campaign to liberate Hue and Da Nang and to drive ARVN troops out of the coastal areas of central Vietnam; and the Ho Chi Minh Campaign to liberate Saigon and nearby provinces.*

*The final offensive was launched in March 1975. On April 21, Thieu resigned, turning the presidency over to Vice-President Tran Van Huong. In his book about the final offensive,* Decent Interval, *Frank Snepp, who was a CIA agent at the time, describes how he drove Thieu to the airport on the night of April 25 when Thieu left the country aboard a US Air Force plane. US Ambassador Graham Martin was waiting there to bid "farewell to the last vestige of three decades of bad policy."[1] On April 28, General Duong Van Minh replaced Huong as president.*

*On April 30, Communist forces reached the presidential palace. Minh surrendered. Denied peace in 1954 and 1973, Vietnam became one country again. Saigon was renamed Ho Chi Minh City. The following excerpts by General Van Tien Dung describe some of what happened on April 30 and May 1, 1975.*

When it was almost light, the American news services reported that [U.S. Ambassador Graham] Martin had cleared out of Saigon in a helicopter. This viceregal mandarin, the final American plenipotentiary in South Vietnam, beat a most hasty and pitiful retreat. As it happened, up until the day he left Saigon, Martin still felt certain that the quisling administration could be preserved, and that a ceasefire could be arranged, so he was halfhearted about the evacuation, waiting and watching. He went all the way out to Tan Son Nhat airfield to observe the situation. Our barrage of bombs and our fierce shelling had nearly paralyzed this vital airfield, and the fixed-wing aircraft they had intended to use for their evacuation could no longer operate. The encirclement of Saigon was growing tighter by the day. The Duong Van Minh card[2] which they had played far too late proved useless. When Martin reported this to Washington, President Ford issued orders to begin a helicopter evacuation. Coming in waves for eighteen hours straight, they carried more than 1,000 Americans and over 5,000 of their Vietnamese retainers, along with their families, out of the South. Ford also ordered Martin to evacuate immediately "without a minute's delay."

The American evacuation was carried out from the tops of thirteen tall buildings chosen as landing pads for their helicopters. The number of these landing pads shrank gradually as tongues of fire from our advancing troops came closer. At the American embassy, the boarding point for the evacuation copters was a scene of monumental confusion, with the Americans' flunkies fighting their way in, smashing doors, climbing walls, climbing each other's backs, tussling, brawling, and trampling each other as they sought to flee. It reached the point where Martin, who wanted to return to his own house for his suitcase before he fled, had to take a back street, using the rear gate of the embassy. When "Code 2," Martin's code name, and "Lady 09," the name of the helicopter carrying him, left the embassy for the East Sea, it signaled the shameful defeat of U.S. imperialism after thirty years of intervention and military adventures in Vietnam. At the height of their invasion of Vietnam, the U.S. had used 60 percent of their total infantry, 58 percent of their marines, 32 percent of their tactical air force, 50 percent of their strategic air force, fifteen of their eighteen aircraft carriers, 800,000 American troops (counting those stationed in satellite countries who were taking part in the Vietnam war), and more than 1 million Saigon troops. They mobilized as many as 6 million American soldiers in rotation, dropped over 10 million tons of bombs, and spent over $300 billion, but in the end the U.S. ambassador had to crawl up to the helicopter pad looking for a way to flee. Today, looking back on the gigantic force the enemy had mobilized, recalling the malicious designs they admitted, and thinking about the extreme difficulties and complexities which our revolutionary sampan had had to pass through, we were all the more aware how immeasurably great this campaign to liberate Saigon and liberate the South was. . . .

The most extraordinary thing about this historic campaign was what had sprouted in the souls of our cadres and fighters. Why were our soldiers so heroic and determined during this campaign? What had given all of them this clear understanding of the great resolution of the party and of the nation, this clear understanding of our immeasurably precious opportunity, and this clear understanding of our unprecedented manner of fighting? What had made them so extraordinarily courageous and intense, so outstanding in their political acumen in this final phase of the war?

The will and competence of our soldiers were not achieved in a day, but were the result of a continuous process of carrying out the party's ideological and organizational work in the armed forces. And throughout our thirty years of struggle, there had been no campaign in which Uncle Ho had not gone into the operation with our soldiers. Going out to battle this time, our whole army had been given singular, unprecedented strength because this strategically decisive battle bore his name: Ho Chi Minh, for every one of our cadres and fighters, was faith, strength, and life. Among the myriad troops in all the advancing wings, every one of our fighters carried toward Ho Chi Minh City the hopes of the nation and a love for our land. Today each fighter could see with his own eyes the resiliency which the Fatherland had built up during these many years, and given his own resiliency there was nothing, no enemy scheme that could stop him.

Our troops advanced rapidly to the five primary objectives, and then spread out from there. Wherever they went, a forest of revolutionary flags appeared, and people poured out to cheer them, turning the streets of Saigon into a giant festival. From the Binh Phoc bridge to Quan Tre, people carrying flags, beating drums and hollow wooden fish, and calling through megaphones, chased down the enemy, disarmed enemy soldiers, neutralized traitors and spies, and guided our soldiers. In Hoc Mon on Route 1, the people all came out into the road to greet the soldiers, guide them, and point out the hiding places of enemy thugs. Everywhere people used megaphones to call on Saigon soldiers to take off their uniforms and lay down their guns. The people of the city, especially the workers, protected factories and warehouses and turned them over to our soldiers. In all the districts bordering the city—Binh Hoa, Thanh My Tay, Phu Nhuan, Go Vap, and Thu Duc—members of the revolutionary infrastructure and other people distributed leaflets, raised flags, called on enemy soldiers to drop their guns, and supplied and guided our soldiers. Before this great army entered the city, the great cause of our nation and the policies of our revolution had entered the hearts of the people.

We were very pleased to hear that the people of the city rose up when the military attacks, going one step ahead, had given them the leverage. The masses had entered this decisive battle at just the right time, not too early, but not too late. The patriotic actions of the people created a revolutionary atmosphere of vast strength on all the city's streets. This was the most precious aspect of the mass movement in Saigon–Gia Dinh, the result of many years of propaganda, education, organizing, and training by the municipal party branch. When the opportune moment arrived, those political troops had risen up with a vanguard spirit, and advanced in giant strides along with now powerful main-force divisions, resolutely, intelligently, and courageously. The people of the city not only carried flags and food and drink for the troops, but helped disperse large numbers of enemy soldiers, forced many to surrender, chased and captured many of those who were hiding out, and preserved order and security in the streets. And we will never forget the widespread and moving images of thousands, of tens of thousands of people enthusiastically giving directions to our soldiers and guiding them as they entered the city, and helping all the wings of troops strike quickly and unexpectedly at enemy positions. Those nameless heroes of Saigon–Gia Dinh brought into the general offensive the fresh and beautiful features of people's war.

As we looked at the combat operations map, the five wings of our troops seemed like five lotuses blossoming out from our five major objectives. The First Army Corps had captured Saigon's General Staff headquarters and the command compounds of all the enemy armed services. When the Third Army Corps captured Tan Son Nhat they met one wing of troops already encamped there—our military delegation at Camp Davis; it was an amazing and moving meeting. The Fourth Army Corps captured Saigon's Ministry of Defense, the Bach Dang port, and the radio station. The 232nd force took the Special Capital Zone headquarters and the Directorate-General of Police. The Second Army Corps seized "Independence Palace," the place where the quisling leaders, those hirelings of the United States, had sold our independence, traded in human blood, and carried on their smuggling. Our soldiers immediately rushed upstairs to the place where the quisling cabinet was meeting, and arrested the whole central leadership of the Saigon administration, including their president, right on the spot. Our soldiers' vigorous actions and firm declarations revealed the spirit of a victorious army. By 11:30 A.M. on April 30 the revolutionary flag flew from "Independence Palace"; this became the meeting point for all the wings of liberating troops.

At the front headquarters, we turned on our radios to listen. The voice of the quisling president called on his troops to put down their weapons and surrender unconditionally to our troops. Saigon was completely liberated! Total victory! We were completely victorious! All of us at headquarters jumped up and shouted, embraced and carried each other around on our shoulders. The sound of applause, laughter, and happy, noisy, chattering speech was as festive as if spring had just burst upon us. It was an indescribably joyous scene. Le Duc Tho and Pham Hung embraced me and all the cadres and fighters present. We were all so happy we were choked with emotion. I lit a cigarette and smoked. Dinh Duc Thien, his eyes somewhat red, said, "Now if these eyes close, my heart will be at rest." This historic and sacred, intoxicating and completely satisfying moment was one that comes once in a generation, once in many generations. Our generation had known many victorious mornings, but there had been no morning so fresh and beautiful, so radiant, so clear and cool, so sweet-scented as this morning of total victory, a morning which made babes older than their years and made old men young again. . . .

Le Duc Tho, Pham Hung, and I leaned on our chairs looking at the map of Ho Chi Minh City spread out on the table. We thought of the welter of jobs ahead. Were the electricity and water still working? Saigon's army of nearly 1 million had disbanded on the spot. How should we deal with them? What could we do to help the hungry and find ways for the millions of unemployed to make a living? Should we ask the center to send in supplies right away to keep the factories in Saigon alive? How could we quickly build up a revolutionary administration at the grass-roots level? What policy should we take toward the bourgeoisie? And how could we carry the South on to socialism along with the whole country? The conclusion of this struggle was the opening of another, no less complex and filled with hardship. The difficulties would be many, but the advantages were not few. Saigon and the South, which had gone out first and returned last, deserved a life of peace, plenty, and happiness. . . .

On May 1 . . . [w]e took a car to Saigon, past areas and positions so vital for the liberation of the city, like Trang Bang and Cu Chi, and past areas which had been revolutionary bases for many years, since the founding of the party, like Hoc Mon and Ba Diem. Along the highway, in the villages, and in the city streets there was no sea of blood, only a sea of people in high spirits, waving their hands and waving flags to welcome peace and the revolution. That sea of people, mingling endlessly with the long lines of our soldiers' trucks, tanks, and cars, in itself proclaimed our total victory. The sides of the road were still clogged with uniforms, rank insignia, guns and ammunition, boots, helmets, vehicles, and artillery the puppet army had abandoned in defeat. Spread out around us were not only the relics of a military force that had been smashed, but the relics of a reactionary political doctrine that had unraveled, the doctrine of a crew of imperialists so arrogant about their wealth and so worshipful of possessions that it blinded them. It was ironic that at every enemy base and barracks a sign had been erected, painted in large letters with the words, "Honor—Responsibility—Fatherland." What the enemy did not have, they had to shout about loudest. The main road to Saigon was very good, built by the enemy in the past to serve their operations. All of the enemy bases and storage depots were vast. The banks, the American billets, the hotels, many stories tall, were imposing advertisements for neocolonialism, implying that it would stand firm here, that it would stand for time without end. In 1968 Westmoreland boasted, "We will always be in Vietnam. Our bombs and bullets will prove it." But in fact the proof was exactly the opposite. We went into the headquarters of Saigon's General Staff. Here, as at the enemy Directorate-General of Police, the files of the enemy commanders' top secret documents remained. Their modern computer with its famous memory containing bio-data on each officer and soldier in their million-plus army was still running. American computers had not won in this war. The intelligence and will of our nation had won completely.

## Notes

1. Frank Snepp, *Decent Interval: An Insider's Account of Saigon's Indecent End Told by the CIA's Chief Strategy Analyst in Vietnam* (New York: Random House, Vintage, 1978), p. 437. Although told from an opposite perspective, Snepp's book, which focuses on the debacle of US withdrawal from Saigon, agrees in many respects with Dung's.

2. This refers to the final move of putting Minh in power.

# Letter That Began
# My Lai Investigation

Mr. Ron Ridenhour
1416 East Thomas Road #104
Phoenix, Arizona

March 29, 1969

Gentlemen:

It was late in April, 1968 that I first heard of "Pinkville" and what allegedly happened there. I received that first report with some skepticism, but in the following months I was to hear similar stories from such a wide variety of people that it became impossible for me to disbelieve that something rather dark and bloody did indeed occur sometime in March, 1968 in a village called "Pinkville" in the Republic of Viet Nam.

The circumstances that led to my having access to the reports I'm about to relate need explanation. I was inducted in March, 1967 into the U.S. Army. After receiving various training I was assigned to the 70th Infantry Detachment (LRP), 11th Light Infantry Brigade at Schofield Barracks, Hawaii, in early October, 1967. That unit, the 70th Infantry Detachment (LRP), was disbanded a week before the 11th Brigade shipped out for Viet Nam on the 5th of December, 1967. All of the man from whom I later heard reports of the "Pinkville" incident were reassigned to "C" Company, 1st Battalion, 20th Infantry, 11th Light Infantry Brigade. I was reassigned to the aviation section of Headquarters Company 11th LIB. After we had been in Viet Nam for 3 to 4 months many of the men from the 70th Inf. Det. (LRP) began to transfer into the same unit, "E" Company, 51st Infantry (LRP).

In late April, 1968 I was awaiting orders for a transfer from HHC, 11th Brigade to Company "E," 51st Inf, (LRP), when I happened to run into Pfc "Butch" Gruver, whom I had known in Hawaii. Gruver told me he had been assigned to "C" Company 1st of the 20th until April 1st when he transferred

369

to the unit that I was headed for. During the course of our conversation he told me the first of many reports I was to hear of "Pinkville."

"Charlie" Company 1/20 had been assigned to Task Force Barker in late February, 1968 to help conduct "search and destroy" operations on the Batangan Peninsula, Barker's area of operation. The task force was operating out of L. F. Dottie, located five or six miles north of Quang Nhai city on Viet Namese National Highway 1. Gruver said that Charlie Company had sustained casualties; primarily from mines and booby traps, almost everyday from the first day they arrived on the peninsula. One village area was particularly troublesome and seemed to be infested with booby traps and enemy soldiers. It was located about six miles northeast of Quang Nhai city at approximate coordinates B.S. 728795. It was a notorious area and the men of Task Force Barker had a special name I for it: they called it "Pinkville." One morning in the latter part of March, Task Force Barker moved out from its firebase headed for "Pinkville." Its mission: destroy the trouble spot and all of its inhabitants.

When "Butch" told me this I didn't quite believe that what he was telling me was true, but he assured me that it was and went on to describe what had happened. The other two companies that made up the task force cordoned off the village so that "Charlie" Company could move through to destroy the structures and kill the inhabitants. Any villagers who ran from Charlie Company were stopped by the encircling companies. I asked "Butch" several times if all the people were killed. He said that he thought they were men, women and children. He recalled seeing a small boy, about three or four years old, standing by the trail with a gunshot wound in one arm. The boy was clutching his wounded arm with his other hand, while blood trickled between his fingers. He was staring around himself in shock and disbelief at what he saw. "He just stood there with big eyes staring around like he didn't understand; he didn't believe what was happening. Then the captain's RTO (radio operator) put a burst of 16 (M-16 rifle) fire into him." It was so bad, Gruver said, that one of the men in his squad shot himself in the foot in order to be medivaced out of the area so that he would not have to participate in the slaughter. Although he had not seen it, Gruver had been told by people he considered trustworthy that one of the company's officers, 2nd Lieutenant Kally (this spelling may be incorrect) had rounded up several groups of villagers (each group consisting of a minimum of 20 persons of both sexes and all ages). According to the story, Kally then machine-gunned each group. Gruver estimated that the population of the village had been 300 to 400 people and that very few, if any, escaped.

After hearing this account I couldn't quite accept it. Somehow I just couldn't believe that not only had so many young American men participated in such an act of barbarism, but that their officers had ordered it. There were other men in the unit I was soon to be assigned to, "E" Company, 51st Infantry (LRP), who had been in Charlie Company at the time that Gruver alleged the incident at "Pinkville" had occurred. I became determined to ask them about "Pinkville" so that I might compare, their accounts with Pfc Gruver's.

When I arrived at "Echo" Company, 51st Infantry (LRP) the first men I looked for were Pfcs Michael Terry, and William Doherty. Both were veterans of "Charlie" Company, 1/20 and "Pinkville." Instead of contradicting "Butch" Gruver's story they corroborated it, adding some tasty tidbits of information of their own. Terry and Doherty had been in the same squad and their platoon was the third platoon of "C" Company to pass through the village. Most of the people they came to were already dead. Those that weren't were sought out and shot. The platoon left nothing alive neither livestock nor people. Around noon the two soldiers' squad stopped to eat. "Billy and I started to get out our chow" Terry said, "but close to us was a bunch of Vietnamese in a heap, and some of them were moaning. Kally (2nd Lt. Kally) had been through before us and all of them had been shot, but many weren't dead. It was obvious that they weren't going to get any medical attention so Billy and I got up and went over to where they were. I guess we sort of finished them off." Terry went on to say that he and Doherty then returned to where their packs were and ate lunch. He estimated the size of the village to be 200 to 300 people. Doherty thought that the population of "Pinkville" had been 400 people.

If Terry, Doherty and Gruver could be believed, then not only had "Charlie" Company received orders to slaughter all the inhabitants of the village, but those orders had come from the commanding officer of Task Force Barker, or possibly even higher in the chain of command. Pfc Terry stated that when Captain Medina (Charlie Company's commanding officer Captain Ernest Medina) issued the order for the destruction of "Pinkville" he had been hesitant, as if it were something he didn't want to do but had to. Others I spoke to concurred with Terry on this.

It was June before I spoke to anyone who had something of significance to add to what I had already been told of the "Pinkville" incident. It was the end of June, 1968 when I ran into Sargent Larry La Croix at the USO in Chu Lai. La Croix had been in 2nd Lt. Kally's platoon on the day Task Force Barker swept through "Pinkville." What he told me verified the stories of the others, but he also had something new to add. He had been a witness to Kally's gunning down at least three separate groups of villagers. "It was terrible. They were slaughtering villagers like so many sheep." Kally's men were dragging people out of bunkers and hootches and putting them together in a group. The people in the group were men, women and children of all ages. As soon as he felt that the group was big enough, Kally ordered a M-60 (machine gun) set up and the people killed. La Croix said that he bore witness to this procedure at least three times. The three groups were of different sizes, one of about twenty people, one of about thirty people and one of about 40 people. When the first group was put together Kally ordered Pfc. Torres to man the machine-gun and open fire on the villagers that had been grouped together. This Torres did, but before everyone in the group was sown he ceased fire and refused to fire again. After ordering Torres to recommence firing several times, Lieutenant Kally took over the M-60 and finished shooting the remaining villagers in that first group himself. Sargent La Croix told me that Kally didn't bother to order anyone to take the machine-gun when the other two groups of villagers were formed. He simply manned it himself and shot down all villagers in both groups.

This account of Sargent La Croix's confirmed the rumors that Gruver, Terry and Doherty had previously told me about Lieutenant Kally. It also convinced me that there was a very substantial amount of truth to the stories that all of these men had told. If I needed more convincing, I was about to receive it.

It was in the middle of November, 1968 just a few weeks before I was to return to the United States for separation from the army that I talked to Pfc Michael Bernhardt. Bernhardt had served his entire year in Viet Nam in "Charlie" Company 1/20 and he too was about to go home. "Bernie" substantiated the tales told by the other men I had talked to in vivid, bloody detail and added this. "Bernie" had absolutely refused to take part in the massacre of the villagers of "Pinkville" that morning and he thought that it was rather strange that the officers of the company had not made an issue of it. But that evening "Medina (Captain Ernest Medina) came up to me ("Bernie") and told me not to do anything stupid like write my congressman" about what had happened that day. Bernhardt assured Captain Medina that he had no such thing in mind. He had nine months left in Viet Nam and felt that it was dangerous enough just fighting the acknowledged enemy.

Exactly what did, in fact, occur in the village of "Pinkville" in March, 1968 I do not know for certain, but I am convinced that it was something very black indeed. I remain irrevocably persuaded that if you and I do truly believe in the principles of justice and the equality of every man, however humble, before the law, that form the very backbone that this country is founded on, then we must press forward a widespread and public investigation of this matter with all our combined efforts. I think that it was Winston Churchill who once said "A country without a conscience is a country without a soul, and a country without a soul is a country that cannot survive." I feel that I must take some positive action on this matter. I hope that you will launch an investigation immediately and keep me informed of your progress. If you cannot, then I don't know what other course of action to take.

I have considered sending this to newspapers, magazines and broadcasting companies, but I somehow feel that investigation and action by the Congress of the United States is the appropriate procedure, and as a conscientious citizen I have no desire to further besmirch the image of the American serviceman in the eyes of the world. I feel that this action, while probably it would promote attention, would not bring about the constructive actions that the direct actions of the Congress of the United States would.

Sincerely,
/s/ Ron Ridenhour

# Address at Johns Hopkins University: "Peace Without Conquest"

## (April 7, 1965)

## President Lyndon B. Johnson

*Mr. Garland, Senator Brewster, Senator Tydings, Members of the congressional delegation, members of the faculty of Johns Hopkins, student body, my fellow Americans:*

Last week 17 nations sent their views to some two dozen countries having an interest in southeast Asia. We are joining those 17 countries[1] and stating our American policy tonight which we believe will contribute toward peace in this area of the world.

I have come here to review once again with my own people the views of the American Government.

Tonight Americans and Asians are dying for a world where each people may choose its own path to change.

This is the principle for which our ancestors fought in the valleys of Pennsylvania. It is the principle for which our sons fight tonight in the jungles of Viet-Nam.

Viet-Nam is far away from this quiet campus. We have no territory there, nor do we seek any. The war is dirty and brutal and difficult. And some 400 young men, born into an America that is bursting with opportunity and promise, have ended their lives on Viet-Nam's steaming soil.

Why must we take this painful road?

Why must this Nation hazard its case, and its interest, and its power for the sake of a people so far away?

We fight because we must fight if we are to live in a world where every country can shape its own destiny. And only in such a world will our own freedom be finally secure.

This kind of world will never be built by bombs or bullets. Yet the infirmities of man are such that force must often precede reason, and the waste of war, the works of peace.

We wish that this were not so. But we must deal with the world as it is, if it is ever to be as we wish.

## The Nature of the Conflict

The world as it is in Asia is not a serene or peaceful place.

The first reality is that North Viet-Nam has attacked the independent nation of South Viet-Nam. Its object is total conquest.

Of course, some of the people of South Viet-Nam are participating in attack on their own government. But trained men and supplies, orders and arms, flow in a constant stream from north to south.

This support is the heartbeat of the war.

And it is a war of unparalleled brutality. Simple farmers are the targets of assassination and kidnapping. Women and children are strangled in the night because their men are loyal to their government. And helpless villages are ravaged by sneak attacks. Large-scale raids are conducted on towns, and terror strikes in the heart of cities.

The confused nature of this conflict cannot mask the fact that it is the new face of an old enemy.

Over this war—and all Asia—is another reality: the deepening shadow of Communist China. The rulers in Hanoi are urged on by Peking. This is a regime which has destroyed freedom in Tibet, which has attacked India, and has been condemned by the United Nations for aggression in Korea. It is a nation which is helping the forces of violence in almost every continent. The contest in Viet-Nam is part of a wider pattern of aggressive purposes.

## Why Are We in Viet-Nam?

Why are these realities our concern? Why are we in South Viet-Nam?

*We are there because we have a promise to keep.* Since 1954 every American President has offered support to the people of South Viet-Nam. We have helped to build, and we have helped to defend. Thus, over many years, we have made a national pledge to help South Viet-Nam defend its independence.

And I intend to keep that promise.

To dishonor that pledge, to abandon this small and brave nation to its enemies, and to the terror that must follow, would be an unforgivable wrong.

*We are also there to strengthen world order.* Around the globe, from Berlin to Thailand, are people whose well-being rests, in part, on the belief that they can count on us if they are attacked. To leave Viet-Nam to its fate would shake the confidence of all these people in the value of an American commitment and in the value of America's word. The result would be increased unrest and instability, and even wider war.

*We are also there because there are great stakes in the balance.* Let no one think for a moment that retreat from Viet-Nam would bring an end to conflict. The battle would be renewed in one country and then another. The central lesson of our time is that the appetite of aggression is never satisfied. To withdraw from one battlefield means only to prepare for the next. We must say in southeast Asia—as we did in Europe—in the words of the Bible: "Hitherto shalt thou come, but no further."

There are those who say that all our effort there will be futile—that China's power is such that it is bound to dominate all southeast Asia. But there is no end to that argument until all of the nations of Asia are swallowed up.

There are those who wonder why we have a responsibility there. Well, we have it there for the same reason that we have a responsibility for the defense of Europe. World War II was fought in both Europe and Asia, and when it ended we found ourselves with continued responsibility for the defense of freedom.

## Our Objective in Viet-Nam

Our objective is the independence of South Viet-Nam, and its freedom from attack. We want nothing for ourselves—only that the people of South Viet-Nam be allowed to guide their own country in their own way.

We will do everything necessary to reach that objective. And we will do only what is absolutely necessary.

In recent months attacks on South Viet-Nam were stepped up. Thus, it became necessary for us to increase our response and to make attacks by air. This is not a change of purpose. It is a change in what we believe that purpose requires.

We do this in order to slow down aggression.

We do this to increase the confidence of the brave people of South Viet-Nam who have bravely borne this brutal battle for so many years with so many casualties.

And we do this to convince the leaders of North Viet-Nam—and all who seek to share their conquest—of a very simple fact:

We will not be defeated.

We will not grow tired.

We will not withdraw, either openly or under the cloak of a meaningless agreement.

We know that air attacks alone will not accomplish all of these purposes. But it is our best and prayerful judgment that they are a necessary part of the surest road to peace.

We hope that peace will come swiftly. But that is in the hands of others besides ourselves. And we must be prepared for a long continued conflict. It will require patience as well as bravery, the will to endure as well as the will to resist.

I wish it were possible to convince others with words of what we now find it necessary to say with guns and planes: Armed hostility is futile. Our resources are equal to any challenge. Because we fight for values and we fight for principles, rather than territory or colonies, our patience and our determination are unending.

Once this is clear, then it should also be clear that the only path for reasonable men is the path of peaceful settlement.

Such peace demands an independent South Viet-Nam—securely guaranteed and able to shape its own relationships to all others—free from outside interference—tied to no alliance—a military base for no other country.

These are the essentials of any final settlement.

We will never be second in the search for such a peaceful settlement in Viet-Nam.

There may be many ways to this kind of peace: in discussion or negotiation with the governments concerned; in large groups or in small ones; in the reaffirmation of old agreements or their strengthening with new ones.

We have stated this position over and over again, fifty times and more, to friend and foe alike. And we remain ready, with this purpose, for unconditional discussions.

And until that bright and necessary day of peace we will try to keep conflict from spreading. We have no desire to see thousands die in battle— Asians or Americans. We have no desire to devastate that which the people of North Viet-Nam have built with toil and sacrifice. We will use our power with restraint and with all the wisdom that we can command.

But we will use it.

This war, like most wars, is filled with terrible irony. For what do the people of North Viet-Nam want? They want what their neighbors also desire: food for their hunger; health for their bodies; a chance to learn; progress for their country; and an end to the bondage of material misery. And they would find all these things far more readily in peaceful association with others than in the endless course of battle.

## A Cooperative Effort for Development

These countries of southeast Asia are homes for millions of impoverished people. Each day these people rise at dawn and struggle through until the night to wrestle existence from the soil. They are often wracked by disease, plagued by hunger, and death comes at the early age of 40.

Stability and peace do not come easily in such a land. Neither independence nor human dignity will ever be won, though, by arms alone. It also requires the work of peace. The American people have helped generously in times past in these works. Now there must be a much more massive effort to improve the life of man in that conflict-torn corner of our world.

The first step is for the countries of southeast Asia to associate themselves in a greatly expanded cooperative effort for development. We would hope that North Viet-Nam would take its place in the common effort just as soon as peaceful cooperation is possible.

The United Nations is already actively engaged in development in this area. As far back as 1961 I conferred with our authorities in Viet-Nam in connection with their work there. And I would hope tonight that the Secretary General of the United Nations could use the prestige of his great office, and his deep knowledge of Asia, to initiate, as soon as possible, with the countries of that area, a plan for cooperation in increased development.

For our part I will ask the Congress to join in a billion dollar American investment in this effort as soon as it is underway.

And I would hope that all other industrialized countries, including the Soviet Union, will join in this effort to replace despair with hope, and terror with progress.

The task is nothing less than to enrich the hopes and the existence of more than a hundred million people. And there is much to be done.

The vast Mekong River can provide food and water and power on a scale to dwarf even our own TVA.

The wonders of modern medicine can be spread through villages where thousands die every year from lack of care.

Schools can be established to train people in the skills that are needed to manage the process of development.

And these objectives, and more, are within the reach of a cooperative and determined effort.

I also intend to expand and speed up a program to make available our farm surpluses to assist in feeding and clothing the needy in Asia. We should not allow people to go hungry and wear rags while our own warehouses overflow with an abundance of wheat and corn, rice and cotton.

So I will very shortly name a special team of outstanding, patriotic, distinguished Americans to inaugurate our participation in these programs. This team will be headed by Mr. Eugene Black, the very able former President of the World Bank.

In areas that are still ripped by conflict, of course development will not be easy. Peace will be necessary for final success. But we cannot and must not wait for peace to begin this job.

## The Dream of World Order

This will be a disorderly planet for a long time. In Asia, as elsewhere, the forces of the modern world are shaking old ways and uprooting ancient civilizations. There will be turbulence and struggle and even violence. Great social change—as we see in our own country now—does not always come without conflict.

We must also expect that nations will on occasion be in dispute with us. It may be because we are rich, or powerful; or because we have made some mistakes; or because they honestly fear our intentions. However, no nation need ever fear that we desire their land, or to impose our will, or to dictate their institutions.

But we will always oppose the effort of one nation to conquer another nation.

We will do this because our own security is at stake.

But there is more to it than that. For our generation has a dream. It is a very old dream. But we have the power and now we have the opportunity to make that dream come true.

For centuries nations have struggled among each other. But we dream of a world where disputes are settled by law and reason. And we will try to make it so.

For most of history men have hated and killed one another in battle. But we dream of an end to war. And we will try to make it so.

For all existence most men have lived in poverty, threatened by hunger. But we dream of a world where all are fed and charged with hope. And we will help to make it so.

The ordinary men and women of North Viet-Nam and South Viet-Nam—of China and India—of Russia and America—are brave people. They are filled with the same proportions of hate and fear, of love and hope. Most of them want the same things for themselves and their families. Most of them do not want their sons to ever die in battle, or to see their homes, or the homes of others, destroyed.

Well, this can be their world yet. Man now has the knowledge—always before denied—to make this planet serve the real needs of the people who live on it.

I know this will not be easy. I know how difficult it is for reason to guide passion, and love to master hate. The complexities of this world do not bow easily to pure and consistent answers.

But the simple truths are there just the same. We must all try to follow them as best we can.

## *Conclusion*

We often say how impressive power is. But I do not find it impressive at all. The guns and the bombs, the rockets and the warships, are all symbols of human failure. They are necessary symbols. They protect what we cherish. But they are witness to human folly.

A dam built across a great river is impressive.

In the countryside where I was born, and where I live, I have seen the night illuminated, and the kitchens warmed, and the homes heated, where once the cheerless night and the ceaseless cold held sway. And all this happened because electricity came to our area along the humming wires of the REA. Electrification of the countryside—yes, that, too, is impressive.

A rich harvest in a hungry land is impressive.

The sight of healthy children in a classroom is impressive.

These—not mighty arms—are the achievements which the American Nation believes to be impressive.

And, if we are steadfast, the time may come when all other nations will also find it so.

Every night before I turn out the lights to sleep I ask myself this question: Have I done everything that I can do to unite this country? Have I done everything I can to help unite the world, to try to bring peace and hope to all the peoples of the world? Have I done enough?

Ask yourselves that question in your homes—and in this hall tonight. Have we, each of us, all done all we could? Have we done enough?

We may well be living in the time foretold many years ago when it was said: "I call heaven and earth to record this day against you, that I have set before you life and death, blessing and cursing: therefore choose life, that both thou and thy seed may live."

This generation of the world must choose: destroy or build, kill or aid, hate or understand.

We can do all these things on a scale never dreamed of before.

*Well, we will choose life.* In so doing we will prevail over the enemies within man, and over the natural enemies of all mankind.

To Dr. Eisenhower and Mr. Garland, and this great institution, Johns Hopkins, I thank you for this opportunity to convey my thoughts to you and to the American people.

Good night.

## *Note*

1. The text of the reply to the 17-nation declaration of March 15 was released by the White House on April 8, 1965. The 17-nation declaration and the U.S. reply are printed in the Department of State Bulletin (vol. 52, p. 610).

NOTE: The President spoke at 9 p.m. in Shriver Hall Auditorium at Johns Hopkins University, Baltimore, Md. In his opening words, he referred to Charles S. Garland, Chairman of the University's Board of Trustees, and Senators Daniel B. Brewster and Joseph D. Tydings of Maryland.

Later he referred to Dr. Milton Eisenhower, President of Johns Hopkins University, and Eugene Black, former President of the World Bank and adviser to the President on southeast Asia social and economic development.

Earlier, on the same day, the White House released the text of the statements, made to the press in the Theater at the White House, by George W. Ball, Under Secretary of State, Robert S. McNamara, Secretary of Defense, and McGeorge Bundy, Special Assistant to the President, which defined the context of the President's speech.

# The President's News Conference of February 2, 1968
## President Lyndon B. Johnson

THE PRESIDENT. [1.] Tom[1] will have copies made of this statement and distribute it to you later, so you don't need to take it verbatim. You may want to take notes as you go along. It is very brief. Then I will take any questions that may occur to you from it.

### Statement on the Situation in Vietnam

We have known for several months, now, that the Communists planned a massive winter-spring offensive. We have detailed information on Ho Chi Minh's order governing that offensive. Part of it is called a general uprising.

We know the object was to overthrow the constitutional government in Saigon and to create a situation in which we and the Vietnamese would be willing to accept the Communist-dominated coalition government.

Another part of that offensive was planned as a massive attack across the frontiers of South Vietnam by North Vietnamese units. We have already seen the general uprising.

General Westmoreland's headquarters report the Communists appear to have lost over 10,000 men killed and some 2,300 detained. The United States has lost 249 men killed. The Vietnamese, who had to carry the brunt of the fighting in the cities, lost 553 killed as of my most recent report from the Westmoreland headquarters.

There were also a number of attacks on United States airfields throughout the country. We have confirmed the loss of 15 fixed-wing aircraft, and 23 helicopters were destroyed. A good many more were damaged but will be returned to service.

This is a small proportion of our aircraft and helicopters available in that area. Secretary McNamara, General Westmoreland, and the Joint Chiefs of Staff do not think that our military operations will be materially affected.

The biggest fact is that the stated purposes of the general uprising have failed. Communist leaders counted on popular support in the cities for their effort. They found little or none. On the other hand, there have been civilian casualties and disruption of public services. Just before I came into the room, I read a long cable from Ambassador Bunker which described the vigor with which the Vietnamese Government and our own people are working together to deal with the problems of restoring civilian services and order in all of the cities.

In the meanwhile, we may at this very moment be on the eve of a major enemy offensive in the area of Khe Sanh and generally around the Demilitarized Zone.

We have known for some time that this offensive was planned by the enemy. Over recent weeks I have been in close touch with General Westmoreland, and over recent days in very close touch with all of our Joint Chiefs of Staff to make sure that every single thing that General Westmoreland believed that he needed at this time was available to him, and that our Joint Chiefs believe that his strategy was sound, his men were sure, and they were amply supplied.

I am confident in the light of the information given to me that our men and the South Vietnamese will be giving a good account of themselves.

As all of you know, the situation is a fluid one. We will keep the American people informed as these matters develop.

Now, I will be glad to take any questions.

## Questions

### Negotiations with Hanoi

[2.] Q. Mr. President, in your State of the Union Message, you said we were exploring certain so-called offers from Hanoi and as soon as you could you would report to the people on that.

Is there anything you can tell us today about the status of possible peace negotiations with them?

THE PRESIDENT. No. I would think that that statement is about as good as I could make on that general subject. That accurately describes what has been going on and what is going on. But I do not have any success or results to report on it.

## Assessment of the Situation in South Vietnam

[3.] Q. Mr. President, does this present rampage in South Vietnam give you any reason to change any assessment that you have made previously about the situation in South Vietnam?

THE PRESIDENT. I am sure that we will make adjustments to what we are doing there.

So far as changing our basic strategy, the answer would be no. I think that there will be changes made here and there as a result of experience that comes from efforts such as they have made. Our best experts think that they had two purposes in mind.

First was a military success. That has been a complete failure. That is not to say that they have not disrupted services. It is just like when we have a riot in a town or when we have a very serious strike, or bridges go out, or lights—power failures and things. They have disrupted services. A few bandits can do that in any city in the land.

Obviously, they have in the Vietcong hundreds and thousands, so it is nothing unexpected to anticipate that they will try in cooperation with their friends from the North to coordinate their activities.

The ferocity and the violence, the deception and the lack of concern for the basic elements that appeal to human beings—they may have shocked a lot of people in that respect.

But the ability to do what they have done has been anticipated, prepared for, and met.

Now so much for the military movements. This is not just a civilian judgment. This is the judgment of the military men in the field for whatever that judgment is worth to us back here as experts—Monday morning quarterbacks.

That is the judgment of the best military advice I have here. I met with them yesterday at lunch at some length. I had General Ridgway[2] come down and spend some time with me and talked to him.

I have spent a good deal of time talking to General Taylor.[3] I had all of the Joint Chiefs of Staff in yesterday. We explored and discussed what had happened, what was happening, what might happen, and so forth.

I have talked to the Pentagon this morning, very early, and have been in touch with Secretary McNamara before his testimony.

Their general conclusion is that as a military movement it has been a failure.

Now, their second objective, obviously from the—what you can see from not only Vietnam but from other Communist capitals—even from some of our unknowing people here at home—is a psychological victory.

We have to realize that in moments of tenseness and trial—as we will have today and as we have had in the past days—that there will be a great effort to exploit that and let that substitute for military victory they have not achieved.

I do not believe when the American people know the facts, when the world knows the facts, and when the results are laid out for them to examine, I do not believe that they will achieve a psychological victory.

I do not want to be interpreted as unduly optimistic at all. I would rather wait and let the facts speak for themselves because there are many things that one far removed from the scene cannot anticipate.

In all of the battles, there are many disappointments for the commanders and even the commanders in chief.

So I think that at this very critical stage I would much prefer to be played low key than to give any false assurances. I can only say this: that based on the best military advice that I have, I feel confident that the men will give a good accounting of themselves.

Now, Sarah,[4] let's get yours, and we'll get through with that if you want.

## The "Pueblo" and Its Crew

[4.] Q. Sir, I was going to shift from that question in view of what you just said to another question.

THE PRESIDENT. Go ahead.

Q. Have you any news on the crew of the *Pueblo*?

THE PRESIDENT. We understand from neutral nations and from reports from North Korea that the men are being treated well; that those who have suffered wounds are receiving treatment; that the body of the man who died is being held. We have received those reports and examined them. That is about the extent of the information we have on it.

Q. Did you say "men" or "man", sir, who died?

THE PRESIDENT. Man.

Q. Mr. President, are you confident that we can get back both the ship and the crew?

THE PRESIDENT. No, I am not. I don't want to hold out any hopes on information that I have that is not justified. All I can say is that these things take time.

The most comparable incident, I am told by the military people, to this one was the RB-47 that went down in 1960 and it took some 7 months of negotiations to get our pilots back.[5]

We are exploring every diplomatic means that is available to us. We have our best military men reviewing all that happened and, as I said in my statement to you and to the country some time ago, we are taking such precautionary steps as we may think the military situation justifies.

## The San Antonio Formula

[5.] Q. Clark Clifford's' testimony before the Armed Services Committee has raised some questions about the San Antonio formula.

THE PRESIDENT. Only in the press, not with anyone in the administration. Mr. Clifford said what I have said, what Mr. Rusk has said, what everybody has said, so far as the San Antonio formula is concerned. The country should know once and for all this morning that Mr. Clifford said just what I said at San Antonio.

## Possibility of Need for Additional Troops

[6.] Q. Mr. President, is it possible that these developments in Vietnam that you had outlined, plus the imminence of this major offensive, could lead to deployment of additional American combat troops in Vietnam?

THE PRESIDENT. I would not want to make predictions. Of course it is possible. The answer is yes. I wouldn't want your lead to say though, "Johnson predicts possibility of troops" because that is not anticipated. We see no evidence of that.

Yesterday I saw that George[7] said that of course we would consider calling up specialists or, of course we could consider some of these things. I must emphasize to you that lots of things would be considered, but so far as adding additional men, we have added the men that General Westmoreland has felt to be desirable and necessary.

There is nothing that has developed there that has caused him to change that estimate. We have something under 500,000. Our objective is 525,000. Most of the combat battalions already have been supplied. There is not anything in any of the developments that would justify the press in leaving the impression that any great new overall moves are going to be made that would involve substantial movements in that direction.

I would not want to foreclose any action in a matter like this. Anything can happen on a moment's notice. But we have constantly under advisement various things that we would want to anticipate. And after reviewing them now for several days, I have not seen the requirement or the necessity, nor have the joint Chiefs, of making any additional requests to the Congress at this time involving additional authority.

It would be desirable, as it was last year, to have legislation a little more generous in one respect or two, or maybe more funds appropriated for military assistance that were reduced. We may have to get some adjustments in those fields, but there is nothing that is imminent at this moment.

## The "Pueblo" Incident and Vietnam

[7.] Q. Mr. President, how much, if any, definite information do you have on the connection between the *Pueblo* incident and what is happening now in Vietnam?

THE PRESIDENT. I do not have evidence that would say that they are definitely, positively one and the same here because I cannot prove that. Practically every expert I have talked to on Korea and North Vietnam and the Communist operation—all of them, I think without exception, believe there is a definite connection.

I would have you know, though, that that is based on their opinion and not on hard evidence that I could establish to CBS's satisfaction in a court of law.

## North Vietnamese Peace Feelers

[8.] Q. Mr. President, in light of what has happened in the last few days, or going back to the *Pueblo* incident, do you have any reason to believe that in the last 2 years there have been any genuine peace feelers put out by the North Vietnamese or other Vietnamese Communists, or have they been phony, except when they were winning in '64?

THE PRESIDENT. We have tried to explore every suggestion made by enemy and friend. I must say that in retrospect I do not think we have overlooked anything, and I do not think that we have found anything that would give an impartial judge reason to be encouraged.

## Validity of Basic Assumptions

[9] Q. Sir, do you see anything in the developments this week in these attacks in Vietnam that causes you to think you need to reevaluate some of the assumptions on which our policies, our strategy there has been based? I am thinking in terms of the security ratings, amount of population that is considered under Government control? Do you think the basic assumption is still valid?

THE PRESIDENT. We do that every week. I see nothing that would indicate that that shouldn't be done. We must do it all the time to try to keep up, and to be sure we have not made errors and mistakes. If you are saying, have we felt that what happened could not happen, the answer is no. As a matter of fact, Mr. Bailey,[8] if you have seen any of the intelligence reports, the information has been very clear that two things would happen:

One is that there would be a general uprising, as I stated.

Two, there would be a general invasion and attempt to secure military victory, and that the objective would be to get a military victory and a psychological victory.

That is one of the great problems the President has to deal with. He is sitting there reading these information reports while his own people, a good many of the best intentioned, are supplying him with military strategy, and the two do not fit in.

So you have to be tolerant and understand their best intentions while you are looking at the other fellow's hole card. That is what General Westmoreland has been doing while all of these Monday morning quarterbacks are pointing out to him that this is the way he should move, or this is the way he should move.

This is a part of what happens when you look at history. It may be that General Westmoreland makes some serious mistakes or that I make some. We don't know. We are just acting in light of the information we have. We believe we have information about what they are trying to do there. We have taken every precaution we know of. But we don't want to give you assurance that it will all be satisfactory. We see nothing that would require any change of great consequence.

We will have to move men from this place to that one. We will have to replace helicopters. Probably we had 100-odd helicopters and planes seriously damaged and we will have to replace them.

Secretary McNamara told me he could have that done very shortly.

We will have to replace the 38 planes lost, but we have approximately 5,900 planes there. We anticipate that we will lose 25 or 30 every month just from normal crashes and so forth.

## Evaluation of the Situation

[10.] Q. Mr. President, do you believe, sir, their winter-spring offensive and their call for an uprising and their attempt to impose a coalition government is based on their belief that they are taking military punishment that they cannot sustain for a long time?

In short, sir, are we still winning the war?

THE PRESIDENT. Well, I see nothing in the developments that would indicate that the evaluation that I have had of this situation throughout the month should be changed.

I do think that the second phase is imminent. What we have expected is upon us. We have gone through the first phase of it. We will have to see what happens in the second phase. If it comes out as expected, I think I can give you a better answer to your question when it is over with.

I do not want to prophesy what is going to happen, although we feel reasonably sure of our strength.

## Vietcong Morale

[11.] Q. Mr. President, one of the problems people seem to be having in making up their minds on the psychological importance of this goes back to our reports that the Vietcong were really way down in morale, that they were a shattered force.

Now people ask: Well, how, then, can they find the people who are so well-motivated to run these suicide attacks in so many places in such good coordination?

Some people say: Well, that proves they know they are licked and this is their dying gasp. And some people say: Well, it proves that we underestimated their morale. How do you feel, sir?

THE PRESIDENT. I haven't read those reports about underestimating all their morale, and their being out of it, and no more problems, and so forth. That hasn't been the information the Government has received.

We do think that we have made good progress there. We are for that. We don't want to overplay it or play it in high key. We just want to state it because we believe it is true.

But no one in authority has ever felt—that I know anything about—that you could not have an uprising of this kind, particularly when they have ordered it and predicted it and we have been expecting it.

As I view history, I think that you have things of this type replete throughout. You can expect it. I see it even in domestic problems. The fact that people's morale may be suffering and they may be having great difficulty doesn't keep them from breaking glass windows and shooting folks in a store or dashing into your home or trying to assassinate somebody. That goes with it. That is a part of the pattern.

Now whether they are doing this from a position of greater strength or greater weakness—I would say neither. I don't think that they are as weak as you picture them in your straw man that you place up there—that the Government has this feeling. I don't think we feel that way.

I think we know that a march on the Pentagon can disrupt traffic and tie up things and cause problems here. I think we can see what happened in Detroit. I think we can see what happened in Saigon.

I think there are times when a few highly energetic and courageous people could seize National Airport. But, could they hold it? Does it endure? Is it a victory? Do they pay more than it is worth and so on and so forth? Those are the things you have to evaluate.

Now, I am no great strategist and tactician. I know that you are not. But let us assume that the best figures we can have are from our responsible military commanders. They say 10,000 died and we lost 249 and the South Vietnamese lost 500. Now that doesn't look like a Communist victory. I can count. It looks like somebody has paid a very dear price for the temporary encouragement that some of our enemies had.

We have approximately 5,900 planes and have lost 38 completely destroyed. We lost 100-odd that were damaged and have to be repaired. Maybe Secretary McNamara will fly in 150 shortly.

Now, is that a great enemy victory?

In Peking today they say that we are in panic. You have to judge that for yourself. In other Communist capitals today they say that we have definitely exhibited a lack of power and that we do not have any military strength. You will have to judge that for yourself.

But General Westmoreland—evaluating this for us and the Joint Chiefs of Staff reviewing it for me—tell me that in their judgment it has not been a military success.

I am measuring my words. I don't want to overstate the thing. We do not believe that we should help them in making it a psychological success.

We are presenting these reports daily to the Armed Services Committee of the Senate where the Secretary of Defense is testifying and will be through a large part of next week.

There will be moments of encouragement and discouragement. And as things go on ahead, we can't estimate them, but they will be given to the committees who have jurisdiction.

Since the Armed Services Committees help draft our people and raise our armies and provide the equipment and so forth, the Secretary is appearing there morning and afternoon. He will be giving periodic reports that will be much more in detail and will supplement what I have said to you.

## Talks Between South Vietnam and NLF

[12.] Q. Mr. President, do you still support talks between the South Vietnamese and the NLF?[9]

THE PRESIDENT. I have not changed the viewpoint that I expressed when I quoted the statement of President Thieu of South Vietnam in my interview with the correspondents.

## Relations with the Soviet Union

[13.] Q. Mr. President, in your judgment, did the interview Premier Kosygin gave to Life's editors reflect any deterioration in our relations with Russia since the Glassboro talks?

392 • Vietnam and America: Readings and Documents

THE PRESIDENT. I don't care to weigh and speculate on the developments in the Soviet Union. We just tabled last week a nonproliferation agreement with them. We have other plans for exchanges of thoughts on various subjects.

We would always like to improve our relations with the Soviet Union and with all nations where we can do that consistently.

## Proposed Civil Rights March on Washington

[14.] Q. Mr. President, some people interested in civil rights, including Martin Luther King, are planning a massive march on Washington this spring. There is some talk that they would like to stop the wheels of Government.

Are you planning to try to talk them out of this? Would you assess that for us?

THE PRESIDENT. I don't know what their plans are. I am not sure that they have developed them yet.

Of course, I would be hopeful that our energies, our talents, and our concerns could be directed in a more productive and a more effective manner.

I would hope that some of these people who are leaders of the causes could recognize that the Congress is having hearings every day on subjects of vital importance to their cause.

By coming there and following constitutional methods, presenting their evidence to the Congress and persuading the Congress, it would be more helpful than just trying to stop the functioning of the Government who is also trying very much to help their cause to eliminate discrimination, get more jobs, and improve housing. Whatever time and attention the Government has to give to these things is taken away from things that they could be doing to help them.

So we will do all we can to work with all groups in this country to see that their views are heard, considered, and acted upon with promptness and understanding.

## Relations with South Korea

[15.] Q. Mr. President, the *Pueblo* incident appears to have put a certain strain on relations between Washington and Seoul. Some political figures in South Korea are saying that the United States appears more interested in getting back the 83 men than in doing something about North Korean incursions into South Korea.

THE PRESIDENT. I don't know which political figures you refer to. I can't comment on that.

We are in very close touch with the President of that country. I think he understands how we feel.

I would be less than frank if I didn't tell you I was deeply concerned about 83 Americans, as I am sure the President of Korea is.

I am also deeply concerned about the situation in South Korea and the obligation we have there. We are going to be equal to that obligation. We are going to be true to our commitment.

We have some 50,000 men there. We are going to see that not only are they adequately informed and supplied, but that all of our plans take into consideration the recommendations of that Government that we have found to be not only a friendly Government but an effective one—and one of our best allies.

I have great respect for the President of South Korea and his judgments. They are being received, considered, and acted upon every day.

I see nothing in any of these developments to justify a concern on the part of South Korea or America that there is a strain in our relations. I think that is largely talk and speculation and so-called reports.

## Meetings with North Korea

[16.] Q. Are we now trying to arrange talks with North Korea at Panmunjom or has there been a meeting since yesterday there?

THE PRESIDENT. Yes, there has been a meeting between representatives of North Korea and the United States. We hope there will be additional meetings.

These meetings have not produced any satisfactory results as far as the United States is concerned.

I know of nothing that I should add to that statement. And I don't plan to.

Merriman Smith, United Press International: Thank you, Mr. President.

## Notes

1. Wyatt Thomas Johnson, Jr., Assistant Press Secretary to the President.
2. Gen. Matthew B. Ridgway, USA (Ret.), former Supreme Allied Commander in the Pacific (1951) and in Europe (1953) and Army Chief of Staff (1953–55).
3. Gen. Maxwell D. Taylor, USA (Ret.), Special Consultant to the President.
4. Mrs. Sarah McClendon, representative of several Texas newspapers.
5. See "Public Papers of the Presidents of the United States, Dwight D. Eisenhower, 1960–61," Item 231; and "Public Papers of the Presidents of the United States, John F. Kennedy, 1961," Item 8.

6. Clark K Clifford, former Naval Aide and Special Counsel to the President (1946–1950), who took office as Secretary of Defense on March 1, 1968 (see Item 104).

7. George E. Christian, Special Assistant to the President.

8. Charles W. Bailey 2d of the Minneapolis Star and Tribune.

9. National Liberation Front, political arm of the Vietcong.

NOTE: President Johnson's one hundred and eighteenth news conference was held in the Cabinet Room at the White House at 12:05 p.m. on Friday, February 2, 1968.

# The President's Address to the Nation Announcing Steps to Limit the War in Vietnam and Reporting His Decision Not to Seek Reelection

## (March 31, 1968)

## President Lyndon B. Johnson

*Good evening, my fellow Americans:*

Tonight I want to speak to you of peace in Vietnam and Southeast Asia.

No other question so preoccupies our people. No other dream so absorbs the 250 million human beings who live in that part of the world. No other goal motivates American policy in Southeast Asia.

For years, representatives of our Government and others have traveled the world—seeking to find a basis for peace talks.

Since last September, they have carried the offer that I made public at San Antonio.

That offer was this:

That the United States would stop its bombardment of North Vietnam when that would lead promptly to productive discussions—and that we would assume that North Vietnam would not take military advantage of our restraint.

Hanoi denounced this offer, both privately and publicly. Even while the search for peace was going on, North Vietnam rushed their preparations for a savage assault on the people, the government, and the allies of South Vietnam.

Their attack—during the Tet holidays—failed to achieve its principal objectives.

It did not collapse the elected government of South Vietnam or shatter its army—as the Communists had hoped.

It did not produce a "general uprising" among the people of the cities as they had predicted.

The Communists were unable to maintain control of any of the more than 30 cities that they attacked. And they took very heavy casualties.

But they did compel the South Vietnamese and their allies to move certain forces from the countryside into the cities.

They caused widespread disruption and suffering. Their attacks, and the battles that followed, made refugees of half a million human beings.

The Communists may renew their attack any day.

They are, it appears, trying to make 1968 the year of decision in South Vietnam—the year that brings, if not final victory or defeat, at least a turning point in the struggle.

This much is clear:

If they do mount another round of heavy attacks, they will not succeed in destroying the fighting power of South Vietnam and its allies.

But tragically, this is also clear: Many men—on both sides of the struggle—will be lost. A nation that has already suffered 20 years of warfare will suffer once again. Armies on both sides will take new casualties. And the war will go on.

There is no need for this to be so.

There is no need to delay the talks that could bring an end to this long and this bloody war.

Tonight, I renew the offer I made last August—to stop the bombardment of North Vietnam. We ask that talks begin promptly, that they be serious talks on the substance of peace. We assume that during those talks Hanoi will not take advantage of our restraint.

We are prepared to move immediately toward peace through negotiations.

So, tonight, in the hope that this action will lead to early talks, I am taking the first step to deescalate the conflict. We are reducing—substantially reducing—the present level of hostilities.

And we are doing so unilaterally, and at once.

Tonight, I have ordered our aircraft and our naval vessels to make no attacks on North Vietnam, except in the area north of the demilitarized zone where the continuing enemy buildup directly threatens allied forward positions and where the movements of their troops and supplies are clearly related to that threat.

The area in which we are stopping our attacks includes almost 90 percent of North Vietnam's population, and most of its territory. Thus there will be no attacks around the principal populated areas, or in the food-producing areas of North Vietnam.

Even this very limited bombing of the North could come to an early end—if our restraint is matched by restraint in Hanoi. But I cannot in good conscience stop all bombing so long as to do so would immediately and directly endanger the lives of our men and our allies. Whether a complete bombing halt becomes possible in the future will be determined by events.

Our purpose in this action is to bring about a reduction in the level of violence that now exists.

It is to save the lives of brave men—and to save the lives of innocent women and children. It is to permit the contending forces to move closer to a political settlement.

And tonight, I call upon the United Kingdom and I call upon the Soviet Union—as cochairmen of the Geneva Conferences, and as permanent members of the United Nations Security Council—to do all they can to move from the unilateral act of deescalation that I have just announced toward genuine peace in Southeast Asia.

Now, as in the past, the United States is ready to send its representatives to any forum, at any time, to discuss the means of bringing this ugly war to an end.

I am designating one of our most distinguished Americans, Ambassador Averell Harriman, as my personal representative for such talks. In addition, I have asked Ambassador Llewellyn Thompson, who returned from Moscow for consultation, to be available to join Ambassador Harriman at Geneva or any other suitable place—just as soon as Hanoi agrees to a conference.

I call upon President Ho Chi Minh to respond positively, and favorably, to this new step toward peace.

But if peace does not come now through negotiations, it will come when Hanoi understands that our common resolve is unshakable, and our common strength is invincible.

Tonight, we and the other allied nations are contributing 600,000 fighting men to assist 700,000 South Vietnamese troops in defending their little country.

Our presence there has always rested on this basic belief: The main burden of preserving their freedom must be carried out by them—by the South Vietnamese themselves.

We and our allies can only help to provide a shield behind which the people of South Vietnam can survive and can grow and develop. On their efforts—on their determination and resourcefulness—the outcome will ultimately depend.

That small, beleaguered nation has suffered terrible punishment for more than 20 years.

I pay tribute once again tonight to the great courage and endurance of its people. South Vietnam supports armed forces tonight Of almost 700,000 men—and I call your attention to the fact that this is the equivalent of more than 10 million in our own population. Its people maintain their firm determination to be free of domination by the North.

There has been substantial progress, I think, in building a durable government during these last 3 years. The South Vietnam of 1965 could not have survived the enemy's Tet offensive of 1968. The elected government of South Vietnam survived that attack—and is rapidly repairing the devastation that it wrought.

The South Vietnamese know that further efforts are going to be required:

—to expand their own armed forces,
—to move back into the countryside as quickly as possible,
—to increase their taxes,
—to select the very best men that they have for civil and military responsibility,
—to achieve a new unity within their constitutional government, and
—to include in the national effort all those groups who wish to preserve South Vietnam's control over its own destiny.

Last week President Thieu ordered the mobilization of 135,000 additional South Vietnamese. He plans to reach—as soon as possible—a total military strength of more than 800,000 men.

To achieve this, the Government of South Vietnam started the drafting of 19-year-olds on March 1st. On May 1st, the Government will begin the drafting of 18-year-olds.

Last month, 10,000 men volunteered for military service—that was two and a half times the number of volunteers during the same month last year. Since the middle of January, more than 48,000 South Vietnamese have joined the armed forces—and nearly half of them volunteered to do so.

All men in the South Vietnamese armed forces have had their tours of duty extended for the duration of the war, and reserves are now being called up for immediate active duty.

President Thieu told his people last week:

"We must make greater efforts and accept more sacrifices because, as I have said many times, this is our country. The existence of our nation is at stake, and this is mainly a Vietnamese responsibility."

He warned his people that a major national effort is required to root out corruption and incompetence at all levels of government.

We applaud this evidence of determination on the part of South Vietnam. Our first priority will be to support their effort.

We shall accelerate the reequipment of South Vietnam's armed forces—in order to meet the enemy's increased firepower. This will enable them progressively to undertake a larger share of combat operations against the Communist invaders.

On many occasions I have told the American people that we would send to Vietnam those forces that are required to accomplish our mission there. So, with that as our guide, we have previously authorized a force level of approximately 525,000.

Some weeks ago—to help meet the enemy's new offensive—we sent to Vietnam about 11,000 additional Marine and airborne troops. They were deployed by air in 48 hours, on an emergency basis. But the artillery, tank, aircraft, medical, and other units that were needed to work with and to support these infantry troops in combat could not then accompany them by air on that short notice.

In order that these forces may reach maximum combat effectiveness, the Joint Chiefs of Staff have recommended to me that we should prepare to send—during the next 5 months—support troops totaling approximately 13,500 men.

A portion of these men will be made available from our active forces. The balance will come from reserve component units which will be called up for service.

The actions that we have taken since the beginning of the year

—to reequip the South Vietnamese forces,

—to meet our responsibilities in Korea, as well as our responsibilities in Vietnam,

—to meet price increases and the cost of activating and deploying reserve forces,

—to replace helicopters and provide the other military supplies we need, all of these actions are going to require additional expenditures.

The tentative estimate of those additional expenditures is $2.5 billion in this fiscal year, and $2.6 billion in the next fiscal year.

These projected increases in expenditures for our national security will bring into sharper focus the Nation's need for immediate action: action to protect the prosperity of the American people and to protect the strength and the stability of our American dollar.

On many occasions I have pointed out that, without a tax bill or decreased expenditures, next year's deficit would again be around $20 billion. I have emphasized the need to set strict priorities in our spending. I have stressed that failure to act and to act promptly and decisively would raise very strong doubts throughout the world about America's willingness to keep its financial house in order.

Yet Congress has not acted. And tonight we face the sharpest financial threat in the postwar era—a threat to the dollar's role as the keystone of international trade and finance in the world.

Last week, at the monetary conference in Stockholm, the major industrial countries decided to take a big step toward creating a new international monetary asset that will strengthen the international monetary system. I am very proud of the very able work done by Secretary Fowler and Chairman Martin of the Federal Reserve Board.

But to make this system work the United States just must bring its balance of payments to—or very close to—equilibrium. We must have a responsible fiscal policy in this country. The passage of a tax bill now, together with expenditure control that the Congress may desire and dictate, is absolutely necessary to protect this Nation's security, to continue our prosperity, and to meet the needs of our people.

What is at stake is 7 years of unparalleled prosperity. In those 7 years, the real income of the average American, after taxes, rose by almost 30 percent—a gain as large as that of the entire preceding 19 years.

So the steps that we must take to convince the world are exactly the steps we must take to sustain our own economic strength here at home. In the past 8 months, prices and interest rates have risen because of our inaction.

We must, therefore, now do everything we can to move from debate to action—from talking to voting. There is, I believe—I hope there is—in both Houses of the Congress—a growing sense of urgency that this situation just must be acted upon and must be corrected.

My budget in January was, we thought, a tight one. It fully reflected our evaluation of most of the demanding needs of this Nation.

But in these budgetary matters, the President does not decide alone. The Congress has the power and the duty to determine appropriations and taxes.

The Congress is now considering our proposals and they are considering reductions in the budget that we submitted.

As part of a program of fiscal restraint that includes the tax surcharge, I shall approve appropriate reductions in the January budget when and if Congress so decides that that should be done.

One thing is unmistakably clear, however: our deficit just must be reduced. Failure to act could bring on conditions that would strike hardest at those people that all of us are trying so hard to help.

These times call for prudence in this land of plenty. I believe that we have the character to provide it, and tonight I plead with the Congress and with the people to act promptly to serve the national interest, and thereby serve all of our people.

Now let me give you my estimate of the chances for peace:

—the peace that will one day stop the bloodshed in South Vietnam,

—that will permit all the Vietnamese people to rebuild and develop their land,

—that will permit us to turn more fully to our own tasks here at home.

I cannot promise that the initiative that I have announced tonight will be completely successful in achieving peace any more than the 30 others that we have undertaken and agreed to in recent years.

But it is our fervent hope that North Vietnam, after years of fighting that have left the issue unresolved, will now cease its efforts to achieve a military victory and will join with us in moving toward the peace table.

And there may come a time when South Vietnamese—on both sides—are able to work out a way to settle their own differences by free political choice rather than by war.

As Hanoi considers its course, it should be in no doubt of our intentions. It must not miscalculate the pressures within our democracy in this election year.

We have no intention of widening this war.

But the United States will never accept a fake solution to this long and arduous struggle and call it peace.

No one can foretell the precise terms of an eventual settlement.

Our objective in South Vietnam has never been the annihilation of the enemy. It has been to bring about a recognition in Hanoi that its objective—taking over the South by force—could not be achieved.

We think that peace can be based on the Geneva Accords of 1954—under political conditions that permit the South Vietnamese—all the South Vietnamese—to chart their course free of any outside domination or interference, from us or from anyone else.

So tonight I reaffirm the pledge that we made at Manila—that we are prepared to withdraw our forces from South Vietnam as the other side withdraws its forces to the north, stops the infiltration, and the level of violence thus subsides.

Our goal of peace and self-determination in Vietnam is directly related to the future of all of Southeast Asia—where much has happened to inspire confidence during the past 10 years. We have done all that we knew how to do to contribute and to help build that confidence.

A number of its nations have shown what can be accomplished under conditions of security. Since 1966, Indonesia, the fifth largest nation in all the world, with a population of more than 100 million people, has had a government that is dedicated to peace with its neighbors and improved conditions for its own people. Political and economic cooperation between nations has grown rapidly.

I think every American can take a great deal of pride in the role that we have played in bringing this about in Southeast Asia. We can rightly judge— as responsible Southeast Asians themselves do—that the progress of the past 3 years would have been far less likely—if not completely impossible—if America's sons and others had not made their stand in Vietnam.

At Johns Hopkins University, about 3 years ago, I announced that the United States would take part in the great work of developing Southeast Asia, including the Mekong Valley, for all the people of that region. Our determination to help build a better land—a better land for men on both sides of the present conflict—has not diminished in the least. Indeed, the ravages of war, I think, have made it more urgent than ever.

So, I repeat on behalf of the United States again tonight what I said at Johns Hopkins—that North Vietnam could take its place in this common effort just as soon as peace comes.

Over time, a wider framework of peace and security in Southeast Asia may become possible. The new cooperation of the nations of the area could be a foundation-stone. Certainly friendship with the nations of such a Southeast Asia is what the United States seeks—and that is all that the United States seeks.

One day, my fellow citizens, there will be peace in Southeast Asia.

It will come because the people of Southeast Asia want it—those whose armies are at war tonight, and those who, though threatened, have thus far been spared.

Peace will come because Asians were willing to work for it—and to sacrifice for it—and to die by the thousands for it.

But let it never be forgotten: Peace will come also because America sent her sons to help secure it.

It has not been easy—far from it. During the past 4½ years, it has been my fate and my responsibility to be Commander in Chief. I have lived— daily and nightly—with the cost of this war. I know the pain that it has inflicted. I know, perhaps better than anyone, the misgivings that it has aroused.

Throughout this entire, long period, I have been sustained by a single principle: that what we are doing now, in Vietnam, is vital not only to the security of Southeast Asia, but it is vital to the security of every American.

Surely we have treaties which we must respect. Surely we have commitments that we are going to keep. Resolutions of the Congress testify to the need to resist aggression in the world and in Southeast Asia.

But the heart of our involvement in South Vietnam—under three different Presidents, three separate administrations—has always been America's own security.

And the larger purpose of our involvement has always been to help the nations of Southeast Asia become independent and stand alone, self-sustaining, as members of a great world community—at peace with themselves, and at peace with all others.

With such an Asia, our country—and the world—will be far more secure than it is tonight.

I believe that a peaceful Asia is far nearer to reality because of what America has done in Vietnam. I believe that the men who endure the dangers of battle—fighting there for us tonight—are helping the entire world avoid far greater conflicts, far wider wars, far more destruction, than this one.

The peace that will bring them home someday will come. Tonight I have offered the first in what I hope will be a series of mutual moves toward peace.

I pray that it will not be rejected by the leaders of North Vietnam. I pray that they will accept it as a means by which the sacrifices of their own people may be ended. And I ask your help and your support, my fellow citizens, for this effort to reach across the battlefield toward an early peace.

Finally, my fellow Americans, let me say this:

Of those to whom much is given, much is asked. I cannot say and no man could say that no more will be asked of us.

Yet, I believe that now, no less than when the decade began, this generation of Americans is willing to "pay any price, bear any burden, meet any hardship, support any friend, oppose any foe to assure the survival and the success of liberty."

Since those words were spoken by John F. Kennedy, the people of America have kept that compact with mankind's noblest cause.

And we shall continue to keep it.

Yet, I believe that we must always be mindful of this one thing, whatever the trials and the tests ahead. The ultimate strength of our country and our cause will lie not in powerful weapons or infinite resources or boundless wealth, but will lie in the unity of our people.

This I believe very deeply.

Throughout my entire public career I have followed the personal philosophy that I am a free man, an American, a public servant, and a member of my party, in that order always and only.

For 37 years in the service of our Nation, first as a Congressman, as a Senator, and as Vice President, and now as your President, I have put the unity of the people first. I have put it ahead of any divisive partisanship.

And in these times as in times before, it is true that a house divided against itself by the spirit of faction, of party, of region, of religion, of race, is a house that cannot stand.

There is division in the American house now. There is divisiveness among us all tonight. And holding the trust that is mine, as President of all the people, I cannot disregard the peril to the progress of the American people and the hope and the prospect of peace for all peoples.

So, I would ask all Americans, whatever their personal interests or concern, to guard against divisiveness and all its ugly consequences.

Fifty-two months and 10 days ago, in a moment of tragedy and trauma, the duties of this office fell upon me. I asked then for your help and God's, that we might continue America on its course, binding up our wounds, healing our history, moving forward in new unity, to clear the American agenda and to keep the American commitment for all of our people.

United we have kept that commitment. United we have enlarged that commitment.

Through all time to come, I think America will be a stronger nation, a more just society, and a land of greater opportunity and fulfillment because of what we have all done together in these years of unparalleled achievement.

Our reward will come in the life of freedom, peace, and hope that our children will enjoy through ages ahead.

What we won when all of our people united just must not now be lost in suspicion, distrust, selfishness, and politics among any of our people.

Believing this as I do, I have concluded that I should not permit the Presidency to become involved in the partisan divisions that are developing in this political year.

With America's sons in the fields far away, with America's future under challenge right here at home, with our hopes and the world's hopes for peace in the balance every day, I do not believe that I should devote an hour or a day of my time to any personal partisan causes or to any duties other than the awesome duties of this office—the Presidency of your country.

Accordingly, I shall not seek, and I will not accept, the nomination of my party for another term as your President.

But let men everywhere know, however, that a strong, a confident, and a vigilant America stands ready tonight to seek an honorable peace—and stands ready tonight to defend an honored cause—whatever the price, whatever the burden, whatever the sacrifice that duty may require.

Thank you for listening.

Good night and God bless all of you.

NOTE: The President spoke at 9 P.M. in his office at the White House. The address was broadcast nationally.

# President Nixon's Speech on Cambodia
## (April 30, 1970)
### President Richard M. Nixon

Good evening my fellow Americans:

Ten days ago, in my report to the Nation on Vietnam, I announced a decision to withdraw an additional 150,000 Americans from Vietnam over the next year. I said then that I was making that decision despite our concern over increased enemy activity in Laos, Cambodia, and in South Vietnam.

At that time, I warned that if I concluded that increased enemy activity in any of these areas endangered lives of Americans remaining in Vietnam, I would not hesitate to take strong and effective measures. Despite that warning, North Vietnam has increased its military aggression in all these areas, and particularly in Cambodia.

After full consultation with the National Security Council, Ambassador Bunker, General Abrams, and my other advisors, I have concluded that the actions of the enemy in the last 10 days clearly endanger the lives of Americans who are in Vietnam now and would constitute an unacceptable risk to those who will be there after withdrawal of another 150,000.

To protect our men who are in Vietnam and to guarantee the continued success of our withdrawal and Vietnamization programs, I have concluded that the time has come for action.

Tonight, I shall describe the actions of the enemy, the actions I have ordered to deal with that situation, and the reasons for my decision. Cambodia, a small country of 7 million people, has been a neutral nation since the Geneva agreement of 1954 an agreement, incidentally, which was signed by the Government of North Vietnam.

American policy since then has been to scrupulously respect the neutrality of the Cambodian people. We have maintained a skeleton diplomatic mission of fewer than 15 in Cambodia's capital, and that only since last August. For the previous 4 years, from 1965 to 1969, we did not have any diplomatic mission whatever in Cambodia. And for the past 5 years, we have provided no military assistance whatever and no economic assistance to Cambodia.

North Vietnam, however, has not respected that neutrality.

For the past 5 years as indicated on this map that you see here North Vietnam has occupied military sanctuaries all along the Cambodian frontier with South Vietnam. Some of these extend up to 20 miles into Cambodia. . . . In cooperation with the armed forces of South Vietnam, attacks are being launched this week to clean out major enemy sanctuaries on the Cambodian Vietnam border.

A major responsibility for the ground operations is being assumed by South Vietnamese forces. . . . There is one area, however, immediately above Parrot's Beak, where I have concluded that a combined American and South Vietnamese operation is necessary.

Tonight, American and South Vietnamese units will attack the headquarters for the entire Communist military operation in South Vietnam. This key control center has been occupied by the North Vietnamese and Vietcong for 5 years in blatant violation of Cambodia's neutrality.

This is not an invasion of Cambodia. The areas in which these attacks will be launched are completely occupied and controlled by North Vietnamese forces. Our purpose is not to occupy the areas. Once enemy forces are driven out of these sanctuaries and once their military supplies are destroyed, we will withdraw. . . .

We take this action not for the purpose of expanding the war into Cambodia but for the purpose of ending the war in Vietnam and winning the just peace we all desire. We have made we will continue to make every possible effort to end this war through negotiation at the conference table rather than through more fighting on the battlefield. . . .

The action that I have announced tonight puts the leaders of North Vietnam on notice that we will be patient in working for peace; we will be conciliatory at the conference table, but we will not be humiliated. We will not be defeated. We will not allow American men by the thousands to be killed by an enemy from privileged sanctuaries. . . .

My fellow Americans, we live in an age of anarchy, both abroad and at home. We see mindless attacks on all the great institutions which have been created by free civilizations in the last 500 years. Even here in the United States, great universities are being systematically destroyed. . . .

If, when the chips are down, the world's most powerful nation, the United States of America, acts like a pitiful, helpless giant, the forces of totalitarianism and anarchy will threaten free nations and free institutions throughout the world.

It is not our power but our will and character that is being tested tonight. . . .

I have rejected all political considerations in making this decision. . . .

Whether my party gains in November is nothing compared to the lives of 400,000 brave Americans fighting for our country and for the cause of peace and freedom in Vietnam. Whether I may be a one-term President is insignificant compared to whether by our failure to act in this crisis the United States proves itself to be unworthy to lead the forces of freedom in this critical period in world history. I would rather be a one-term President and do what I believe is right than to be a two-term President at the cost of seeing America become a second rate power and to see this Nation accept the first defeat in its proud 190-year history. . . .

# Vietnam Veterans Against the War
## Statement by John Kerry to the Senate Committee on Foreign Relations (April 23, 1971)
## John Kerry

I would like to talk on behalf of all those veterans and say that several months ago in Detroit we had an investigation at which over 150 honorably discharged, and many very highly decorated, veterans testified to war crimes committed in Southeast Asia. These were not isolated incidents but crimes committed on a day-to-day basis with the full awareness of officers at all levels of command. It is impossible to describe to you exactly what did happen in Detroit—the emotions in the room and the feelings of the men who were reliving their experiences in Vietnam. They relived the absolute horror of what this country, in a sense, made them do.

They told stories that at times they had personally raped, cut off ears, cut off heads, taped wires from portable telephones to human genitals and turned up the power, cut off limbs, blown up bodies, randomly shot at civilians, razed villages in fashion reminiscent of Ghengis Khan, shot cattle and dogs for fun, poisoned food stocks, and generally ravaged the countryside of South Vietnam in addition to the normal ravage of war and the normal and very particular ravaging which is done by the applied bombing power of this country.

We call this investigation the Winter Soldier Investigation. The term Winter Soldier is a play on words of Thomas Paine's in 1776 when he spoke of the Sunshine Patriots and summertime soldiers who deserted at Valley Forge because the going was rough.

We who have come here to Washington have come here because we feel we have to be winter soldiers now. We could come back to this country, we could be quiet, we could hold our silence, we could not tell what went on in Vietnam, but we feel because of what threatens this country, not the reds, but the crimes which we are committing that threaten it, that we have to speak out. . . .

In our opinion and from our experience, there is nothing in South Vietnam which could happen that realistically threatens the United States of America. And to attempt to justify the loss of one American life in Vietnam, Cambodia or Laos by linking such loss to the preservation of freedom, which those misfits supposedly abuse, is to us the height of criminal hypocrisy, and it is that kind of hypocrisy which we feel has torn this country apart.

We found that not only was it a civil war, an effort by a people who had for years been seeking their liberation from any colonial influence whatsoever, but also we found that the Vietnamese whom we had enthusiastically molded after our own image were hard put to take up the fight against the threat we were supposedly saving them from.

We found most people didn't even know the difference between communism and democracy. They only wanted to work in rice paddies without helicopters strafing them and bombs with napalm burning their villages and tearing their country apart. They wanted everything to do with the war, particularly with this foreign presence of the United States of America, to leave them alone in peace, and they practiced the art of survival by siding with whichever military force was present at a particular time, be it Viet Cong, North Vietnamese or American.

We found also that all too often American men were dying in those rice paddies for want of support from their allies. We saw first hand how monies from American taxes were used for a corrupt dictatorial regime. We saw that many people in this country had a one-sided idea of who was kept free by the flag, and blacks provided the highest percentage of casualties. We saw Vietnam ravaged equally by American bombs and search and destroy missions, as well as by Viet Cong terrorism—and yet we listened while this country tried to blame all of the havoc on the Viet Cong.

We rationalized destroying villages in order to save them. We saw America lose her sense of morality as she accepted very coolly a My Lai and refused to give up the image of American soldiers who hand out chocolate bars and chewing gum.

We learned the meaning of free fire zones, shooting anything that moves, and we watched while America placed a cheapness on the lives of orientals.

We watched the United States falsification of body counts, in fact the glorification of body counts. We listened while month after month we were told the back of the enemy was about to break. We fought using weapons against "oriental human beings." We fought using weapons against those people which I do not believe this country would dream of using were we fighting in the European theater. We watched while men charged up hills because a general said that hill has to be taken, and after losing one platoon or two platoons they marched away to leave the hill for reoccupation by the North Vietnamese. We watched pride allow the most unimportant battles to be blown into extravaganzas, because we couldn't lose, and we couldn't retreat, and because it didn't matter how many American bodies were lost to prove that point, and so there were Hamburger Hills and Khe Sanhs and Hill 81s and Fire Base 6s, and so many others.

Now we are told that the men who fought there must watch quietly while American lives are lost so that we can exercise the incredible arrogance of Vietnamizing the Vietnamese.

Each day to facilitate the process by which the United States washes her hands of Vietnam someone has to give up his life so that the United States doesn't have to admit something that the entire world already knows, so that we can't say that we have made a mistake. Someone has to die so that President Nixon won't be, and these are his words, "the first President to lose a war."

We are asking Americans to think about that because how do you ask a man to be the last man to die in Vietnam? How do you ask a man to be the last man to die for a mistake? . . . We are here in Washington to say that the problem of this war is not just a question of war and diplomacy. It is part and parcel of everything that we are trying as human beings to communicate to people in this country—the question of racism which is rampant in the military, and so many other questions such as the use of weapons; the hypocrisy in our taking umbrage at the Geneva Conventions and using that as justification for a continuation of this war when we are more guilty than any other body of violations of those Geneva Conventions; in the use of free fire zones, harassment interdiction fire, search and destroy missions, the bombings, the torture of prisoners, all accepted policy by many units in South Vietnam. That is what we are trying to say. It is part and parcel of everything.

An American Indian friend of mine who lives in the Indian Nation of Alcatraz put it to me very succinctly. He told me how as a boy on an Indian reservation he had watched television and he used to cheer the cowboys when they came in and shot the Indians, and then suddenly one day he stopped in Vietnam and he said, "my God, I am doing to these people the very same thing that was done to my people," and he stopped. And that is what we are trying to say, that we think this thing has to end.

We are here to ask, and we are here to ask vehemently, where are the leaders of our country? Where is the leadership? We're here to ask where are McNamara, Rostow, Bundy, Gilpatrick, and so many others? Where are they now that we, the men they sent off to war, have returned? These are the commanders who have deserted their troops. And there is no more serious crime in the laws of war. The Army says they never leave their wounded. The marines say they never even leave their dead. These men have left all the casualties and retreated behind a pious shield of public rectitude. They've left the real stuff of their reputations bleaching behind them in the sun in this country. . . .

We wish that a merciful God could wipe away our own memories of that service as easily as this administration has wiped away their memories of us. But all that they have done and all that they can do by this denial is to make more clear than ever our own determination to undertake one last mission—to search out and destroy the last vestige of this barbaric war, to pacify our own hearts, to conquer the hate and fear that have driven this country these last ten years and more. And more. And so when thirty years from now our brothers go down the street without a leg, without an arm, or a face, and small boys ask why, we will be able to say "Vietnam" and not mean a desert, not a filthy obscene memory, but mean instead where America finally turned and where soldiers like us helped it in the turning.